fiction will ~~except~~

most outlandish idea...

publishers will only give them

a chance to demonstrate their

appetite.

I'm proud of the story,

but in a way I'm even

more proud of the leadership

that proved the cynics wrong;

the leadership which will take

honor, fiction kicking and screaming

into the 21st Century because

it wants to stretch its imagination

CLIVE BARKER'S
DARK WORLDS

PHIL & SARAH STOKES

CLIVE BARKER'S
DARK WORLDS

PHIL & SARAH STOKES

CERNUNNOS

CONTENTS

Sir Michael Tippett said of his operas that he wanted hearing them to be "like breathing the air of another planet."

It's an extraordinary phrase, not least because it would be understood in a heartbeat by writers, filmmakers, painters, and poets alike. What artist would not want their art to be that strange, that frightening, that ecstatic?

The answer is: most.

If I've learned anything in my years of making films, books, and pictures, it's that there's definitely an Us and a Them.

Us? Well it's pretty plain who We are. You, you reading this, you're one of Us. You seek out the odd, the off-kilter, the threatening. You want the novels you read and the music you listen to and the paintings you look at to remove you from the commonplace, the ordinary, the conventional.

The Them, of course, want what they had yesterday, and the day before; they want their art to reflect them, to reinforce their beliefs. They want something comforting, something soporific.

The act of creation has, for me, always been driven by a feeling deep in my gut that certain stories need to be told, that the status quo needs to be challenged, and that I have a duty, perhaps even an obligation, to invent anarchic alternatives to the wretched banalities of life as it is barely lived in this over-polished but under-nourished virtual world we are supposed to be pleasured by.

CLIVE BARKER

INTRODUCTION

"Clive Barker? Oh, *Hellraiser*, right?"

More than three decades after *Hellraiser*'s release, Clive Barker's name remains synonymous with the movie and with its Lead Cenobite character, dubbed Pinhead, though never referred to as such in the screenplay or the film.

This enduring connection reflects both the unexpected impact of the movie's content and subject matter and that its 1987 release was the moment that Clive Barker—the *enfant horrible*, the future of horror, the master of the macabre, the titan of terror—burst irrepressibly into the public consciousness, declaring there to be "no limits" and that it was far, far better to see the monster in plain sight and great detail—and to embrace its monstrousness—than it was to suggest through subtlety, nuance, or tease.

Interviewers were consistently surprised at his boyish charm, his eloquence, his simultaneous passion for highbrow and lowbrow culture, and his insistence that horror stories and graphic images represent powerful and important sources of transcendence, allowing readers and movie audiences to confront deep-rooted and important issues and to emerge changed, transformed, by the experience.

Stephen King—horror fiction's heavyweight—had already dubbed Clive to be "the future of horror" and declared that "what Barker does in the Books of Blood makes the rest of us look like we've been asleep for the last ten years." *Hellraiser*, though, took its author and director into every cinema in every town and established his reputation as the man guaranteed to shock and terrify you. To the surprise of audiences and interviewers, he did it with a seriousness of intent and no apparent restraint: he meant his work to scare you and he didn't view a horror movie as a tongue-in-cheek, ninety-minute distraction—his film dealt with believable adult lives confronted by the extraordinary.

For some, of course, *Hellraiser* was proof positive that Clive was a poster child for a dangerous and depraved threat to civilized society and that this particular film represented the worst excesses of the late 1980s, mixing sex and death and weird fetishistic practices into entertainment and thereby threatening morality, decency, and beliefs.

The impact of *Hellraiser* was huge, and remains so today—something that its creator has come back around to embracing, though at times over the years, as he worked in other areas, it felt somewhat of a millstone around his neck: a movie filmed by a first-time director across three and a half months in late 1986 and early 1987, and released in September 1987, had what he sometimes regarded as undue prominence in a creative life that encompassed painting, poetry, novels, short stories, theatre, photography, and much more.

This book showcases a creative life. For many he'll always be "the *Hellraiser* guy, right?" For others, Clive Barker is an imaginer, an artist who challenges and provokes us to think in new ways and to appreciate our human condition in new lights, through different eyes, such that we emerge, in the words of one of his heroes, William Blake, capable of "making our own laws, not slaves to the laws of others.

OPPOSITE PAGE

Christopher Carrion Resurrected, circa 2006.

9

1987 HELLRAISER

"There are no limits."

Cricklewood, North London, perhaps not the obvious place to create a nightmare that would propel Clive Barker to worldwide fame, but close to Clive's Crouch End home—coincidentally located on the same street where Peter Straub had lived for several years and written *Ghost Story*, and the same neighborhood that inspired Stephen King's short story "Crouch End." So maybe not so far-fetched after all.

Hellraiser was filmed largely in a residential house on Dollis Hill Lane and on sets at the Production Village studio. At the heart of its cast were Andrew Robinson, Clare Higgins, Sean Chapman, and Ashley Laurence, playing the Cotton family of Larry, Julia, Frank, and Kirsty, as Larry and his second wife, Julia, move into Larry's recently deceased mother's old home. We see early on that all is not well in the marriage, and that stepmother and stepdaughter do not get along particularly well, but that everyone is trying to make this new life work as a fresh start.

The boldness of the opening five minutes of the film sets the tone for audiences and tells them in no uncertain terms that they are not about to enjoy the at-times campy, comedic horror of a *Nightmare on Elm Street* movie or the murder-by-numbers stalk and slash of a *Friday the 13th* movie. An unnamed man kneels at the center of a ritualistic, candlelit formation in an otherwise bare room. He invokes otherworldly figures by solving an elegantly constructed puzzle box, twisting and caressing it like some demonic Rubik's Cube into obscure configurations, ultimately succeeding in summoning pale-skinned, wounded, leather-clad figures that speak calmly, logically, and then impale him with hooks on chains that tear him apart. A scene in which the leader of these visitors patiently reassembles pieces of the man's shattered face among lumps of bloody flesh signaled the movie's intent.

As Clive recalls, "I took my mum and dad to see the cast-and-crew showing of *Hellraiser*, and my name appeared in the opening credits, and my mum burst into tears: finally, Clive gets his name on the big screen . . . I leaned over and said, 'That's going to be the most fun you're going to have for the next ninety minutes!' "

The unnamed man, his spirit living in the room, is revealed to be Frank Cotton, Larry's brother, and the room in which he met his demise is revealed to be in the house that Larry and Julia have just moved into, sometime after the events of the opening sequence. Frank and Julia have a history—a short-lived but intensely passionate affair at the time of her wedding to Larry—and the accidental spilling of blood in the room triggers Frank's reincarnation, aided by Julia's subsequent agreement to commit murders in order to supply Frank with more blood to complete his corporeal return.

The film has many reasons for success. Its seriousness of intent was an antidote to much of the decade's horror movie output. It has serious actors playing serious roles—Andrew Robinson has a dual role as bland, cuckolded Larry and later as the back-in-business bad-boy brother Frank, ably demonstrating the sibling relationship between two very different men; Clare Higgins is wholly believable as the fervent lover who will do anything to win back the source of her only real taste of passion. Both were already well-established actors, with Andrew a worldwide name from his role as Scorpio in the first Dirty Harry movie, and their on-screen portrayals lend weight to the drama. Sean Chapman oozes sensual allure and danger. Newcomer Ashley Laurence was put through a grueling shoot as Kirsty, seeking to protect her father and herself, unwittingly summons the pale-skinned enigmas with the puzzle box. She is a strong, determined female character and carries the audience through the terrors she encounters.

Oliver Smith, though dubbed in the final edit and therefore losing his English accent, gives a gracious, elegant performance as a skinned man, the improvised moment where he lights a cigarette as he glistens and oozes showing his humanity and encouraging empathy at a point when other films may have emphasized repulsion. At other moments his unsuppressed rage and desire fuel the action.

The four Cenobites—explorers in the further regions of experience, demons to some, angels to others—were played, under heavy make-up and prosthetics, by three of Clive's friends and one member of his family. Clive's acting relationship and friendship with Doug Bradley, who played the Lead Cenobite, went back sixteen years prior to filming, starting with school productions in Liverpool and continuing through many years of creative work together. Simon Bamford (Butterball Cenobite) and Nicholas Vince (Chattering Cenobite) had both attended Mountview Theatre School in North London and met Clive through theatre work, Simon taking a role in one of Clive's plays alongside Doug. Grace Kirby, Clive's cousin, played the Female Cenobite.

The stylized look of the Cenobites was a collaboration between Clive, a creative team at Image Animation headed by special effects supremo Bob Keen, and Jane Wildgoose, another friend of Clive's from his theatre work. The physical look of the facial and bodily scarring and prosthetics were honed over several beer and pizza sessions between Clive, Bob, Geoff Portass, and others over a period in which Clive and his producer Christopher Figg were seeking funding. The striking costumes, with their leather designs interwoven with the mutilation and wounds, were Jane's response to Clive's request for "repulsive glamour" and "areas of revealed flesh where some kind of torture has, or is, occurring."

The now iconic puzzle box was designed by another Image Animation creative, Simon Sayce, who invested meaning and intrigue into each of the six brass plates on the wooden cube, whose hieroglyphic designs reward close inspection and have helped inspire the ongoing mythology of the Cenobites.

Robin Vidgeon played a vital role as Clive's director of photography, helping his first-time director with the technicalities of lenses and camera angles. Mike Buchanan worked wonders within the limitations of a single house location as production designer.

Stephen Jones as unit publicist was instrumental to building anticipation for the film. In an unusual move for a British movie of the time, he encouraged journalists to visit the set throughout filming and key imagery was released to select horror fanzines, film magazines, and trade journals during the shoot.

The publicity department of the film's production company, New Word Pictures, settled on a photograph of Doug Bradley as the Lead Cenobite for the film's poster and it was marketed heavily ahead of its September 1987 release in the UK, the US, and Canada.

In his numerous press interviews, Clive stressed his unapologetic view that horror movies should unsettle and provoke audiences. Press reaction to the movie itself reflected the strength of its impact—both good and bad. Headlines proclaimed:

"NEW BRITISH HORROR FILM HITS THE NAIL IN THE HEAD"

"INTELLIGENT IT IS, TASTEFUL IT IS NOT"

"LIFESTYLES OF THE SICK AND SKINLESS"

"GRISLY EXCESSES ROB *HELLRAISER* OF ITS HORROR"

"*HELLRAISER* WEDS SEX AND DEATH IN IMAGINATIVE STOMACH-TURNER"

"WORDSMITH ALSO DIRECTS RELENTLESS HORROR FILM"

"*HELLRAISER* IS NOT UNLIKE A FEATHER IN THE THROAT"

"'ENGLAND'S STEPHEN KING' GOES FOR THE GORE WITH GUSTO"

and reviews also ran the full spectrum:

"This is a literate, suspenseful and truly scary experience, a wonderful combination when your aim is to see a movie that will make you want to turn from the screen."

"*Hellraiser* will be a hideous treat for the hard-core, nearly unshockable audience that's ready for it; those of more tender tastes may have to wait until Barker's radical sensibility catches up to his viciously adroit visual expertise."

"For anyone but hard-core gore addicts, *Hellraiser* is a movie to be endured, not enjoyed."

"The film is pretty disgusting and quite scary—in short, quite an auspicious debut from Clive Barker, a man to watch."

HELLRAISER. 18

ABOVE

Clive Barker (center) on the *Hellraiser* set with (l to r) Nicholas Vince, Simon Bamford, Grace Kirby, and Doug Bradley as the Cenobites. UK lobby card, 1987.

OPPOSITE PAGE

Clive's sketch of Frank, used as the cover for Clive and Christopher Figg's 1986 pitch document for the first *Hellraiser* movie.

Clive's own favorite headline was from Joe Bob Briggs's review: "Sex in the attic with devilhead slime." Clive said, "I can't think of a better description myself!"

Screen International noted: "If there are occasional signs of bottom-dollar film-making and a few slightly iffy creatures from the other world, *Hellraiser* remains the best slam-bang, no-holds-barred, scare-the-shit-out-of-you horror movie for quite a while."

Roger Ebert, however, was rather less forgiving: "This is a movie without wit, style or reason, and the true horror is that actors were made to portray, and technicians to realize, its bankruptcy of imagination. Maybe Stephen King was thinking of a different Clive Barker."

On its opening week the movie was number three at the US box office. Its director, though, reflects today, "I know it sounds silly but I had no comprehension of the importance of that. I was in England, I was writing *Cabal*—was it? I was certainly writing. I got a call on Monday from Chris Figg, who said—Chris is a delightful man, a very English man, a very Oxford Englishman—he said, 'You know the movie was number one over the weekend!' And then of course once the *L.A. Times* came round then we started to get the calls: I got calls, Chris got more calls, obviously, being the movie's producer, 'God almighty, the picture made all this money and you're number one and boom-boom-boom,' and you know what? It didn't signify anything to me—I wish I could tell you I was dancing in the street naked with a bottle of champagne in my bottom, but I wasn't!

"The world has changed radically since that time. We weren't in the industry we are now where everybody knows Friday's take on Saturday. We weren't so obsessed with all of the crap which has since stolen a certain magic away from film. I think now we know each weekend what's number one, we know what's happened to the picture that was number one and how much it fell off by. Now, whether I could have had access to that information and just didn't know how to get to it, I don't know. My guess is that it was just not something that appeared twenty years ago, before the internet.

"I think we were naïve. I don't mean that in a bad way, I think we were just a lot less informed and I've tried to continue that. It was Cronenberg, actually: David was very useful; he was the one who gave me the advice not to get caught in that game, that it was a waste of time. I mean, if you were to ask me what was number one last week, here in America, I wouldn't have a clue.

"I didn't care, frankly. It wasn't where my head was at. I'd had a great time with the press, but I knew that a lot of people hated the movie. . . ."

1984 BOOKS OF BLOOD, VOLUMES 1-3

"Everybody is a book of blood; Wherever we're opened, we're red."

While Clive Barker was new news to mainstream filmgoers in 1987, horror fans had been eagerly anticipating *Hellraiser*'s release, having already experienced Clive's written work.

His first published fiction was three slim paperback volumes of short stories with odd photographic covers, each with a print run of ten thousand copies released onto UK bookshelves. Clive Barker's Books of Blood series contained a total of sixteen stories that he had been working on in 1981 and 1982 alongside his theatre projects with the Dog Company, having signed a contract with Sphere Books in June 1982.

"I got started," he reflects, "as a writer of plays, out of a passion for theatre and out of a passion for fantastical storytelling of one kind or another. And when I realized that this was not going to keep me in the manner to which I intended to become accustomed . . . it became necessary to really think about organizing my creative life a little better. I'd been a little lackadaisical about really focusing on it.

"Then I read this massive Kirby McCauley–edited horror story collection called *Dark Forces* and I thought, 'This is great; here's a book full of all these great guys'—it had Isaac Bashevis Singer and Stephen King and Ramsey Campbell, Joyce Carol Oates, Ray Bradbury, Robert Bloch, and many others: all these first-rate writers in their various ways, doing completely different things, but they could all fit in one book. . . . It was a really marvelous and very eclectic compendium that drew several kinds of horror together.

"I thought, 'I know what I'll do, I'll put together my own book and I'll try as many ideas and stylistic techniques as I possibly can.' It became almost a game, to see how many kinds of stories I could generate. So there would be a comic story, some erotic stories, a couple of psychological horror stories, a ghost story or two, and some extremely brutal, visceral tales.

~~Wavarad~~
Wyburd

~~Wyburd~~ looked at the book, and the book looked back. Everything he'd ever been told about the boy was true.

'How did you get in?' McNeal wanted to know. There was neither anger nor trepidation in his voice. Only casual curiosity.

'Over the wall.' ~~Wyburd~~ Wyburd told him.

The book nodded. 'Come to see if ~~were~~ ̶t̶h̶e̶ rumours were true?' ~~Wyburd said.~~

'Something like that.'

~~Amongst connoisseurs of the bizarre the~~
~~story of McNeal's story described.~~
~~the McNeal's story was told amongst~~

Amongst connoisseurs of the bizarre McNeal's story was told in reverential whispers.
How the boy had ~~particularly~~ passed himself off as a medium, ~~fobbing several credulous para-psych-ologists that he had contact with the spirit~~ inventing stories on behalf of the departed for his own profit; and how the dead had finally tired of his mockery, and broken into the living world to exact ~~their~~ an ~~ever~~ awesome revenge.

[chap heading] 22 COMING TO GRIEFOE

taken the short-cut along

21 — Miriam had not ~~walked~~ the gravel path
around the rim of the quarry for almost eighteen years.
Eighteen years of another life, quite unlike the life she'd lived
in this all-but-forgotten city. She'd left Liverpool to taste
the world: to grow; to prosper; to learn to live; And, *by* God,
hadn't she done just that? From the/frightened nineteen-year-old
naive and
she had been when she had last set foot on the quarry path, she
had blossomed into ~~a woman of some beauty and considerable élan.~~
~~A perfect hostess, a valued guest, a raconteur,~~ a wholly
sophisticated woman of the world. Her husband idolized her, her
daughter grew ever more like her with every year; she was
universally adored.

Yet now, as she stepped on to ~~that~~ *the* ill-lit, ill-bred path
that skirted the chasm of the quarry, it was as though a wound
and
had opened in her heel/that hard-won ~~sophistication~~ *poise* and ~~strength~~
self-reliance
was draining
~~had drained~~ out of her and ~~ran~~ *running* away into the dark; ~~Worse, it~~
her native city
~~was~~ as though she'd never left ~~Liverpool~~, never grown wiser with
experience. She felt no more prepared to face this hundred-
yard stretch of walled walkway than she had been at nineteen.
Same Same as had always haunted her on this spot, clung now
The doubts, the imagined horrors, ~~clung~~ to the inside of her
and whispered
brain-pan, ~~whispering~~ about the certainty of secrets. ~~Damn it,~~
~~was she still prey to these adolescent fears? Surely not~~
~~Surely all those nightmares had slipped away forever~~
~~been erased by the joy of marriage~~

They still lay in wait here; idiot fears concocted of cheek-corner
gossip and childish superstition. Even now the old myths

-3-

came running back to embrace her. Tales of hook-handed men,
and secret lovers slaughtered in the act of love; a dozen rumoured atrocities
that, to her burgeoning and over-heated imagination had always had
their source, their epicentre, here : on the Bogey walk.

That's what they'd called it; and that was what it would
always be to her: the Bogey-Walk. Instead of losing its
it had grown gross.
potency, ~~it had grown gross~~ with the passage of the years, It
it had
had prospered as she had prospered; ~~it had~~ found its vocation
perhaps
as she had done. Of course she had grown into contentment, and
had weakened her; o
may be that made her weaker than she had been. But it, *Oh it*
fed on its own frustration and
had merely ~~matured~~ longing, ~~and becoming~~ encrusted with desire
as time had passed
to take her for itself. Maybe, it had fed a little to keep its
its to keep it alive. Of this
strength up: but it needed, in its immutable heart, only the
certainty of ~~its~~ final victory ~~that's what kept it alive. It~~
she was suddenly and in contestably certain; that the battles she had fought
into own weakness were not over. They had scarcely begun.

she attempted to advance a
few yards along the but
familiar Walk, ~~she~~ faltered and stopped, the so-
panic turning her feet to lead weights.
The night was not soundless. A jet winked over, a longing roar *roar*
drowned on the walk itself.
in the dark: ~~traffic hooted on the highway~~. But here,
such signs of life were a world away, and could not comfort her. Cursing her own vulnerability,
she turned
back the way she'd come and traipsed home through the warm
a more roundabout
drizzle by ~~the~~ route.

battered on and
Grief, she half-reasoned, had ~~weakened her~~ sapped her will
to fight.

In two days' time perhaps, when her mother's funeral was
sudden
over and the loss was more manageable, then she would see the
its proper
future plainly and that pathway would fall into perspective.
recognise
She'd ~~see~~ the Bogey-Walk as the ~~excrement~~ ridden, weed-lined

---

that
gravel path it was. Meanwhile, she'd get wetter than she
needed taking the safe road home.

in itself to any but her, was
The quarry was not such a terrifying spot, nor the path
along its ~~~~ rim.

rapes or
There'd been no murders there that she knew of: no ~~atrocities~~
muggings
committed along that sordid little track. It was a ~~thoroughfare~~
no less and no more: a walk-way public foot-path,
badly-kept, badly-illuminated ~~path~~ around the edge of *what had once been*
a productive quarry, and was now the communal rubbish-tip.
The wall that kept the walkers from falling a
hundred feet to their deaths below was built of plain red brick.
that
It was eight feet high, so nobody could even see the depth on the
other side, and it was lined with pieces of broken milk-bottles
op
set in concrete, to dissuade adventurous boys from scrambling on
to it.

The path itself had once been tarmac: but subsidence had
opened cracks in it, and instead of the Council resurfacing,
they had seen fit simply to dust it with loose gravel. *It was seldom, if*
ever weeded. Stinging nettles grew to child height in the meagre
dirt at the bottom of the wall, as did a sickly-scented flower whose name she
did not know but which, at the height of summer, was a Mecca to
wasps. And that - wall, gravel and weeds - was the sum of the place.
In dreams, however, she'd scaled that wall—her palms
magically immune to the pricking glass, and in those vertiginous
and cliff
adventures she'd peered down down the black, sheer ~~side~~ of the
dark heart. gloom
quarry into its ~~deep~~. It was impenetrable, the ~~darkness~~ at the
that and
bottom, but she knew there was a lake of green brackish water
somewhere below. It could be seen, that choked pool of filth, from
the other side of the quarry; from the safe side. That's how she
knew it was there, in her dreams. And she knew too, walking on

---

"I just wrote some stories which I hoped my friends would enjoy, and in some ways it wasn't dissimilar to the nine-year-old boy retelling stories to his friends."

OPPOSITE PAGE
December 1981
typescript pages from
Coming to Grief, hand-
corrected by the author
in 1982.

"Sometimes I used colloquial language, sometimes not; sometimes large paragraphs, sometimes really quick and broken down. So there was an attempt to write a range of things.

"I had read two of Stephen King's novels and seen a lot of horror movies. I'd read Ramsey Campbell and a lot of other stuff that might loosely be described as horror fiction—early Ray Bradbury, for instance—but I hadn't gone into it thinking, 'Hey, I can really make some bucks from this stuff.' It was more accident than intention."

Recognizing this unknown author would benefit from endorsement, his publisher asked if he could secure any cover blurbs. Clive approached Ramsey Campbell, Liverpool's leading horror writer, who had been invited by Clive's teacher, Helen Clarke, to talk to Clive's sixth-form class a dozen or so years before. The two had met sporadically over the years since but had not seen each other for a long time until, as Ramsey would recall:

> Most of ten years later he rang me. Could I advise him about the publication of horror sto-
> ries, collections of them? Aaargh—but wait a minute, I once crawled out of the slush pile
> myself and would have got nowhere without the advice and patience of August Derleth:
> The least I could do was try to emulate him. And so I have, I think, in my various anthologies,
> but in general, reading unpublished work simply in order to advise the author is a bit much,
> especially if the author's opinion of the importance or originality of his work is impregnably
> high. Still, the caller was a friend of Helen Clarke's, and so I awarded myself an entry in
> whichever ledger records good deeds and went in to Liverpool to meet Clive Barker.
>
> Seldom if ever has my sense of literary duty been so spectacularly rewarded.

Ramsey agreed to write an introduction to the first three Books of Blood, which he duly completed in May of 1983, having already sent a letter to Clive's publishers allowing them to add his recommendations to the covers of the first editions. "Clive Barker is the most important new writer of horror since Peter Straub," proclaimed volume 1, while on volume 2 Ramsey confessed: "I thought I was past being profoundly disturbed by horror fiction, but these books proved me wrong." The third volume promised this was "the most exciting debut in horror fiction for many years."

The books were released in March 1984 without fanfare, and although success was not immediate, they did start to gain a reputation as something fresh and startling among specialist horror and fantasy circles.

Clive's earliest mainstream interviews in the *Liverpool Echo*, the *Birmingham Evening Mail* and London's *Time Out* saw him setting out his stall:

"I suppose it's because I love anything that's taboo. I dare to talk about things which others push to the back of their minds.

"Things still growl in the dark but they have to be put in a new context, in the environment that people know. This is where the monsters are, not in some dusty old vault. People in 1984 are aware of so much more than one hundred years ago—and the more you know, the more there is to be scared of.

"I never actually stopped reading horror stories or seeing the movies, I just became less public about it. There's a terrible attitude of condescension—even now, people who find out what I do tend to ask what else I do, what I do when I'm being 'serious' . . . ! There's nothing in any of the books that I'd consider gratuitous. To me a book or a film—something like *The Driller Killer* or *I Spit on Your Grave*, say—it's only gratuitous if the violence is all there is. There's got to be something else. But on the other hand, you have to remember that if you pick up a horror book in the first place you're asking to be horrified, to be frightened. And I've got to deliver; I set out to scare people. And one of the tools I deal with is sinews and blood."

The stories, though, didn't break out to a wider audience until they caught the attention of the biggest name in horror fiction of them all.

Stephen King's initial comment arose from a panel discussion at the October 1984 World Fantasy Convention in Ottawa—before he'd read any of Clive's work. It was part of a longer observation that other convention-goers, such as Peter Straub and Douglas E. Winter, were talking in glowing terms about these new Books of Blood, an indication to King that something new was in the air. He responded, "Well, I haven't read this guy, but from what I understand it's like what Jon Landau said: 'I have seen the future of rock and roll, and his name is Bruce Springsteen.' Sounds like Clive Barker might be the future of horror."

Having read the books, King's endorsement became more fulsome; in April 1985, for the US release of the Books of Blood, he told Berkley Publishing: "I think Clive Barker is so good that I am almost literally tongue-tied. Yes, I stick by it: I have seen the future of the horror genre, and his name is Clive Barker. . . . What Barker does in the Books of Blood makes the rest of us look like we've been asleep for the last ten years."

Ramsey Campbell also updated his introduction for Scream/Press's debut US publication of the first three Books of Blood later that year. (Berkley's mass-market paperbacks were kept on ice until mid-1986.) Stephen King wasn't done yet either, and Poseidon Press used quotes from praise he wrote for the 1986 Albacon III convention program for their advance sampler of *The Inhuman Condition*:

> He doesn't just have the goods, he *is* the goods. . . .
>
> Never in my life have I been so completely shaken by a collection of stories. Never have I actually put a book aside because I was alone and knew I must soon turn off the lights . . . or at least turn in. I have never experienced such a combination of revulsion, delight and amazement. The first encounter with Barker's work was a little like eating anchovy ice cream. That's really the only way I can put it.

Over twenty years later, Clive reflected on the impact of this in a heartfelt speech delivered to Stephen King in person as the Canadian Booksellers Association presented the latter with their Lifetime Achievement Award:

> When my English publishers put out my first stories, the Books of Blood, they were greeted with a very English silence. Polite and devastating. I don't know what I was expecting, but it certainly wasn't this smothering shrug.
>
> And then, a voice. Not just any voice. The voice of Stephen King, who had made people all around the world fall in love with having the shit scared out of them. He said, God bless him, that I was the future of horror. Me! An unknown author of some books of short stories that nobody was buying. . . .

Stephen had no reason to say what he said, except pure generosity of spirit. The same generosity he has shown over the years to many authors. A few words from Stephen, and lives are changed forever.

> Mine was. I felt a wonderful burden laid upon my shoulders; I had been seen, and called by name, and my life would never be the same again.

The sixteen stories in these volumes were:

Volume 1	Volume 2	Volume 3
The Book of Blood	Dread - Hell's Event	Son of Celluloid – Rawhead
The Midnight Meat Train	Jacqueline Ess: Her Will	Rex – Confessions
The Yattering and Jack	and Testament	of a (Pornographer's)
Pig Blood Blues	The Skins of the Fathers	Shroud – Scape-Goats
Sex, Death and Starshine	New Murders in the Rue	Human Remains
In the Hills, the Cities	Morgue	

Clive was already looking ahead, and at the British Fantasy Society's Fantasycon in September 1984 he declared he had no intention of being defined by or within the horror genre:

"After I finish the stories for Books of Blood, volumes 4, 5, and 6," he said, "I would like to write a big thriller and also some fantasy novels. I don't want to be labeled as a horror writer, not because I don't like horror, but because I want to do a lot of other things. I want to do whatever it's possible to do in the field of imaginative writing. It excites me. I want to write science fiction. I want to write fantasy, and so on. I would love to do illustrated books.

"I don't think it's very wise to be put in a certain slot. People say, 'Oh, he's a horror writer,' and that's it. It's much better to do a lot of things. The trouble is, you have to go slowly, and I'm very impatient; I want it to happen fast, and it takes some time to get these things done, but next year I hope to do several of them, including the first part of a big fantasy novel, and I would like to write an erotic novel, a big, erotic novel."

© Clive Barker (1985)
53, Fullfield Avenue
London N8.
Tel. 01-348-1167

Clive Barker's Books of Blood.
Volume One

53.4

1985 THE DAMNATION GAME

"Hell is reimagined by each generation."

OPPOSITE PAGE

Manuscript page for
the opening of *The
Damnation Game*, 1983.

Having delivered the first three Books of Blood, and before addressing the next three, Clive turned his attention to writing a debut novel that had been commissioned by Barbara Boote and Nan du Sautoy at Sphere Books.

The Damnation Game is a story of empire, power, money, and social class. Spanning four decades from the end of World War II through to its mid-1980s setting, the novel tells the tale of a Faustian bargain and its impact.

Clive drew on his interactions with the family of Sir Peter and Gillian Parker, who he had met after their youngest son, Oliver, had auditioned for and joined the Dog Company. "I could not have written *The Damnation Game* without the Parkers," he confirms. "It was interesting to enter into a world and a life that was so radically different from anything I'd ever seen before.

"When I was with them, in their apartment in London or in the Oxford house—which had, on its grounds, Richard III's castle, which I always thought was so funny—there was always a sense that, where they gathered, there was something special about them. I never had that in my family at all. I don't think it's good or bad, I just think it's a description.

"All the Parkers are games people; they love to play games of every possible kind: rugby, football or whatever, but also card games, word games. . . ." But this wasn't the aspect that Clive drew on most closely; instead it was: "Power. Sealed units of power. They definitely had an idea that they were a unique circle, the Parkers, they were high-flyers, all of them."

Although, the Books of Blood had been conceived as paperback originals, Sphere had also arranged a hardcover reprint with Weidenfeld & Nicolson, who picked up a similar arrangement for a hardcover release of *The Damnation Game*, this time more traditionally, as the first edition.

Published in the UK in August 1985, the book's publicity was able to benefit from Stephen King's endorsement, and an eight-page marketing book for the UK trade asked, "Who is so terrifyingly good even Stephen King cannot read him alone?" before challenging booksellers: "Enter if you dare . . ."

Clive had written the novel under working titles of *Fleshlands* and *Mamoulian's Game* before settling on the Faustian aspect with *The Damnation Game*.

1

The air was electric the day the King crossed
the city, certain that tonight, after so many
weeks of frustration, he would finally locate the
card-player. It was not an easy journey. Eighty-
five percent of Warsaw had been levelled, either
by the months of mortar bombardment that
preceded the Russian liberation of the city, or
by the programme of demolition the Nazis had
undertaken before their retreat. Several (sectors/sections)
were virtually impassable by vehicle.
Mountains of rubble, — still nursing the dead
like bulbs ready to sprout as the spring weather
warmed — clogged the streets. Even in the more
accessible districts the once-elegant facades
swooned dangerously, their foundations
growling.

   But after almost three months of plying his
trade here, the King had become used to navigating
the urban wilderness. Indeed, he took pleasure in
its desolate splendour; perspectives
tinged lilac by the dust that still settled from the
stratosphere; its squares and parkways so unnaturally
silent; the sense he had, trespassing here, that this

"Very seldom are my protagonists viewing their circumstances without ambiguity, and to write the straightforward type of horror fiction that leaves the reader rigid with fear you need to remove ambiguity, you need the dyed-in-the-wool villain you don't understand, and certainly don't sympathize with. *The Damnation Game* either has four villains or none, and my conclusion is that it has none. Everybody is morally tainted. I wanted to do a covenant-with-the-devil story without a devil."

The book's cover flap described the plot as:

When Marty Strauss is offered parole and becomes the bodyguard of one of the richest men in Europe, it seems Fate has finally dealt him a good hand. On Charles Whitehead's estate he tastes a life of luxury. And of love.

But there is something terrifying in the air, a mustering of forces which makes the great tycoon tremble, despite his dogs and his electrified fences.

Within weeks, the idyll is shattered as—in a series of ever more appalling nightmares—Marty comes to know the nature of the ancient enemy which has appeared to turn Whitehead's privileged world on its head.

Though he and Whitehead's daughter make a bid for freedom, the immortal Terror at their heels has powers beyond their comprehension. In its shadow, the worst depravities of the modern world come to seem minor crimes. At its behest the vengeful past erupts into the present. The dead walk. The Deluge looms.

For Whitehead and his opponent the approaching Apocalypse is merely the final phase of a game which has lasted decades.

But for those innocents trapped between the players—and for the readers who share their fears and their frail hope of salvation—it will be a breath-snatching ride into hell, which will bring new meaning to the word *damnation*.

Whether your taste in dark fantasy is for the teasingly suggestive, or for the shockingly explicit, *The Damnation Game* will take you to fresh heights of visionary terror.

"I had a couple of notions about the Faust story," Clive said as the book was released. "I mean, there's no argument that Faust must be one of the oldest horror stories extant as a basic formula: 'Man makes pact; pact-keeper comes seeking retribution; now read on . . .' is a basic structure and, I think, a very potent one. I wanted to see what sense I could make of these notions in the late part of the twentieth century. What does damnation and all that stuff actually mean now? What would a man sell his soul for? What is it that we could call a soul which we could sell in the first place? And under those circumstances, assuming that such a sale was made, what would Hell be? What would the Devil have in his arsenal to claim a new Faust?

"I looked at all these things and *The Damnation Game* is the result. The book has done a lot of things I wanted it to do; it's a horror book in one obvious sense and a thriller in another sense. I've attempted to write a horror novel that is also a mainstream novel.

"The chief perspective for me comes when Mamoulian says, 'Every man is his own Mephistopheles.' This is the Faust story without the Devil. They finally work out that 'they have no devil on their back, just old humanity, cheated of love and ready to pull down the world on its head. . . .'"

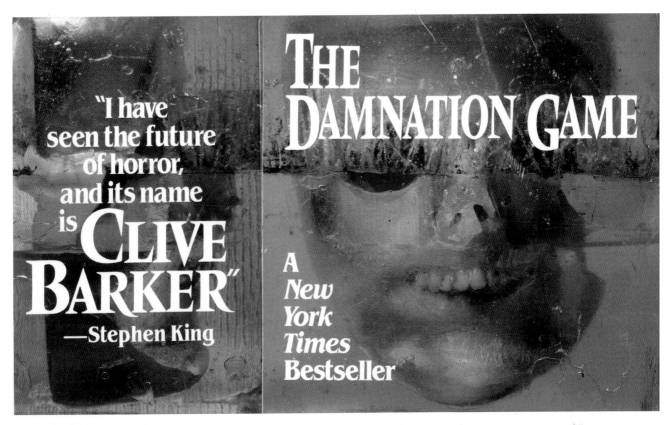

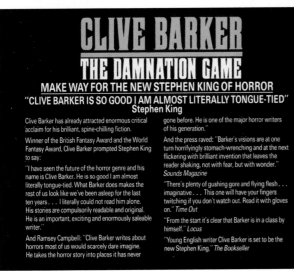

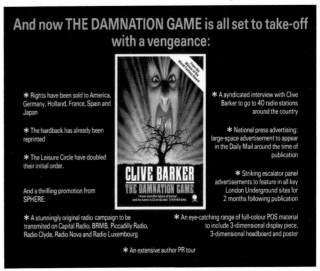

London's *Time Out* reviewed the book: "Barker seduces and subverts the reader with a world where any perversion (from cannibalism to necrophilia) is acceptable, and where the boundaries of reality, nightmare and illusion constantly blur together to provide further disorientation. He also knows that more subtle horrors, such as the debauched drinking party culminating in the humiliation of Strauss, are as effective as the explicit set pieces."

Author James Herbert offered: "The most impressive first novel I've read for a long, long time. Touches of sheer brilliance throughout."

Adding to Clive's growing reputation, a collectible slipcased and signed edition of 250 copies of the novel was also published, retailing at £25.00, compared to the regular edition's more modest £8.95.

1985 BOOKS OF BLOOD, VOLUMES 4-6

"What the boy had said was true. The dead have highways. Only the living are lost."

The second installment of Clive Barker's Books of Blood was published in the UK in June 1985, again as a trilogy of paperbacks with photographic covers. The print run of each remained a modest fifteen thousand copies.

Ahead of their release, Clive had been interviewed by Neil Gaiman for the May 1985 edition of *Penthouse*, protesting against "cozy" horror fiction, saying instead: "Horror fiction can dramatize the fact that when we wake up in the morning, everything is up for grabs. Too often horror fiction says, 'It's up for grabs—but normal service will be resumed as soon as possible.' I don't *want* normal service. My vision of horror is that it celebrates the moment of breakout. Horror throws people off balance, and it can never be the way that it was again. That's what human beings are terrified of, deep down. We cling to the notion that if we grit our teeth and hold on, the world will stay the same. And it *won't*."

The fourteen new stories were:

Volume 4	Volume 5	Volume 6
The Body Politic	The Forbidden	The Life of Death
The Inhuman Condition	The Madonna	How Spoilers Bleed
Revelations	Babel's Children	Twilight at the Towers
Down, Satan!	In the Flesh	The Last Illusion
The Age of Desire		The Book of Blood (a Postscript): On Jerusalem Street

ABOVE
Cover art, by the author,
for volume 4 of the
Books of Blood, 1986.

Part of the six books' commercial success can be found in Barbara Boote's decision to publish them as small individual paperbacks with an accessible price point, in a style long familiar to genre readers of the Pan Book of Horror Stories series. As fellow British author Christopher Fowler observes of the stories, "I suspect that if he'd delivered them now, he would have been told to knit them into a single framework and publish the whole thing in one go."

To cater to a different market, hardcovers followed the paperbacks and, as with the signed limited edition of *The Damnation Game*, the Books of Blood were issued as a limited edition of two hundred boxed sets, each of the six books individually signed and numbered, and each sporting covers newly painted by Clive, the first major public indication that he was a talented artist as well as a writer.

The books also started to win genre awards. In September 1985, Clive won his first British Fantasy Award with "In the Hills, the Cities," named the year's best short fiction story. Reviewing the awards ceremony for the *BFS Newsletter*, Simon MacCulloch recorded Clive as "trying hard for the much-coveted accolade for the Shortest Acceptance Speech ('All I've got to say about "In the Hills, the Cities" is the publishers didn't want it in the collection'), only to be outdone by veteran Ramsey Campbell ('Well, this is a surprise. Thank you')."

The following month, Clive boarded a plane for Tucson, Arizona, for the 1985 World Fantasy Convention.

Attending this annual gathering for the first time—the previous year's event at Ottawa, Ontario, had been the setting for Stephen King's now familiar quote about the then "unknown" Clive Barker—Clive was nominated for both the year's Best Anthology/Collection Award (for *Books of Blood, Volumes 1–3*) and Best Novella Award (for *Jacqueline Ess: Her Will and Testament* from volume 2).

Clive was welcomed to the traditional Friday Autograph Party between 8:00 and 10:00 p.m., sitting alongside one of his heroes, Fritz Leiber, to sign his first two US publications. With import copies of the UK editions being hard to come by, this was the first chance for many in the US to finally read something by "Britain's answer to Stephen King."

The first publication was a printed trade sampler of upcoming titles from Berkley which included the introductory tale, "The Book of Blood." Susan Allison of Berkley had secured the US rights to both *Books of Blood, Volumes 1–3* and *The Damnation Game* the previous year at the Ottawa convention and this was an opportunity for Berkley to celebrate its new author on US soil.

The second was the first collected edition of volumes 1, 2, and 3 in a single volume from Scream/ Press, the Santa Cruz–based specialty publisher. Illustrated by J. K. Potter and Harry O. Morris, it showcased the sixteen stories within suitably crimson red covers.

The World Fantasy Awards judging panel awarded the Best Novella Award to Geoff Ryman for *The Unconquered Country* but handed Clive his first World Fantasy Award for the Books of Blood

"Dark Forces . . . was the most extraordinary cross-section that one could imagine of kinds of talent, writing stories that could scarcely be more different from each other. I thought it was a really exciting notion—that one could actually put so many kinds of stories into a collection and call it a horror anthology, for want of a better word—and I thought I should have a go at that."

at the Sunday afternoon awards banquet. One of judging panel, George R. R. Martin—still a decade away from publication of *A Game of Thrones*, the first in his Song of Ice and Fire series, but already a well-respected short story writer, novelist, and editor—was lined up to work with Clive, having agreed to edit a collection called *Night Visions 3* for publication in 1986.

Clive's contribution would be the novella *The Hellbound Heart*.

As 1985 came to a close, Clive was not only well underway on a first draft of his next novel, *Weaveworld*, but he had also recently made his first foray into cinema. *Underworld*, for which he wrote the screenplay, premiered at the London Film Festival in November 1985. Film rights to five of the Books of Blood had been sold to the same producers, and Clive had already turned in his adaptation of the first of them, "Rawhead Rex."

In addition, his discussions with a kindred spirit he'd met at the Tucson convention, fellow author and screenwriter Michael McDowell, convinced him to adapt *The Hellbound Heart* into a movie . . .

The year ahead was about to be a busy one.

1952– **EARLY CHILDHOOD**

Clive Barker was born in Liverpool, England, on October 5, 1952, the eldest son of Len and Joan Barker. He would be joined in February 1956 by a younger brother, Roy.

Len's family had Irish roots, Joan's had Italian heritage, and his two grandmothers were profound influences. "My grandmother Flo," says Clive, by way of example, "had an appetite for the macabre and the horrific, the excessive, in the news—it had to be real otherwise she wasn't interested. She had a friend called Kitty and they both knew where the whiskey was. . . . They would partake liberally of this once Gran had finished her two Guinnesses for the day (which she warmed in front of the fire) and Kitty would come round and off they'd go into brandy or whiskey—and tales would come out, and it didn't matter that I was there."

The urban setting of postwar Liverpool features heavily in Clive's work, alongside his childhood holidays to North Wales and visits to two sets of couples who were friends of his parents, the Wetheralls on Guernsey in the Channel Islands and the MacKinnons on the Hebridean island of Tiree, off the west coast of Scotland.

"I have escaped into dream worlds all my life," he admits, "even as a small child. My mother says I had these secret worlds that I would tell everybody about, you know, relatives, people who would come to the house. If they asked me, I would be able to describe these secret worlds that I went to and the friends that I met there. And this was a great source of amusement to my relatives.

"If you were to go into a time machine to 1956 when I was four and ask my mum what I was like, she'd probably roll her eyes and say I was strange. 'He tells stories to himself and makes up characters and I don't know what's going to become of him.'"

He recalls a chilly morning in 1957, at the age of five, when he was captivated by a window display in his local co-op in which a Sugar Puffs branded locomotive puffed around a track. He saw this miniature universe, far removed from the unremarkable streets of Liverpool, as a wonderful alternative reality in which he could lose himself. Such parallel worlds and fantastic journeys would fuel recurring themes in his work on the page, onstage, and on-screen.

"The problem was that the fifties were very drab in England—we were still using ration cards until 1955. It was as if the first eight years of my life were all monochrome. I think that's why I'm such a fantasist. All my adventures had to be internal. I had to create my own world inside my mind because the outside world was so dreary."

At a bookstore event in 1992, Clive recalled a conversation: "My mother said, 'We just didn't know what to make of you, you were just such a strange little boy,' and I said, 'Well, I'm a strange big boy now, and very proud of it.' She said, 'The thing that used to disturb us was that you were so happy with your imagination, you were so happy with these little demons and things that you would draw.' I gather that when crayons were put into the hands of children to the left and right of me they would be drawing little houses and picket fences and flowers and suns and so on—and I would be drawing these raging, be-toothed things chewing the heads off innocent people. My mother thought this was some sign of psychosis. . . .

"Mum said, 'Of course you were a weird kid, dear,' you know, like, 'Wow, why would you ever imagine otherwise?' which I sort of found confusing in a way. They then sent me a picture from when I was six, I guess, of my class all sitting, and I am this rather worried-looking kid with his hair slicked back and a little bow tie looking rather fiercely at the camera and I think I probably was a damn weird little kid. I didn't have a lot of friends—I had a lot of imaginary friends. My mother tells the tale of just being able to park me in the corner and allow me to talk to the imaginary friends. I conversed with these invisibles and I think, sometimes, that what I write is a continuation of that conversation.

"I don't believe my parents ever put pen and paper in my hands and said, 'Get on with it,' or 'Write whatever your imagination directs you.' Far from it! I think they had the conventional belief of making sure that I somehow found a purpose in life which would pay the mortgage and allow me to be a sane and productive member of society. So they let me get on with my interests, but they certainly didn't encourage them.

"Around school age, four, five, or six, I really did realize there are two worlds. One I liked, and the other one . . . ehh, if I *have* to be there, you know. I had monster figures for toys instead of soldiers or weapons and I looked at these monsters as friends. And I always read the fiction of the imagination, fantasy fiction, science fiction, comic books, anything in which reality was blown to bits. There's a great quote from Herbert Read in an introduction to a book he once did on surrealism. He says, 'Reality is a bourgeois prejudice.' I loved that!

"But I'm sure if I tried that line on my parents, they would have looked at me askance. They were looking at the kinds of things I liked and just completely not relating. There's a division in the world, Thems that understand and Thems that don't. But for the most part they left me alone to do my

kind of reading. It was just my stuff, and I was thought of as the family wacko. And whenever I came across a quote like Read's, I'd be inspired. But there weren't many of those. During my childhood, I felt quite isolated as a consequence.

"I was very scared of the world outside—I was a fat, shortsighted kid who was basically the definition of 'nerd' and very socially uncomfortable. Very bruised by the way my father treated me and very insecure. And a lot of what was out there in the world, either by day or by night, intimidated me massively, massively. I had secrets, and any child has secrets but some children have bigger secrets than others! I had desires and hungers and appetites for work, for sex, for all kinds of things which I knew very early in my life. And because I knew them so early in my life, my life seemed from the age of let's say seven or eight onwards to be on an autobahn, heading towards a distant place that I knew was defined and awaiting me, and what frightened me was that things out there might stop me.

"The imaginative tool is in us all, you only have to go to a schoolyard and hear four-year-olds and five-year-olds playing and see that there isn't a kid in the schoolyard who doesn't have this vital thing blossoming, flowering in them all the time. What happens is that we get educated and there's a lot of good things about education but one of the bad things is that the capitalist system is preparing us for a forty-hour week in which our imaginations must not be overstimulated."

In 1998, from his Hollywood home and with a successful career to his name, Clive reiterated, "We're not very comfortable with people in our culture who are deeply imaginative. We tend to hold them at arm's length. In my own family, my propensity to tell stories was viewed very suspiciously. In some respects I think it still is. Years later and some money in the bank and they still look at me suspiciously. . . .

"There are adults who forbid and there are adults who encourage. My parents were forbidders; my father was a very forbidding, in both senses of the word, man. My mother simply was oblivious to what I did, which isn't forbidding; it's just oblivion."

"He was a perfectly normal lad . . . we're quite normal."
—Joan Barker

Although Clive paints a picture of a lack of understanding and encouragement at home—and indeed his father's resistance to Clive's later work would lead him to deliberately make his output more intense than it might otherwise have been—this underplays the creative influence that both parents had in his earliest years.

His father's practical skills led to Clive constructing puppet theatre sets and other props, and the stories his mother read to him encouraged his own flights of fancy. Their own artistic interactions together would also be significant, their habit of singing songs to each other echoing down the years through Clive's love of musicals.

In fact, for all his protestations about a lack of parental encouragement, the more restrictive environment of school was where he felt most constrained.

"Right through my childhood I was supplied with all of the things I needed in the way of imaginative materials. My mother was keen that I should be reading, and allowed me to range through the library. I suppose for imaginative kids, deprivation comes not in the home, but in school. That's certainly where I felt it most keenly because that's where the world is divided up into the real and the unreal. That's where you learn the gross national product of Chile. That's where live things are dissected—and I speak both literally and metaphorically. That's where people bully you and shame you into pretending that you don't actually like the things you actually like.

"As I grew older and I went to school and teachers dealt with me, one of the things I realized was they want you to be just like everybody else, because it's easier if you're like everybody else. It's more convenient for them. That's why, in England, they put everyone in school uniforms; everybody looks the same. And, if they could, they'd make you all the same height and all the same weight; it would be so much easier if they could do that! And instead of bathing you, they could just line you up and hose you down.

"So, as a kid, I was really aware that I was not like the others. I was really embarrassed about that. I felt really vulnerable and stupid."

33

LIVEPOOL LIVES

C live went to Dovedale Primary School from September 1957 to the summer of 1964, then pro-gressed to Quarry Bank Grammar School in September 1964 through to the summer of 1971.

While he cites particular staff at Quarry Bank for their profoundly positive encouragement—Norman Russell, his English teacher, Alan Plent, his art teacher, Helen Clarke in liberal studies, and the influence of Bill Pobjoy as headmaster—others made intensely negative marks on Clive's second-ary school experience and it took him time to adjust.

"We had a French teacher," he says. "In my day, they wore black gowns, you know, the classic black gowns. He had ball bearings sewn into the lower lining of his gown. And when he didn't like what you were doing, he had a way, in one swift, even elegant motion, of taking it up, swinging it round, so as to make a ball bearing–weighted club, and bringing it down on your hand or your head or your shoulder. Or wherever he could catch you. I spent a lot of time as a child plotting elaborate, morbid revenges on these people, many of which I have enacted out in my books.

"It may not be about power as we conventionally know it," he reflects, bringing up a more serious area of interest for him, "but the occult has to do with gaining power in strange ways—magical power. I know as a kid, for instance, the notion of having magical powers was deeply attractive and it was about being able to, frankly, dominate other kids. I was this kind of nerdy kid. I thought, 'Gee, it would be nice to fly rings around people, be able to give them the evil eye, and watch them keel over. That would be kind of cool.'"

Clive returned to Quarry Bank in the early 1990s and recalls with relish a moment of revenge that would have satisfied his childhood dream. It involved a teacher whom Clive was convinced thought him "a dreamer and a waster" as a child.

"I went back to my school in Liverpool to do a TV show about me—they were re-creating my child-hood: would you believe it? I went in, and there was a sublime moment at the front door, because one of the members of the staff—he'd never scared me but he'd been deeply condescending in my child-hood some twenty-four years before—he was at the door holding back this mass of kids who were trying to watch the filming of this thing. I made my way through these kids, and he laid his hand—not knowing who I was—heavily on my chest. And I guess I looked younger than my forty years. He said, 'Stay back. We're making a film about one of the ex-boys.' And I said, 'I am the ex-boy.' And it was completely worth waiting twenty years for, to watch the look on his face. It was the artist's revenge."

Quarry Bank offered both creative opportunities and a captive audience that Clive took full advantage of, acting in school plays, then graduating to coauthor an alternative school newsletter, *Humphrei*, and to stage original plays in the school hall with a group of like-minded friends.

His earliest collaborators were his oldest friend, Adrian Phillips, who had also been at Dovedale, and three other boys he had met at Quarry Bank: Philip Rimmer, Malcolm Sharps, and David Fishel. This group of five staged their own plays: *Voodoo* in spring 1967, *Inferno* in late 1967 and *Neongonebony* in December 1968.

"Any artist in their youth is a pasticher," says Clive, "and everything I was taking in I was pastiching and passing out again and, you know, it was comic strips, it was books I was reading, it was whatever movies I could get to see (though that was a relatively limited number), and I would just mix these in an unholy mix; it was really exploitation theatre! And we actually—I want to say Phil may have done this—had some cool special effects for some of the stuff, which was kind of very fun and I think it was fun for the audience because they were my contemporaries and they were watching a bunch of their friends make complete pricks of themselves, you know? In funny costumes, I mean, the whole thing probably lasted an hour but the point is it was brought off; it actually worked enough for us to do it another time, and even though I'm sure it was really terrible and amateurish and silly, it allowed me the confidence to feel that I could go and do it again."

In March 1970, Nikolai Gogol's *The Government Inspector* was selected as the school play and the cast for this show would introduce Clive and his closest friends to several others who would join their "inner circle" for the remainder of their school days—and, in some cases, well beyond. They included Jude Kelly, Ann Taylor, Doug Bradley, and Les Heseltine. The two girls had joined the school when Calder High had merged with Quarry Bank; Doug had been two years below Clive at Quarry Bank throughout; and Les had joined from the former Morrison Secondary Modern.

In late 1970, the group mounted another original play, *The Holly and the Ivy*, improvised from a storyline by Clive. Sometime in 1970 or 1971, Jude then directed a performance of T. S. Eliot's *Murder in the Cathedral* at venues including All Hallows Church in Liverpool, casting both school friends and staff.

Clive went to Liverpool University in September 1971 through to the summer of 1974 but he maintained close links both with his contemporaries who had also gone to university and his younger

OPPOSITE PAGE

Class photo at Quarry Bank Grammar School, in 1963, Clive's first year at the school. Clive is in the back row, fourth from the right.

ABOVE

Returning to Quarry Bank in 2004, Clive takes a moment to sit in the school hall again.

"As a kid I had a picture of a ship on the wall and it set my imagination going, not just about the ship but where it was from, where it was going. I think children are blessed by time to have lots of possible destinations; it's kind of wonderful from that point of view."

school friends still at Quarry Bank. In July of 1972, in a significant step for the group, they took over Liverpool's professional Everyman Theatre for two nights and presented a farce written by Clive and Philip called *Is There Anybody There?* Julie Blake and Susan Bickley, both of whom had acted in *Murder in the Cathedral*, were now also firmly established within the group, as was Lynne Darnell, another friend from school. Susan's younger brother, Graham, would also join for their April 1973 performances of Clive's latest play, *Hunters in the Snow*, again at the Everyman.

Together, Clive, Ann, Doug, Graham, Julie, Lynne, Philip, and Susan would film an adaptation of the Salomé story on 8mm black-and-white film in 1973 before moving on to stage two new Clive Barker plays, *A Private Apocalypse* and *The Scream of the Ape*, just around the corner from Clive's house at IM Marsh, where Julie was at university. "He felt that he could make his dreams come true," remembers Julie. "He wanted more than anything to create; he believed that it was more important than anything to bring new things into being, to get inside people's minds, and to influence and change them. He believed that people's lives could be more than they were."

The group, now called the Hydra Theatre Company, returned to the Everyman for three nights in July 1974, with new material presented each night: four short plays in "An Evening of the Fantastic" on the Tuesday; *A Dream* on the Thursday; and *The Wolfman* on the Saturday.

New to the company for these plays but destined to become a key friend and collaborator was Peter Atkins, introduced to Clive and the others by Graham. Peter features as the main character who is skinned at the conclusion of Clive's short silent film *The Forbidden*, with sequences shot between 1975 (in Liverpool) and 1978 (in London).

Renamed again as the Mute Pantomime Theatre Company, the friends staged *A Clowns' Sodom* in April 1976 and then an iteration of that play, called *The Day of the Dog*, at London's first International Mime Festival in February 1977. In ones and twos, the group moved to London that year and the capital became home to Clive, Philip, Doug, Lynne, and Julie, with Peter joining them after his summer 1978 university final exams.

OPPOSITE PAGE

TOP LEFT

(l to r) Jude Kelly as Beth Barton, Nick Suckley as Flash Harry, and Clive as bookmaker Alfred Tubbe, onstage in a school production of John Chapman's Whitehall farce, *Dry Rot*, directed by Bruce Prince (1971).

TOP RIGHT

Having left school, Clive founded the Hydra Theatre Company with friends, some of whom were still at Quarry Bank. Ann Taylor was also involved in the Everyman Youth Theatre and Jude Kelly had been a folk singer in the theatre's bistro, which gave them the connections to secure the prestigious Liverpool Everyman in dark weeks. Clive co-wrote the black farce *Is There Anybody There?* with Philip Rimmer for Hydra, and it played for a two-night run in July 1972. Here, Clive plays Bishop Norman Duckworth against Jane Abbott's Gloria Goodbody in *Is There Anybody There?*

CENTER LEFT

(l to r) Susan Bickley, Julie Blake, Philip Rimmer, Ann Taylor, Doug Bradley, and Lynne Darnell pose on Hale Beach, circa 1973. Hale Beach was a favorite haunt and was used as an outdoor location for filming *Salomé*.

CENTER RIGHT

(l to r) Philip Rimmer, Doug Bradley, Clive, Julie Blake, Lynne Darnell (masked), and Ann Taylor, rehearsing in costume on Hale Beach, circa 1973.

BOTTOM LEFT

Julie Blake as the Sphinx with Doug Bradley as the Pilgrim in rehearsal for *A Dream*, one of the sequence of productions at the Everyman, 1974.

BOTTOM RIGHT

(l to r, standing) Julie Blake, Doug Bradley, and Ann Taylor with (seated) Philip Rimmer, Lynne Darnell, and Susan Bickley on Tiree with Clive in 1974.

Clive on a day trip out with his friends, circa 1975.

In late 1976/early 1977, Peter Atkins wrote a short thesis, "The First Manifesto of Clive Barker's Mute Theatre, Europe's Most Articulate Mime Company," as an academic argument for the importance of the company's agenda. Photo portraits were included from this shoot including Clive (with plaster relief of an angel), Doug Bradley (with portrait of Jean Cocteau), Peter Atkins and Lynne Darnell.

Doug Bradley, Anu, and Clive in 1976.

Doug Bradley with paper birds from The Forbidden 16mm film (1975-78).

Peter Atkins, circa 1976.

Clive, in 1976, in make-up as Herlequin.

Clive applies make-up before a photo session, 1976.

Portrait of Doug Bradley, Tiree, 1974. Over the next few years, particularly while the group of friends lived together, Clive and Philip Rimmer would continue to experiment with still photography. Although his use of black-and-white film was largely an economic choice, it gave Clive a strong sense of how he might manipulate light and shadow.

In a precursor of Pinhead's gridded head of nails, Clive explores light and shade using a similarly gridded nail board in this portrait of Philip Rimmer, circa 1977.

Clive from a series of mirrored poses shot by Philip Rimmer, circa 1977.

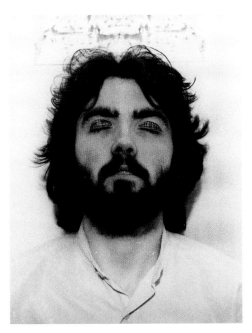
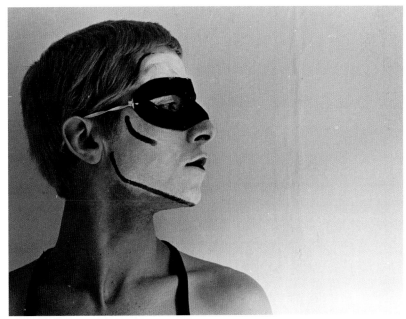

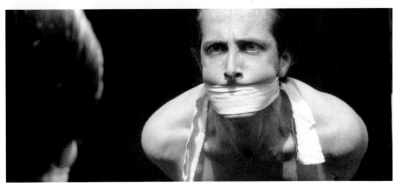

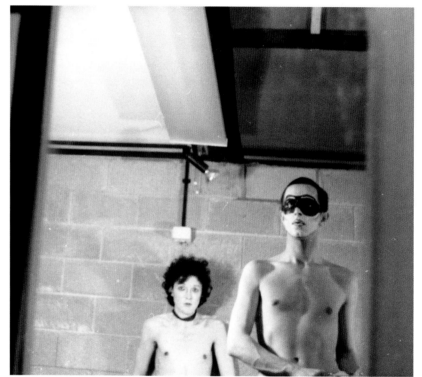

OPPOSITE PAGE
TOP LEFT

Having moved into the
flat of his boyfriend,
John Gregson, Clive
found a new energy for
theatre work. He began
work on a Commedia
dell' Arte mime piece
that reflected his
growing interest in
clowns, *A Clowns'
Sodom*. Here, Doug

Bradley as the Patriarch
(Lot) backstage at *A
Clowns' Sodom*. The
production was staged
at Liverpool University's
Eleanor Rathbone
Theatre in April 1976.

TOP RIGHT

Lynne Darnell as
Grimaldi, backstage at
A Clowns' Sodom, 1976.

CENTER LEFT

The cast of *A Clowns'
Sodom* backstage:
(l to r, back row) Philip
Rimmer as Pulcinella,
Peter Atkins as Pierrot,
and Clive as Herlequin
(center, seated) Doug
Bradley as the Patriarch
and Lynne Darnell
as Columbine; (front
row) Julie Blake as the
Surgeon, 1976.

CENTER LEFT

Lynne Darnell as
Grimaldi behind Julie
Blake as the Surgeon,
backstage at *A Clowns'
Sodom*, 1976.

CENTER RIGHT

Peter Atkins as Pierrot
and Clive as Herlequin
backstage at *A Clowns'
Sodom*, 1976.

BOTTOM LEFT

Clive, circa 1973.

BOTTOM RIGHT

Clive, circa 1974.

THIS PAGE

Clive filming for *The
Forbidden*, circa 1975.

1978–1983

THE DOGS IN LONDON

Now called the Dog Company, and with mime left behind, the group performed two new plays by Clive in 1978: *The Sack* in June and *The Magician* in December. These were both staged back in Liverpool and it was not until October 1979, when they debuted *Dog* (a reworked version of *The Day of The Dog*, now with words), that London witnessed its first Dog Company performances.

Nightlives then debuted in November 1979 and became the group's longest-running play to date, playing fifteen times at various small venues through to May 1980.

Despite having had a good reputation and relationship with the Merseyside Arts Association and having received funding from that body for projects, the London-based Arts Council was far less impressed. Times were tough for the group; money was hard to find and Arts Council critics were blunt before eventually awarding Clive a writing grant on a project-by-project application basis.

"You know, my method for getting past those bad times," reflects Clive, "is to just get on and work and it always helps me—you move on, you get engaged with another project, and before you know it the stings have passed away."

Peter Atkins would later reflect on the whirlwind of creative activity: "I miss the drive and confidence and ambition that you can only have at that age. It was a blind faith and complete commitment to what we were all doing. I miss the sense of a very fruitful artistic collaboration with a peer group that you loved, admired, and respected . . . the togetherness in the face of adversity."

Peter left the company over the summer of 1980 and returned to Liverpool, while Clive decided to cease acting in order to concentrate on writing and directing. New company members joined, including Oliver Parker, Mary Roscoe, and Jay Venn, just ahead of the Dog Company's break-out success, *The History of the Devil*, which they played on sixty-four occasions between September 1980 and September 1981, touring it outside London to various venues in England as well as in the Netherlands and at the Edinburgh Fringe Festival, with Konni Burger replacing Mary halfway through the year.

Their most successful project thus far, *The History of the Devil* was the Dog Company's coming-of-age production, replacing the succession of plays that had been staged just once or a handful of times each with a production that toured and brought the company to new audiences across Britain and beyond.

"With these things from the Everyman," says Doug reflecting on the contrast, "we would spend a year rehearsing and do one, maybe two, and at most three performances. Now we were working with

ABOVE

Clive's character sketches and poster designs for *The Day of the Dog*, 1977.

OPPOSITE PAGE

Clive onstage as Dog in *The Day of the Dog*, February 1977.

"Studying _Frankenstein in Love_ with fresh eyes, I was taken aback by how unrelentingly grim it is. There are some dark journeys taken in the Books of Blood, to be sure, but I can't think of a tale even there that so obsessively circles on images of death and taboo."

a fixed rehearsal time. We were a proper theatre company. A limited company with directors and patrons. There was an opening date to aim for, and for the first time we brought actors in from outside, some of whom simply came in for one or two productions and then went on to other jobs."

"It is appealing," says Clive of _The History of the Devil_. "You can have fun. It was tremendous fun to do and once you get up a kind of speed it's almost like a kind of circus, you know, it's an actor's circus: it plays fast and furious and it's funny one moment and poignant the next and it has a great punch line and I was always astonished how much people loved it. I mean, we had audiences in Edinburgh, people who would come night after night after night. It was the first time that I really had a sense I could make something, really make something that would really capture a decent-sized audience, and I will have to say in a way, therefore, that it is the flame that ignited the fuse that led to the Books of Blood."

The creation of the acting troupe as a separate entity, excluding Clive, allowed the play to extend its life without the previous restless nature of its author to stop the run of performances.

"I think there was a general sense that we were all growing up by doing this. . . . It made sense all round, no question. The previous circumstance wasn't helped by the fact that I never really enjoyed acting that much, so that when I had a chance to move on from the experience I was happy to do so. Once, I remember . . . you know how you're blessed in youth by moments of epiphany: I was sitting on a bench outside the British Museum, eating an ice cream, and I realized, in this little moment, that I was incredibly, perfectly happy. The day was bright and breezy, and it must have been early fall, because there were leaves around my feet, and I was eating an ice cream, which, of course, always made me happy, and I had a play that was playing at that time at the York and Albany. I think we had gone back to the York and Albany for a second time to play _History of the Devil_ again and it was playing; we had full houses for the week. It played pretty flawlessly and I remember very clearly feeling, 'This is as good as it gets!' It's one of those moments that fixes in your head, you know?"

In early 1981 the company also added to its repertoire a new play devised by Doug and Oliver, *Dangerous World*, which used the words of William Blake to tell the story of his life in his final hour alive.

Paradise Street, Clive's next play, debuted in July 1981 and the Dog Company played *The History of the Devil*, *Dangerous World*, and *Paradise Street* during July, August, September, and October 1981 before reappearing on stage with Clive's *Frankenstein in Love* in March 1982—another production that they took on an overseas tour, adding venues in Belgium to ones in the Netherlands this time. *The Secret Life of Cartoons* debuted in August 1982, with both shows being performed at the Edinburgh Fringe Festival later that month.

Clive did not travel to Edinburgh in 1982 and had already made another conscious step into focusing on his writing, having handed his *Frankenstein in Love* text to an outside director for the first time. Instead he was hard at work completing short fiction to add to pieces he had been writing through 1981 and early 1982 and had just sold, in his first book publishing deal, to Sphere Books.

With Clive now writing contracted books for a publisher and plays commissioned for other troupes, the Dog Company was left without its resident playwright. Despite a fundraising performance in November 1982 and plans for a tour of *The Secret Life of Cartoons* around the UK and Europe, the company disbanded in 1983.

The artistic director of London's Cockpit Theatre, where the Dog Company had staged several of its plays, commissioned Clive to write three plays, all for the Cockpit Youth Theatre: *Crazyface* staged in December 1982, *Subtle Bodies* in June and July 1983, and *Colossus*, which explores Goya's approach to art, in September 1983.

"It took forever to write *Colossus*," Clive recalls. "I remember sitting on the Underground, writing, delivering pages to the theatre, and going home to write more pages. There were some terrible typos as they were being typed from my handwriting.

"I was trying to find a kind of new language for this play that was less literary and was much more naturalistic; people speak in these relatively short phrases and have very different ways of speaking; there isn't a single kind of style that people use. It was me really trying to experiment pretty strongly, knowing that I had the director Geoff Gillham's support to do that."

Goya's work had long fascinated Clive, as he later reflected: "Let me take this chance to name Francisco de Goya as a hugely influential figure in my life. "He was a documentarian of the first order, who was also a brilliant fantasist and a man who found the profoundest universal truths in images that were plucked from his personal dreamscape."

Colossus would prove to be Clive's final play to date. Other avenues awaited. . . .

THE HISTORY OF THE DEVIL

TOP LEFT

The Dog Company, always short of income, held this fundraising evening in January 1982, hoping to raise sponsorship funding. This display included press clippings and some early rehearsal shots of *Frankenstein in Love* ahead of the production later that year.

TOP RIGHT

Oliver Parker as Shay Bonner looks over the shoulder of Doug Bradley as his brother, Quinn, onstage in *Paradise Street*, 1981.

CENTER LEFT

Company photo, including (back row) Jay Venn, Doug Bradley, and Konni Burger, (kneeling) Oliver Parker, and (seated) Philip Rimmer, 1981.

BOTTOM LEFT

(l to r) New company member Konni Burger, Lynne Darnell, and (seated) Oliver Parker in costume for *The History of the Devil*, 1981.

BOTTOM RIGHT

Doug Bradley as Quinn entertains Lynne Darnell as Caroline, onstage in *Paradise Street*, 1981.

Konni Burger as Elizabeth I in *Paradise Street*, 1981.

(l to r, foreground) Jay Venn as Jude is entertained by Konni Burger as Elizabeth I while (background) Lynne Darnell as Lucy Lovelace looks on in *Paradise Street*, 1981.

Two masquers debate the nature of theatre as they announce the opening of a play for the pleasure of Gloriana, Queen Elizabeth I, in *Paradise Street*, 1981.

Doug Bradley as Quinn and Oliver Parker as Shay in *Paradise Street*, 1981.

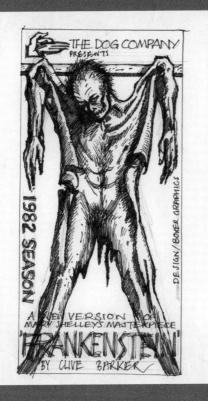

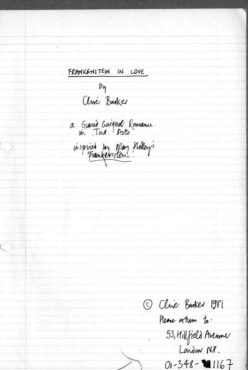

TOP LEFT

Working on the stylized poster design for *Frankenstein in Love*, Clive directs Clare O'Donnell and Oliver Parker in a photo shoot for reference images, which would be used by artist and designer, Chris Priestly, 1982.

TOP RIGHT

Final poster design for *Frankenstein in Love* at the Cockpit Theatre, London, 1982.

BOTTOM LEFT

Clive's poster design for *Frankenstein in Love*, 1982.

BOTTOM RIGHT

Manuscript title page from *Frankenstein in Love*, 1981.

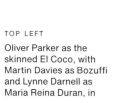

TOP LEFT

Oliver Parker as the skinned El Coco, with Martin Davies as Bozuffi and Lynne Darnell as Maria Reina Duran, in *Frankenstein in Love*, at the Cockpit Theatre, London, in April 1982.

TOP RIGHT

Doug Bradley as Dr. Frankenstein with Clare O'Donnell as Veronique in *Frankenstein in Love*, 1982.

BOTTOM LEFT

Clive's character design for Frankenstein's "monster as romantic hero," 1981.

BOTTOM RIGHT

Lynne Darnell as Maria Reina Duran, 1982.

'The Secret Life of Cartoons'
by
Clive Barker
an entertainment

TOP LEFT
Oliver Parker as El Coco attacks Doug Bradley as Dr. Frankenstein in a publicity still for *Frankenstein in Love*, 1982.

TOP RIGHT
Clive's manuscript title page from *The Secret Life of Cartoons*, 1982.

BOTTOM
The Dog Company's late-night show in Edinburgh, 1982, was Clive's one-act comedy *The Secret Life of Cartoons*, in which the 2D world of animation collides with the 3D world of its creators. Its success would bring it back to down to play in London after the festival. (l to r) Clare O'Donnell as Lorraine Caplan, Lynne Darnell as Betty B., and John Elnaugh as Dick Caplan impersonate A Certain Rabbit to try to throw Oliver Parker, as A Certain Mouse, off the rabbit's trail. Onstage in *The Secret Life of Cartoons*, Edinburgh, 1982.

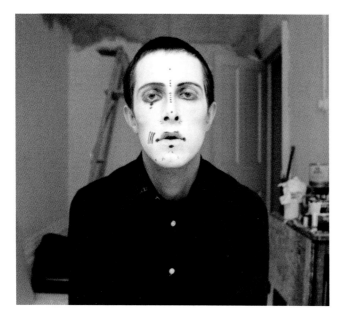
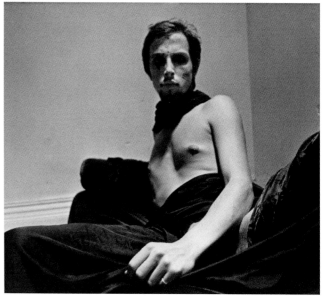

1972–1978

EARLY FILMS—SALOMÉ AND THE FORBIDDEN

Dance of the Seven Veils

The short film *Salomé* draws inspiration from the biblical tale and followed Clive's earlier staged production with the Hydra Theatre Company in Liverpool of Oscar Wilde's play of the same name. Filmed partly on Hale Beach, partly in a florist's cellar at night, the film is a poetic interpretation of the famous story.

Asked about the subject matter, Clive responds enthusiastically: "The Salomé story: boy, there are layers to that story. It's a very sexual story; it's a very ritualistic story; it's a bargain story. The story had always attracted me. The Bible is a source of inspiration constantly for me and remains a significant source of inspiration. The references to Salomé in the Bible are I think slight, but, nevertheless, biblical stories, if they are good stories, have a kind of primal quality to them."

Clive used the film to attempt to attract funding for his next proposed film project, *The Forbidden*, and despite his feeling about the technical quality of the footage compared to the movie in his mind, his concerns were not shared by others. "I remember when we got three hundred pounds from the Liverpool Film Association or whatever, I showed the man *Salomé* and I was squirming with embarrassment at how rough it was, but he was astonished at what we had achieved."

The Forbidden is a personal interpretation of Faust's bargain with the Devil, a scenario that would eventually be reemployed by Clive as the driving force behind both *The Damnation Game* and *The Hellbound Heart*.

Fade up on a room, empty. It has a square latticed window (very simple), white walls, white floor boards, black window frame and latticework. No curtains. Firstly, in a series of long, very evenly paced pans, the camera examines this room to set the limits of this film, to assert the room's coolness, its total lack of complicity. On one wall, opposite the

You want to know
what
The Forbidden
is
?

Go ask your hearts.

window, a reproduction of Géricault's *Horse Frightened by Lightning*. No other ornament. A blue bulb.

Whiteness: titles. Move away from a piece of paper on a small black table. The table has a drawer in it. A young man (25) sits at the table and proceeds to fold the piece of paper into an origami form. He does it without thinking. His white face registers nothing, his black hair is short and slicked back. The music that plays in a different room may or may not be his choice. It is Schubert.

OPPOSITE PAGE
Manuscript note,
circa 1975.

ABOVE
Clive and Peter Atkins
in costume for *The
Forbidden*, 1976

Writing in *Sight and Sound* magazine in 1995 as the two films were released, Clive recognizes their limitations. "In short, they are technically extremely crude and their storylines obscure. *Salomé* vaguely follows the biblical tale of lust, dance, martyrdom, and murder, but only vaguely; *The Forbidden*, though derived from the Faust story, is steeped in a delirium all of its own. Notwithstanding, the images still carry a measure of raw power some two decades on, in part perhaps because the context is otherwise so unsophisticated."

What remains fascinating about the projects is how they offer an early visual snapshot of the narrative themes Clive wanted to explore.

"I think *The Forbidden* has a weird sort of life to it and it's interesting because it contains all those imagistic prophecies of things that would later appear in either the short stories—tattooing, voyeurism, and so on—or in the *Hellraiser* movies, obviously. So put together with *Salomé*, even though they were movies made at the *most* primitive level . . . actually, I think it has a strange poetry about it—they both have a poetry about them—and they do fix in time who we were at a certain point and what our obsessions were—perhaps more particularly what *my* obsessions were. . . . And so when Frank is skinned, obviously, in *Hellraiser*, it is a *direct* development from the moment in *The Forbidden* when Pete has his skin removed."

"When Frank is skinned, in *Hellraiser*, it is a direct development from the moment in *The Forbidden* when Pete has his skin removed."

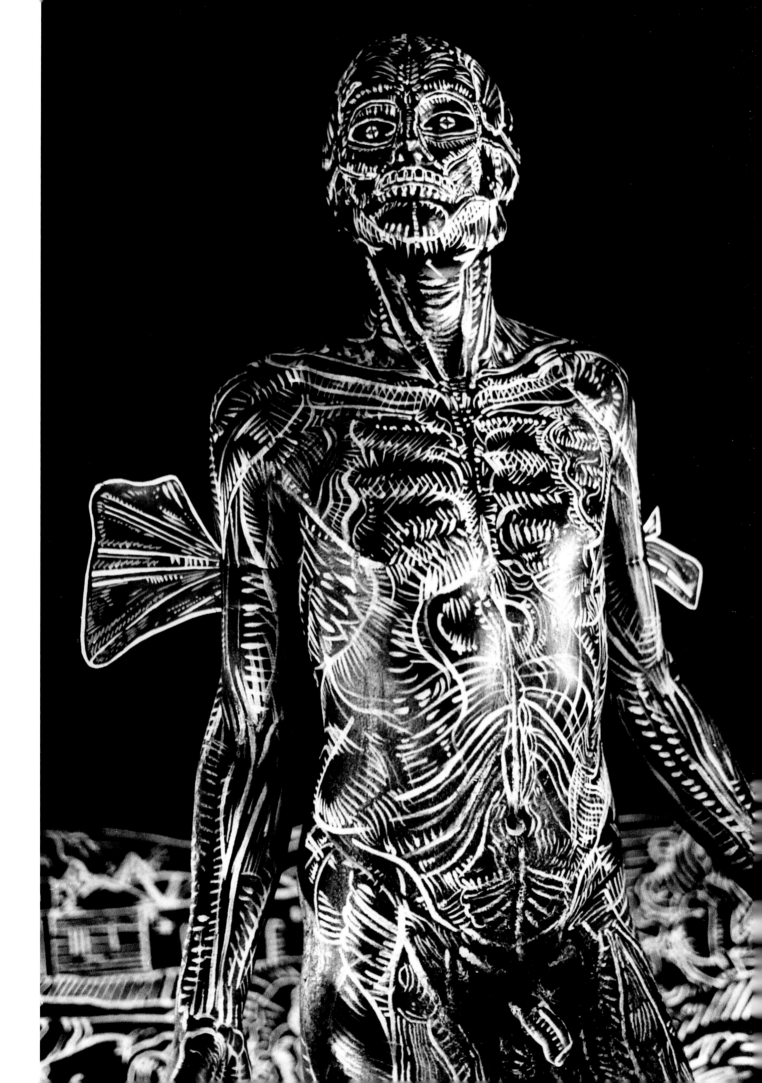

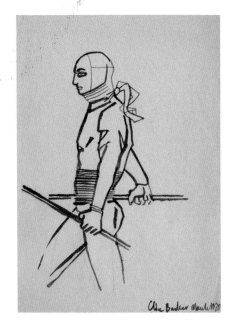
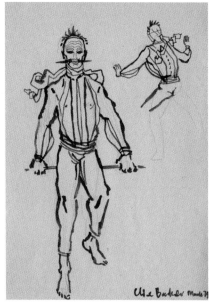

EARLY ARTWORK

Clive has long been known as a weaver of stories, be they for page or screen, but what was less obvious in the late 1980s was that his ideas were often manifesting as images before they became words. From childhood he has constantly drawn, sketched, and painted his dreams and ideas.

As those themes and visions evolve, they cross back and forth across media; handwritten notes for narratives are populated with character sketches wherever the words take a pause. An oil painting might inspire a fresh plot point or be the catalyst for an entirely new world, and an idea for a story will be fashioned as a movie, comic, or game to find its best home. In the same way, Clive has always captured and shared his ideas in whichever medium happens to work best in the moment—often visually.

Despite being badged as a horror writer and a director intent on the dark and distressing, he has always expressed a desire to explore a full spectrum of metaphysics, spirituality, and the human condition. That applies no less to his artwork. Admittedly graphic and unconstrained in subject, the extent of his body of work was a surprise to many when it was explored across two volumes of monographs in 1990 and 1993—*Clive Barker: Illustrator* and *Illustrator II: The Art of Clive Barker*, both by Fred Burke and published by Eclipse—and Clive's first solo exhibitions in New York in 1993 brought his artwork to the attention of a still wider audience.

In his introduction to the first volume, artist Stephen R. Bissette calls Clive's work "a mercurial alchemy," an observation that very much speaks to Clive's experience of creation and empowerment through his art, both at school and at home.

"When I drew things people looked, people smiled, took pleasure, asked me questions about what I was sketching, which allowed me in turn to invent stories about the things I was drawing, those stories leading on to more drawings.

"I never drew from life. I couldn't understand why anybody would want to. I also wasn't very good at it, which remains true to this date. It was my mental world I was interested in; the things my inward turning eye could see. I was calling things forth with my pencils and my brushes; summoning the shapes of beasts and the heroes that battled them, in wholly invented landscapes."

Clive's art teacher at Quarry Bank, Alan Plent, observed, "Dinosaurs and monsters played a large part in his thinking and drawing, even then! His art always invited a story from it. You never looked at

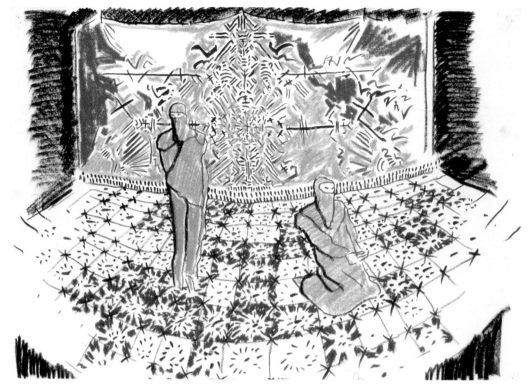

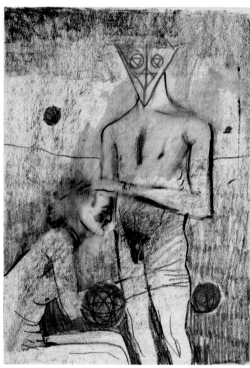

TOP

Clive would often spend time designing various characters and settings for theatre work, including this *Design for Unnamed Theatre Piece*, 1976.

BOTTOM LEFT

Clive's sketched the male form for theatre projects and portraits. Circa 1977.

BOTTOM RIGHT

The Blues, 1977.

it and said, 'Oh, well there's a lovely landscape'; you were inclined to say, 'What's going on in there?' and you would look for the next one."

It's a view that Clive shares. "I never really was that attached to the process of writing or drawing. It was the results I liked. For me, it's all about the story, the metaphysical and visceral thrills of the story, not just style.

"What I'm doing all the time when sketching is making visual notes for things which may eventually pop into being in a novel or a short story, a movie, or may simply become a painting. I sometimes wake in the middle of the night and sketch. I keep ink and brushes right alongside the pens on my

62

"His art always invited a story from it. You never looked at it and said, 'Oh, well there's a lovely landscape'; you were inclined to say, 'What's going on in there?' and you would look for the next one." —ALAN PLENT, art teacher

desk. In many cases, the preparatory drawings are extremely crude, just a few lines done with brush and India ink. They're things that I pen down, put aside, and then one day think, 'That was a weird idea.' Then I'll go back to it, and suddenly it has a life of its own."

Drawing became the natural language of his teeming imagination and a way to discharge cascading thoughts when words might take more crafting. But it would also serve as a vital tool in his collaborative work with friends as they fashioned narratives into the plays of the 1970s and early '80s. His artistic ability meant he could not only consolidate a fleeting thought with a quick pencil sketch, he could also communicate ideas to others—a methodology he employs to this day—with a clarity that could otherwise be lost.

Publicity posters for the plays would also benefit from Clive's artistic talents, which could marry a visual conceit with a striking call to "come see our fantasy played out for you." As Peter Atkins, who codesigned many of the Dog Company's posters, recalls: "The process for our mutual posters was that Clive would do a pencil sketch of the main image and then I would take them and turn them into the heavily stylized, strict black-and-white images and add the lettering.

"What's fascinating to me now," he continues, "is that they were genuine handcrafted artworks—because we hand-printed them ourselves on silkscreen equipment. Phil Rimmer would prepare photographic mattes/screens from my actual-size finished artwork and Clive and I (along with Phil and whoever else was around to help) would hand-pull them, applying the ink and working the squeegee ourselves. We only ever made about a hundred of each one."

Immersed in the plays for the Dog Company and the Cockpit Youth Theatre, and in the tales that would become the Books of Blood, Clive's art was strongly character-driven. Following a journalistic sense of observing characters as concrete presences in his head as he wrote them, Clive's sketchbooks abounded with fools, demons, princes, and madmen. Giving them sketched lives on paper helped give their words and actions a depth and credibility onstage that they would need to lead an audience from a grimy streetscape to a world peopled with angels.

TOP LEFT
Untitled, circa 1972.

TOP CENTER
Untitled, circa 1972.

TOP RIGHT
Untitled, circa 1972.

BOTTOM
Clive's portrait of Simon Bamford, circa 1981.

1982–1987 UNDERWORLD AND RAWHEAD REX

We Are What We Dream

"**U**nderworld started with George Pavlou, the director," recalls Clive. "I had met George at a dinner party in 1982. All we talked about were movies. He wanted to direct them and I wanted to write them. It seemed a perfect match, as we could learn the ropes together—the basis being the possibility of us both becoming a unit. He asked me to write a screenplay with him so I said, 'Let's do a gangster-versus-mutants horror picture. . . .'"

Although Clive had experimented with filmmaking for many years, he'd never at this point put pen to paper on a full-length screenplay, so rather than race headlong into the unfamiliar format he drafted a shorter outline treatment. Running to twelve typed pages, the story mixed gangsters, monsters, scientists, dreams, desires, and bodily transformation. Inspired by his own sense of claustrophobia, Clive confined his characters bodily and psychologically and set the action both above-ground and in a world below the city streets.

"Our hero is stuck between the overworld and the underworld; between a world which is brutal and superficially, glossily attractive—a world of money and influence—and an underworld which is physically filthy and repulsive but which contains the one woman he has ever loved. I was keen to create an environment at once identifiable yet strange, and we have this labyrinth of sewers that act as a sort of no-man's-land where someone from above may meet something from below. It's a bit like Dante's *Inferno*, in fact. I'm posing the question, 'What happens when our dreams go out of control?'"

Clive completed the treatment in September 1982 and discussed various possible plot points with George Pavlou but it was decided to leave further drafting until financing could be found. This took two years, until November 1984, when George put the treatment into the hands of two producers, Don Hawkins and Kevin Attew of Green Man Productions.

Someone has awakened him.

RawHeadRex

...He lives again to feed again.

ALPINE PICTURES Presents A GREEN MAN Production RAWHEAD REX
Starring DAVID DUKES and KELLY PIPER Director of Photography JOHN METCALFE Music COLIN TOWNS
Screenplay CLIVE BARKER Executive Producers AL BURGESS PAUL GWYNN Produced by KEVIN ATTEW DON HAWKINS
Directed by GEORGE PAVLOU

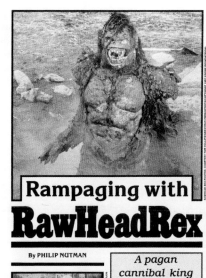

Introducing *Rawhead Rex*, the monstrous giant from the pen of Clive Barker.

Rampaging with

RawHeadRex

By PHILIP NUTMAN

Director George (*Underworld*) Pavlou (pointing) brings his second Clive Barker film to the screen with *Rawhead Rex*. Empire releases it this year.

A pagan cannibal king returns from its tomb in director George Pavlou's latest Clive Barker adaptation.

Beneath the thin crust of earth, Rawhead smelt the sky. It was pure ether to his dulled senses, making him sick with pleasure. Kingdoms for the taking, just a few inches away. After so many years, after the endless suffocation, there was light

on his eyes again, and the taste of human terror on his tongue . . . .

Since the multi-talented Clive Baker's short horror stories exploded upon an unsuspecting genre two years ago (in Britain, at least), excitement has been building steadily. *Underworld* (Fango #50), the first film based on his work, an original screenplay, has yet to be released on either side of the Atlantic, but a second project, *Rawhead Rex*, went before the cameras in spring 1986. It's an adaptation of a short story from volume three of *Books of Blood*. And expectations are running high.

Lensed entirely on location in Southern Ireland, *Rawhead* is an Alpine Pictures/Greenman Productions film. The two companies were responsible for bringing *Underworld* to the big screen, and George Pavlou directs for a second time. Empire International plans to release both Pavlou-Barker movies.

During *Underworld's* shooting schedule, Pavlou informed Fango that he would have preferred to have made *Rawhead Rex* as his motion picture debut. With hindsight, he admits his comments were naive. "*Rawhead* proved to be a more difficult movie than *Underworld* in almost every area, particularly in terms of effects," explains the British director.

"We're dealing with one creature and the whole movie depends upon him. To make him credible, totally believable, is quite an undertaking. We only had eight weeks to prepare the film, and to create an animatronic creature within that period of time is incredibly demanding. Actionwise, there's much more going on in this one compared with *Underworld*. We have several explosions. And we even beat the world record for setting men on fire at the same time! In one scene [when Rawhead causes the pyrotechnic destruction of a camper site], we have nine people covered in flames."

Rawhead Rex is a nine-foot tall warrior monarch from a pre-Christian era, a fearsome, ferocious being with an appetite for human flesh. He is accidentally unearthed by a hapless farmer and begins to lay waste to the surrounding countryside. When the cannibal king eats the son of visiting American Howard Hallenbeck (David Dukes), it proves to be the turning point in the creature's reign of terror. Hallenbeck, feeling responsible for his son's death, decides to kill the monster by drawing on his research into pagan legends, thereby

34 FANGORIA #61

The movie was greenlit as a coproduction with Limehouse Productions contingent on production starting almost immediately, so Clive was asked to produce a script at a breakneck pace, with just two weeks to turn his treatment into a screenplay.

Writing the key conceit—"We Are What We Dream"—on the front page, he set to work and turned in two drafts before the start of filming on January 7, 1985. The plot involves an experimental drug that a man named Dr. Savary is testing to disfiguring effect on his subjects, all except on one beautiful young sex worker, Nicole.

Thinking about the physical embodiment of dreams, facilitated in the film by the mind-altering drug and through Nicole's control of its effects, Clive reflected on the metaphor during filming: "The rational encounters the absurd, its distorted mirror image, in the imaginative process. The drug theme of the movie makes that explicit and we are asking what happens when our dreams go out of control, thus we have characters caught between both worlds. Personally, I find something immensely satisfying about a metaphorical structure like that."

Steven Berkoff, playing Motherskille, one of the villains from London's East End, noted Clive's genre-mixing intent, saying, "I think *Underworld* is going to be great, as it's a very unusual kind of gangster/science fiction/fantasy film—I think the combinations of things are what make things successful. When people dare to juxtapose opposites. Mostly they don't dare: SF is SF, gangster fiction is gangster fiction, documentary is 'North Country poor kid gets a girl in trouble.' Everything is very simple-minded. Here, the guy has mixed everything up. . . ."

"But I've tried to take it further than just that," continued Clive. "I have inverted the conventions of the genre in that the surface characters, the representatives of society, which in most monster movies are authoritarian figures, usually scientists or other people responsible for order and stability, are models of moral depravity—they are criminals, bastards of the first rank. So the situation raises, hopefully, if they get on-screen what I've written, a number of moral complexities which the audience will have to form their own conclusions about."

Clive's "if they get on-screen what I've written" comment reflects the fact that his draft scripts, written in haste by a self-admittedly inexperienced screenwriter, had been considered by Green Man as unfit for locking as the shooting script. In parts they were as densely written as a novel. With the start of principal photography looming, they hired a second writer, James Caplan, to work on the screenplay in parallel with Clive.

Ultimately, the movie was altered beyond Clive's original intention and he was unhappy with the finished result.

The film screened at the London Film Festival on Friday, November 29, 1985, and was advertised this way:

> *Underworld* provides a rich (and decidedly unBritish) feast of sci-fi, myth and Gothic horror, which begins with the abduction of Nicole (Nicola Cowper), a beautiful young prostitute, by a pack of mutant beings. "Retired" henchman Roy Bain (Larry Lamb) is tempted back onto the payroll of gangland boss Hugo Motherskille (Steven Berkoff) in order to find the girl they both love ("I don't want to see her come back in bits and pieces," Motherskille tells him. "Call that sentimental if you like"). Bain's search leads him to the unsavoury Dr. Savary (Denholm Elliott), and to the cavernous underworld where the victims of Savary's experiments are plotting revenge. Director George Pavlou and a first-rate cast play the thrill (and the grim humour) of this grisly chiller on just the right side of credibility, re-working the Orpheus myth through two kinds of futuristic underworld. Denholm Elliott, Steven Berkoff and an almost unrecognisable Miranda Richardson relish the meatier roles. Nicola Cowper makes a breathtaking Eurydice, and Sydney Macartney's stunning photography deserves special praise.

Despite its well-respected cast, *Underworld* would not receive a UK theatrical release after the festival, while its US theatrical debut the following spring came under the rebranded title *Transmutations*.

"It's worth pointing out," noted Clive ahead of the festival, "that this story does not exist in Books of Blood. *Underworld* is a completely separate original treatment. . . . Kevin and Don, who are always approachable with new ideas, then became very interested in doing *Underworld* as part of a series. It just so happened that the first three Books of Blood were about to be published. I was able to get the galley proofs to them and they secured options on the movie rights of five of the short stories—'Human Remains,' 'Confessions of a (Pornographer's) Shroud,' 'Jacqueline Ess: Her Will and Testament,' 'Rawhead Rex,' and 'Sex, Death and Starshine.'"

This was a significant next step for the intended life of Clive's works on-screen. He signed the option contract in the summer of 1985. The first story selected for adaptation was his tale of Rawhead Rex, "nine feet of lumbering death."

He wrote the first draft in July 1985, discussed notes, and wrote and delivered a second draft in late summer 1985, saying, "Right now all I'm doing is working on the screenplay to *Rawhead Rex*—rewrites basically. It's going very well and the production company has been very agreeable about all the violence. I think they're getting used to me. I don't like 'polite' in literature or in film. I want the filmmaker to constantly press my imagination, you know. To me, 'polite horror' doesn't work."

Later he would lament, having turned in the second draft, "That was literally the last I ever heard from anyone." Perhaps the *Underworld* experience could have prepared him for more disappointment, but the speed of that first production was very different from the seemingly more relaxed schedule for this first movie under the new five-picture deal.

"I know, it does seem a dumb thing to do," sighed Clive, reflecting on signing further stories over to Green Man, "but I'm an optimist, so when they came back to me and bought 'Rawhead Rex,' which was a monster story about a horrid beast unleashed from the earth to kill children and piss on virgins, I didn't think there was any way they could ruin it. . . ."

66

The movie was greenlit but Irish funding came with the condition of an Irish location, and the timing of the shoot undermined Clive's narrative intentions.

"It was meant to be an English equivalent of *Jaws*, in which you had sun and jolliness and people holidaying and there's this shark eating them. I wanted the same kind of thing, only in a quintessen-tially English fashion. I'd purposely written 'Rawhead' during one of our rare hot summers—the sort of atmosphere where flies bred in dead creatures in two hours flat. England, midsummer, blue skies, bright sunshine, birds everywhere—and behind the barn lurked this child-eating creature.

"So I knew it was bad news when they decided to film it in Ireland in February. . . . All the contrast that I'd written into the screenplay went to the wall. Immediately, a whole counterpoint of this blazing English summer and this ravaging monster just went out of the window. I wanted to smell thunder in the air but it ended up as a cold, Celtic, lumbering excuse for a horror movie instead."

Unlike *Underworld*, where he had visited the set and been actively involved in rewrites during filming, this time principal photography took place without him.

"I was never invited on the set, never saw the promised plane ticket for Dublin, and all I kept hearing were pretty lousy things about the way the film was progressing. . . . I'll never understand why I was ignored. It still remains a complete and utter mystery to me. Even to this day I've never received an explanation why I was never consulted over any of the major decisions to change the thrust or details in my original script. Either they thought I was useless and wouldn't have anything to contribute or else they worried I might have some valid opinions which would make too many waves.

"At least on *Underworld* I used to come off the phone shaking with rage because I knew they were heading in the wrong direction. On *Rawhead* the phone never rang once—I was in the dark and still being fucked over and there was nothing I could do about it."

In the second half of 1985, as *The Damnation Game* and the second set of Books of Blood were published and six months before *Rawhead Rex* had even gone before George Pavlou's cameras, Clive started to hatch plans to direct a movie himself.

"I had a friend who had a brother who had a friend," says Clive. "The friend was Oliver Parker, the brother was a guy called Alan Parker, and his friend was a fellow called Chris Figg. Chris Figg wanted to produce movies and I wanted to direct a movie and we were both without any experience, really, in our fields, but two inexperienced people is always more interesting as a combination than one inexperienced person, and we kind of gave each other courage, I think."

ABOVE
Promotional brochure for the VHS and Betamax releases of *Rawhead Rex* and *Underworld* (before *Underworld*'s change of title in the US to *Transmutations*). Vestron Video, 1987.

NEXT SPREAD
Manuscript opening pages from Clive's screenplay for *Underworld*, 1984.

1. <u>Title Sequence</u>

In darkness, the belly-churning thunder
of ~~rushing~~ rushing water. As the volume of the
roar rises, the image of a tunnel appears.
We ~~glide~~ glide through this ~~tunnel~~ passage as the rushing
continues — the ~~noise~~ Noise coming first from one
direction, then another. From beneath the
sound of water, music. It is slow at first,
matching the eerie environment, and our
slow progress through it. <u>Titles</u> start to ~~be~~ appear.
The music begins to gather pace and
excitability as we move <u>upwards</u> through
the tunnels — passing through grilles, and between
narrow walls, climbing steps shiny with slime. By
the time we reach a ladder, the music is a
~~furious~~ feverish tattoo. We ascend the ladder;
at the top, a man-hole cover. A hand reaches
up and ~~pulls~~ pushes the heavy cover aside. The
camera rises to the Overworld. As it crosses
the threshold of one world into another, the
music abruptly stops. We are left with the
natural sounds of a city night: music heard
through an open window, the sound of a

place-siren fading into the distance. Close by, ~~the~~ a
sigh of satisfaction from those who have
ascended from the Underworld.

2   Ext : Brothel — Night

Long-shot of a large well-appointed house

Long-shot of a large, well-appointed house.
Lights burn in many of the windows. The
front door is open. On the step, an argument
between Pepperdine, the   Madam of
exclusive
this, establishment, and Abbott, a customer.
We move closer. Pepperdine is a ripe, powerful
woman, Abbott is middle-aged, very well-dressed
and drunk.

Abbott

I haven't finished with her—

Pepperdine

Go home.

Abbott

I want Nicole!

Pepperdine

She's had enough. We've all had
enough—

Abbott attempts to get past Pepperdine

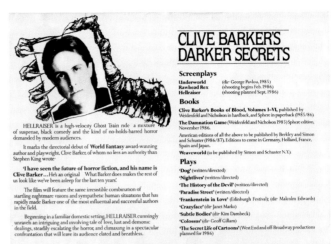

1986 THE HELLBOUND HEART AND HELLRAISER

"Come to Daddy . . ."

ABOVE LEFT

Clive would carry small red notebooks with him, particularly on London Underground journeys to and from rehearsals and meetings, filling them with ideas. An early version of a figure peering around a doorway or wall is a precursor to *Hellraiser*'s Frank Cotton image. Circa 1983.

ABOVE RIGHT

An early *Hellraiser* flyer, produced in January 1986 as part of the sales pitch, detailing Clive's work to date.

"We started with a simple idea—three people in a house together—and worked from there," recalls Christopher Figg. "The film synopsis came first, and out of that Clive developed a novella as a way of working the story out."

HELLRAISER
Synopsis

In the upper room of a house in a suburban backwater, Frank Cotton is raising Hell.

His method? A Chinese puzzle-box, called the Lament Configuration, which—if solved—will summon spirits from the Outer Darkness.

His motive? The promise of untold physical pleasure at the hands of these spirits, the Cenobites, creatures who have dedicated an eternity to the pursuit of sensuality.

But when the Cenobites come, they bring pain not pleasure. Frank is tortured, and finally torn apart . . .

————————————-

A year passes, and Frank's younger brother, Rory, moves into the house with his wife Julia. They are hopelessly mismatched; the marriage is on the rocks. Increasingly it is Frank, with whom she had a brief and heated affair, that Julia dreams of.

She's not the only one in love with the wrong person. One of the visitors to the house is Kirsty, a young, dreamy girl much infatuated with Rory.

As the moving goes on, noises begin in the upstairs room.

The odd atmosphere of the room in which Frank died does not go unnoticed by Julia. Indeed she is in the room when, a few days later, Rory injures himself, and appears,

bleeding badly, at the door. Calmly, Julia takes him off to the hospital, leaving the blood that has splashed on to the bare boards to mysteriously evaporate . . .

A week later. The house-warming. Julia, bored with the company, retires early. Drawn back to the mystery room she finds Frank, or rather a horrifying shadow of Frank, alive in the darkness. He has fed on Rory's blood and has escaped his captors. But he is far from whole. For that, he will need more blood.

For love's sake, Julia obliges.

In the following days she seduces a man back to the house, and murders him. Feeding off the corpse, Frank becomes stronger.

Julia's odd behaviour starts to concern Rory, who is ignorant of what is happening, and he asks Kirsty to talk with her. Arriving at the house, Kirsty sees Julia inviting another victim inside.

She investigates, and upstairs finds the monstrous Frank draining life from a second victim, slaughtered by Julia.

Frank comes within a hair's breadth of killing Kirsty in the subsequent pursuit, but she distracts him by throwing his precious box out of the window. She thus escapes, picking up the box as she flees.

She wakes up in hospital, terrified and alone . . .

Back at the house, Julia and Frank plan their escape together. First, says Frank, I need a skin . . .

At the hospital, Kirsty solves the puzzle of the box, and raises the Cenobites. Once summoned, they are not willing to leave empty-handed: they want her body and soul. She makes a bargain with them. If she can lead them to their escaped prisoner Frank, she can go free.

She returns to the house, and finds Rory there, much the worse for a confrontation with Frank. The truth is out, Julia tells Kirsty, and Frank's unnatural life has been ended.

Kirsty is horrified. With Frank already dead, her bargain with the Cenobites is rendered useless. Her soul will be forfeit.

She starts to leave the house, but as she does so Rory addresses her, using a turn of phrase Frank has used several times earlier. She becomes suspicious, and in the subsequent struggle with the man she assumes to be Rory, the skin of his face slides off.

Beneath is: Frank.

Together, he and Julia have killed Rory, and now Frank is wearing his brother's skin.

ABOVE LEFT

Illustrated letter of authenticity from the bound, hand-amended, typescript of *The Hellbound Heart*, 1986.

ABOVE CENTER AND RIGHT

Clive's *Hellraiser* storyboards: Kirsty escapes the Engineer and summons the Cenobites by solving the Lament Configuration, 1986.

Julia attacks Kirsty, but in the confusion of the struggle Julia is fatally stabbed by Frank, leaving Kirsty to escape by the only route available to her—upstairs.

With Frank in pursuit she stumbles first over the corpses of Julia's victims, and then in the spiralling hysteria of the chase, over Rory's skinned body.

Finally, Frank corners her, and boasts of how he has successfully stolen his brother's identity.

His celebration is cut short, however, as the Cenobites appear.

Realising Kirsty has conspired against him he tries to slaughter her, but the visitors quickly have their hooks in him. Telling Kirsty to leave the house before all Hell breaks loose, the Cenobites tear Frank limb from limb.

On the lower floor Kirsty encounters another demon, nursing Julia's head on its lap. Hungry for fresh victims, it pursues Kirsty, but she escapes with soul and sanity intact, leaving the demons to finish their business within.

TOP LEFT

Backstage on Day 34 of filming. In the busy make-up room for *Hellraiser*, Bob Keen (far left) works on Grace Kirby's Female Cenobite make-up with Little John while Nicholas Vince (center) has touch-ups to his Chatterer costume and make-up by Jane Wildgoose and Paul Catling, November 1986.

TOP RIGHT

On location at Paddington Basin on Day 40 of *Hellraiser*'s shoot for the end sequence of the bonfire and the derelict. Clive discusses a shot with Robin Vidgeon and crew. November 1986.

BOTTOM LEFT

On location at the Zen W3 bar on Day 13 of *Hellraiser*'s shoot, October 1986. Clive (far right) directs Clare Higgins as Julia (center left) and Anthony Allen as Prudhoe.

BOTTOM RIGHT

Christopher Figg and Clive pose with the drained torso of Prudhoe at Production Village, Cricklewood, on Day 16, October 1986.

OPPOSITE PAGE

Clive poses on set for promotional photos with the Engineer to share with journalists. Day 35 of filming, November 1986.

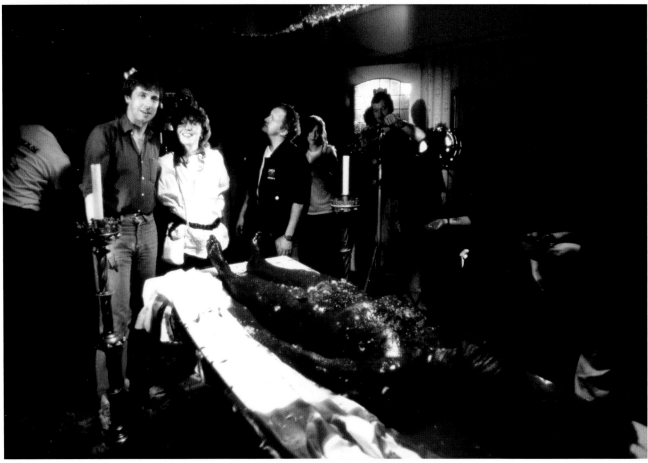

> **"I wanted Frank to be able to stand around and talk about his ambitions and desires because I think what the monsters in movies have to say for themselves is every bit as interesting as what the human beings have to say."**

In the street outside, a shadowy figure collides with her, and then runs off into the darkness. In her hands Kirsty finds the box, the Lament Configuration, sealed up once more and waiting to seduce some fresh innocent into raising Hell.

Describing it later as "a sort of a Jacobean tragedy: everybody falls in love with the wrong people and kills them," Clive set to work on the story, calling it *The Hellbound Heart*—a novella, rather than a screenplay.

"*Hellbound Heart* suggested itself as something we could turn into a movie for very little money," he notes. "For me it was a chance to see if I could put what I felt I was putting onto the page onto the screen: to form a narrative that would allow me imaginative latitude with the visuals but which wouldn't be too large in terms of set pieces. The only way to do this was to write the novella with the specific intention of filming it. This was the first and only time that I have done that, but it was useful in that I worked through a lot of the visual problems in the novella and the final screenplay didn't take that long to draft."

Earlier in 1985, Clive had been invited by Dark Harvest to write thirty thousand words for the third volume of its groundbreaking anthology series Night Visions, contributing alongside Ramsey Campbell and Lisa Tuttle. Clive happily accepted the opportunity.

Revisiting the text of *The Hellbound Heart* in the context of other work that Clive wrote around the same time, it's immediately obvious that its tone is considerably grimmer. It's less playful in its plotting, its subject matter, and its use of language than many of the stories in the final three Books of Blood and is at odds with the more upbeat tone of *Weaveworld*, which he was also writing at the time.

Clive today cites two major influences on the topics of love and pain/pleasure in the novella:

"I was in a very damaging relationship that was coming towards its end. It had been wonderful for a time and had soured horribly. It had become abusive—him towards me—and I, being much physically slighter than he, found myself . . . not frightened, but certainly not happy. The relationship finished when he broke a vase over my head—which was the end of a journey full of incidents like that. Not all of it, of course, but the last two years. It was a relationship between his anger towards me and my growing confidence in the world—my sense that I had a place in the universe. . . . I was in this failed relationship with a lot of anger which *poured* into the story. That was half of it.

"The other is that I had explored S/M pretty extensively at that time. I had done an illustration for an S/M magazine which was famously taken by Scotland Yard and burned. I received the letter saying, 'Dear Sir, we are writing to inform you that under Section So-and-So of the Obscenities Act, the illustration you did, along with all copies of the magazine and your original work, have been destroyed. If you do this again, you'll be thrown in jail!' So S/M was not a designer choice at the time, which is what it's since become. It had a genuine bite to it, a very forbidden quality.

"The drama of S/M is fascinating to me," Clive later told Charles Isherwood for the *Advocate* magazine. "The more formalized elements of the S/M fraternity have never really drawn me, but I'm very interested in the power struggles in sexual relationships, the dramas of sexuality. I *love* sex as drama."

Reflecting on these influences in his work, Clive offers that "the pursuit of sensual extremes is part of *The Hellbound Heart* and several of my other stories. I've always been interested in how we pursue pleasure—and how soon the pleasurable road turns into a cul-de-sac. Then we have to turn and look around and look elsewhere. It's the law of diminishing returns. It's 'Well, I've done this. What can I do next? I've taken that drug, what's the next one available . . . ?' If hedonism doesn't satisfy us—and plainly it is the law of diminishing returns—what next . . . ? The flesh has its limits. . . ."

OPPOSITE PAGE, TOP
Clive directs Oliver Smith as Frank, locking eyes with Clare Higgins as Julia. Day 19 of filming, October 1986.

OPPOSITE PAGE, BOTTOM
Clive sets up a shot for Kirsty's dream sequence on the set of *Hellraiser*, with Ashley Laurence watching from the doorway. Day 7 of filming, October 1986.

NEXT SPREAD, LEFT
Clive and Ashley Laurence on the set of *Hellraiser*. Day 45 of filming, November 1986.

NEXT SPREAD, RIGHT
Clive directs Doug Bradley as Pinhead on the set of *Hellraiser*. Day 26 of filming, November 1986.

1986 A YEAR OF BOOKS, SCREENPLAYS, AND THE WEST END STAGE

"Que será, será . . ."

The beginning of 1986 saw Clive and Christopher Figg taking the newly completed *Hellraiser* screenplay out to seek financing, and in May the movie was greenlit by New World Pictures, initially in coproduction with Virgin Films, although the latter dropped out before filming began, leaving New World as the sole production company.

In the meantime, however, Clive had other projects ongoing. Having sold a new idea for a novel, *Weaveworld*, to Poseidon Press/Simon & Schuster and Pocket Books in the US the previous summer, he was busily working on completing it before the *Hellraiser* shoot began.

He also found time to write an adaptation of his Books of Blood story, "The Yattering and Jack," for the US anthology TV series *Tales from the Darkside*. The episode was filmed later that year and aired in December 1986. Speaking to Larry King two years later, he would confess that he wasn't totally happy with it: "The problem with network television, the thing you're faced with all the time—with horror on network TV—is that it has to be so mild, and my horror fiction is not mild, so we're always dealing with the problem of censorship, I'm afraid."

In August 1986, Clive undertook a US promotional tour to support Berkley's publication of the first three Books of Blood and combined the trip with casting sessions for *Hellraiser*, including finding Ashley Laurence to play Kirsty. Andrew Robinson had already been secured by New World to play Larry Cotton and other casting was finalized in England ahead of the start of principal photography in the last week of September 1986.

"This assignment. Jack Polo. I can't do anything with him. I've tried everything I know. I've turned the house upside down, I've slaughtered his pets, I've spent night after night giving him bad dreams. And he doesn't break."

The initial seven-week shoot was extended to ten weeks with additional funding granted by New World to expand the scale of the narrative outside the main location of the Cricklewood house and to reshoot certain sequences.

Away from the film set, Clive had earlier expanded his 1982 one-act comedy play *The Secret Life of Cartoons* into a two-act version, which premiered as a professional production in Plymouth in September 1986, directed by Tudor Davies, and then transferred to London's West End in mid-October, in week three of *Hellraiser*'s shoot. It was not a success and closed a month later.

"It's a weird piece of work," says Clive, "and it needed to stay weird. The problem when you go into legitimate theatre in the West End is that it costs a lot of money to mount the thing and they have to clean up your act because they are cleaning it up for a tourist audience. Suddenly you find that you're losing control of the stuff that you really loved. And a lot of the nice stuff goes and it gets coarsened in a curious kind of way because it gets simplified. Suddenly it's vaudeville, and it lost it. The reviews were disastrous. They deserved to be, because it was a bad production."

The paperback of *The Damnation Game* was published in the UK in November, but, more significantly, Clive completed the sale of UK rights to *Weaveworld* and to his next book, selling them to Collins Books in a well-publicized and highly lucrative auction process involving four publishing houses.

The proliferation of all these endeavors at the same time allowed Clive to talk to journalists visiting the *Hellraiser* set about a variety of projects, rather than just his debut movie, and helped them to frame him as someone who explored multiple media and genres—from books to stage to screen—and from comedy to horror to fantasy.

Indeed, as Kim Newman noted in the *New Statesman*, reviewing the July 1986 hardcover reissue of *Books of Blood, Volumes 4–6*:

> According to Stephen King, "the future of horror is Clive Barker." The latest step in this young British writer's consolidation of his position in the genre is the republication, in hardback with evocative cover art by the author himself, of the second three volumes of Books of Blood (Weidenfeld, £8.95 each).
>
> This reversal of the usual process—later editions having more literal and metaphorical weight than ephemeral originals—parallels Barker's emergence from the ghetto of paperback horror. He can afford to have the mandatory recommendation from Stephen King discreetly on the flyleaf, rather than blatantly on the cover. He can, in his final story, bid a kind of adieu to the up-market splatter that has made his name and promise to expand in other directions. The monster is getting perilously close to respectability.

-table, the book he has been reading. The din gets louder above. He turns the tele-vision up louder still to cancel it. Then he sits down in his armchair beside the lamp, his back to the television (which is showing news of blizzards) and opens his book. It is <u>War and Peace</u>, and he's almost through it.

The din of the television and the noise from above are deafening, but he settles down to read as though hearing nothing.

<u>Jack</u> (to himself)

Che sera, sera....

Now the television channels are being flipped, at a maddening rate — images appearing in nonsensical abandon: news and weather reports; soap operas; advertising jingles and game shows.

~~End of Act One.~~

Jack reads on, as the lights in the room flicker, and the television cavorts in this lunatic fashion.

Then, we see something moving in the corner of the room. The lights go out completely before we can make more than a moment's sense of the creature however.

Now, with the lights out, only the flickering channels of the television illuminate the room, ~~the~~ like coloured lightning, while the mingled voices of game-show hosts and soap opera stars become deafening.

Jack refuses to be distressed by this. He stands up and goes to the lamp to try and put it on again. As he does so a creature appears — its teeth sharpened to points, its flesh pale, its eyes wild — and stands behind Jack as he fiddles with the light.

By the ghastly illumination from the television, which flickers too much for us to gain any detailed impression of the Yattering, we see the beast staring at Jack, malice in its eyes.

<u>Jack</u> (to the lamp)
Come on, damn you. Come on.

We are genuinely afraid that the Yattering is going to do Jack some serious damage. It has the claws for the job, and its limbs twitch to take out Jack's throat. But, even as it approaches Jack, the light (see insert #2

80

OPPOSITE PAGE

Hand amended typescript page from Clive's teleplay for *The Yattering and Jack*, 1986.

ABOVE

Clive's two-act version of *The Secret Life of Cartoons* was picked up as a professional production which transferred to the Aldwych Theatre in London's West End in October 1986. Starring roles went to well-known UK comedy actors of stage and television including Una Stubbs and Derek Griffiths, directed by Tudor Davies.

1987 WEAVEWORLD

"That which is imagined need never be lost."

The streets of Liverpool provide a recurring urban backdrop for Clive's work: from the mythical hook-handed Candyman, to the dockside streets of *Everville*. In *Weaveworld*, he resolved to write a novel that would capture the poetic sensibility of his former hometown. The book has remained one of his bestselling and most-loved novels.

Five years earlier, Clive had brought the fabulous world of Elizabeth I's court to the streets of Liverpool in the play *Paradise Street*, and he now revisited his memories of the city from his new home in London. With this new perspective he devised a more sophisticated way to illuminate the miraculous hidden in the everyday and address his sense of separation from home.

"I wanted to write a novel in which the world of magic and the world of the real collided. The world of visions, the world of transformations, the world of William Blake colliding with the gritty, brutal reality of living in the later part of the twentieth century in a dehumanized, de-deified, de-mythologized world. . . . I wanted to see what would survive."

Weaveworld's narrative opens in the back garden of a terraced house in Liverpool as a young man tends his dad's half-neglected racing pigeons. It's an inauspicious location for a grand fantasy, but the enchantment begins well before that. Having opened the richly decorated cover, readers have to turn past five pages of contents, with even the casual eye being engaged by lyrical titles like "Never, and Again," reminiscent of English fantasies like *The Once and Future King*. Reassessing those chapter titles recently, Clive agrees: "T. H. White, absolutely! And what's interesting is they are all encoded in a pretty fast-moving novel. I don't know how long the next thing—the chief model for it is *Moby-Dick*: a massive number of chapters, each with a title, each very short and the language moving from the commonplace—"Call me Ishmael"—to the James I translation of the Bible.

"I wrote *Weaveworld* in a sense to become a populist and one of the ways I thought that might happen was by breaking the chapters down so they could be read in the car or on a bus or a tube journey, so you could read a chapter, put it away, read another chapter on the way home that night—that turned out to be true, I get that from a lot of people: 'It became a book I pocketed.'"

Announcing itself on the front cover as "an epic adventure of the imagination," *Weaveworld* gave

fair notice that this was not a stylistic follow-up to *The Damnation Game*, and its opening invocation is both mournful and beguiling:

> Nothing ever begins.
>
> There is no first moment; no single word or place from which this or any other story springs.
>
> The threads can always be traced back to some earlier tale, and to the tales that preceded that: though as the narrator's voice recedes the connections will seem to grow more tenuous, for each age will want the tale told as if it were of its own making.
>
> Thus the pagan will be sanctified, the tragic become laughable; great lovers will stoop to sentiment, and demons dwindle to clockwork toys.
>
> Nothing is fixed. In and out the shuttle goes, fact and fiction, mind and matter, woven into patterns that may have only this in common: that hidden amongst them is a filigree which will with time become a world.

"*Weaveworld* is a meditation on memory," Clive says, reflecting on the novel. "Yes, it also tells about magic and demagoguery and angelic judgments, but the central drama of the tale is the way the characters remember—or fail to remember—the glimpse they've had of paradise. When I go back and look at *Weaveworld*, I realize that buried beneath its rather chummy surface is a lot of very dark material and very melancholy material. *Weaveworld* is filled with yearning, for a time that has passed and for a place that you've lost."

Although the magical world of the Seerkind is certainly a visionary place, it's not a simple wonderland with a single doorway through which to tumble. Joanne Harris notes of the novel, "The world of memory, so close to that of dream, is rebuilt every time we conjure it; each of us experiences it in a unique and personal fashion," and in *Weaveworld* Clive strives to create intimate connections between what is imagined and what is more immediately real.

While completing stories for the earlier Books of Blood, he'd drawn together ideas for an ultimately unwritten story called "Out of the Empty Quarter." Long enchanted by images of the Rub' al Khali, Clive still tells delightedly of meeting explorer Wilfred Thesiger in Collins's offices. In his book

ABOVE LEFT

Weaveworld UK first edition with cover design by fantasy artist Tim White, 1987.

ABOVE RIGHT

Illustration for an unpublished novel, *Magic Night*, 1985.

"Don't You Dare!", said the Salesman. There was panic in his voice. He's afraid, thought Nat, afraid of what I can do.

Arabian Sands Thesiger wrote of this desert region, "I found a freedom unattainable in civilization, a life unhampered by possession," but Clive found the idea of emptiness distinctly unnerving. In his hands, the barren land becomes the location for an ancient evil, thrown out of Paradise, and together with another exile, Immacolata, *Weaveworld* is given characters who display unbridled venom and generate tangible, vicious jeopardy for Suzanna and the Seerkind.

The nature of human frailties, of the grief of forgetting who we are and from where we came, is balanced against latent powers of creation. Both Cal and Suzanna reach back into their separate heritages, and while Cal integrates his within his new enlightened self, Suzanna goes further, evolving into something greater than her human self, to match the enormity of the obligation she has inherited.

Just a month after his round of press for *Hellraiser*'s release, Clive was back on tour for the novel, with interviewers taking note of his diversion from horror to fantasy.

The book's flap copy read:

Weaveworld is an epic adventure of the imagination.

It begins with a carpet in which a world of rapture and enchantment is hiding; a world which comes back to life, alerting the dark forces from which it was hiding, and beginning a desperate battle to preserve the last vestiges of magic which Humankind still has access to.

Mysteriously drawn by the carpet and into the world it represents are Cal Mooney and Suzanna Parrish, two young people with no knowledge of what they are about to live through and confront. For the final conflict between the forces of good—the Seerkind—and of evil, embodied by the terrible Immacolata and her ravening twin wraith sisters, is about to take place.

Weaveworld is a book of visions and horrors, as real as the world we live and breathe in, yet opening doors to experience, places and people that we all dream of, but daren't hope are real. It is a story of quest, of titanic struggles, of love and of hope. It is a triumph of imagination and storytelling, an adventure, a nightmare, a promise . . .

A publishing event of the year, Clive's novel drew praise from other writers as well as from critics.

J. G. Ballard's praise was quoted extensively in UK advertisements: "A powerful and fascinating writer with a brilliant imagination . . . an outstanding storyteller."

Peter Straub's observations were included on the back cover of US paperbacks for years to come:

"It's such a simple idea, but it still seems to me miraculous: that in words we may preserve ideas and images precious to us. Not only preserve them, but pass them on."

NEXT SPREAD, LEFT

Manuscript page for the opening of *Weaveworld*, 1986.

NEXT SPREAD, RIGHT

Clive's brush-and-ink artwork for the UK limited edition of *Weaveworld*, released as a limited-edition print to booksellers, 1987.

"Clive Barker has been an amazing writer from his first appearance, with the great gifts of invention and commitment to his own vision stamped on every page. *Weaveworld* is pure dazzle, pure storytelling. The mixed, tricky country where fantasy and horror overlap has been visited before—though not very often—and *Weaveworld* will be a guide to everyone who travels there in the future. I think it'll probably be imitated for the next decade or so, as lesser talents try to crack its code and tame its insights."

Nothing ever begins.

There is no first moment; not single, not a place from which this or any other story springs. The threads can always be traced back to another, and a tale that preceded them — other tales, some real, some dreamt, merely — will have only this in common; that in them is a filigree which may with time become a world. & in which a seed was planted, or a tear shed, which may have only this in common: that hidden in them is a filigree which will with time become a world.

It must be arbitrary, then, this place/spot from which we chose to travel from. Somewhere between a past half forgotten and a future as yet only glimpsed.

This place, for instance. now?; it's as good as any.

Clive Barker

171/175

1988 HELLBOUND: HELLRAISER II

"Time to play."

OPPOSITE PAGE

Magazine advert for
Hellbound: Hellraiser II
using Peter Atkins's
"Time to play" tagline
to prefigure Pinhead's
more central role in the
sequel, 1988.

The second film in the *Hellraiser* franchise followed hard on the heels of the first, with the screenplay commissioned before the first film arrived in theaters.

"I didn't see a series when I wrote the novella," Clive said, "but when I came to write the script, I did. The box exposes the possibility of opening up lots of different doors. I also liked the idea of bringing the film around full circle—at the conclusion of *Hellraiser*, the box is returned to the old man from whence it came; it's elegant, and that's often missing. I also don't like sub-*Carrie* endings, so I used what I think is a neat visual device."

Clive did not write or direct the sequel, explaining, "At the beginning, I didn't want to hand the project over, but there's a window of opportunity for a sequel and if you miss it you will lose both the momentum and the money. I had just signed a four-book deal with Collins, my publishers, and I was in the middle of writing *The Great and Secret Show*, so there was no way I could get involved with a movie at that time, and I'm not even sure that, having written the original book and the screenplay and directed the movie of *Hellraiser*, I would have been ideally placed to generate the kind of freshness of innovation the movie needed anyway."

For the screenplay, Clive instead turned to his old friend, Peter Atkins.

"I got a phone call on the Wednesday of a week in July '87," says Peter, "to meet with Clive and Chris. *Hellbound* was a story that Clive and I came up with together. It hadn't been fully detailed. Basically we bashed out a skeletal plot outline in one night at Clive's apartment in London. From there we presented that to Chris Figg and New World and they approved that and I went off and did the screenplay on my own.

TIME TO PLAY

HELLBOUND
HELLRAISER II

CLARE HIGGINS

ASHLEY LAURENCE

KENNETH CRANHAM

dirigida por TONY RANDEL

HELLBOUND: HELLRAISER II

"Clive did not at any stage come in and say, 'Don't say that, say this.' Obviously, when he read the first draft he had comments to make, as did Chris Figg and the people at New World. He had input, but it was positive, encouraging input."

Peter and Clive brought their shared love of myth and story to the plot, as Clive reflected: "*Hellbound* is a sea of mythological images and allusions. There is the Frankenstein myth—the mad doctor who loses control. There's certainly the theme of Orpheus in the underworld, the difference being that it is a daughter in search of her father as opposed to Orpheus searching for Eurydice. There is the classic imagery of the labyrinth, the Minotaur, and a whole bunch of allusions to other horror movies. But I don't think any of these things are essential to the picture. They are there for whoever wants them, but for those who want a good time on Friday night, the picture is a roller-coaster ride."

After Michael McDowell, Clive's first choice as director, had to decline, Tony Randel—who had been New World's on-set representative for the first film and was working with Clive to set up the sequel—took up the reins himself for his first film as a director.

"Tony was flown over in October 1987," Peter says, "and in London I produced the second draft, working closely with him. At that stage Tony's ideas started to come into play, joining the melting pot."

"Having done so much work on the original film," says Tony, "I had become very familiar with the material and obviously had an affinity for it because I was able to create material for *Hellraiser* that felt like it belonged; it didn't feel out of left field. In a way, *Hellbound* felt like my second picture because I was so closely involved with the first one."

The film shot for forty-three days of principal photography from late 1987 through to March 4, 1988 (with a new ending filmed the following week) and was released in December of that year.

HELLBOUND: HELLRAISER II
Press Kit Synopsis

For Kirsty Cotton (Ashley Laurence), the nightmares never end . . . With a scream, she abruptly awakens in a strange hospital bed, the events at 55 Lodovico Street still fresh in her fevered memory. During a night of unspeakable terror, she discovered her father's skinned corpse, watched as the life-force was sucked from the body of her murderous step-mother Julia (Clare Higgins), defeated the evil machinations of her Uncle Frank's reanimated body, and eluded the perverse pleasures of the demonic Cenobites.

Now, only a few hours later, she is a patient at the Channard Institute—a psychiatric hospital for the mentally disturbed.

Cold, rational, competent and powerful, Doctor Channard (Kenneth Cranham) is a man at the peak of his profession. But behind his veneer of cool proficiency he conceals deep and dark secrets. Although he listens to Kirsty's story with apparent detachment, his young assistant, Kyle Macrae (William Hope), is more sympathetic towards the obviously distraught girl.

"The most difficult thing I had to do in *Hellbound* was walk down the wind tunnels with a jet engine blowing at me, keep my eyes open and look evil at the same time!" —CLARE HIGGINS

Kirsty tries to make friends with another patient, the enigmatic Tiffany (Imogen Boorman), a girl in her early teens who never speaks. But Channard holds an inexplicable power over his young charge, ensuring that she develops her skill at solving more and more difficult puzzles.

Meanwhile, during the inevitable police investigation at the house at Lodovico Street, a young officer is tagging the grisly evidence of Julia's crimes in the junk room when he discovers the gore-stained mattress upon which the hammer-wielding woman died . . .

Despite Kyle's suspicions, Channard convinces the police to deliver the blood-splattered mattress to his home ostensibly to be used in the treatment of Kirsty's 'nightmares.' But unbeknown to his colleagues, the doctor has spent a lifetime delving into the secrets of the ornate puzzle box—the Lament Configuration—which opens the dimensions to ultimate pleasure or unlimited pain. Now, with the information he has elicited from Kirsty, Channard is prepared to go to any lengths to unlock the portals that lead into the Outer Darkness.

Using the blood of Browning (Oliver Smith), one of the more deeply disturbed patients he keeps confined in the basement of the Institute, Channard succeeds in releasing Julia's flayed remains from the mattress.

Soon an unholy alliance has been struck between the seductive woman and the obsessed doctor: in return for supplying her with innocent victims on which to feed and restore her flesh, Julia will reveal to Channard the secrets beyond time and space.

But while the innocent Tiffany is being used to manipulate the box and open the corridors between the dimensions, in Kirsty's hospital room a vision of her skinned father manifests itself in a pool of blood, which he uses to write a message on the wall, entreating her help.

Once again, Kirsty must venture beyond the limits into the Stygian passageways in an attempt to rescue Tiffany, thwart her step-mother's manipulations and release her father from his eternal torment. For a second time, she must elude Frank's damned soul, and her quest will set her against the dark desires of the Cenobites and ultimately force her to confront the awesome powers of their omnipotent master: Leviathan the Lord of Hell's Labyrinth . . .

The film was released in the US on December 23, 1988, which made possible such review headlines as "Hellbound Holiday: Scary Christmas, All You Horror Fans" in the *Seattle Times*.

Critical reaction was split, with many celebrating *Hellbound* as a deeper exploration into the themes of the first film, while others were unable to see it as anything beyond a blood-drenched shocker—and couldn't help but note the absence of the director and writer of the first movie. Either way, the *Hellraiser* franchise was well and truly underway.

JOSE FRADE
Producciones
Cinematográficas, S.A.

CLARE HIGGINS

ASHLEY LAURENCE

KENNETH CRANHAM

dirigida por **TONY RANDEL**

NEW WORLD INTERNATIONAL

HELLBOUND: HELLRAISER II

1989– GRAPHIC NOVELS
1994

Tapping the Vein

The images, setting, and plotlines of the Books of Blood were ripe for visual interpretation, and
Clive—a lover of comic books since his childhood—was keen to see them come to life in adaptations and through the lenses of talented artists.

"Part of the pleasure of working in the comics medium is that other minds, other visions, are brought to bear on the underlying material. So when John Bolton takes "The Yattering and Jack" or "In the Hills, the Cities" or when [P.] Craig Russell takes "Human Remains" or when Scott Hampton takes a tale, and they redefine the way the images appear in the mind's eye, I could not be happier. It's a great talent."

Between late 1989 and early 1994, no fewer than eighteen of the thirty stories were published as graphic novels.

Ten were presented in a five-book series edited by Fred Burke called Tapping the Vein, published by Eclipse Books, a pair of stories in each.

94

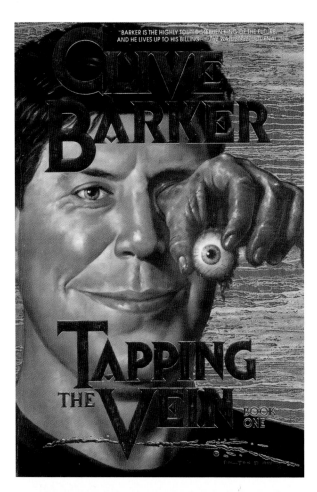

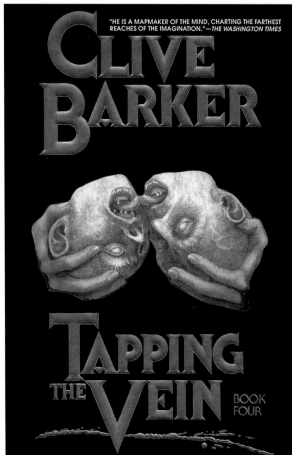

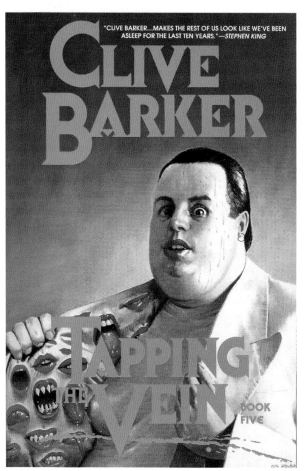

"I think the two major narrative impulses which brought me to the way I write were comics and movies, no doubt about that."

"Human Remains" was adapted and illustrated by P. Craig Russell, whilst "Pig Blood Blues" was adapted by Chuck Wagner and Fred Burke and illustrated by Scott Hampton.

"Skins of the Fathers" (adapted by Chuck Wagner and Fred Burke and illustrated by Klaus Janson) was followed by "In the Hills, the Cities" (adapted by Chuck Wagner and Fred Burke and illustrated by John Bolton).

"The Midnight Meat Train" was again adapted by Chuck Wagner and Fred Burke, with illustrations by Denys Cowan and Michael Davis, while "Scape-Goats" was adapted and illustrated by Bo Hampton.

"Hell's Event" was adapted by Fred Burke and illustrated by Steven E. Johnson, Alan Okamoto, and Jim Pearson, and "The Madonna" was adapted by Fred Burke and illustrated by Stan Woch, Mark Farmer, and Fred Von Tobel.

In the final volume, Steve Niles joined the team to adapt "How Spoilers Bleed" with Fred Burke, with illustrations by Hector Gomez. "Down, Satan!" was also adapted by Steve Niles and illustrated by Tim Conrad.

Two further pairings were presented outside the Tapping the Vein title: "The Life of Death" (adapted by Fred Burke with art by Stewart Stanyard) and "New Murders in the Rue Morgue" (adapted by Steve Niles with art by Hector Gomez); and "Rawhead Rex" and "Twilight at the Towers" (both written by Steve Niles with art by Les Edwards and Hector Gomez, respectively).

Stand-alone publications included "Dread" (written by Fred Burke with art by Dan Brereton), "Son of Celluloid" (written by Steve Niles with art by Les Edwards), "Revelations" (again adapted by Steve Niles with artwork by Lionel Talaro) and "The Yattering and Jack" (written by Steve Niles and illustrated by John Bolton).

Eclipse produced the series with die-cut covers for some titles and foil lettering and presented them as square-bound graphic novels—all denoting that this was a significant line of books and a high-profile tie-in for the publisher.

A nineteenth story, "The Book of Blood" itself, was presented visually as a collectible thirty-two-card boxed set illustrated by Tristan Schane and published in 1993 by Eclipse Enterprises.

One that got away, "The Age of Desire," was adapted by P. Craig Russell and illustrated by Tim Bradstreet, but fell into limbo when Eclipse ceased operations. For years the first thirty-seven pages of artwork were feared lost. Happily, they were rediscovered and reunited with the remaining pages and subsequently published by Desperado Publishing in 2009, along with pages by P. Craig Russell, who had initially also been lined up to illustrate the adaptation.

OPPOSITE PAGE

Covers by John Bolton, Dave McKean, John Totleben, and Les Edwards for *Tapping the Vein*, books 1, 3, 4, and 5, Eclipse Books, 1989, 1990, 1990, and 1992, respectively.

1988   CABAL

"At Last, the Night Has a Hero!"

Cabal was written over the course of eight months in 1987 and published in 1988. Its release came hard on the heels of Clive's two most successful projects to date: the screen debut of the first *Hellraiser* movie and the massive popularity of *Weaveworld*.

Weaveworld had documented the story of a tribe of "monsters" in hiding within a specially woven carpet; a tribe with magical powers that had coexisted with humanity—not always comfortably—but now faced a greater enemy, the Scourge, that seemed intent on wiping the existence of such "otherness" from the face of the earth.

Cabal shares similar themes with *Weaveworld*'s tribe; like the Seerkind, the Nightbreed are hidden from humanity, this time in an underground refuge. "They're both about magic fighting against reason when reason is corrupt," agrees Clive. "They're both about societies in flight, societies taking refuge. *Weaveworld* is a 'lost tribe' story, and again, in *Cabal*, the story is very clearly a 'Moses and the Lost Tribe' tale.

"I set out very consciously, though, to write the flip of *Weaveworld*. In *Weaveworld*, you enter a world of enchantment and mystery which turns out to have dark elements in it; in *Cabal*, you enter a necropolis which turns out to have within it the capacity for transcendence. The Seerkind possessed a holy magic in a secular and rationalist world but was an essentially benign species. The Nightbreed are not. They're the monstrous flip side of the coin; a collection of transformers, cannibals, and freaks."

This idea of abandoned tribes looking for redemption and salvation had also figured strongly in his screenplay for *Underworld* and in several of the Books of Blood. "The whole idea of a lost tribe being led to safety has religious connotations. Biblical themes such as Revelation and Armageddon run behind all my work, though my interest is in folklore and legends as much as it is in Christian iconography. The idea for *Cabal* had been around for a long time, however; the book became bigger and bigger and then I ended up with a mythology, or at least the beginning of a mythology, which was larger than I ever thought it was going to be. That's intriguing to me, that's exciting because I have the chance of expanding that on the page."

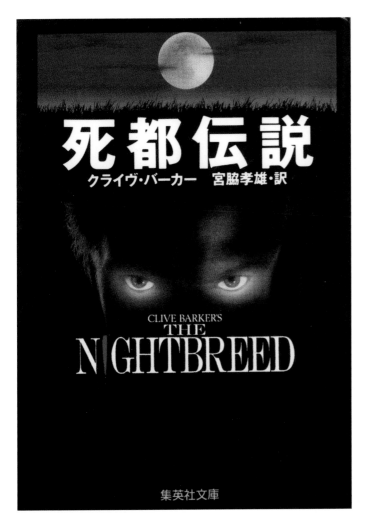

Putting Aaron Boone at the heart of Cabal, the novel opens with his vows to his lover, Lori: "I'll never leave you." In a similar way, a promise made to a lover that had unlocked experiences unlike any other was the driver behind *The Hellbound Heart* and its adaptation, *Hellraiser*. When Frank petitions Julia to "heal me . . . please," she responds, "I will, I promise you I will" (in the novella) and (in the screenplay), "I'll do anything you want. Anything," which captures her motivation to bring back the lover who has given her unmatched sexual satisfaction.

Boone, by contrast, is a failure sexually and his relationship with Lori is more complex. He may be handsome but he's also damaged and has been in therapy for years; the qualities Lori brings to their relationship are ones we sense that no other human has given him: patience, encouragement, and, above all, love. Her unquestioning devotion—and her demand that Boone follow through on his promise—resolutely drives her side of the story.

While Clive describes the book in overview as "a romance for dead people," he admits that "the romance is sometimes very perverse; I mean, what's going on between Boone and Lori is extremely perverse—they fall more and more deeply in love the deader they get!"

Although Boone is our gateway into the world of the Breed, it is Lori who is given the more heroic role, overcoming trials and proving her strength of character. In sharing the burden of the uncertain future of the Nightbreed, she accepts otherness and rejects Eigerman's view of the world that tomorrow should go back to "normal."

"This theme of acceptance, accepting even contradictions, ugliness, and pain as part of life, is the most powerful theme in *Cabal*," Clive offers. "Midian is full of monsters, but each monster is monstrous in a different way, and their life, diverse as it is, is shown to be valuable."

ABOVE LEFT

The Japanese first edition of *Cabal* as *The Nightbreed* in paperback, Shuesha Bunko, 1989.

ABOVE RIGHT

The Italian first edition of *Cabal* in hardback, Sonzogno, 1990.

"It's my hymn of praise to the monstrous. It's a book in love with monsters."

Clive also explores his characters' hidden selves and the masks that are worn—physical masks, uniforms, and behaviors deployed as mental defense mechanisms. Clive's own childhood ritual of screwing up his face at the window at night to scare away the outside world is an example of one of his own masks in action, as is his showman's face in promotional interviews, which shields an intensely private persona. Using it in his fiction, he subverts stereotypes and reveals unexpected appetites and passions in his characters. "The mask is, of course, both a means of concealment and one of confession," he says. "It covers the human and reveals the inhuman. The man disappears, and a creature of mythic proportions replaces him: some demon or divinity, a terrible intelligence."

As the masks are surrendered in *Cabal*, true selves emerge. Transforming between states, the shape-shifters reveal different personas and this metamorphosis within tribes of "others" played a central part in Clive's plays, *The Wolfman* and *Dog*, in some of the later Books of Blood in which flesh and gender are proved mutable, and on into later works, including *Imajica* and the Books of the Art.

Clive wrote *Cabal* in a way that he never had before, and never has since, dictating the book into a voice recorder; thus it is the only one of his books without a handwritten manuscript. In contrast to the epic scale of *Weaveworld*, this book was far shorter.

"In *Cabal* I wanted to present a piece of quicksilver adventuring in which you were just seeing flashes of things: Boone, Lori, the Breed, each character's psychology reduced to impressions," Clive explained to Philip Nutman in *Fangoria*. "Part of the fun for me was to write it in short, sharp bites. It's the right size for the novel. I think you've got to allow stories to occupy the length that they need to occupy. I could have certainly made it into a much, much bigger novel—whether it would have been all the better for that I think is a moot point. I think, probably, it's better short and sharp."

The Ontario press office for Collins focused on its local connections with the story to draw attention to the upcoming release of both *Cabal* and its movie adaptation, *Nightbreed*:

CLIVE BARKER
CABAL

Clive Barker spins fantastic yarns but his own story makes fascinating reading. A solitary child who preferred to play with his imagination than with other kids, Barker grew up off Penny Lane and attended the same schools as John Lennon.

He first came to the public eye when he became involved in fringe theatre in Crouch End eleven years ago, having moved to London from his native Liverpool. On the dole for 9 years, his writing was done more for fun than profit, but when his theatrical agent sent along his short stories to publishers, they were snapped up. Since then he has forged a successful relationship with Collins with the hardback and paperback success of *Weaveworld*. He achieved film success with *Hellraiser*, which he wrote and directed and has just completed filming for *Hellraiser 2 : Hellbound*. No wonder that the 35 year old Liverpudlian describes what's happened to him as 'unreal'.

CLIVE BARKER
CABAL

Stunning Point-of-Sale Package

"The realm in which the Nightbreed dwell is located in a cemetery in a ghost town east of Peace River, near the town of Shere Neck, north of Dwyer, Alberta. During his author tour for *Weaveworld*, Clive Barker managed to spend a few days traveling in Alberta, to and from Banff. The landscape so inspired him that he was able to begin writing *Cabal* the minute he returned to his home in London. . . . And [he] will be in Alberta in February scouting sites in which to set the film."

The book's press kit said:

Boone knew there was no place on this earth for him, no happiness here, not even with Lori. Just as certain, there was no salvation possible for him in Heaven. He would let Hell claim him, let death take him there.

But death itself seemed to shrink from him. No wonder, if he had indeed been the monster who had shattered, violated and shredded so many others' lives. Decker had shown him the hellish proof—the photographs where the victims were forever stilled, splayed in the last obscene moment of their torture.

The only place left to him was Midian, that awful legendary place which gathered in its monstrous embrace the half-dead, the Nightbreed.

Boone made his way there, not knowing, and caring even less, if Decker or Lori would follow. All he wanted was to leave the nightmare behind. But the real nightmare had yet to begin . . .

Collins Canada added:

In *Weaveworld* Clive Barker took us on an epic adventure, beginning with a wonderous rug into which a magical world was woven. With his trademark graphic vision balanced by a spirit of transcendent promise, Barker explored the darkness and the light. Now in *Cabal* he expands on this metaphysical conflict through a perverse and terrifying story of the ultimate clash between two monstrosities, and a young woman willing to cross the borders of the human to be with the man she loves.

ABOVE LEFT

Clive's UK press kit biography for *Cabal*, 1988.

ABOVE RIGHT

UK press kit point of sale advert for stockists of *Cabal*, 1988.

NEXT SPREAD

Clive's artwork for *Cabal* as he started to prepare it as a film, retitled *Nightbreed*. 1988.

1990 NIGHTBREED

"Everything's true . . . God's an astronaut. Oz is over the rainbow. And Midian's where the monsters live."

Despite his prior success in writing and immediately adapting *The Hellbound Heart* into a screenplay, Clive did not write *Cabal* with a plan to film it. "I'm nervous of the idea of doing books as first-draft screenplays. I'm wholly committed to the word, wholly obsessed with the word. Ideas get rerouted to the movies, if you like, but they don't start off that way. It would be very disruptive to the way I write to think that way. However, as I was finishing it, I realized that it would lend itself very nicely to movie adaptation."

Clive had initially set his sights on a different big-budget feature—the still unmade *Harry D'Amour and the Great Beyond*—but a three-picture deal with Morgan Creek Productions turned his attention instead to a first-draft screenplay adaptation in September 1988 under a new title, *Nightbreed*.

"When Morgan Creek bought the film rights they insisted on a more commercial title. They thought *Cabal* didn't mean anything and they could be right. Who knows?"

The new title also reflected Clive's clear intention to make a subtle shift of focus for the filmed story as he recognized the different demands of film.

"The movie is the book deconstructed and then reconstructed in a different formulation," he explains, "so the movie is less about how two human beings come to be involved with the Nightbreed and more about the delirium of monsterdom. The book is about Boone and his journey. The movie is about the Nightbreed, this hidden tribe of mythological beings, shape-changers, and strange people who come from the Old Country of the imagination.

"You lose the complexities of how somebody gets from the rejection of the monsters to embracing them, because much of that is internal workings. You also lose Lori moving forward through the erotically charged dream-states which are in the book."

Rather than dwelling on such losses—redemption and forgiveness, self-doubt and self-renewal—Clive embraced the exotic possibilities conjured by the creation of a bizarre and enthralling world in

VIEW OVER THE BEAST AS IT STOPS, SCENTING ASHBERRY + OR OTHER HUMANS, ACROSS MIDIAN. 2.

both sound and vision. "What you gain, however, is two things: Firstly, the music, which in the fantastique is very important as an indicator of feeling, and a way of sweeping people along; the other is the power of the image—you gain the ease of presenting a creature which turns into a little girl, and there is something immediately poignant about showing that little girl.

"One of the things I love about making a movie from something I've written is the pleasure of being able to reinvent your imagination: you've done it once, you know the way it looked when you wrote it, and then you reinvent it entirely. All the walkways and stuff isn't the Midian described in the book—it's all very, very vaguely described. *Nightbreed* doesn't look the way I imagined it when I was writing *Cabal*. It turned out to be much larger in scale than I originally anticipated. . . . For example, Baphomet isn't even described in the book. Baphomet is 'in flames,' and the technical problems of making that work on film made me think about it until I dreamt it. I literally dreamt it, and there he was. I think in the film he is actually better than I described him in the book!

"A subtle thing in one way, though it's mammoth in another, is that in the book the Breed are represented very impressionistically, you only get two or three paragraphs about them, but you can't do that in a movie. In the movie they have to be realized in great detail."

Well ahead of the start of principal photography on March 6, 1989, says Clive, "my first job was to go to Bob Keen and his boys and tell them, 'My vision of the Breed is this.' They had to translate those notions into concrete forms, make them into prosthetic reality. Hieronymus Bosch was my inspiration: I was trying to create onscreen his pictures of beasts in every corner. You'll get glimpses of stuff. I like the idea of all this stuff going on behind the level of the story. . . . I want people to get the impression that there's this great gallery of characters and you're not seeing them all; almost a sense of frustration that you're not seeing it all, like the cantina sequence in *Star Wars* the first time you see it.

"On film, the Breed exist; they have a lifestyle, a religion, a concrete sense of life. We have life histories for them, little family units, a sense of them developing as a colony."

Like any full-fledged colony, the Breed has a collective history too, as documented on the walls of the necropolis—a mythology that Clive delights in exploring.

"That wasn't really present in the book, and I felt that this was the perfect time to examine that. Certain mythological elements have increased, such as the fact that Boone is now revealed as the

ABOVE

The stop motion animation of Diadaria/Nesta and the Mezzick-Muul was one of twelve animation sequences initially approved for development under the control of Rory Fellowes as animation designer. During production, the number of shots was cut back sharply and ultimately the few completed shots were edited out of the theatrical release, before being reinserted in the director's cut. Storyboard, 1989.

seventh savior come to save Midian, as opposed to just being a guy who happens along. He is someone who has been prophesied—and I love the chance to increase the mythological resonances. . . ."

As a foil for the Breed, Clive needed to cast his true monster—the psychopathic Dr. Decker—with care and he turned to award-winning Canadian writer/director David Cronenberg.

Speaking to press during filming, Clive elaborated: "For me it couldn't be more perfect casting—it's great genre casting for one thing. I don't think I'd realized how good he actually looks until I saw him on film. He looks very chilling. He offers up these wide, sympathetic grins, then they suddenly vanish off his face. . . . He wrote a little speech for himself, which will be obvious when you see the film—it's absolutely pure, essential Cronenberg!"

David Cronenberg added, "There are certain similarities between what I do and what he does, and then there are some extreme differences. For me, it's the differences which are exciting rather than the similarities. We're both interested in transcendence through transformation, considered in a very physical sense rather than a metaphysical sense. Those are themes that we both return to again and again. But he is much more exuberant in his sense of invention and his creation of new mythologies without any rational explanation. That's where we become different: I would never create the Cenobites, for example, I would never create the Nightbreed. Those are the differences there, I think."

Clive cast Craig Sheffer as his hero, Boone, and Anne Bobby as Lori. Charles Haid, famous as Officer Andy Renko from *Hill Street Blues*, was cast as Captain Eigerman; Hugh Quarshie was Detective Joyce; Hugh Ross played Narcisse; Catherine Chevalier was Rachel; and Malcolm Smith, who would become Clive's partner, played Reverend Ashberry.

In other roles, several familiar faces were back, albeit under deep latex in some cases, with Doug Bradley as Dirk Lylesberg, Nicholas Vince as Kinski, Oliver Parker as Peloquin, and Simon Bamford as Ohnaka. Peter Atkins directed some second-unit material.

106

ABOVE

Image Animation's workshop with just some of the headpieces used for characters In *Nightbreed*, 1989.

Danny Elfman wrote a distinctive and evocative score. David Barron and Gabriella Martinelli produced. Steve Hardie led the production design. Image Animation created the inhabitants of Midian, with Geoff Portass leading alongside Bob Keen. Several key *Hellraiser* and *Hellbound: Hellraiser II* crew members returned, including Robin Vidgeon as director of photography and, initially at least, both Christopher Figg as producer and Richard Marden as editor.

The set was welcoming and many from the fantasy-horror community visited and found themselves conscripted in bit parts as members of the Breed or as crowd members at Lori's gig—or victims murdered in bloody fashion. The writers John Skipp and Craig Spector were both Breed members and murdered motel guests. . . .

Clive reflected in the movie's press kit: "*Hellraiser* was unapologetically a movie that set out to make your palms get clammy and make you shift around in your seat. You weren't sure you wanted to see what was coming next. That isn't the case with *Nightbreed*. It is much more benign in its intentions. This picture is much more upfront about the fact we don't want to see the monsters die. We actually find them interesting. And sexy. We're not really on the side of the cross-wielding Christians, we're actually on the side of the creatures of darkness."

With *Nightbreed* Clive had hoped to subvert the growing fad of serial killers as antiheroes. Unfortunately, the studio seemed determined to capitalize on that precise trend, with Philip Decker positioned to be the next Freddy Krueger. After nine weeks of principal photography at Pinewood ended in May, there were another two and a half weeks of additional photography there in September 1989. The following month Clive headed to Los Angeles to undertake even more reshoots, and then a painful editing process began, with Mark Goldblatt replacing Richard Marden.

"You start with a stalk-and-slash character," says Clive, "but this time you're going to understand that this isn't something you want to applaud. I'm saying to the audience, 'Here's the tradition you've

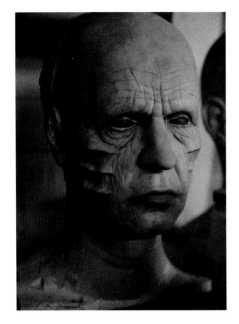

ABOVE LEFT

The design for Lylesberg, 1989.

ABOVE RIGHT

On set for *Nightbreed*: Catherine Chevalier as Rachel looks on as Clive directs, 1989.

been applauding, but there's another tradition which is rich and various and witty and warm and poetic. Isn't that what we should be celebrating?'"

Studio executives had a different response, adding to earlier difficulties for Clive. "*Nightbreed* was an incredible challenge from the very beginning. Chris Figg, the producer of the *Hellraiser* movies, was sacked from the project six weeks in, and then my executive producer Joe Roth became the head of 20th Century Fox. *Nightbreed* was just one small movie on a whole list that Fox was releasing and Roth didn't want to be seen to be playing any favorites, so he almost willfully distanced himself from the picture.

"Next they put out what was probably the worst ad campaign known to man. David Cronenberg actually wrote to Fox saying, 'How dare you do this to our movie?' Of course in the end it didn't do anywhere near as well as we expected. In fact, it ended up being pretty much of a disaster at the box office."

The creative joy that *Nightbreed* had been to develop turned into a bitter personal disappointment for Clive as his footage was edited down from an epic sweep to a roller-coaster ride with key plot elements excised to leave the remainder confusing if tantalizingly visually elegant. A tacked-on ending and other reshoots focusing on Decker's character moved the emphasis back to the twentieth-century monster at the expense of the intended celebration of the inhabitants of Midian.

"The lesson I've learned is that a lot of people don't want anything different. They don't want you to have a unique vision. But why make movies anybody else could have done? Well, I've paid the consequences, but I'm unrepentant. Again and again I listened to deprecating comments about low literacy levels. There was supposedly no point showing *Nightbreed* to critics because the people who see these movies don't read reviews, in brackets, even if they can read at all! Immediately it was disqualified from serious criticism. Therefore it had to be sold to the lowest common denominator. Nobody cares for the product I, and a host of other horror directors, make. One guy at Fox never saw it through because he felt it was morally reprehensible and disgusting—the two very things it's not. Their imaginations are limited and they have a very unadventurous sense of what to do. Someone at Morgan Creek said to me, 'You know, Clive, if you're not careful, some people are going to like the monsters.' Talk about completely missing the point! Even the company I was making the film for couldn't comprehend what I was trying to achieve!"

Many years later, in 2009, rough-cut VHS workprints of the movie from 1989 were uncovered at Clive's home. An edit called *Nightbreed: The Cabal Cut*, put together by Russell Cherrington and Jimmi Johnson, spliced footage from these tapes into scenes from the original theatrical version and this cut toured film festivals in 2012 and 2013. An extensive fan campaign, dubbed "Occupy

"I've always loved monsters. I think there's a corner of all of us that envies their powers and would love to live forever, or to fly, or to change shape at will. So, when I came to make a movie about monsters, I wanted to create a world we'd feel strangely at home in. I called it Midian."

Midian" by Anne Bobby, was launched in 2012 by three fans, José Leitão, Ryan Danhauser, and Roger Boyes of *The Clive Barker Podcast*, which generated new impetus for a studio release of an extended cut.

Feared lost for many years, the original film elements were, against all the odds, finally tracked down by Cliff MacMillan and Scream Factory in 2014, which allowed a director's cut to be assembled and released in 2015. Mark Alan Miller and Andrew Furtado oversaw the editing process.

As Clive reflected on his decades-long quest to be able to present "his" *Nightbreed*, he said, "Even if we did find some footage (which we did in 2009 in the form of heavily degraded VHS tapes) and even if we did find a company willing to release the film (which we did in 2013 with Scream Factory, God bless them), the prospect of finding the actual lost film materials was remoter than I'd wanted to admit out loud. If the footage could not be found by those who had worked closest on it the same year it had been released, then what were the odds we'd be able to find anything twenty years on? But Scream Factory, in their commendable determination, kept up the search, and thanks to them, total reconstruction has been made a possibility. There's never been a reconstruction that's had as little chance of succeeding and yet has succeeded on as many fronts as this film has. It's unprecedented. To now have a movie that we can put together in the way that I fully intended it to be seen when I first set out to make this film in 1989 is extraordinary."

A hymn to variegation and a celebration of the Other, *Nightbreed* in its truncated, frustrating original form was nevertheless embraced by many as a queer film that gave fans the confidence to be different. It established a cult following on VHS and then DVD and its mythology was even expanded in comics, but its creator could not be happier that the director's cut now allows his full cinematic vision to be shared and experienced as he intended.

ABOVE LEFT

On location for *Nightbreed*: Anne Bobby and Clive, 1989.

ABOVE RIGHT

Cast and crew photo at Pinewood for *Nightbreed* including, in the front two rows, Stephen Jones (unit publicist), Anne Bobby, Clive, producer Gabriella Martinelli and Craig Sheffer, 1989.

1989 THE GREAT AND SECRET SHOW: THE FIRST BOOK OF THE ART

"Memory, prophecy, and fantasy—the past, the future, and the dreaming moment between—are all one country, living one immortal day. To know that is Wisdom. To use it is the Art."

As Clive began to write the Art trilogy in late 1987 (originally plotting it as a story called "Immortals"), the success of *Hellraiser* and his excitement to create new films meant that, despite living in London, he was spending a lot of time in Hollywood. The unique surroundings he found there inspired him to relocate the story from East Coast to West. "I'm looking to do a book which will do for the American scene what *Weaveworld* did for the British. . . . I want to do for a particularly attractive part of America—California—something similar."

The Dream Factory was a perfect location for a novel in which we find "that sleep is a door, that dreams are more than casual fictions we whip up for our own delectation: dreams are part of a matrix of mythologies where we are given clues for our survival."

"When I was young," Clive reflects, "I was told that my dreams would never get me anywhere, that the fantasies that I had were distractions from the business of getting on with living. Whereas I don't think that's the case at all—I think the fantasies that we have as imaginative people are the ways that we help understand reality."

Following the huge success of *Weaveworld*, and with the setbacks of *Nightbreed* not yet apparent, Clive carried a self-confidence into the novel, allowing him to open it in heroic fashion: "Homer opened the door."

"It's no accident," he notes, "that the man who opens the door at the beginning of *The Great and Secret Show* is called Homer. We are about to be told a story about Love, War, and Sea Voyages. The first of those epics known in the West comes from a man with the same name."

This sense of assurance was vital to match the growing scope of the novel as Clive decided it would be the first of a trilogy—such was his ambition for, but also the depth of, the subject matter that one novel would not do it justice.

"The Art took four months to research and, even if I was busy at the studios during the day, I would make the time in the evenings. I found this little town in Ventura County just outside Los Angeles and renamed it for the book. Sometimes an image comes along which is so perfect you absolutely have to have it, and who could possibly improve on the symbolic significance of a perfect little town—the lawns all evenly mowed, everything working like clockwork—constructed on a fault line?"

The novel introduces the notion of a sea named Quiddity—a word that in philosophy means the essence of someone or something—as it explores the dream-lives of its characters, sparked by Clive's university philosophy studies.

"One of the lecturers made a brief and somewhat disparaging reference to Carl Jung's theory of the collective unconscious, and it instantly piqued my interest. Jung's psychoanalytical writings offer a variety of descriptions of the collective unconscious, and they're not always consistent. But it comes down to this: he suggests that despite the fact that we seem—as nations, as tribes, as individuals—very different from one another, there is a pool of ancient and archetypal images that lies beneath our myriad variations, and these images recur with uncanny frequency in dreams and visions, in mythology and folklore and urban myth. . . . Jung was clearly drawn to the idea that the collective unconscious offers us some glimpse of how we might interact with the divine.

"The notion appealed to me for many reasons, not least that I could immediately conjure up its physical analogue. It was a sea. A place where we swim—in sleep, or some other altered state—and there encounter forms that we bring back with us into the waking world. Sometimes we encounter one another there. Sometimes we encounter the divine. We also, inevitably, meet forces that mean us harm. In short, the collective unconscious is another world: a world both strange to us—filled with images remote from our domestic lives—and closer than the concrete reality in which we live, because the door that leads into it lies inside us.

"This idea stayed with me for several years before I found an adequate way to express it. I called the sea Quiddity and slowly developed a mythology around it. Human beings would enter Quiddity, the dream-sea, three times, I decided. Once when they were born, once when they slept beside the person they would love most in their lives, and once before they died. Three life-changing immersions in the sea of the unconscious. Three confrontations with the secret show of our dreams."

Clive also employs the nirvanic notion of "one immortal day," a motif which has often surfaced in his work, especially in the Books of Abarat series, where it is fabricated as an island—"a time out of time" where everything exists in all times at once. In this moment, and in visiting Quiddity, we are reminded both of our common mortality but also our drive to evolve toward some rarer state where we might know more, feel more, and be more than we are. The novel explores the ways in which its characters seek to pull aside a curtain that keeps them from the Show, but also hints at countering forces from beyond. Referencing Plato's Atlantis, Clive introduces the antagonistic lad Uroboros who follows a quest for purity, singularity, and madness and whose probes against the veil reach into our sleeping minds. . . .

The Art would be continued in a second novel, *Everville*, but as Clive reflected on this opening novel some years later, "the stage is set, as it were, for another show, another series of spectacles and revelations. By the time I'd finished this book, I knew, at least vaguely, what form that show would take. It would be a book in which I unpicked some of the knots I'd tied at the close of this novel, in order to demonstrate something central to the Books of the Art: the uncertainty of things, especially of finality. Nothing, I had come to believe by the end, was more illusory than the idea of ending."

The book's flap copy read:

Armageddon begins quietly.

It is 1971. In the small Californian town of Palomo Grove four girls go swimming in a mysterious and haunted lake. Nine months later several children are born. Two are the offspring of the Jaff, a man-spirit obsessed with darkness and depravity. The other is the son of Fletcher, a force for light who has fought the Jaff across America.

Their prize is the Art, the greatest power known to mankind. A doorway to the dream-life of the species, on the other side of which lies a force that pales every human evil into insignificance . . .

To finally possess it, the two men intend to fight through their children. Until their children fall in love.

"We're living in a world which is full of metaphor, in which our dream lives are, any minute, about to break into our real lives... look, there are angels sitting in the corner, and one of them has a werewolf on its knee."

7th August 1989　　Collins　　£12.95

Then all hell breaks loose, as an innocent passion between two lovers escalates the war between their fathers to a new ferocity.

This time, they will fight to the death, gathering their armies from the souls of Palomo Grove. Nightmares will walk the streets. Dreams will be made real. At last, the Grove will see the Great and Secret Show.

It will never be the same again.

Nor will the world.

The Great and Secret Show is the work of a master fabulist at the height of his powers. Clive Barker has already astonished readers with the extraordinary, visionary range of his previous work, including *Weaveworld*. Now in this—the First Book of the Art—he has produced a fable for our times set in the sultry landscape of California and Hollywood. It is a story about love, lunatic ambition and the incalculable power of our secret lives. *The Great and Secret Show* is in our heads and in our hearts. Only Clive Barker could have brought it to light.

"Clive Barker's career has been building up to *The Great and Secret Show*," wrote Ken Tucker in the *New York Times Book Review*, adding, "[I]t is nothing so much as a cross between [Thomas Pynchon's] *Gravity's Rainbow* and J. R. R. Tolkien's *Lord of the Rings*, allusive and mythic, complex and entertaining."

Harper & Row borrowed from that review for its US press ads, along with two more:

"Barker's most ambitious work yet, topping even *Weaveworld*: a massive and brilliant Platonic dark fantasy that details an eruption of wonders and terrors—as the veil between the world of the senses and the world of the imagination is rent in a small California town." (*Kirkus Reviews*)

"He proves himself an expert tactician, smoothly deploying over 40 characters and any number of careening, converging plots. He renders it all in a precise, ironic, measured style that avoids both campy humor and pretentious solemnity." (*Chicago Tribune*)

Meanwhile, William A. Henry III wrote in *Time*: "The images are vivid, the asides incisive and the prose elegant in this joyride of a story."

113

1991 IMAJICA

"Magic is the first and last religion of the world."

What might it mean to forget one's own nature? Is it a particular kind of self-consciousness that connects to a fear of aging and lost agency? Clive explores those questions in *Weaveworld* as Cal becomes preoccupied with the humdrum reality of living a colorless life in a gray city. Later, in *The Thief of Always*, we're shown Harvey's selfish, childish ability to live in the moment without care for consequences or for others; this idea is inverted in the Abarat series, as we see the filigrees of distant memories returning to a hero who has no prior awareness of their absence. In *Imajica*, however, we share Gentle's slow realization that he bears responsibility for righting an epic failure that he has wiped from his own mind.

"*Imajica* started with my thinking about the images which appear in the great paintings of Christian mythology. Whether or not they're true, they seemed to me to be a potent, powerful, and important cyphers of image and meaning. So I considered writing a book which would be a fantasy but which would also be about God, about belief, about a man who discovers that all his life he has been prepared for an act of massive consequence but didn't realize it. . . . A lot of this came from the feeling that there is so much more in us than we completely comprehend, that our day-to-day lives with their petty annoyances perhaps shouldn't distract us from a grander and deeper perception of ourselves."

The Great and Secret Show had proved to Clive that he could explicitly tackle weighty ideas of existence and spirituality within a novel without it becoming dull or dry, and in *Imajica* he expands his scope even further by setting the narrative across five fully populated worlds.

"The worlds which open up in *Imajica*, just in terms of their physical scale, not to mention their metaphysical scale, are so much larger than I would have dared attempt even a couple of years ago," Clive admitted at the time, cautioning that "the horror, the darkness, has never gone. *Imajica* has still got some very dark passages in it. . . . What's been added is this, hopefully, transcendental level. What's also been added is a sense of thoroughly created worlds; I mean worlds with names, tribes, flora and fauna, religions, cults, and so on. I did hint at dimensions hidden in secret places in the horror fiction, obviously, and a lot of it contains the sense that if you open the wrong door you're

going to find yourself lost in another world. The way I'm doing it now, it's not just opening the door but knocking down the whole damn wall and saying, 'Here it all is.' "

While editing *Nightbreed* in Los Angeles in October 1989, Clive began making notes for the new novel, centering on a strange being uniquely sensitive to its surroundings. He then returned to London, to the home he shared with his partner, David Dodds, and devoted 1990 to writing the novel.

Clive had long been entranced by Hollywood and, with fresh filmmaking prospects ahead of him, he was now making plans to move there permanently. He'd met Malcolm Smith on the set of *Nightbreed* and been encouraged by him to take the leap. David took charge of the practicalities and began to arrange moving their belongings to Beverly Hills in late 1990. In the latter stages of this, Clive was left alone in an almost empty house, with little more than his writing desk and the *Imajica* manuscript remaining with him.

"Between, I think I'm going to say the middle of December and when I left for America permanently, which was, I think, in March, I finished the book. I was alone in this huge place, this huge Georgian house, utterly alone. I mean there was nothing: the rooms were entirely empty and it both induced profound loneliness and a profound sense of departure because the things that I owned had departed before me and the man I loved had departed before me, so I was there in that house and what could I do but fill the pages with visions?

"In order to get through a big novel like *Imajica*, both as a reader and as a writer, you need mystery—and you can't have one mystery, you need to have many. There's a pulling away of the veils constantly. What I've tried to do to the reader is say, 'There isn't the solid moral clarity of *Lord of the Rings*.' I do the reverse of that. *Imajica*'s characters are human beings like you and I, who, of course, discover a larger purpose for themselves. But in discovering a larger purpose, rather than becoming more themselves—like the hobbits out there in the wilderness becoming more hobbity—my characters skin themselves. The lives they have fall away."

Imajica's unflinching embrace of life lost is the cornerstone of its gravity, giving the novel an emotional depth that is felt keenly by readers and grows out of Clive's own loss at the time—of his friend Alton, who was killed, and of his cousin Mark, who died from AIDS.

As *Imajica* was published in 1991, Clive explained the importance for him of writing narratives that embody ideas of weight: "I come back to something which is very certain in me—that death is simply a point of transformation, that the adventure that we are having, the three-score-years-and-ten adventure, is just idling on a railway station platform, waiting for the train onward, and I feel as though fiction is a doorway—good imaginative fiction particularly—to our own personal heavens, our own personal hells. We're opening those doors and saying, 'What might the future be beyond this body?' 'What might the future be beyond the limitations, beyond the cage of flesh?'

"Over and over again in my books, whether it be in the early horror fiction or now, a big fantasy book like *Imajica*, people are set free; they shuffle off this mortal coil and they take new kinds of adventures."

The book's flap copy read:

> Amid a seamless tapestry of erotic passion, thwarted ambition and mythic horror, Imajica picks out the brightly-coloured threads of three memorable characters: John Furie Zacharias, known as Gentle, a master forger whose own life is a series of lies; Judith Odell, a beautiful woman desired by three powerful men, but belonging to none of them; and Pie'oh'pah, a mysterious assassin who deals in love as well as death. United in a desperate search for the heart of a universal mystery, all three discover the truth that

"*Imajica* is audacious, arrogant and subversive in the most imaginative and visionary of ways. It's Barker's best work yet."
—W. C. STROBY

lies in a place as mysterious as the face of God, and as secret as the human soul. They discover the Imajica.

The Imajica: five Dominions, four reconciled, and one, the Earth, cut off from them, her inhabitants living in ignorance on the edge of a sea of possibilities, an ocean of mystery and magic. Only a few know of the Imajica, and many of them are frightened. For a time is coming, a time of great risk, a time of great promise—a shining mystical moment in which Earth can be reunited with the other four Dominions. A time of Reconciliation.

As Judith, Gentle and Pie race to capture that moment, other forces are gathering to keep the Earth forever bound in the darkness that surrounds her. Their quest will carry them on an epic journey through all five Dominions to the very border of the greatest mystery of all: the First Dominion, on the other side of which lies the Holy City of the Unbeheld, where their highest hopes, or their deepest fears, will be realised.

Imajica is many things: an epic tour de force that soars in celebration of the power of magic and the imagination; a brilliant compilation of visionary splendours, heart-stopping terrors and fundamental myths that reinvent mythology itself; a novel of vast panoramas and intimate, obsessive passions, embracing ghosts and reflections as well as the human and the divine. Above all, *Imajica*—a book of revelations—is Clive Barker's outstanding achievement to date. Spellspinner, master fabulist, he takes us on a voyage to worlds beyond our knowledge, but within our grasp. Long after you have turned the final page, you will be yearning for *Imajica*'s wonders, believing they are just a breath away.

Critical reaction to *Imajica* was positive. The *Times Literary Supplement* wrote that the book's "tears and blood and nightmare imagery are passionate and ingenious. *Imajica* is a ride with remarkable views."

The *Washington Post* said: "Rich in plot twists, Byzantine intrigues, and hidden secrets, *Imajica* is a Chinese puzzle box constructed on a universal scale. . . . Barker has an unparalleled talent for envisioning other worlds."

1989–1994 GRAPHIC ADVENTURES

Terror the Movies Don't Dare Unleash

The Books of Blood were far from the only comics and graphic novels bearing Clive's name in the late 1980s and early 1990s. Around the time of the first of the Tapping the Vein series, Clive had met with Archie Goodwin at Marvel and the pair struck a deal for an anthology series of comics based on the *Hellraiser* series.

D. G. Chichester authored a series bible with input from Clive and Archie, as well as from writers Erik Saltzgaber and Philip Nutman. A series bible is a collection of guidelines and background information that establishes the mythology and mechanisms of a series's universe, in order to maintain consistency across installments. The *Hellraiser* series bible was especially guided by the conception of Hell as a place of order, rules, and precision.

Clive Barker's Hellraiser: Book 1 was published in 1989 with a lineup of writers for the first three tales comprising Erik Saltzgaber, Shelly Fische, and Jan Strnad. The respective artists for each were John Bolton, Dan Spiegle, and Bernie Wrightson, with Ted McKeever completing the quartet of tales and illustrating his own story.

In his introduction to this first book in the series, Clive wrote:

> The extraordinary thing is this: that the moment you make a story or create an image that finds favour with an audience, you've effectively lost it. It toddles off, the little bastard; it becomes the property of the fans. It's they who create around it their own mythologies; who make sequels and prequels in their imagination; who point out the inconsistencies in your plotting. I can envisage no greater compliment. What more could a writer or filmmaker ever ask than that their fiction be embraced and become part of the dream-lives of people who it's likely he'll never even meet?
>
> *Hellraiser*, and to a lesser extent the novella upon which it's based, *The Hellbound Heart*, were pieces of work that elicited these welcome responses from their first appearances on page and screen. That the Lament Configuration and the Cenobites its solving summons—Pinhead especially, of course—be taken to the hearts and imaginations of so many healthily perverse folks around the world was both surprising and reassuring

MARVEL COMICS

ART PAPER FOR BLEED PAGES
(BOOKSHELF FORMAT OR SADDLE STITCH)

65%

KEEP ALL LETTERING INSIDE BROKEN-LINE BOX

XEROX | STATS | CODE

M-05
4/89

Book HELLRAISER BOOK 2   Issue   Pg. #15

PRINTS AT 60%

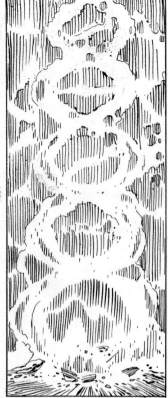

ABOVE

Comic store ad templates for Marvel's/ Epic's Hellraiser and Nightbreed comic book series, sent to retailers in 1991 and 1992.

to me. The former because the film had been made very cheaply—as much to prove to myself and the overlords of Hollywood that I could turn a modest amount of money into a marketable film; the latter because the images and ideas in the picture were extremely dark, and I was delighted that there was a sizable audience for a horror film that didn't dice adolescents in the shower, or have its tongue buried so deeply in its cheek it could lick out its ear from the inside.

But back to what I was saying about the work being possessed by others. After *Hellraiser* came *Hellbound: Hellraiser II*, in which writer Peter Atkins and director Tony Randel took the open threads of the first movie and wove their own sequel. It wasn't the movie I would have made, but it was immensely interesting to see how other minds and other talents dealt with the ideas; exploring avenues I hadn't even contemplated when I first set pen to the paper.

Which brings me on to the comic book in your hands, the first of what I hope will be many such little monsters. Its twin godfathers are Archie Goodwin and Dan Chichester, and its many parents are listed in the pages that follow. Though my name's on the cover I am, you see, just a bystander at this baptism. But I'm proud nevertheless. Not just that so many fine creators were sufficiently attracted by the conceits of *Hellraiser* to expand its fictional world with tales of their own, but because—lo and behold!—the little bastard movie I made's got a life of its own.

Who'd have thought it? Who'd have ever thought?

Subsequent issues showcased a strong lineup of writing talents attracted to the series, including Marc McLaurin, Philip Nutman, Randy and Jean-Marc Lofficier, and Lana Wachowski, alongside artists including Kevin O'Neill, Scott Hampton, Bo Hampton, Bill Koeb, Mike Hoffman, John Ridgway, John Van Fleet, Miran Kim, Mark Bloodworth, Mike Mignola, Colleen Doran, Ray Lago, and Paul Johnson.

The series also allowed Clive's earlier collaborators on the *Hellraiser* movies to contribute, with stories written by Peter Atkins in issue 3 and by Nicholas Vince in issues 4, 7, 10, 12, and 14. Clive's partner, Malcolm Smith, wrote stories for issues 16 and 19.

120

"I think it's very exciting to see my ideas and characters in new and fresh ways. Some of the stories are erotic, some are sociological, some have a political sense. It looks great, too, the artists are really in top form."

Clive waited until issues 17 and 18 to contribute his own storyline, "The Harrowing," to the series, written by Malcolm Smith, Anna Miller, and Fred Vicarel and brought vividly to life by the art of Alex Ross.

Issue 20, the final issue in the run, was published in 1992 and featured Neil Gaiman and Dave McKean's take on the *Hellraiser* mythos, the duo having already broken new ground in comics together with *Violent Cases* and *Black Orchid*, and with Dave McKean having contributed covers to Neil Gaiman's *The Sandman* since its debut in 1989.

Along with three seasonal specials, four *Hellraiser* spin-off Books of the Damned and a comic adaptation of the *Hellraiser III* movie, the latter written by Peter Atkins with art by Miran Kim, the twenty issues of *Hellraiser* set a high bar. Their success had already led to plans at Marvel for another of Clive's movie storylines to breed a similarly expansive set of comics.

In April 1990, Epic's run of *Nightbreed* comics began with four issues, written by the pair behind *2000 AD* and *Judge Dredd*, Alan Grant and John Wagner, and drawn by Jim Baikie. These followed Clive's original screenplay relatively faithfully (the version before reshoots, such that issue 4 gave readers Clive's original intention for its concluding scenes, as compared to the theatrically released movie version). The series then set off on new adventures for the Breed from issue 5 onwards.

As Archie Goodwin noted, "The thing that appealed to me is the potential beyond the movie, as a regular ongoing series. It walks a very fine line to covering the world of superheroes. The main characters of *Nightbreed* are monsters, but you could also call them 'mutants.' Suddenly, they could be a regular comic. They are the supernatural characters of society. If people have gotten a little tired of 'regular superheroes,' *Nightbreed* is kind of a logical step for them to take."

Twelve issues, from 5 to 16, were written by D. G. Chichester before Lana Wachowski wrote issue 17, Gregory Wright penned 18 to 20, and Nicholas Vince took over from issue 21 onwards, with the final installment, issue 25, published in May 1993.

Hellraiser and *Nightbreed* were combined in a crossover story in *Jihad*, a two-part series written by D. G. Chichester with artwork by Paul Johnson, published in 1991, and both *Hellraiser* and *Nightbreed* featured in an Epic Comics anthology series in 1992.

The comic collaborations continued; late 1992 also saw the publication of *Primal* by Dark Horse Comics, written by Clive with D. G. Chichester and Erik Saltzgaber, with John Van Fleet providing the artwork.

Weaveworld also received a three-part adaptation published by Epic Comics in 1991 and 1992, written by Erik Saltzgaber with art by Mike Manley, Ricardo Villagran, and Gloria Vasquez.

Clive also contributed to another series in 1993: "Steve Niles and Tom Skulan came to me and said, 'We publish *Night of the Living Dead* and we want to do something with London. You used to live there, so how about populating London with zombies for a couple of issues?' I said I'd be happy to offer them a storyline and then let them run with it, which they've done quite wonderfully, with Carlos Kastro providing the artwork. I think it'll make absolutely certain that I never receive a knighthood, because it really does have a dig at the monarch and the Church of England."

As Clive prepared a new world of ten different storylines for Marvel—the Razorline universe—his previous creations continued to breathe new life in comic form. Pinhead gained a six-issue run as a stand-alone eponymous comic, written by D. G. Chichester and Erik Saltzgaber, and was also featured in a two-part crossover, *Pinhead vs. Marshal Law*, written by Pat Mills and illustrated by Kevin O'Neill. Meanwhile, the Harrowers, a group of characters created for the *Hellraiser* graphic novels, got their own six-part comic series, published monthly from December 1993, written by Malcolm Smith and McNally Sagal, with art by Gene Colan and Joe Rubinstein.

1992   CANDYMAN

"Be my victim . . ."

Clive's short story "The Forbidden" was brought to vivid, cinematic life by the film adaptation, written and directed by Bernard Rose, with Tony Todd's central performance as the Candyman kickstarting another film franchise.

Originally published in 1985 in volume 5 of the Books of Blood, "The Forbidden" was inspired by cautionary tales Clive was told as a child.

"With children, their beliefs are stronger than adults and they exist in that magical state where anything is possible. Children disseminate urban legends because they're at that age where it's difficult for them to tell the difference between reality and fiction. The story about the little boy who had his genitals cut off by the hook-handed man was told to me by my grandmother when I was six years old. She was trying to tell me to be careful of strangers, but I remember being terrified for weeks. Of course, that didn't stop me telling that story to all my friends at the playground, and I used that story in the first *Candyman*."

Marrying common elements and fears—the hook-handed man, castration, the uncatchable killer, and urban brutality—the story explores not only the narrative of an urban myth but the very nature of mythology, playing on the fame of a whispered myth as it spreads:

"I am rumour," he sang in her ear. "It's a blessed condition, believe me. To live in people's dreams; to be whispered at street corners, but not have to be."

"I was writing about the experience of horror," says Clive. "This was about why we write those tales, why we hear those tales. The story was about story itself."

The character of the Candyman draws upon a motif Clive had long been developing since writing his 1973 play *Hunters in the Snow*—that of the calmly spoken gentleman-villain—who seduces Helen with the poetry of Shakespeare and the measured rhythms of a lover. *Hellraiser*'s Pinhead would later share some of these characteristics and be all the more terrifying for it.

"I use a quote from Hamlet in the story: 'Sweets to the sweet,'" Clive says. "The earlier origin of the quote is biblical, from Judges 14:14: "And he said unto them, Out of the eater came forth meat, and out of the strong came forth sweetness." It references a riddle decipherable only to Samson, who

ABOVE LEFT

Virginia Madsen as Helen
Lyle in *Candyman*, 1992.

ABOVE RIGHT

Tony Todd as the
Candyman, 1992.

had once killed a lion and found bees and honey in its corpse, and the answer to the riddle comes in Judges 14:18: "What is sweeter than honey? And what is stronger than a lion?"

As Clive notes: "In England, we have golden syrup. The makers of this syrup put on their can a picture of the partially rotted corpse of a lion with bees flying around it, and the biblical quote." The syrup, called Lyle's Golden Syrup (made by Tate & Lyle), inspired Bernard Rose, a fellow Englishman, to change Helen's last name from Buchanan to Lyle—yet another way to weave the biblical allusion into the story.

As Clive notes today, the figure of the Candyman in "The Forbidden" wears a motley: his appearance is multicolored, standing for every kind of "other"—making his universal story adaptable to resonate widely with all who are outsiders or marginalized.

> He was bright to the point of gaudiness: his flesh a waxy yellow, his thin lips pale blue,
> his wild eyes glittering as if their irises were set with rubies. His jacket was a patchwork,
> his trousers the same. He looked, she thought, almost ridiculous, with his blood-stained
> motley, and the hint of rouge on his jaundiced cheeks. . . .
> And she was almost enchanted. By his voice, by his colours, by the buzz from his body.

The setting of "The Forbidden" was relocated from Liverpool to Chicago for the movie, a choice made by Bernard Rose as he and Clive discussed the adaptation. Bernard also added a Bloody Mary element of invoking the titular presence by repeating his name in a mirror, and the Candyman was reimagined to reflect the majority-Black, urban environment of Chicago's Cabrini–Green public housing project.

"*Candyman* was Bernard Rose's baby from the beginning," says Clive. "We shared an agent at CAA, Adam Krentzman, and I'd enjoyed *Paperhouse*—I thought it was tremendous, a smashing picture. Adam said, 'You know, Bernard really likes your short stories and there are two or three he's interested in and would like to get going. . . .'

"Anyway, his favorite story was 'The Forbidden,' because he wanted to deal with the social stuff. He liked the idea of taking a horror story with some social undertones and making a movie of it. This was while I was still living in London, and we sat down several times and talked it through. We agreed that it needed to be relocated to the United States because it was American money and they weren't going to be interested in a story set in Liverpool. But the Cabrini–Green setting I think worked perfectly well. He took the thematic material in the story and expanded it and turned it into something that was very much his own. I watched over the thing and worked with him and story-conferenced with him and did all those things, but at the end of the day it's Bernard's movie and I think he did a tremendous piece of work.

"It's a very elegant exploration of certain themes found in 'The Forbidden.' It touches the spirit of the story and is a very accurate echo of that spirit. The narrative has been repositioned . . . but, in terms of what's going on in the story—the exploration of the myth, and the clash between a subculture which believes in its own urban legends and the woman who helps make them—it's all very much intact in the movie."

"Candyman really poses the question that if God exists because we believe in him, what would happen to him if the worship ceased?"
—BERNARD ROSE

The Candyman in the movie is a wronged Black painter, Daniel Robitaille, and his death at the hands of a white mob decades earlier roots the screenplay in a conflict of racial injustice.

"In the original story," says Clive, "the Candyman is all kinds of colors. Bernard had to argue strongly for being able to make the Candyman Black. There had been Black horror movies before *Candyman* but they had tended to be very campy. One of the things Bernard did is really make this character have some real nobility."

"I decided to set it in America," said Bernard in 1992, as the film was released, "because I felt it would make it more accessible to a world audience. I chose Chicago because I went there for a film festival and felt it was extraordinary looking in terms of its architecture. The film is about modern architecture. Cabrini-Green has got the highest murder rate per square foot in the world. It's a very, very, very scary place. . . . What's also true is the series of murders committed by coming through the backs of medicine cabinets. . . . A murder was committed in Cabrini-Green in exactly that fashion.

"*Candyman* is a horror film in the real sense of the word. It deals with the elements of dread and death, not just a man with a big knife. *Candyman* invokes our primal fears more than simply the fear of dismemberment. This is modern Gothic horror, a genre which traditionally deals with the romantic horror of death.

"It's a romance of death, like *The Tomb of Ligeia*—a nineteenth century idea of lovers dying together being the ultimate consummation of some kind of sex act. I saw the relationship between Candyman and Helen in those terms, a doomed love affair where death is the ultimate love act. Candyman only goes after people he loves. He's not going after people for the joy of killing. First you've got to call him, and second there has to be some kind of connection. His relationship to Helen is very complicated."

Virginia Madsen, cast as Helen, and Tony Todd as the Candyman realize this romance in gritty, realistic performances that elevate the movie to its mythic conclusion.

Alongside the strong cast, the evocative urban setting and the dread unfolding in the storyline, Philip Glass's soundtrack had an extraordinary impact on the movie.

"One of the things I always wanted to do," says Bernard, "was not to have the score behave in a way that it normally does in a horror movie, telling you when you're supposed to be scared, which is the same thing as telling me I'm not going to be scared."

As Clive noted on the soundtrack's liner notes,

> Philip elevates horror and suspense to an epic plateau. Moving between the gentle toy piano touches of a child's grim fairy tale and the sinister pipe organ of the most fearsome of fire and brimstone sermons, Philip Glass has found a way to evoke the web of the collective fears woven across the span of a human lifetime and lay it like a shroud across an hour and a half of our lives. To this very day, this music still sends chills down my spine.

"*Candyman* isn't going to change people's opinions of me," Clive said as it debuted, "especially with audiences who don't like horror. It's an intimidating story and movie. *Candyman* is less florid and baroque than *Hellraiser*. You don't have to believe in Lament Configurations to enter its world. Bernard has made something that's less supernatural and broader in its appeal. Though *Candyman* will be coming out at the same time as *Hellraiser III*, the two films couldn't be more different. *Candyman* is a new style of Barker, and it's going to be the scariest film of the year."

HELLRAISER III: HELL ON EARTH

"What started in Hell will end on Earth."

"I love the fact that material that originated from the same mind can result in pictures that are stylistically so different," said Clive at the time of the release of *Hell on Earth*. "*Hellraiser III* is a brightly colored, special effects–heavy gross-out, which I had a good time with. *Candyman* is the reverse of it—very low on special effects and high on shock and subtext. I've always loved variation. It's one of the few things that makes life worth living.

"*Candyman* is a very classy package. *Hellraiser III* is a very different proposal. The *Hellraiser* movies are low-budget shockers which go into profit after the first weekend and manage to put some images on the screen which you would not see in any other movie. They're not art pictures by any stretch of the imagination, but they are Grand Guignol and excessive, and I like that. And they're 'poppy'—I mean they're fun pop culture. They have a kind of hold on the imagination which is very different from the hold that *Candyman* has. But when you see the *Hellraiser* movies with an audience that's revved, you have a really great time at the pictures and you come away with some wonderfully disturbing imagery at the end."

The path to *Hellraiser*'s second sequel was not smooth, having been complicated by New World falling into financial difficulties and the eventual purchase of the *Hellraiser* sequel rights and other assets from the failed company by a new entity.

Finally, though, the sequel went before the cameras on September 23, 1991, in High Point, North Carolina—the franchise's first time filming in the US.

Peter Atkins again provided the screenplay and, initially at least, Tony Randel was set to return too to direct the movie, but this changed shortly before filming; Anthony Hickox was tapped as Tony's replacement.

Clive was not involved in the initial stages of the movie's development. "All monsters totter off into the night on their own at some stage," he noted. "Now it's happened to one of mine. Quite honestly, I'm not too concerned. The script is spicy, has superb thrills, and goes like a locomotive. It recalls the original's black perversity—except written on a more extensive, intriguing canvas. Peter's grasp on what makes the mythos work is very strong, and I really have no terrible cause for complaint."

"*Hellraiser* was a very strong story," says Peter, "and the whole mythos is so rich in itself that it can inspire many stories going in so many different directions. Being given such a central mythology as Clive created for the first movie is a gift for any writer. I think the *Hellraiser* movies, and the character of Pinhead itself, offer an intensity of vision that the audience hasn't seen before. People are fascinated by puzzles, by gateways, and I think that the *Hellraiser* movies we've made so far are about gateways, about puzzles, about stepping through and going beyond. Half the fascination is that something awful might happen to you when you go beyond, but there is also the promise that something marvelous might happen as well, and I think that is really at the core of the appeal of all fantasy and horror."

Doug Bradley, back as Pinhead, noted, "Pete's done a terrific job. He and I have had hours of discussions concerning Pinhead's character since we finished *Hellbound*. Between us, we've really discovered who this demon is and, equally as important, who he was as a human being.

"At the end of *Hellbound*, we split the character into the human and Cenobite parts. The human side saved Kirsty and Tiffany. We last saw Pinhead frozen on the torture pillar, and it's through that pillar that the character is reincarnated. The whole of *Hellraiser III* is driven by the question of how Pinhead is reincarnated and what happens when he is. This time, we meet a Pinhead who is freed from the rules, the laws, and the constraints of the Lament Configuration box. The title 'Hell on Earth' tells you he's out there, on the streets, menacing. This is a more sinister, more malevolent character, one who is prepared to—and does—get his hands dirty."

HELLRAISER III: HELL ON EARTH
Synopsis (from the original press kit)

Get ready for the final confrontation! Pinhead, the Black Prince of Hell once again walks
the earth in an orgy of blood and desire.

Rich and spoiled nightclub owner J. P. Monroe (Kevin Bernhardt) purchases a six-
foot-tall, intricately carved pillar in a mysterious art gallery. Among the writhing figures
and distorted faces etched into the surface of the Pillar of Souls are the marbled features
of Pinhead, menacingly frozen in time and space.

Joey Summerskill (Terry Farrell) is a young, ambitious television reporter who, on a
dead-end assignment at the local emergency room, has her life changed forever as she
witnesses a tormented teenage boy being torn apart by bloody chains hooked into his
writhing flesh. In the midst of the gore, Joey finds the boy's trendy girlfriend, Terri (Paula
Marshall), who flees back to J. P.'s nightclub, The Boiler Room.

Joey follows and finally corners Terri, demanding to know where the chains came
from. There, amidst the pounding, satanic music and gyrating bodies, Terri reluctantly
reveals that the chains came from a small puzzle box that her boyfriend had stolen from
the Pillar of Souls.

Meanwhile, in his apartment above the nightclub, J. P. admires his sculpture. Bitten
by a rat hiding in the hole the puzzle box had been taken from, he drips blood on the
pillar. And so begins the release of the soul of Pinhead (Doug Bradley).

Freed by J. P.'s hedonistic greed and lust for power, Pinhead walks the earth again,
creating a new band of Cenobites from the transmuted flesh of his victims. Their one
desire: to reclaim the box and liberate themselves forever from the powers of hell.

"Don't flee from yourself. If you have a quality, let it define you. Cultivate it. It is you." —Pɪɴʜᴇᴀᴅ

Through videotaped interviews with Kirsty Cotton, who vanquished Pinhead in *Hellraiser I* and *II*, Joey and Terri discover the source of the demonic Cenobites and the secret and power of the Lament Configuration box—and that only through controlling the box can they banish Pinhead forever back to hell.

Pinhead's rampage overwhelms the city, and he leaves a horrifying trail of death and destruction. Now only Joey and Terri stand in the way of Pinhead achieving his ultimate triumph. But Joey is tortured by recurring dreams and visions of her dead father, and Terri, jealous of Joey's access to the other plane of reality, would give anything to dream . . .

Finally, the ultimate battle between good and evil provokes a cataclysmic confrontation. Dreams become reality; reality a nightmare. And the only hope of salvation comes from a most unexpected source . . .

In late November 1991, three weeks after completion of filming, Clive was shown a rough cut and, when asked for his opinion, said, "Although it contained some great moments, there was a lot of stuff missing; the end wasn't right, there was no climax, I didn't understand some sequences, and in parts the story was incomprehensible."

The US distribution rights had been bought by Miramax, who very much wanted Clive's name to be on the picture when it was marketed. "A few weeks later I got a call from Bob Weinstein (who owned Miramax with his brother Harvey). He asked for my honest opinion of *Hellraiser III* and I reiterated to him what I thought the problems were . . . and they agreed to finance whatever changes I felt were necessary. While I hadn't been invited to the party at first, I turned out to be the surprise guest only too happy to join in the festivities late in the day!

"I added Terry Farrell's bondage scene at the climax, the monstrous thing coming up through the floor in front of her, the extra computer graphics for the girl being skinned, and many insert death scenes for the nightclub victims. Pete Atkins did all the extra writing. I threw in my ideas and everything was cut into the movie. The result is a pretty seamless patchwork, but a patchwork nevertheless. The best one can say about the movie is it's abundant and there's loads of fun stuff going on.

"It's actually easier for me to comment on it than it would be if I had made the picture, because sometimes when you finish a book or a movie, you're so close to the thing that you don't know what's there. But I have sufficient distance from *Hellraiser III* to know that it's stylish, and it's slick, it's well made, and it's got a damn good performance bang in the middle for Doug Bradley as Pinhead.

"I think Pinhead is the reason people go to see these movies and he must be in fifty percent of *Hellraiser III*. . . . Where Freddy Krueger has turned, especially in the latter movies, into a teenager-hating jokemeister, Pinhead emerges in this one with even more seriousness of intent and means to express that intent [more] than ever before. I think we're actually seeing, as Doug gets more and more confident with the role, a darkening of what he does.

"The danger with seeing Pinhead on earth, in an urban setting, was that the character would be diminished. I mean, the moment you see Freddy by the side of a swimming pool, you know that something's seriously wrong. But they pulled it off. Part of it is Anthony Hickox's great visual skill. He's managed to contextualize the character every step of the way, and not at any point diminish him. And I'd be the first to blow the whistle if Pinhead was diminished, because I feel very close to the character."

In a further sign that he was back on the team, Clive also directed Doug as Pinhead for the first time since the first *Hellraiser* movie, in a music video for Motörhead's song from the movie soundtrack that received airplay on MTV and elsewhere, further promoting the film.

"It was a one-day shoot—seventeen hours," he recalls, "and towards the end Doug came in and everybody was getting rather reverential. It was like, 'The Lord of Hell is here.' The image carries a

kind of potency. It's almost impossible to shoot Pinhead and not have it look good. It's one of those images—very, very cold!"

Clive pitted Pinhead against Lemmy, Motörhead's lead singer, in a game of cards, as written in his outline for the video:

> We open on Motörhead's performance, set in a large, cavernous space. Dante-esque, dimly lit with pools of light on the band members and their instruments. As the camera moves around the space, various creatures are revealed, oily bodies shining through their ragged bits of clothing, prosthetic pieces (a claw, a beak, etc.) and bandages, stylized make-up all showing that they are The Damned. All of this is shot in shadowy black and white. We also see Props from *Hellraiser 3* (the baby, signage, etc.), which become match dissolves to footage from the film itself.

> Back in our black and white cavern a roadie sits in a large overstuffed chair toward the back of the space, smoking, watching the band's performance. Suddenly light streams in when a door crashes open. We switch to colour as Pinhead makes his grand entrance, rim-lit, a delicate presence. The demons begin to writhe madly to the music. The band's performance builds as Pinhead moves across the floor, throwing the roadie out of his chair and out of frame. Pinhead takes the seat and gulps virgin's blood from a smoking cup. From Pinhead's point of view we watch the band.

> We cut to a scene of Lemmy and Pinhead in two chairs at a gaming table. Intercutting with performance footage and *Hellraiser III* footage, we see Lemmy and Pinhead playing cards, drinking, serious competitors having fun. The demons writhe behind Pinhead, the band stands behind Lemmy as the tension builds between the two.

"And, of course," adds Doug, "Lemmy plays the ace of spades . . ."

PINHEAD

"Make him confess himself. And maybe we won't tear your soul apart."

When *Hellraiser* was released in 1987 the most startling figure was the Lead Cenobite, swiftly tagged "Pinhead" by both the production crew and subsequent viewers of the film, and his features have remained front and center of every entry in the continuing franchise. But Clive had long been toying with the character who would later be found far and wide, from posters to T-shirts to comics.

Back in 1973, Clive was directing his play *Hunters in the Snow*, with Doug Bradley in the role of the Dutchman, an undead inquisitor and torturer. Both writer and actor recognize him as the earliest incarnation of *Hellraiser*'s Pinhead, his bleakly eloquent delivery strangely prescient: "Why do you murmur? Why do you dread the calm symmetry of death? Is there not succor to be drawn from oblivion?"

"The character I played in *Hunters*, the Dutchman, I can see echoes of later," Doug Bradley agreed some years later, in conversation with Peter Atkins for the book *Clive Barker's Shadows in Eden*. "This strange, strange character whose head was kind of empty but who conveyed all kinds of things. I remember getting the best note ever from a director when I was the Dutchman; Clive said, 'Dougie, I want you to say this line as if the North Wind was blowing through your eyes. . . .'"

Around the same time, Clive was experimenting with positive and negative shadows cast by a grid of nails while filming *The Forbidden*. "Clive had built what he called his 'nail-board,' which was basically a block of wood which he'd squared off and then he'd banged six-inch nails in at the intersections of the squares," recalls Doug. "He spent endless hours playing with what happened if a light was swung around in front of it to see the way that the shadows of the nails moved and what happened if it was top lit and so forth. Of course, when I saw the first illustrations for this gentleman, it rang a bell with me that here was actually Clive putting the ideas that he'd been playing around with the nail-board in *The Forbidden*, now ten, fifteen years later or whatever; here, he'd now put the image all over a human being's face. Which is typical of the way that he will work with ideas: you'll find little bits of ideas that he would play around with that ten, fifteen years later, when apparently it's all forgotten with, that idea is suddenly brought up again and dealt with in a much bigger way."

23rd July 1993 ; Austin , Texas.

Clive Barker

ABOVE

Simon Bisley's cover artwork for *Clive Barker's Book of the Damned: A Hellraiser Companion*, volume 1, Epic Comics, 1991.

The Forbidden would not see the light of day until the early 1990s, but the image persisted in Clive's mind. While adapting his treatment for *Underworld* into a screenplay in 1984, Clive wrote a notable death scene for Dr. Savary that survived extensive rewrites to be filmed but would ultimately land on the cutting room floor.

"I had a great scene where the villain of the piece has these dreams, and nightmares manifest themselves through him physically. He was forced by the monsters to take some of his own drug—he was a doctor, and all the way through we'd seen him using hypodermics on people. These pricks appeared on his face one by one and hypodermics pushed through so his face became a mass of needles—an image I finally used in *Hellraiser*, of course."

Incorporating the theme of bodily disfigurement in *The Hellbound Heart*, Clive was determined to put his unfiltered ideas on-screen as he worked with Christopher Figg, and with the support of Alan Parker, to generate a sales package for *Hellraiser*.

"One of those pages contained the original drawing of Pinhead. And God knows where that drawing came from. It wasn't in a dream. But it came from somewhere in my psyche. I probably drew it around the time that I wrote the story because *The Hellbound Heart* . . . contains quite a specific description of Pinhead. The whole geometry of him, the scarification of his face, the pins driven in at each intersection of the lines, and the kind of priestly garb which the Cenobites wore in *Hellraiser* were also described. So really there was quite a solid jumping-off place for Pinhead. But I don't know where those images came from. Maybe it's great that I *don't* know. It's one of the secrets of the psyche."

Christopher Figg notes, "We worked incredibly hard on the business plan and presentation pack. . . . Pinhead was one of the first creatures we scratched out in Clive's house in Crouch End; we thought it would be great to have this guy with bits and pieces of metal stuck in his face. Lighting-wise, we designed it so that shadows would swirl round his head. In post-production, it became very clear that Pinhead was going to be the hook on which to hang the marketing."

Working on the design in pre-production, Clive spoke with Bob Keen and Geoff Portass at Image Animation, and with Jane Wildgoose, who had designed many of the Dog Company's later stage costumes. By late July 1986 the shooting script clearly identified the scarified Cenobite as the leader, with the now-familiar pattern of pins in his head.

Geoff Portass says, "Pinhead was basically Clive's design, as seen on the *Hellbound* T-shirts. There was a lot of discussion with Clive, then I did a few drawings. First we just had spikes coming out of his head. I wanted it to be more geometrical. Originally he had pins all over the head, but Clive and I thought it would be nice to make it look more like a mask with pins around his chin, over his ears and at the back of his head. We modeled it about six times and did loads of drawings. If you look at the first test pictures that came out of *Hellraiser* there are actually pins in there rather than nails and the pins got lost—you couldn't see them. So we clipped the ends of the pins off and made our own hollow brass nails that inserted over the top and they were much more visible."

Jane Wildgoose adds, "My notes say that he wanted '1. areas of revealed flesh where some kind of torture has or is occurring; 2. something associated with butchery involved' and then here we have a very Clive turn of phrase, I've written down, 'repulsive glamour.' And the other notes that I made about what he wanted was that they should be 'magnificent super-butchers.' There would be one or two of them with some 'hangers-on' as he put it, and there would be four or five altogether."

Reflecting back on his thinking for the character in 2004, Clive observed that "nothing springs into my imagination without having inspiration in other things I've seen or experienced. The Cenobites were no exception. Their design was influenced amongst other things by punk, by Catholicism, and by the visits I would take to S/M clubs in New York and Amsterdam. Of course the make-up and costume designs only do part of the job. We were blessed (if that's the right word when it comes to such unholy labors) to have marvelous actors beneath the latex, particularly Doug Bradley, who played a character unremarkably dubbed 'Lead Cenobite' in the credits of the first *Hellraiser* film. He so perfectly married threat and elegance that he quickly caught the affections of the audience and was given a name which I think originated in the make-up studio: Pinhead. . . .

"There was another source of inspiration for the Cenobites, more particularly for Pinhead himself. I had seen a book containing photographs of African fetishes: sculptures of human heads crudely carved from wood and then pierced with dozens, sometimes hundreds of nails and spikes. They were images of rage, the text instructed."

Reflecting back on the initial movie, Clive notes: "You can't predict what's going to strike the collective psyche because if you could predict it you'd do it more often. The fact is, when we made Pinhead I was aware this was an image which hadn't been seen on the screen before but I was not prepared for the level of devotion that that character has aroused in people—and I think 'devotion' is correct because it has faintly Catholic undertones.

"When we were shooting the picture, we got a lot of bad vibes off the producers at New World because they said he wasn't making any jokes—Freddy was on the rise at that point so he was one of the areas of focus—and one of the notes I got repeatedly was: 'He wasn't making any jokes; why wasn't he making any jokes?' 'He's moving really, really slowly and good monsters move fast.' He was 'rather too literary.'

"What they were saying was, this is not going to work because he wasn't like Freddy and they were very negative about that. And they also went through a phase where they wanted him to say nothing at all because the other tradition at that time was the Friday the 13th stuff, indeed the Halloween stuff, which had Jason and Michael Myers going around being mute, and my argument was that Pinhead hailed back to a much earlier tradition of monsters—primarily, obviously, Dracula who is very articulate, very aristocratic. Part of the chill of Dracula surely lies in the fact that he is very clearly and articulately aware of what he is doing—you feel that this is a penetrating intelligence—and I don't find dumb things terribly scary: I find intelligence scary, particularly twisted intelligence; it's one of the reasons why Hannibal Lecter is scary, isn't it? It's because you always feel that he's going to be three jumps ahead of you."

Doug Bradley recalls that, before filming began, "I went to Clive, worried, saying, 'Give me a clue about him.' He was magnificent and irritating at the same time, because he has a wonderful imagination but it's difficult to lock down. He told me he thought of him as a cross between an administrator and a surgeon who's responsible for running a hospital where there are no wards, only operating

"Pinhead is the aristocrat. If you put Jason and Freddy and the rest of them down at a table, Pinhead is the only one of them that would know which fork to use." —Neil Gaiman

theaters. As well as being the man who wields the knife, he's the man who has to keep the timetable going. Armed with that, I went back to the script and said, 'But how do I play him?'"

In his book, *Sacred Monsters*, Doug wrote, "I asked—politely—if everyone would leave the room. I sat and stared in the mirror, letting a flood of sensations and emotions wash over me. After all the preparation that had gone before, most of my real decisions about the character and how I wanted to play him were probably made in about twenty minutes right there. On the one hand it is a genuinely unsettling experience. Where was I? Left behind somewhere, an identity in my head, but according to the mirror not here anymore. On the other, it was thrillingly exciting: this idea, sketch, description, was now three-dimensional and real.

"I moved my head a little, this way, that way: I went close to the mirror, moved back from it. Then I began to tentatively move my mouth and face. A frown. A sneer. Raise an eyebrow. Smile. Laugh. Scream. Then words . . . I'll tear your soul apart . . . Angels to some, demons to others . . .

"To put no finer point on it, I fell in love! I bathed in the sense of power and majesty that the make-up gave me. I felt a sense of beauty; a dark mangled, inscrutable beauty. This detached, ordered piece of mutilation or self-mutilation, so carefully and lovingly executed. The head had a sense of peace and stillness about it, quite at odds with the horror the image was presenting. And beneath it all, a sense of tremendous melancholy, a feeling of a creature fundamentally lost. A line from one of Clive's plays swam into my mind: 'I am in mourning for my humanity.' At this point there was no backstory for the character, but I had discussed this with Clive and we had agreed that he had once been human. But whether this was yesterday, last week, last year, ten, a hundred, a thousand years ago, I didn't know. I didn't need to. Sufficient to have that idea lodged into my brain. A perpetual, unconscious grieving for the man he had once been, for a life and a face he couldn't even remember. And a frozen grief. I felt now that Pinhead existed in an emotional limbo where neither pain nor pleasure could touch him. A pretty good definition of Hell for me."

Peter Atkins offers, "It's undeniably true that Pinhead—the name and the face—is more well-known than Doug Bradley is. Is it possible then that it's just the character, the dialogue, the make-up, that have done the trick? Does Doug really have anything to do with the monster's popularity?

"I can answer that with an emphatic *yes*. At Clive's invitation, I took over the writing of the *Hellraiser* series with the second movie. I've now written three of them. I know just how vital Doug's talent is to the success of the pictures. I've watched Doug at work on the soundstage. I've seen him in the dailies. I've seen him in the rough cuts. I've seen him in the finished movies. He's quite brilliant. I can sit down and write piss-elegant dialogue for our little black Pope of Hell as much as I want. It's only when an actor of Doug's caliber gets hold of those lines that they come to life. He never goes for the surface reading, never goes for the obvious, the hammy—which, God knows, the lines would allow. His interpretations are always subtle, fully rounded, and thoroughly thought through. He thinks about the role of Pinhead as much as if he was essaying Macbeth or Lear. To Doug, Pinhead is not a silly movie monster with a latex face and an attitude. He's a character. With subtleties. With light and shade. Doug's ironic, mannered, and darkly knowing performance is absolutely the single most important element in Pinhead's success."

> **"The basic concept is, if you had all the other Clive Barker books, this is the one that goes on the end of the shelf next to the rest."** —STEPHEN JONES

1991–2006   INSIGHT AND APPRECIATION

"It's all the work of another man entirely."

As the breadth of Clive's work became apparent, so did a demand to know more about his history and the events that had shaped him and his worldview.

In 1991, the year after the first of the Illustrator volumes was published, two more nonfiction works arrived in bookstores, each offering insights into Clive's early years prior to the Books of Blood, sharing previously unpublished texts and images, and digging deeper into Clive's passions and concerns.

The first was a comprehensive and beautifully designed collection of original and previously published interviews and essays, edited by Stephen Jones. Published by Underwood–Miller in the US, *Clive Barker's Shadows in Eden* devoted more than 450 pages to showcasing Clive and his work, including biographical and bibliographical detail that made it an indispensable reference work.

Stephen Jones wrote in it that "this is *not* a biography, nor is it intended to be a definitive work. *Shadows in Eden* is a mosaic sampling of facts and opinions by a selection of writers who have chronicled Barker's polymorphic career to date, and it will hopefully allow the reader an unbiased insight into Barker's talent and the multifarious imagination that guides it."

The lineup was a powerful tour de force assembled by its editor and the volume included contributions from Stephen King, Ramsey Campbell, Dennis Etchison, Lisa Tuttle, Philip Nutman, Neil Gaiman, Kim Newman, Gary Hoppenstand, Peter Atkins, Stanley Wiater, Douglas E. Winter, and many others.

It got the full treatment in terms of production effects, hitting the market as a trade hardcover and a five-hundred-copy limited edition in a slipcase—each signed by Clive—as well as a traycased deluxe lettered edition, only fifty-two copies printed, each not only signed by Clive but also containing its own unique original piece of Clive's art drawn directly onto a special limitation page.

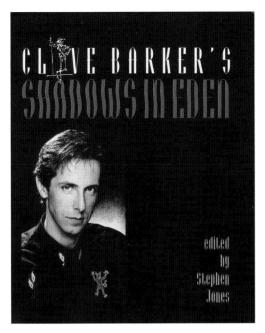 

The second nonfiction monograph about Clive was *Pandemonium*. Edited by Michael Brown, it was published by Eclipse Books as a signed limited edition hardcover (only three hundred copies printed), as well as a trade hardcover and paperback. *Pandemonium* had more of a magazine digest format but included many never-before-seen photographs and artwork images as well as interviews with Clive and many others, including Alan Plent, Peter Atkins, Doug Bradley, Nicholas Vince, and Simon Bamford. John Bolton provided cover artwork and an interior portfolio.

It also featured the first publication of one of Clive's playscripts, presenting the full text of *The History of the Devil*.

The following year, Michael Brown also launched The Breed: The Authorized Clive Barker Fan Club and its official newsletter, *Dread*, which would run for twelve issues and two special editions over its two-year life. Published by Phantom Press/Fantaco Enterprises, *Dread* featured regular interviews with Clive and with his collaborators in film and comics, including Peter Atkins, Malcolm Smith, D. G. Chichester, Doug Bradley, Bob Keen, Anthony Hickox, Bernard Rose, Nicholas Vince, John Bolton, and Steve Niles. It also published a second play by Clive, *A Clowns' Sodom*, as well as an original short story, "On Amen's Shore."

Issue 12 came with a trading card featuring Clive's artwork, advertising a release from Fantaco, again edited by Michael Brown, of a fifty-card set of Clive's artwork, which also had a deluxe signed version that included four additional art cards.

Issue 11 had featured articles by two members of The Breed, Cheryl Bentzen and Stephen Dressler. Two years later, after The Breed and *Dread* folded, Cheryl and Stephen would launch the Lost Souls official Clive Barker fan club and online fan site. The first issue of the club's self-published magazine came out in 1995 and featured a short story by Clive: the titular "Lost Souls." For the next eight years *Lost Souls* magazine regularly supplied fans with exclusive interviews with Clive, as well as news, essays, and conversations with key collaborators such as Peter Atkins and Douglas E. Winter.

In its later years, Lost Souls was run by Craig Fohr, and by Deborah Gordon, who had previously been editor of the Clive Barker Appreciation Society and had published a separate newsletter.

Hellraiser, rather than Clive Barker, had also had its own fanzine from an early point. *Coenobium*, launched and published by Diane Keating, who was joined from issue 1 by Ed Martinez, ran from 1989 to 1996 and branched out to cover all aspects of Clive's wider work over that period. Alongside articles documenting film-set visits and visits to conventions and Clive's art gallery installations, issues included interviews with Clive, Bob Keen, Peter Atkins, Nicholas Vince, Doug Bradley, Valentina Vargas, Bruce Ramsay, and Bill Condon, as well as with model makers including Jeff Brower of Screamin', who was sculpting the Cenobites into vinyl life.

ABOVE LEFT
Shadows in Eden, edited by Stephen Jones and published by Underwood-Miller in 1991, gave a comprehensive view of Clive's work to date that showcased his art and written work alongside articles and interviews.

ABOVE RIGHT
In 1991, Michael Brown's *Pandemonium* volume compiled Clive's artwork with a miscellany of articles and photographs from films and theatre productions and interview material with Clive and his collaborators. This untitled artwork was used for a signature sheet in the hardback limited edition.

1992 THE THIEF OF ALWAYS

"The great grey beast February had eaten Harvey Swick alive."

Subverting expectations was becoming a habit for Clive, an inconvenience that the HarperCollins US press team wryly noted in their sales material: "With every new book published, renowned author Clive Barker manages to re-create his style, always expanding the realm of fiction as he explores the subtle nuances of the human heart and mind."

And when Clive raised the possibility of writing a book for young adults, it was not initially received well. "The story had occurred to me a while ago and I'd written it down in short form called 'The Holiday House.' And I showed it to my agent who wasn't particularly eager about it, so I went into a corner and just did it, because it was a story I wanted to write. It took about three months to write, probably another couple of months to do fixes on, and then I gave it to HarperCollins and said, 'I realize you're taking a huge risk with this, because here's a children's book coming from Clive Barker, and maybe nobody will buy it! So I'll sell it to you for a dollar.' Actually, they ended up giving me a silver dollar for it.

"It felt like exactly the right time to cast back to the fantasies and ambitions that touched me as a child. There was a purity of evil and a purity of good in those books which is very much a part of the fiction I write as an adult. For the eight-year-olds, *The Thief of Always* is an adventure about a kid who goes to a house that seems to promise everything but has a dark, terrible secret. And to an adult, it's a story about the problems of time and childhood, and what you give away in the moments of your youth that you can never get back again. I was striving for the same kind of layered effect you get with *Alice in Wonderland* or *The Halloween Tree*—books that are wonderful tales, where even as a child you sense that there's something going on beneath the surface which you can't quite grasp, and once you go back as an adult, you find it to still be fresh."

Contributing a piece to accompany sales material, Clive wrote:

I had long wanted to write a fable that might find its way into the hands of a child like me. I don't mean the child I was, I mean the child I am, indeed that we all are in some corner of our

CLIVE BARKER

> *The tales we are told as children are with us, I believe, for life. We may read greater works, filled with finer prose and profounder emotion, but the place those first stories have in our hearts is unassailable.*
>
> *The works of childhood (I'll avoid the word literature, it sounds too like hard work) introduce us to the primal themes of art, and on occasion their very simplicity may allow them to carry weight that far more elaborate fictions lack. On Pan's Island and in Alice's Wonderland, in Oz, Narnia and Middle-Earth, we first encounter the power of the imagination, and of the words that serve it.*
>
> *I had long wanted to write a tale for the child in all of us. A fable with enough shudders to make opening it a little nerve-wracking, enough weird adventure to give any imaginer a taste for further explorations along the book shelf, enough mystery to invite all manner of private musings on the nature of Love, Time and Magic.*
>
> *The subject, THE THIEF OF ALWAYS, stole up on me. But when I saw it plainly, there in my head, I knew its purpose in a moment. I would write, at the age of forty, about how the years fly, hoping I might learn from the telling how to slow the next forty. And I would revisit the haunted boy who is pictured at the back of the book, to see how far I had come from there.*
>
> *Not far, it seems. I loved to let my imagination fly then, as I do now; now, as then, I sought the company of demons and divinities.*
>
> *In one regard, however, I have changed. As a boy I looked to books of enchanted travel as a substitute for the magic I longed to have erupt into the real world. Now I know the words themselves are an enchantment, and the dreams conjured by a succession of marks on the page - dreams that can transform our hearts and minds - proof of the miraculous.*
>
> *In his battles for life, little Harvey Swick, the hero of THE THIEF OF ALWAYS, uses every speck of imagination he possesses. His victory over the darkness that would take love and meaning from him is the victory of any reader (or writer, come to that) whose imagination survives the banalities of our daily lives. The dreaming child endures, and reaching for us from the page reminds us what power resides in tales and their telling.*

psyches. A fable with enough shudders to make opening it a little nerve-wracking, enough weird adventure to give any imaginer a taste for further explorations along the book shelf, and with enough mystery to invite all manner of private musings on the nature of Love, Time and Magic.

The subject, *The Thief of Always*, stole up on me. But when I saw it plainly, there in my head, I knew its purpose in a moment. I would write, at the age of forty, about how the years fly, hoping that I might perhaps learn from the telling how to slow the next forty. And I would revisit the haunted boy who is pictured at the back of the book, to see how far I had come from there.

Not far, it seems. I loved to let my imagination fly then, as I do now. I sought the company of demons and divinities and there too, things remain the same.

In one regard I have changed, however. Then, I looked to books of enchanted travels as a substitute for the magic I longed to have erupt into the real world. Now I know the words themselves are an enchantment, and the worlds conjured by a succession of marks upon a page—worlds that can transform our hearts and minds—are proof of the miraculous.

In his battle for life, little Harvey Swick, the hero of *The Thief of Always*, uses every speck of imagination he possesses. His victory over the darkness that would take love and meaning from him is the victory of every reader (or writer, come to that) whose imagination survives the banality of our daily lives. The dreaming child endures, and reaching for us from the page reminds us what power resides in tales and their telling.

ABOVE
Author's introduction to *The Thief of Always* in the HarperCollins press kit, 1992.

"It was a neat writing experience, in the sense that I really knew what the narrative was going to be." Clive smiles. "I laid it out in chapters before writing it; I laid out what I thought the action was going to be. I had a really clear sense of it. I wish novels were always this easy, but they're not. But of all the things I've written, this was probably the simplest process."

Reflecting nearly thirty years later on the importance of how a play or a story leaves its audience or reader feeling at its close, Clive says of *The Thief of Always*, "Resolutions to narratives move me if they're working and it's almost a test as to whether a narrative is working; if I am dry-eyed or crying at the end of the narrative. It took me a day to write that last paragraph and if you look at it you can see why it took a day, because I was going through seasons and I was going through feelings—'Love enough for a thousand Christmases . . .' Every nuance of feeling that is in the book is not just in that last sentence but the fact that it is about being separated from your parents, being given a second chance. It's a redemptive book, I think, and I know as a kid you don't think about redemption but I think that's one of the reasons why the book works for adults as well as kids."

"At the heart of the book there is a very simple idea: live in the moment and understand that the moment is miraculous."

The book's original flap copy read:

> Mr. Hood's Holiday House has stood for a thousand years, welcoming countless children into its embrace. It is a place of miracles, a blissful round of treats and seasons, where every childish whim may be satisfied . . .
>
> There is a price to be paid, of course, but young Harvey Swick, bored with his life and beguiled by Mr Hood's wonders, does not stop to consider the consequences. It is only when the House shows its darker face—when Harvey discovers the pitiful creatures that dwell in its shadow—that he comes to doubt Mr Hood's philanthropy.
>
> The House and its mysterious architect are not about to release their captive without a battle however. Mr Hood has ambitions for his new guest, for Harvey's soul burns brighter than any soul he has encountered in a thousand years . . .

Despite the misgivings of his publisher, the novel was a huge hit with both critics and readers alike, with London's *Time Out* declaring that it "puts the grim back into fairy tales" and *Locus* describing it as "Bradbury with razored edges." Regarding Bradbury, Clive has long admired his ability to write for all ages. "There are things in *The Thief of Always* that have a simple beauty to them which take me back to Ray Bradbury, who is one of the great masters of writing. If you read *Something Wicked This Way Comes* when you are ten, it means something very different to you than if you read it in your thirties or forties. And I hope *Thief of Always* is the same. I know that the children who read it love the adventure, and love Harvey getting turned into a vampire, and they love the fight at the end, and all that stuff. And they tend to find other things in the book."

What no one foresaw was the longevity of *The Thief of Always*—in an arena where books for younger readers can drop out of fashion with every turning generation, it continues to sell around the world, driven in part by its recurrence on teachers' lists of recommended reads. While classes of new readers find both the storyline and the emotional weight engaging, teachers point to its narrative complexity and use of language, with which they can encourage those readers to also become deft writers.

As Clive reflects, "It wasn't bad for a book that cost them a dollar. . . ."

THIS SPREAD

Clive's wraparound cover
artwork for *The Thief of
Always*, 1992.

144

"The Thief of Always" Clive Barker 1992

1993– ART GALLERIES
1994

"Nothing but monsters, anywhere."

One of the most striking things about *The Thief of Always* is its full-color wraparound cover art, painted in watercolor by Clive himself. Matched in style by the black-and-white interior illustrations he created for the novel, it was an extension of his occasional work for various editions of *Weaveworld* and *Cabal*. The ability to add visual nuance to his written work had made these editions much sought-after by readers.

In 1993, Clive prepared a selection from both his artwork on paper and his oil paintings (a new medium for him at the time) for his first gallery exhibition, which would open at the Bess Cutler Gallery in New York. Yet again, his disregard for the boundaries of genre and medium led interviewers to question whether he was truly a writer, a filmmaker, a painter, a brand, or something else entirely.

"Labels are the curse of our culture," Clive countered. "A lot of people have said, 'Well, you do all these things—what do you want to be known as?' and I say, 'I want to be known as an imaginer.'

"I want to be known as somebody whose business it is to set things out on celluloid, on canvas, on the page, in a sufficiently powerful way that they will move people and maybe delight people, and arouse people, and anger people. . . . The whole point is to make your imagination work in the most potent way possible."

Gallery owner Bess Cutler offered an overview of Clive's work ahead of the exhibition opening:

His drawings reveal a surprisingly broad range of mark-making, and while many display the artist's known flourishing brushwork, many others startle with the degree of angry jabbing of the artist's pen. And as the general import of the drawings, given Clive's novelistic and filmic background, is his excursions into the horrific, I suppose what was most pleasantly surprising to me is the extent to which Clive's work fits the surrealistic movement of the 20th century.

The paintings, of course, are an even grander experience—certainly to be surprising to Clive's many viewers and readers. His illusionistic, crowded spaces on the canvas are filled with figures and shapes radiating unnatural light and color. All striking, to say the least—some literal and some expressionistic pushed to embody in their wet, rich, oil paint the extraordinary world that embodies and inhabits the imagination of one Clive Barker.

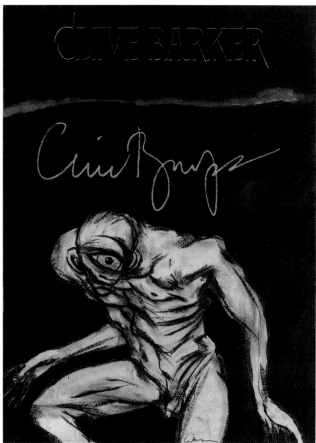

If Clive is a born mark-maker, he is no less a born painter of oil on canvas. Clive sees his painting as seamlessly connected to his writing, arguing that he selects a medium for expediency and that there's always been a merging of media in his artistic expression:

"In a way the techniques I end up using are all in service of something else; they're in service of trying to put down on the canvas or on the piece of paper what's happening in my head, my dream imagery if you like. And so I don't think a whole heap about the technique of it. I just think about how I can most forcibly, most strongly communicate these things to people. I don't really mean ideas, I mean the images, the things that are in my mind's eye. How can I get these onto the canvas?"

Introducing the 1993 exhibition, Keith Seward wrote:

Clive Barker has a wandering eye. While most artists doggedly pursue their medium of choice into the deepest recesses of tunnel vision, Barker has a vision—often a horrible one—that he injects into whatever medium his sights are set on, like a glass eye that he pops out of his head and plugs into a movie camera or a writing machine. Oftentimes this glass eye gets plugged into another machine as well, a sort of art machine that has produced scores of paintings and drawings over the course of some twenty years. Or would it be more precise to say that, when Barker paints, he becomes an art machine, puts the glass eye back into his head and uses his very own hands to transcribe the visions it transmits to him? Either way, the vision migrates from the glass eye to the canvas or paper. . . .

There are nothing but monsters, anywhere. Horror is simply what you feel when you see someone (or something) more monstrous than yourself. By consequence, if Clive Barker is a master of horror, it is because his glass eye wanders out to the furthest limits of the human and spies on the monsters that live out there. As his stories are their history, so is his art their collective portrait.

"The primal urge to create forms that are half animal, half man—the blurring of the human role—is central to the idea of the fantastique," Clive agreed. "The movies, the writing, the image-making, are

ABOVE LEFT

As the extent of Clive's artwork became more apparent, Clive worked with Steve Niles and Arcane/Eclipse to publish a collected portfolio. With text and interview transcripts written by Fred Burke, the volume featured Clive's *Seated Man*, 1989, as cover art for the first of two Illustrator volumes (published 1990 and 1993).

ABOVE RIGHT

A promotional postcard featuring *Cyclops*, 1991, produced to accompany Clive's first New York exhibition at the Bess Cutler Gallery, March to April 1993.

all finally expressions of the same bundle of concerns. The medium inevitably dictates certain ways of stating those concerns. There are certainly the rudiments of a narrative in a lot of the drawings—a story, a drama, a subtextual life to their various defamations and conditions. All kinds of experiments with the body—and therefore, by extension, with the mind—are going on in my work, and those experiments can sometimes be bloody painful. My characters are not exactly rising to meet the new day with smiles on their faces. They're saying. 'This is painful, this is difficult, but this is also inevitable.' And there's no fourth wall: they exist in full knowledge of themselves; they demand that we look at them, assess them, completely unabashed at their twisted, reconfigured conditions."

The portraits of mutated bodies or strange beasts exhibited at these early shows often look directly at the viewer from their fantastical landscapes, dispassionately reporting their condition to the viewer.

"It's that thing about wanting to be a documentarian in some way or other," Clive explains. "I learned this from Goya, this idea that what you really want to be doing is just making an account of what your mind's eye is seeing. You want to be almost journalistic in it. My approach is one where you actually say, 'Here's this kind of rather dry and unmelodramatic rendering of something which is going on in my mind's eye and I'm not going to make it more epic than it needs to be.' I just want to make a few marks and say, 'Well, here's what it is.' For me, part of it is the multiplicity of the images. Part of it is that there's a huge amount of stuff just churning in my head and I want to find simple ways to put it down. I just want to make these accounts."

Across 1993 and 1994, Clive's art was exhibited twice at the Bess Cutler Gallery and at the Tunnel Gallery, both in New York, as well as at the Dallas Fantasy Fair and the Los Angeles Art Fair.

His materials of choice had evolved over many years, from his use of Rotring pens at a younger age, to his discovery of the fluidity of sumi-e brush and ink, to paintings done in oil, which he found to be physically demanding. He first began experimenting with oil painting while staying in rented accommodations in Hollywood during reshoots for *Nightbreed* in 1989. After that experience he decided to embrace the challenge of large-scale canvases, having moved to Beverly Hills and created a space in which he could paint with the freedom of being able to make a mess without upsetting a landlord.

He took huge pleasure from this new free-form way of working, a love of oil that would blossom in coming years.

CLIVE BARKER

BESS CUTLER GALLERY

"Barker mixes paint
as if he were tending
a witch's brew."
—ARTFORUM

1990– DOCUMENTARIES AND
1997 THE SMALL SCREEN

"My fiction is my confession."

While exhibiting at the first Bess Cutler show, a short film was made to give people beyond New York new insight into Clive's visual work and some of his thought processes. In it, Clive says, "I never think through exactly what the image is expressing for fear of it becoming literal, for the fear of it becoming something it would have been better to make a novel of."

A more major boost to Clive's mainstream artistic standing arrived in May 1994 in the form of *The South Bank Show*, the UK's premier arts and culture television program. Clive's episode filmed him in his Beverly Hills home; observing him create artwork on paper and showing his oil paintings; walking around Los Angeles with him; and tracing, via various interviews, his work with the Dog Company through to the *Hellraiser* films, *Nightbreed*, and *Candyman*. In the episode Clive also reads from *The Thief of Always*, and cameras follow him to London's Forbidden Planet for a signing. The show was an ideal opportunity for Clive to articulate his work and ambitions to a national audience.

"I keep a notebook beside the bed," he told the show's presenter, Melvyn Bragg, "so I keep what roughly might be called a dream journal. So dreams are very important—and so are daydreams. In a sense what am I doing for ten hours a day when I'm writing a novel but dreaming with my eyes open? That's the whole business of writing this kind of material, I think—is that you're plunging down through layers of your consciousness into hopefully fairly primal areas."

Clive's episode also aired in the US after the release of *Lord of Illusions* the following year, as a part of A&E's *Biography* series.

An earlier UK documentary had been filmed in Liverpool in 1990 and aired in the Granada television region under the title *The Dissection of Clive Barker*. Opening with a tongue-in-cheek segment with Clive on an operating table in a setting that's somewhere between an operating theater and a

152

"Face to face with a monster, I like to think I could handle myself pretty well: charm a vampire, sidestep a werewolf, but of all the horror archetypes, zombies have always scared me witless."

mortuary, a surgeon is seen working on Clive. The guests—who look down on the "surgery," then later stand around the table, glasses of wine in hand, with food on a plate balanced on Clive's motionless body—include Doug Bradley, Peter Atkins, Philip Rimmer, and Lynne Darnell. They then go on to talk about Clive and their work together. Norman Russell, Clive's English teacher, is also interviewed. Clive reads two or three extracts from the Books of Blood, and there's a partial dramatization of the Book of Blood story "The Madonna."

"I've never really understood why so few writers of the fantastic want to write about sex," Clive offered. "If we're talking about horror fiction, horror fiction has a lot to say about the body and about our relationship to the body and our control over our bodies—or the lack of control we have over our bodies—so I've always seen sex as being very much a part of fantastical writing. And, you know, it is fun to write, it really is! It puts a bloom on your cheeks at eight o'clock on a Monday morning. . . ."

Another documentary, Christopher Holland's 1992 *The Art of Horror* from Zig Zag Films, was included on certain VHS, LaserDisc, and DVD releases of *Hellraiser* and *Hellraiser III*. In it, Clive offered: "I am telling my life every time I write a page. My fiction is my confession. Everything that was ever important in my life is written. I'm putting it down. That's what I do. And the more absurd and ridiculous and rococo and baroque the imaginings, the closer it is to me."

Later, in 1995, Peter Whittle and Daniel Wiles, who had produced and directed *The South Bank Show* segment, compiled extended interview footage of Clive in his writing study, left over from the show, into a short documentary for the Redemption Films release of *Salomé* and *The Forbidden*.

In 1996 the Sci-Fi Channel visited Clive at home and documented an early painting session in his studio for its series *Masters of Fantasy*. The episode also featured interviews with Quentin Tarantino, Peter Straub, Neil Gaiman, Peter Atkins, and Douglas E. Winter about Clive and his work.

By now a regular on television talk shows, Clive was a familiar face, but these documentaries gave depth and context to his work in ways that the two- or three-minute plug for his latest book or movie did not.

Turning the tables in 1997, Clive hosted *Clive Barker's A–Z of Horror*, recording on-screen introductions to all twenty-six segments for the BBC documentary series, produced by Dev Varma, and with an accompanying hardcover book edited by Stephen Jones. While there are the traditional twenty-six separate chapters in the book, the six-part series as it first aired had just twenty-one segments—and two of these were different from those in the accompanying book. . . . In a curious release schedule, some of the "missing" segments eventually aired in different countries, in differently edited episodes.

In the segment on his own work, "V is for Vice Versa" (which did not air in the UK), Clive discussed paradox, illustrated through a second partial dramatization of "The Madonna," and Peter Atkins discussed *Hellbound*.

Other segments covered topics as diverse as Ed Gein in "A is for American Psycho," the Grand Guignol theatre in "K is for Killing Joke," special effects legend Tom Savini in "P is for Pain," fairy tales in "G is for Grim Tales," Barbara Steele in "M is for Mistress of the Night" and H. P. Lovecraft in "C is for Chaos."

"If ever there was a medium made for overachievers, it's comics. Where else can a creator make mischief on a cosmic scale?"

1993 RAZORLINE

"Superheroes from the mind of Clive Barker."

In late 1992 and across the early months of 1993, Clive unveiled the Razorline universe with interviews in a number of comics-related magazines, teasing details ahead of the launch of the imprint that September. In July 1993 he then wrote a piece for *Comic Buyer's Guide*:

What could be more exciting than standing on the threshold of a new world?

The door is open, just a crack, and through it we catch a glimpse of what lies beyond. A panorama of untold wonders. A heaven set with unnamed stars. A crowd of faces—some radiant with goodness, some corrupted by ancient evil—ready to swarm into our world . . .

I write these words standing upon such a threshold. And the sights I can see are about to spring to life in four new comic books from the Marvel/Razorline imprint. They are the beginning of what I am certain will be a unique exploration into uncharted regions: those 10 realities that I have called the Decamundi, and which Mr. Carl Potts wittily dubbed the Barkerverse.

• *Hyperkind*—which will be the first of the quartet to appear—is a revisionist superhero title, featuring a group of teenagers chosen by fate to inherit the powers of a far older tradition, powers which they are ill-equipped to comprehend or wield.

• *Hokum and Hex* is a visit to a world of magic and absurdity, a mingling of thrills, chills, and wild lunacies that will, I trust, revive the fortunes of the tale dedicated to both nerve-wracking action and spine-chilling mystery.

• *Saint Sinner*—which is perhaps the darkest of the four books—introduces us to states of flesh and spirit that I truly doubt have appeared on any page hitherto: states so powerfully portrayed they will haunt you for weeks.

• And *Ectokid* is a narrative which leaps, I hope nimbly, between our world, the realm of the living, and the Ectosphere, a place haunted by all manner of supernatural terrors.

None of these titles is, I think, quite like anything you will have seen from either Marvel or Barker before. Though I have been associated for several years now with films on the cutting edge of horror, my life in publishing has moved further from the blood-soaked

MARVEL COMICS

SPECIAL PREVIEW ISSUE!

First Cut

RAZORLINE™

SUPER HEROES FROM THE MIND OF CLIVE BARKER

TRISTAN

ground of the *Hellraiser* mythos with each book, into evermore fantastical territory. When the chance came to expand my imaginative horizons and open, as it were, 10 new doors to 10 new kinds of reality, setting down what my mind's eye saw, the invitation was irresistible.

Now, after a little over a year, the first four Marvel/Razorline books are ready to be shipped. In them you will find the speed and power of first-rate Marvel style storytelling married to the complex mythologies which I like to bring to my narratives—the state-of-the-artwork style for which Marvel is renowned used to create vistas and visions that could only leap, I suspect, from my fevered head. In short; a marriage of minds, which we all hope will not only catch the eyes, hearts, and imaginations of loyal Marvel readers, but find new devotees amongst those who had previously dismissed the medium as being too predictable.

A brief word here about how these ideas came into being. "Where do you get your ideas from?" is, of course, the most feared of fan questions, simply because it is the most difficult inquiry to answer. But if there is one methodology that I use more regularly than any other, it is the what if? method.

What if a boy was born from the passion of a living woman and a ghost, able to see the real world with his right eye and the Ectosphere with his left?

What if a stand-up comedian was given the power of a minor divinity and stood alone between humanity and an invasion of genocidal forces from another dimension?

What if a bunch of kids inherited the powers of a group of heroes whose tragic history went back to the pyramids?

What if there was a man in the world who could advance the evolution of living tissue with a touch? What if? What if? I sometimes think that every sentence I set down, every notion I suggest for a comic book, every painting I make, every movie I produce is an attempt to answer that question. What if?

All the questions in the world are pointless, of course, if there's nobody there to share the answers with you, which is why I have been spending so much time this summer talking with readers and retailers at conventions and stores, spreading the word about Razorline. I want these tales to be read and enjoyed by many tens of thousands of people, some of whom may never have considered comic books as an entertainment form before, but will perhaps be drawn to the titles because they enjoyed *Weaveworld* or *Candyman*.

If the mysteries I've conjured here intrigue you, as I hope they do, and if this summer you would like to enter a comic-book universe that does not resemble any other, then please join us on our collective journey into the wilds of the Decamundi. And then, spread the word. There are numerous titles waiting in the wings, numerous tales to be told, but it will be your Open Sesame that will turn the handles of those doors, your enthusiasm and appetite for fresh new worlds that will bring the next wave of wonders over the threshold.

Explaining his motivation for each of the four launch titles, Clive said, "I wanted to do a superhero comic, something which would be my take on what superheroes were going to be like in the nineties. . . . *Hyperkind* fell into that category. I wanted to do something that was magical and mystical in the way that *Doctor Strange* was and still is. *Doctor Strange* was one of my favorite comics from when I was a kid. So I suppose *Hokum and Hex* is my take on that. *Ectokid*, which is perhaps the second weirdest of the bunch, is a kind of dream story for the fifteen-year-old that's still alive to me—the tale of an adolescent who lives in two worlds and has access to a whole other sphere of reality. And *Saint Sinner* is just a wild one, the series which hopefully will press the limits of what comics can do.

"So each of these books hopefully offers a different kind of pleasure, and the thrill of doing all four, and hopefully doing more in the course of time, is that you are sort of creating a mini-universe, the Marvel Universe of course being well-established over a period of many decades. I'm universe-creating in my novels all the time—in *Imajica*, I've created a whole series of worlds and rules and species and so on which are unique to that book, the same with *Weaveworld*. I thought it was time to try it in comics.

156

"My first career was as a painter, and then I turned to writing. From writing I turned to filmmaking. And now I do all three. In a sense, comics stand at an intersection of those things. They're very visual. They depend on good storytelling. They allow you what can be loosely called cinematic effects.

"I feel as though I'm trying to express my imagination in a whole slew of different ways. There are definitely pieces of connective tissue between these various activities, even though the manifestation of these activities may look very different. The underlying concerns of an *Ectokid* or *Hyperkind* are absolutely to be found buried deeply in the novels—ideas about heroes and about the afterlife, and about responsibility, and about transformation, and about the force of storytelling and so on. Concerns which are there for analyzers to pick up if they want to, and if, as is more likely the case, not, then they're there for my entertainment. But I do think of these things as essentially springing from the same place, which is my desire to tell stories, and to create worlds."

The series was overseen by Clive alongside Marc McLaurin as editor, Malcolm Smith as consulting editor, and Carl Potts as executive editor. They assembled a team of writers and artists, several with preexisting work in the Hellraiser and Nightbreed comics, to bring the Razorline universe to life.

"I've gotten used to and come to enjoy the process of collaboration. . . . You have to be willing and able to fold your ideas into the mix and encourage people. If the creators are having a good time and producing good, original material, I let them go their own way. If they're having problems, I'm there to step in and help solve them. I'm not about to take my ball home if someone doesn't do things quite the way I've anticipated. Part of the pleasure of life is to be in business with other imaginations. It's not to my advantage to stultify other people's creative urges.

"I watch over all of this stuff very closely. Not to catch anybody out, but to help if there are problems, to illuminate some of the darker parts of the mythology so that people know what we're trying to achieve here. Stories are written for purposes. Stories should leave you with a new piece of information in your head. You have to say to the writers, 'Look, have all the fun in the world, but remember that, at the end of the day, there should be a reason for telling the story.' People should feel, in the best of worlds, a little bit changed by a story. Something that is alive in their hearts that wasn't there when they opened up the comic book."

Hyperkind was written by Fred Burke, with art by Paris Cullins and Bob Petrecca. "Comics have been very dark recently," said Fred, "and that's fine but fighting darkness is what *Hyperkind* is all about."

James Robinson was the launch writer on *Ectokid* before handing it over to Lana and Lilly Wachowski after issue 3. Steve Skroce and Bob Dvorak provided the artwork. Lana Wachowski offered that "the Ectosphere is not eternity—I picture it more as this metaphysical bus station. It's a place for people who never finished their business in our world, so they're still attached to the land of the living. You'll see Kennedy chatting away with Oswald in the background."

Frank Lovece wrote *Hokum and Hex*, noting about his stand-up hero, "Two gags and a beheading, that's what we've got in the first story. . . . Through all these insane circumstances, humor is the only thing keeping Trip sane." Anthony Williams and Andy Lanning provided the artwork.

"If a young, morbid teenager's worst horror fantasy came true, that would be what happens to this boy," said *Saint Sinner*'s writer Elaine Lee about poor Philip Fetter and the competing entities within him. Noting the sweep available to the narrative within this Decamundi, she said, "*Saint Sinner* answers people's prayers, and those prayers can be a bridge between dimensions." Max Douglas provided art for the initial issues, followed by Richard Pace for issue 5, and Larry Brown for the final two issues.

Three of an additional six comics series were lined up to appear in 1994: "Wraitheart," written by Frank Lovece with artwork by Hector Gomez; "Fusion Force" (or "Schizm," which was being considered as a possible title), written by Fred Burke with art by Franchesco and Mike Halbleib; and "Mode Extreme" by Sarah Byam with art by Josue Justiniano and Mike Halbleib; but a glut in new titles had saturated the comics market and, within this, superheroes and hardware were deemed hot, while the market was less keen on mystical elements, a strength of Razorline. Instead of the new titles appearing, the four existing titles ceased publication—*Saint Sinner* after seven issues and the other three after nine issues, although *Hokum and Hex* and *Ectokid* both got a subsequent one-issue *Unleashed!* special before closing.

NEXT SPREAD, LEFT
Clive's character art for Ectokid, lead character in one of the Razorline comics, 1993.

NEXT SPREAD, RIGHT
Clive's character art for Razorline's *Saint Sinner*, 1993.

Clive 1993 "Saint Simon"

1994 EVERVILLE: THE SECOND BOOK OF THE ART

"Open your mind. . . ."

In 1992, Clive turned his thoughts towards *Everville: The Second Book of the Art*.

"*Everville* was an interesting challenge," he noted, "because it's the middle book of a trilogy. The danger with the middle book of a trilogy is that it is just a recap of the first book and a warm-up to the third. The thing I promised myself and the readers as I stepped into the writing of *Everville* was that it would be a book unto itself; that by the end of the book the characters who entered it would be unrecognizable. That it would genuinely be a journey. It would not be a recapitulation, but a further exploration of the themes and ideas that motivated me to write *The Great and Secret Show*. It was sort of fun going back to characters I had written about five years previously and changing their lives out of all recognition."

In this second novel, Clive offers a change of perspective: although mankind looks at Quiddity as a place of wonder, there are those looking back at the Cosm (the world as we know it) as their source of the miraculous. He had already played with this idea in the short fable "On Amen's Shore," in which two clownish travelers, Beisho Fie and Ruty, in the fishing town of Joom, on the shores of Quiddity, ponder the possibility that they are descended from the dreaming men and women who visit the sea beside them:

"Does that trouble you?" Beisho enquired of Ruty.

"To be descended from a dreaming species?" Ruty said. "Yes . . . that troubles me."

"Why?"

"Because it means we're accidents, Fie. Bastard children. Without purpose. Without meaning."

For all the comedy of his characters, "On Amen's Shore" conveys many of the weighty themes important to Clive in the Art trilogy, and in the space of just a few pages.

160

"The idea," Clive notes, "that occult forces may make themselves visible in public ways, that the unconscious is on constant display in the world—the Ultimate Show—intrigues me because it refers back to the very process of making art."

In *The First Book of the Art*, the glimpses we have of Quiddity and the somewhat oblique references to the Art itself match the lack of real understanding held by the characters in the book. In the sequel, Clive elaborates on that narrative by setting a portion of the story on the far side of the veil, in Quiddity itself, on its shores and on its islands. The names of those who dwell there sound faintly tribal, sometimes biblical or ancient. The 'Shu who swim in Quiddity are described as part of the Creator—a fascination with threads of connectedness that Clive would revisit in the Books of Abarat where the gentle acts of the creatrix, Princess Breath, take place amid the Sea of Izabella. Later, we learn of otherworldly avatars, drawn to watch the human show and experience it vicariously.

"This is a book about the threads between things, about how the past influences the present, how our private desires shape our public faces, about the intricate cross-knitting of believer and divinity.

"In the middle of *Everville*," Clive points out, "is a symbol, which is a representation of this connectedness. It is a kind of map representing the crossroads between this world, called the Cosm, and the other world, the world of Quiddity, called the Metacosm. The passage from one to another is symbolically represented along the horizontal axis. The vertical axis, north of that central bar, represents the ascent of mind into the oneness of the divine state, and its descent, south of the central bar, to the primal simplicity of a single cell. It's a kind of compass, if you like, by which the readers may chart their position. But it's also my reworking of the crucifix, for at the center of the device—at the intersection of the physical journey and the spiritual—is the spread-eagled figure of a human being.

"The image is a kind of goad to me. My ambition for this trilogy—which will be completed when I write *The Third Book of the Art*—is clear whenever I look at the image: I want to put my readers, for a time, into that sacred spot; to make them feel the flow of energies between states of being."

Looking forward to that much-anticipated third volume, Clive explains: "I need to feel that the metaphysical life of the piece is right. . . . I need to feel that whatever this book is saying is true. 'Well,' you might say, 'this is fantasy, so why does it matter whether it's true or not?' By 'true,' I mean metaphorically true. True to what I believe about the world. Tesla Bombeck has been released into this place about stories, this place where all stories happen with equal validity, in a way. So, the final book, to some extent, is about what story is. And it's a big subject for a storyteller. For a storyteller not to simply write 'Once upon a time . . .' but to write about what 'Once upon a time' means is a big subject. And I want to make sure that when I tell it I have the right answers.

"It was always a show, always the idea that there was a presentational element to the story and the sense that there were narrative solutions which were about people taking roles: Kissoon takes a role, Tesla takes a role, the idea that there's a massive toy theatre which is the size of the world and with a narrative which is ten thousand years long. And what we're going to watch is that theatre go up in flames to find out which of those characters are made of paper and which are made of steel . . . and the lad Uroboros, waiting in the wings, behind all of this from the very beginning. . . .

"I believe we coexist with all sorts of extraordinary forces. I believe we live in one plane of reality which is, if you like, one groove on a record, and there are melodies being played to right and left of us all the time. I believe we are living a stretch of physical life which will have all kinds of spiritual consequences when this life is over. I have a sense that this is just the beginning of an adventure, not the end, nowhere near the end!"

The book's flap copy read:

> On a mountain peak, high above the city of Everville, a door stands open: a door that opens onto the shores of the dream-sea, Quiddity. And there's not a soul below who'll not be changed by that fact . . .
>
> Phoebe Cobb, once a doctor's receptionist, is about to forget her old life and go looking for her lost lover Joe Flicker in the world on the other side of that door; a strange, sensual wonderland the likes of which only Barker could make real.
>
> Tesla Bombeck, who knows what horrors lurk on the far side of Quiddity, must solve the mysteries of the city's past if she is to keep those horrors from crossing the threshold.
>
> Harry D'Amour, who has tracked the ultimate evil across America, will find it conjuring atrocities in the sunlit streets of Everville.
>
> Enthralling, chilling and charged with an unbridled eroticism, Everville is above all a novel about the deepest yearnings of the human heart. For love. For hope. For understanding.
>
> And it's about the forces that threaten those dreams. The monsters that are never more terrible than when they wear human faces . . .
>
> Step into Everville's streets, and enter a world like no other fiction, created by a man whom the *Washington Post* called: "a mapmaker of the mind, charting the furthest reaches of the imagination."

Bruce Allen in the *New York Times Book Review* said, "Our most accomplished contemporary purveyor of horror fiction strikes again in *Everville*, a tale of worlds in conflict in which, you might say, Hieronymus Bosch paints before-and-after pictures of our town," concluding that "Mr. Barker is much more than a genre writer, and his extravagantly unconventional inventions are ingenious refractions of our common quest to experience and understand the mysterious world around us and the mysteries within ourselves."

The city of Liverpool is again important in the text.

Describing his memories of growing up in Liverpool, Clive has mixed emotions. "Liverpool is a great city, but a gray one, especially in winter. Leaden skies and a muddy Mersey; grimy civic

"The fact that Maeve is the founder of Everville is obliterated because history represses things we don't want to know about. It is the old story: the founding mothers are forgotten while the founding fathers are enshrined."

buildings and rain-soaked streets bounded by row houses, built back-to-back with refuse-strewn alleys between: a deeply dispiriting spot. I know, I passed twenty winters there and, apart from those few snowy Christmases of my childhood, it was a wet, gloomy place through the long winter months.

"I was a huge walker; I walked everywhere. . . . I was completely happy on my own and one of the places I used to go was down to the docks—not to the real docks part where the ships were, but to the part which was kind of run-down . . . and it was cool because there were a lot of wharves that were disused; there was grass growing up in them and it was just a cool, empty place, a lot of rusted machinery, empty warehouses, and, later on, Phil [Rimmer, Clive's best friend at school] and I would go and shoot little movies there and it was great."

Clive had already shown his desire to bring illumination to the city in his 1981 play *Paradise Street*: a transformative visitation from Elizabeth I and her court from the Golden Age of England, bringing spring vibrancy, color, and excitement to the wintry domestic drama of the Bonner family's Liverpool lives. In his production notes he wrote:

"This play, named after a real thoroughfare, Paradise Street, imagines what it would be like if, in the depths of that season, magic were to transform the city, replacing the gray with green blossom, and lending the people trapped in its streets a new perspective and a new purpose.

"Elizabeth I is the progenitor of this miracle. Time-traveling on the beatific light of her own glorious presence, she arrives in the frigid city with a few members of her court: a group of masquers prepared to perform a piece by Ben Jonson, Jonson himself, the royal lady-in-waiting, a willful ape called Benny Butterblood, and the even more willful Earl of Essex, Robert Devereux. And with them comes a miraculous spring. Trees crack the concrete and blossom overnight, balmy winds blow; the eponymous street, which has previously been walked by a lonely Irish derelict, is suddenly buzzing with plots and counterplots."

Having both set *Weaveworld* in his home city, giving the novel its gritty reality and its love of poetry and humor, and written a dream of the city into *Everville*, Clive plans to revisit Liverpool in the final installment of the Art trilogy: "I love Liverpool and I always will and I was thinking actually—as I've been very tentatively looking at Art 3 and just beginning to focus my attentions there, knowing that in the next few years I'm going to tackle that—you know that Liverpool obviously has a part to play in *Everville* and has another part to play in the third book and it's interesting: I've got to be careful about this, I've got to make sure I'm describing a city which still exists, given its rapid transformation.

"I would like people to be able to go to Liverpool with Art 3 in their hands and be able to go to a given place, and I'd like to make sure that I get the geography right with Art 3 because I'd like to think, as I say, that people would be able to have Art 3 under their arms and go to a given place and find it there. . . .

"There's some very magical backwaters, particularly actually in central Liverpool—little alleyways which lead onto squares—and I've always had, I think, a love of the secret side of cities; it's particularly clear in *Imajica* when the idea of a city as a body is offered up, that cities enthrall me and the first city I was ever in thrall with was of course Liverpool."

1995 LORD OF ILLUSIONS

"Illusionists get Las Vegas contracts, D'Amour. Magicians get burned."

Although bruised by the studio and distributor's treatment of *Nightbreed*, Clive's passion for filmmaking was undimmed and his move to the US in 1991 had placed him closer to Hollywood's decision-makers.

His next film project as screenwriter and director was *Lord of Illusions*, an adaptation of his Books of Blood story, "The Last Illusion," with his iconic private investigator, Harry D'Amour, at its heart.

Harry had appeared in that short story and another, "Lost Souls," which reinforced his role as everyman detective: the reluctant, diligent, but weary worker battling those from the other side of the Schism. He'd had a cameo part at the end of *The Great and Secret Show* and would soon play a lead role in its sequel, *Everville*, which Clive was working on around the same time as he began drafting the movie adaptation of "The Last Illusion."

This new screenplay was not even the first potential movie appearance for Harry, as, having filmed *Hellraiser*, Clive had originally turned to him for his next film project. *The First Adventure* (later titled *The Great Unknown*) had been intended as the first of a trilogy of Harry D'Amour pictures and Clive wrote three drafts between 1987 and August 1988. Assessing it at the time against other possible film projects he was considering, he noted:

"It's a very elaborate screenplay with lots of creatures in it; it's the largest and the most extensive, special effects–wise—and also the most expensive. I guess we have to describe it as a fantasy rather than a horror movie. "The Last Illusion" will probably constitute a hefty part of the second of the three Harry pictures. The first one sets up a whole series of events which will be dealt with through the subsequent pictures. I want to create a mythology so strong that if it works [it] will sustain us through three pictures. In this case, it is really important to get it right in the first instance. Even by my own standards the events in the first Harry D'Amour screenplay are deeply weird. I was in L.A. a couple of weeks ago taking the material round and there were certain people who said, 'This is simply too weird,' and I thought, 'I must be doing something right.'"

'The Devil and D'Arc'
magic show design
Arthur 1974

The planned sequence of Harry films was overtaken, however, and *Nightbreed* ended up being prioritized in Clive's schedule.

Unhappy with a 1990 adaptation by a writer hired by A&M, Clive decided to take "The Last Illusion" back into his own hands. In his first draft of the screenplay, dated 1992, he introduces William Nix as a cult leader based in the Nevada Desert—the foundation of a narrative that would become familiar to moviegoers three years later—with Butterfield as his loyal young follower. Nix is killed by former cult member Philip Swann and four of Swann's friends; then the story moves into the present, twenty-five years later, where Swann presents the grand spectacle of his illusion shows in Los Angeles. In his third draft, Clive puts the dichotomous theme of "magic and illusion" right up front:

TITLE SEQUENCE

The credits appear against a shifting background of posters for the great magicians of the century. Garish and grotesque, fetishistic and fabulous, here are the illusions that have mystified generations. The death-defying escapes and miraculous transformations of Harry Kellar, Houdini, Chung Ling Soo and the rest. Then as the credits come to end, the posters fade away, and against pitch darkness the title of the picture emerges. After all the miraculous performances that have gone before, this is: The Last Illusion.
FADE IN

EXT. NEVADA DESERT—DAY
A violent wind raises billowy veils of sand, but through them we can just make out a large, solitary building: the home and temple of William Nix. Its walls are white-washed and scrawled with graffiti. There are a half-dozen cars parked haphazardly around it. On screen, the words: Nevada—Nine Years Ago.

The next draft, dated July 1993, is titled for the first time: *Lord of Illusions*.

Over the following year, Clive wrote three more drafts of the script as well as multiple revisions to the fourth draft as pre-production was finalized in June and July 1994. Ultimately, Clive relocated the desert across the border, in California, and settled on a gap of thirteen years between Nix's death and the present-day action, so that the sixteen-year-old Butterfield, nineteen-year-old Philip Swann, and twelve-year-old Dorothea from the opening cult sequences could be played in the present day by Barry Del Sherman, Kevin J. O'Connor, and Famke Janssen. Famke would go from filming *Lord of Illusions* to filming her role as Xenia Onatopp in *GoldenEye*, the first James Bond film to star Pierce Brosnan, which started shooting in January 1995. Nix would be played by Daniel von Bargen, while our hero, Harry D'Amour, would be brought to life by Scott Bakula, fresh from finishing his five-season run as Sam Beckett in *Quantum Leap* the previous year.

Comparing the short story to the screenplay, Clive offers, "'The Last Illusion' was almost a Philip Marlowe type of thing, but the movie isn't an homage to forties noir: it isn't full of immaculately back-lit women with a lot of smoke; it's not about venetian blinds and ashtrays with cigarettes left burning with lipstick on them. What we have is a brave everyman who is drawn into the heart of darkness over and over again because of some karmic thing which he has no power over.

"One of the things you have in your head when you're writing a script, or I have in my head when I'm writing a script, is some very specific pictures, and only a handful of them, which are by no means enough to spread throughout a movie. I had four or five images in my head which were starting places for scenes: the look of the magic show—Swann's spectacular—which we've staged at the Pantages; the look of Nix's lair; the cultists' house; the look of the Bel-Air mansion where Swann and his wife, Dorothea, reside—and actually Harry's apartment; that was a late addition, but that would be another one where I had a clear idea."

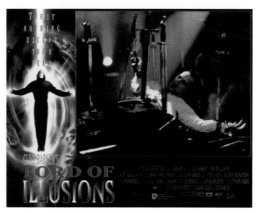

LORD OF ILLUSIONS
Synopsis (from the press kit)

Between what can be seen and what must be feared

Between what lives and never dies

Between the light of truth and the darkness of evil

Lies the future of terror.

It should have been routine. Private detective Harry D'Amour comes to Los Angeles to get out of the cold, gray New York winter as much as to solve his latest case. Harry should have known better; nothing was ever routine where he was concerned. But nothing could have prepared him for the cold, gray darkness of pure evil.

Harry's routine case takes an ominous turn when he stumbles upon a mystery involving the world-famous magician, Philip Swann, and his beautiful wife, Dorothea. When something goes fatally wrong during a performance of Swann's spectacular magic show, Harry is drawn into a frightening spiral of secrets, deceit and unimaginable terrors. As his world steadily darkens, Harry finds himself falling in love with Dorothea. Only then does he unearth the horrific secrets of her past . . . and come face to face with her enemy, Nix, the diabolic power who gave Swann his dark magic. In the climactic final battle, Harry confronts the monstrous Nix and discovers that illusion is trickery . . . but magic is real.

Clive led the cast through a read-through on July 19, 1994, followed by two days of rehearsals and a day of camera tests and publicity stills.

The first day of principal photography, July 26, captured the New York look of Harry's office and apartment at the Lacy Street Production Center in Los Angeles, where *Cagney & Lacey* had been shot for several years. The production moved efficiently through its fifty-two-day shoot through to its end date on October 6: day three saw the crew at Angelus-Rosedale Cemetery; days five to nine

ABOVE

Behind the scenes on
Lord of Illusions, Clive
(upper left) directs Scott
Bakula as Harry D'Amour
(center) on the set of the
cultists' sanctuary, 1994.

staged Swann's set piece magic act at the Pantages Theatre; day eleven was a day at the Magic Castle; and days twenty-one to twenty-three were in the desert at Nix's house and grave. The main part of the movie was shot at studios in Los Angeles.

JoAnne Sellar produced the movie with Steve Golin and Sigurjón Sighvatsson as executive producers. Steve Hardie led on production design, Rohn Schmidt was director of photography, and Alan Baumgarten was film editor. Simon Boswell provided a memorable score that underpinned the menace, magic, and relationships onscreen. Special effects and make-up effects came principally from Steve Johnson's XFX and from Robert Kurtzman, Greg Nicotero, and Howard Berger at KNB EFX Group, with Gary J. Tunnicliffe adding some additional effects. Visual effects were supervised by Thomas C. Rainone. Seraphim Films and Propaganda Films produced the movie.

Released in the US on August 25, 1995, by MGM/UA as distributors, the theatrical version ran at 109 minutes, missing twelve and a half minutes of footage that was subsequently restored for Clive's director's cut, which was released for home video in 1996.

"This extra stuff," notes its director, "includes intense material, dialogue material, subtext material— a lot of stuff that helps people understand what the movie is all about. It's not twelve and a half minutes of blood and gore, it's actually the thematic guts of the movie. What MGM/UA did—and I'll think they're wrong till the end of my days—was say that 'this isn't enough of a horror movie, we want to make it more intense.' It was a bad commercial decision in my view. They wanted to take out some of the detective elements. I said no. Part of the point of the movie is that it's a genre-breaking movie. It moves from film noir to horror and back and forth and that's what makes the movie work. But MGM/UA was adamant. They said, 'We're gonna take this stuff out, either you do it or we do it.' So I said I would take it out, so long as they promised me that a director's cut would come out on video and LaserDisc."

Ultimately, Clive got to show the world his vision despite the studio's reluctance: "I got to do all kinds of shit that I wanted to do: the bondage stuff in there, the girl and the ape, all kinds of shit. It's

very funny because Frank Mancuso [Jr.] was head of MGM/UA at that time, and he didn't like the movie at all. There was one shot of a dead child on the floor, and he said, 'This shot will never appear in an MGM/UA movie.' As it turns out, it did, because I took it out, and then when he wasn't looking I put it back in. I knew he'd never bother to see the film again!

"You know, I can look through the movie and every two or three minutes I'm saying, 'Geez, why did I do that? Why did I do this?' Well, the answer is, you know, I got fifty things right and thirty things wrong and that's a pretty good batting average for me! You make your work and you move on—and you do that whatever medium you work in."

"I've long considered Harry D'Amour an interesting character to put into movies, partly because horror movies of the last ten years have been dominated by the villains . . . and there are limitations that come with that."

TOP
Scott Bakula in conversation with Clive on location for *Lord of Illusions*, 1994.

BOTTOM
Famke Janssen with Clive at a launch event for *Lord of Illusions*, 1995.

169

MAGIC

"Clive Barker is a magician of the first order" —New York Daily News

"*L*ord of Illusions*," says Clive, "uniquely parallels something that's going on in my own art all the time. It deals with illusions and illusionists, and illusionists provide, for bourgeois audiences, narratives—they are, loosely speaking, narratives in the form of tricks or illusions—that seem to be pieces of frivolous entertainment but are, at root, extremely rich and dark tales of death and resurrection.

"What is fantasy for? To me it's all about convincing people that these extraordinary things are plausible, where reality is reconfigured completely, where the rug of reality is pulled away from beneath the reader/spectator, and the painter/artist/writer says, 'OK. Begin again. I have a new world to show you.'

"There's a little exchange in *Lord of Illusions* in which Valentin is making the distinction between magic and illusions. He and Harry are driving and Valentin says, 'Illusions are trickery,' and produces a flower out of his hand. Then he scrunches the flower up and shows his bare hand, saying, 'Magicians do it for real.' There's a beat and then Harry leans across and says, 'Where did the flower go?' And in that line—which, by the way, was an ad-lib by Mr. Bakula—is the voice of the audience. 'Where did the flower go? I know it's a trick, I know it's not real magic, but where did the flower go?'"

We grow up with stories of magic: witches, be they benevolent godmothers or wicked stepmothers, from Baba Yaga to the Wicked Witch of the West to Hermione Granger; wizards with a twinkle in the eye and an air of distraction; malevolent imps like Rumpelstiltskin; dark tales of misbehaving children, fairy dust and pixie lore and enchanted forests with distant castles—where does that love of myth and mystery go when we grow up? Using these childish delights as touchstones in thoroughly grown-up stories, Clive is working with the very stuff of our dreams and nightmares—powerful things, whether we believe we've outgrown them or not.

Shakespeare of course happily grabbed fistfuls of the mythic and magical, as did some of our most revered artists. But should a character in a novel today make mention of "such stuff as dreams are made on"—or indeed nightmares—it's likely a postmodern signifier of a troubled superego and

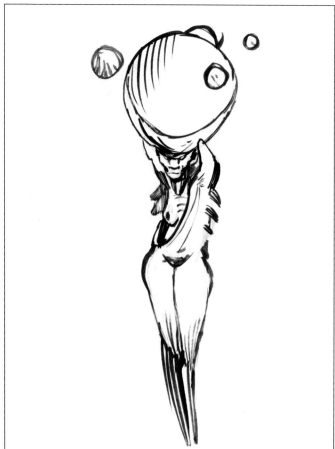

nothing more. So where would Shakespeare—or Milton, or Blake—fit into the literary world today? It's not by accident that Clive embraces his poetic language and lets it infuse his characters: the Candyman murmurs, "Sweets to the sweet," as he seduces his victim, as double-edged as Gertrude's elegy for Ophelia. Pinhead and his precursor, the Dutchman, speak with unexpected gravity: "Why do you dread the calm symmetry of death? Is there not succor to be drawn from oblivion?" The charm of Clive's monsters is the power of illusion and rapture.

Clive happily sees himself as a son of a tradition that stretches back to the storyteller shaman of old, weaving tales that use spirits, demons, gods, and other worlds without a glance back to see if we are following—of course we are; how could we resist?

He grew up with J. M. Barrie's Peter Pan, the boy who was "betwixt and between a boy and a bird," and Tinker Bell, whose blessing with fairy dust grants the Darling children the ability to fly to Neverland—a huge source of enchantment for a boy living in postwar Liverpool.

Many years later, introducing his publishers to the idea of his Abarat series of books, he referenced a production of *Peter Pan* by the Royal Shakespeare Company: "I saw the show six times. And there's no doubt in my mind that much of the hunger to create the books of the Abarat was fueled by those visits. I saw how eloquently and bittersweet fantasy could be, watching it move adults to tears and children to laughter, often at the same moment."

Writing his first full-length fantasy, *Weaveworld*, Clive's aim was "to write a novel in which the world of magic and the world of the real collided," taking inspiration from William Blake to seek out the wondrous while also documenting life in the streets around him. Similarly, in the short story "Pidgin and Theresa," he references his love of Arthur Machen's "The Holy Things" when bringing miracles and a heavenly presence to the otherwise lackluster Crouch End in a curious love story: "The streets of North London are not known for miracles. Murder they had seen, and rape, and riot. But revelation? That was for High Holborn and Lambeth."

171

Just as Cal envisions a flight with the pigeons over Liverpool in *Weaveworld*, Rachel articulates a dream of transformation in *Nightbreed*; Clive's stories of metamorphosis touch on desires that are intrinsically human, from the delight of flight to the horror of deformity.

```
Rachel: To be able to fly? To be smoke, or a wolf; to know the night and
live in it forever? That's not so bad. You call us monsters but when you
dream, it's of flying and changing, and living without death. You envy
us. And what you envy . . .
Lori (softly, understanding): . . . We destroy . . .
```

In the Books of the Art, Clive continues to explore preternatural reality rather than conjured illusions. "My reality is open every minute to transformations, to transfigurations—a ghost-haunted, vision-haunted world in which magic and demonic doings can erupt at the slightest invitation. . . . What preoccupies me in The Art is the idea of the dream show, what happens to us in the twenty-five years of our lives when we sleep."

The press material for *Imajica* highlighted its magical elements: "Magic is the first and last religion of the world. It has the power to make us whole, to open our eyes to Dominions, and return us to ourselves." However, Clive was at pains to point to the novel as an extension of his exploration of spirituality and its ever-present place in our lives. "I don't believe that our consciousness has fully grasped the complexity of reality, or, perhaps I should say, realities, in which we live. Our imaginations seem to offer us glimpses of other possibilities, other states of beings, other dimensions. I believe we will one day access those dimensions. The book came about because I wanted to write a spiritual quest story in the form of an enormous religious/metaphysical fantasy."

Rebelling against the adult dismissal of magic as mere illusion, *Lord of Illusions* directly tackles the "fine line between trickery and divinity" as the illusionist Philip Swann uses real magic gleaned from a shaman magician, Nix, and finds there's a heavy price to pay for his abilities.

"The subtext of magic shows is so often death and resurrection. They're entertainments which contain very profound primal symbols. The magician cuts the lady in half and she's dead. He then

"I've seen every 70mm spectacle there is to be seen and I've sat with my teeth chattering while THX has made the whole theater shake and I'm still a three-year-old in the face of magic acts. Partly it's the extraordinary skill with which the trick is executed, but partly it's that you are reminded of how much you want to believe. It reminds you of how eagerly you will run into the arms of the miraculous if it's offered."

puts her back together again; she's alive. . . . It interests me that in this form of popular entertainment we're being presented with these images of the miraculous.

"A great magician, for a moment, suspends everything you believe about the world. It's an extraordinary power: They stand back with that smug smile that says, 'Look what I did—I'm a miracle worker!' As a writer and director, I understand that. I'm trying to do exactly the same thing to my audience—make them believe for a moment that these miracles are real."

Some years later, as Clive turned his thoughts towards the Abarat project, he wrote the following note:

> If magic is an invisible science, which makes what seems immutable flow and become
> other than itself, then love is its most certain proof.

In the colorful world of Abarat, an archipelago of islands inspired by childhood holidays on Tiree in the Scottish Inner Hebrides, a teenage girl from Minnesota named Candy finds a profusion of magic— but not wielded by singsong imps and benevolent fairies. Politicians and power-hungry figures use the ancient language of the Abarat to their benefit; it is wielded both in love and in hatred. As the reader follows Candy's adventures through the world of the Abarat it becomes increasingly clear that she too has ancient powers of creation and transmutation that are strangely awoken within her.

We see magical power embodied in objects like the hats stolen and worn as trophies by the wizard Wolfswinkel, or the wand-like summoning clavicle of Mater Motley. But Clive also explores something more fundamental to the existence of this created world. The pages of the Abarataraba are connected to the spiritual, creative meaning of the Abarat; they are "Pieces of Life."

Sensing Candy's abilities even from her selected tarot card, the blind seer Zephario entrusts her with a square of the Abarataraba with which she orchestrates the creation of a mighty flying glyph. The glyph takes sparks of Candy's soul and the Abarataraba remakes her as "a constellation . . . pieces of her soul speeding in search of Deity," leaving Candy to face ever more unpredictable forces as the series approaches its conclusion.

Clive eagerly adopts the role of literary magician to take his readers almost seamlessly from the familiar, comfortable notions of magic as illusion and trickery—witches, wands, and hats—to the magic of life, creation, and our place and purpose.

CANDYMAN: FAREWELL TO THE FLESH AND THE CANDYMAN FRANCHISE

"I am the writing on the wall, the whisper in the classroom."

After the success of *Candyman*, a sequel was inevitable. Bernard Rose was keen to continue in the theme of urban legends and to weave the mythology of "The Midnight Meat Train" alongside the British Royal Family in a London setting for the next installment.

"I wrote a sequel, but it was a cannibal movie and they were all horrified by it. I sent it to Clive and he said, 'Pardon me for asking, but where is the Candyman in all of this?' However, I love that script. It's a brilliant story and it ends with the Queen feasting on the body of prostitutes and throwing their entrails into the fire while her corgis look on."

Deciding this wasn't the right direction and that Tony Todd's Candyman character should remain the focus for the sequel, Clive instead wrote a treatment that set the action in New Orleans at Mardi Gras. Naming it "Farewell to the Flesh," he set down the storyline for the movie.

Rand Ravich worked the treatment up into a first-draft screenplay, finished in November 1993, which he then refined. Mark Kruger subsequently wrote a final draft, dated July 1994, which he and director Bill Condon then worked on together in the final weeks of pre-production.

"I'd worked in New Orleans before, on *Sister, Sister*," notes Bill Condon. "You know, when you go to New Orleans, it sets the entire mood. This whole movie is about our heroine finally being dragged into the earth where she was born and where Candyman was born, and throughout we have a lot of rain and mud. You stand on any street in New Orleans and that's the story of that city, nature reclaiming its own, because all these great buildings have vines growing out of them; some of them have tree limbs growing out of them. Everywhere there's decay and earth overpowering what man has created.

FROM THE CHILLING IMAGINATION OF CLIVE BARKER

"I admire the first *Candyman* because it put horror in broad daylight. I loved the way Bernard Rose looked around and said, 'What does a haunted house look like today? What's a place where we are really going to be afraid to step into?' and those tenements in Chicago's Cabrini–Green are really scary. That was brilliant. Nothing is really scary anymore and I thought it was very interesting, a completely original take on traditional horror conventions. This movie," he continues, "is a family melodrama that I think goes maybe a little deeper into some of the racial dynamics that were suggested in the first movie but, visually, instead of a daylight-realistic approach, it sort of demanded going into the gothic."

Filming took place in New Orleans and Los Angeles, with principal photography starting on August 16, 1994, at the same time that Clive was directing *Lord of Illusions*. Initially scheduled to run for thirty-nine shooting days to October 10—fifteen in New Orleans and twenty-four in Los Angeles— additional days were added, bringing the total to forty-eight, ending on October 19, 1994.

For the sequel Tony Todd returns as the titular character, as does Michael Culkin, whose character, Phillip Purcell, has written a book about the Candyman since his discussion over the dinner table with Helen Lyle in the first movie. Other cast members include Veronica Cartwright (who had worked with Bill Condon on *Dead in the Water*) as the matriarchal Octavia Tarrant, and Kelly Rowan as her daughter, Annie Tarrant.

"When I prepared for the first film," says Tony Todd, "I went to a lot of museums and studied the art of the 1870s and '80s. Before he was the Candyman, Daniel Robitaille was an artist, educated in the highest European society, so I took fencing, riding, and waltzing classes in preparation for the role. I wanted to really concentrate on the things that would reflect the way he dealt with people. . . .

"The lines are all Clive's, even though I did all the background and came up with the idea that he was an artist. Bernard Rose incorporated it, and it's in the script for the second movie. I really think

"To hear that sound that bees make, that lazy droning, it's very lulling, very seductive. Like the Candyman, they have this ability to frighten, to hurt, and yet they're beautiful, magical creatures that make honey." —TONY TODD

that making him an artist brings his sense of loss and frustration into focus: the mutilation to his painting hand fuels a great deal of that anger.

"Audiences sympathize with the Candyman. He's a Black man who has had this horrendous act of racism and prejudice committed against him for a universal right—to be able to love another human being. But in Robitaille's case, he committed a taboo act in the 1890s—he loved a white woman. The audience is able to relate to the Candyman because of their own knowledge of racism. Everyone's felt discrimination in some form.

"Annie's family are living in denial. If I can get them to recognize my existence, then I can rest; my soul will evaporate. It's almost like I want to create my own suicide. In the first one, he needed people to continue the myth—he was more driven. In this one, he's calmer—actually, he's more violent, but he's calmer."

"The Candyman is more understandable in this movie," agrees Clive. "We see how he became the Candyman and we get some sense of his backstory, but he's still pretty mean. After all, we're not making a polite little family movie. These movies aren't made for kids: they're made for adults who are sixteen years and upwards. Horror films are always being blamed for all kinds of things. When Charlie Manson was looking for inspiration, he used 'Helter Skelter,' a perfectly innocent Beatles song, as his motivation. So crazy people will find signals everywhere and anywhere."

However, Clive had to go on American television around the time the film came out to defend the premise of the movie. The film (and its poster in particular) had stoked some controversy due to the timing of its release in March 1995: O. J. Simpson's murder trial had just begun in January of the same year. Those who were outraged had made a connection between the portrayal of Candyman's relationship with the movie's white female protagonist, and Simpson (a Black man and former football player and actor), who was accused of murdering his wife Nicole Brown Simpson, a white woman, as well as her friend Ron Goldman, who was also white.

Clive issued a statement that read:

I am disturbed and appalled regarding the allegations that Gramercy Pictures and the creative team behind *Candyman: Farewell to the Flesh* have been riding the coattails of the O. J. Simpson trial because of the image depicted in our poster. The one-sheet for

Inside the promotional press book image:

WHAT'S BLOOD FOR, IF NOT FOR SHEDDING...?

Clive Barker is a prolific writer of novels and screenplays that explore the darkest corners of the human psyche. His short story "The Forbidden" was the basis of the original Candyman movie which Barker also executive produced. At the age of 31, Barker shot to fame with the publication of his first novel "The Books Of Blood". Following its success came such chilling works as "The Damnation Game", "Weaveworld", "Cabal", "The Great and Secret Show" and "Imajica", all of which achieved status as national best-sellers.

In 1987, Barker began his film career with the adaptation of the novel "The Hellbound Heart" for his feature debut HELLRAISER. Though produced on a shoestring budget of $1.5 million, the film grossed over $30 million at the box-office and Barker was acclaimed for his twin role of writer and director. He went on to make its sequel HELLRAISER II as well as NIGHTBREED which was based on his novel "Cabel".

Along with Stephen King, Clive Barker is now ranked as one of the world's foremost horror writers and his stories have achieved success in all media - stage, screen and television as well as in literature.

Now, from the chilling imagination of Clive Barker comes FAREWELL TO THE FLESH, a second terrifying encounter with the hook-handed demon introduced in the box-office hit CANDYMAN.

According to legend, The Candyman was an 18th century slave who was savagely beaten to death on the orders of a local landowner whose daughter he had fallen in love with. He revenges himself upon their descendants and anyone who refuses to believe in his existence. The Candyman is first encountered when Helen Lyle (VIRGINIA MADSEN), a student in urban mythology, accidentally summons the blood-thirsty demon and so begins a battle for her very sanity. After a confrontation with The Candyman whereby Hellen loses her life, it seemed that his blood-lust had been satisfied but the nightmare refuses to go away...

In FAREWELL TO THE FLESH, the location is now New Orleans during Mardi Gras and therapist Annie Tarrant uncovers the terrifying secrets of her family's past which link her to the Candyman in a way she would never dare imagine.

Candyman: Farewell to the Flesh depicts the character of the Candyman (Tony Todd) with a hook in hand standing behind the heroine of the picture (Kelly Rowan).

There have been parallels made by the public regarding the two "stories" and while some may view them as a strange example of Life imitating Art, the two situations are very different.

Candyman: Farewell to the Flesh is a supernatural thriller, with its focus being an anti-hero in much the same tradition as Frankenstein's Monster, Dracula, and the Werewolf. Following in this tradition, the Candyman is a sympathetic character who has been wronged by his enemies and is trying to clear his name. He is a contemporary mythical figure who has found a home in the imagination of the American public: part Man; part Myth; part Lover; part Avenger.

Gramercy Pictures has been receiving calls from the public who have been responding to the "Life imitating Art" aspects of the campaign. Ironically, it is the public that has begun to make the correlation between O.J./Nicole and the Candyman poster. It is my belief that the comparisons with the O.J. case say more about the public's obsession with celebrity tragedy than they do about the movie we have made."

Nevertheless, the film opened well, reaching number two at the box office in the US on its opening weekend.

Another sequel, released in 1999, had no involvement from Clive. Once again starring Tony Todd, alongside Donna D'Errico and Alexia Robinson, and directed by Turi Meyer, the movie was set in East Los Angeles and linked Daniel Robitaille's artwork with the Day of the Dead festival.

In 2019, Nia DaCosta directed what she described as a "spiritual sequel" cowritten with and produced by Jordan Peele and Win Rosenfeld, again without Clive's involvement. The movie was set back in Chicago's Cabrini–Green, and explored the gentrification of the area. Vanessa Williams returned to play Anne-Marie McCoy a second time. Yahya Abdul-Mateen II played her son, the baby rescued from the bonfire at the end of the first film, now an artist who becomes inspired by the legend of the Candyman. Teyonah Parris played Brianna Cartwright, Nathan Stewart-Jarrett was Troy Cartwright, and Colman Domingo played William Burke. Delayed several times due to the Covid-19 pandemic, the movie was released in August 2021.

ABOVE

Interior pages from the *Candyman 2* UK promotional press book featuring Tony Todd as Candyman and Kelly Rowan as Annie Tarrant, 1995.

1996 HELLRAISER IV: BLOODLINE AND THE HELLRAISER FRANCHISE

"I am so exquisitely empty."

At the same time as pre-production for both *Lord of Illusions* and *Candyman: Farewell to the Flesh*, pre-production was also underway on a fourth *Hellraiser* movie. The initial storyline ideas for Pinhead's next outing had been set down by Clive as story notes in early 1993 and screenwriter Peter Atkins refined them and wrote a first-draft screenplay that August.

"Creatively, the most interesting thing as far as I was concerned," says Peter, "was that they got Clive back and involved, because he hadn't really been part of *Hellraiser III* at all. . . . His involvement with *Bloodline* meant, for me, a similar situation to the one we'd had on *Hellraiser II* . . . where Clive and I would knock some ideas around, and then I would go away and turn it into a complete story and a screenplay.

"As far as I was concerned, part three was the end creatively. It seemed to round things off. I had taken away the remnants of the human soul that had driven Pinhead at the end of *Hellbound* when Kirsty reminded him that he was human. Part three, what I wanted to do was tell the story of the dissipated soul, to have the ghost of the English officer who had become Pinhead in 1921 be a driving force in one strand of the narrative and the thoroughly soulless Pinhead the other force. The ending brought them back together, thus putting Pinhead more or less in the position he'd been in at the beginning of the first movie. I thought we'd rounded everything off nicely there.

"But Miramax wanted to do a fourth part and I have to give Clive credit for the idea of a movie split into three parts, across three time zones, which excited my interest. In passing, Clive suggested that what we should do was maybe follow the fortunes of a single family. As soon as he said that, I said, 'Well, if we're going to do a family, let's do the Lemarchand family. Let's set it in eighteenth-century France, and make it about the family of the man who created the Lament Configuration box.' My

暗黒の恐怖——

無限の苦痛——

〈善〉と〈悪〉の最終決戦！

ヘルレイザー4

HELLRAISER
BLOODLINE

2/14

RENTAL RELEASE

TOHO VIDEO

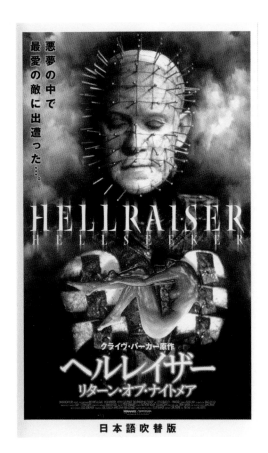

ulterior motive was that I thought it would nicely frame the trilogy created by the first three movies. . . .

"What I was trying to achieve with *Hellraiser IV: Bloodline* was to bracket the whole mythology that we'd created in the other three films. I wanted to tie up some loose ends. I thought that if someone was sufficiently motivated to do it, they could re-edit the four films in the way they created *The Godfather Saga*. One epic, five-hour-long saga, '*Hellraiser Chronicles*' film."

Doug Bradley was back as Pinhead, Valentina Vargas played Angelique, and Bruce Ramsey played three generations of the Lemarchand family.

Kevin Yagher, the make-up effects artist who had also directed the Cryptkeeper wraparound segments and two episodes of *Tales from the Crypt*, was the movie's director, although he would remove his name from the project before it was complete. The director of photography was Gerry Lively, who had shot the two Waxwork movies and *Hellraiser III* with Anthony Hickox, as well as *Children of the Corn III: Urban Harvest*, for which Kevin Yagher had provided special make-up effects. Production design was by Ivo Cristante. Gary J. Tunnicliffe created make-up designs, including the design of Angelique. The producer was Nancy Rae Stone. The initial budget was for a thirty-six-day shoot through to September 21, 1994.

The movie started filming in Los Angeles on August 9, 1994, seven days before Bill Condon started filming the second Candyman film in New Orleans, but this Hellraiser film would be plagued by budgetary problems and creative disagreements and would appear a full twelve months later than the Candyman film, hitting theaters in the US on March 8, 1996.

Kevin Yagher recounts that, "essentially, I wanted to make a story about the box and be true to the fans by detailing the history of where it came from. My whole idea was that I didn't want to do a *Hellraiser IV* where Pinhead slaughters a bunch of people. It's been done before, and *III* was a good example of that, turning people into CD Heads and Cameraheads. I wanted to do something a little different. The script was wonderful: it was a Frankenstein monster story about the maker of the box and how his box—the monster—is killing people.

"The problem was that the moneymen came up with a budget they thought the picture could be made for, but they didn't really talk to the filmmakers about it. They were looking into it, but nobody was putting any more money into it. Even Clive told them we needed three more weeks. So we just started pulling scenes out, which can be good and bad."

Peter Atkins had completed a fifth draft of the screenplay back on May 17, 1994, weaving in comments from Kevin Yagher; then he turned in a sixth draft on June 17. As the start of filming drew closer, Peter was asked to revise again, completing his edits on August 3; then again, on August 12 and 30, even though filming had begun August 9. After yet another set of requested changes came in on September 2, 1994, Peter elected to remove himself from the project, saying to the producer, "The changes proposed in your fax might do wonders to the schedule and the budget but they will do nothing but damage to the film. I might be powerless to stop the movie going up in flames but I can certainly refuse to strike the first match."

Fresh from his work on *Candyman*'s sequel, Rand Ravich stepped in to provide revisions on September 6, 12, and 14—as the shoot continued.

A revised schedule on September 12, 1994, extended the production to thirty-eight days of shooting, to finish on September 24. Even so, Miramax was unimpressed with the results.

"When I delivered my director's cut," says Kevin Yagher, "we knew the kills were missing and we had to put those in, but the big concern was that Pinhead was not in the first part of the movie—he came in about forty minutes into it. Pinhead is in the film, though for me it's not about him. But they wanted to restructure it and essentially turn it into one long story. The script was tight to begin with, and to go back and forth between the time periods is impossible if you want to believe this character is going through any change. Plus, the second act wasn't long enough to make it into a full feature."

Peter Atkins noted later, "I'd written six versions of this script: six drafts. And they always knew that the eighteenth century came first and Pinhead didn't appear until the twentieth-century story. So it's not that anyone could blame Kevin for delaying Pinhead's entrance because that's the way it was written, that's the way it was approved by Miramax. But I think that when they saw the movie they suddenly felt, 'Hey, wait a minute, where's our monster? We made a terrible mistake!' They didn't finger-point. They didn't say, 'Oh, it's Pete's fault or it's Kevin's fault!' They just figured, 'We should have known this originally. We should have brought Pinhead in earlier.'"

"In terms of 'servicing the franchise' Miramax wanted to focus on the prime character, Pinhead," Clive confirms. "Now, my argument about Pinhead has always been that less is more. But audiences just go crazy when this guy comes onscreen, so the studio said, 'No, more is more.' And I said, 'Well the more you put this guy on the screen, the less scary he's going to be.' And their response to that was 'Well then, we'll just put more blood in.'"

In support of his argument, Clive wrote to the studio in January 1995, saying, "If the picture's to be worth a damn, the story needs to be made more involving and consistent. Simply re-cutting the picture to make it quicker will not solve its difficulties. Yagher was never given the production support or a viable schedule; as a consequence he did not shoot the script as Pete wrote it, and the resulting material does not tell the story properly. We never get to feel anything for the characters, and as we've agreed many times, horror movies are not scary if the audience remains uninvolved. If this *Hellraiser* is to work, time has to be taken to fill in its considerable narrative and motivational gaps. A few quick-fix gore scenes will not make the picture more commercial. You'll simply be wasting money."

Clive drafted suggested changes and additional sequences and, agreeing that investing in reshoots and delaying the film's release date was required, Miramax spent the additional time and money.

Kevin Yagher was not involved in the additional filming. Instead, Joe Chappelle, fresh from directing *Halloween 6: The Curse of Michael Myers*, was hired to direct the enhancement reshoot, which was undertaken in April and May 1995 and followed by a shoot later in the year to rework Pinhead's final scenes in the movie.

The film's direction was eventually credited to Alan Smithee, the Hollywood pseudonym used when a director removes his name from a film. "On an artistic level," says Kevin Yagher, "the final cut I saw did not represent my vision, and it changed enough that I no longer wanted credit. There was a lot of me in there, but there were a number of things in there that I wasn't involved in. That's why I removed my name."

Doug Bradley adds, "It was the shoot from hell, literally! If anything could go wrong, it did. There was a whole raft of bad employment decisions that the producers were rectifying while we were shooting it. Two directors worked on it and we had a total of four directors of photography. How they managed to sort out the color grading, God alone knows.

"That's not to say that the film is without merit; some of it is outstanding. The first sequence, in eighteenth-century France, is as good as anything we shot in all four films. We had the same amount of money as *Hellraiser III*, but the film was just too ambitious, technically. Part III was character driven, but *Bloodline* had a complicated script and specified a major special effect on just about every page. The problems were not helped when the art department and camera crew were sacked at the end of week one. There was a fire, a flood, and a strike, and the young boy got chickenpox. Try to pick a movie out of that lot!"

Clive agrees: "I think there are some fine things in *Hellraiser IV*, actually—at the beginning and the end—but I don't like the middle very much. Even so, there are some things that return almost to the tone of the first one. It's uneven, no question, but overall I prefer it to number three."

"I wish I could take credit," reflects Peter, "but I can't and it's very fitting who does take the credit for this: Doug's very kind to say there are some good lines in *Bloodline* but one of the best lines in it was not written by me and happens right at the end. At the time we thought it was going to be the last words Pinhead would ever utter onscreen because we figured the series was going to be over; we didn't know there were going to be direct-to-video sequels.

"I'd already done three sets of free post-production rewrites for them but I was off writing *Wishmaster*, so they brought in Rand Ravich to write a couple of scenes and he did a fine job, but almost the last important line Pinhead speaks was actually written by Clive.

"They asked Clive to come and view the edit—and I'd given him lots of good shit to say beforehand, like 'Do I look like someone who cares what God thinks?'—all that good stuff—but the last line was just a free gift from Clive, so I thought it was very fitting that the guy who created the whole thing in the first place wrapped it up. And the line is: 'I am so exquisitely empty.'"

Clive's involvement with the franchise ended after *Bloodline*, though the movies continued without him. *Hellraiser V: Inferno*, directed by Scott Derrickson and released in 2000, features Craig Sheffer (*Nightbreed*'s Aaron Boone) in a return to the world of Clive Barker. In *Hellseeker*, which came out in 2002 and was directed by Rick Bota, Ashley Laurence reprises her role as Kirsty Cotton, and Dean Winters plays her husband, Trevor. Rick Bota became the first person to direct more than one *Hellraiser* movie when he returned for both *Hellraiser VII: Deader* and *Hellraiser VIII: Hellworld*. The two movies were filmed back-to-back in 2002 but both had their releases delayed until 2005. *Deader* starred Kari Wuhrer and Paul Rhys, with Marc Warren also in the cast, and *Hellworld* starred Katheryn Winnick and Lance Henriksen alongside Henry Cavill. Doug Bradley, as Pinhead, appeared in all of these, but *Hellworld* would prove to be his final entry to date in the series.

Clive almost came back into the world of *Hellraiser* at this point when, in October 2006, while writing *The Scarlet Gospels*, he announced, "They're going to remake *Hellraiser I* with a lot more money and they've invited me to write it—the invitation came from Bob Weinstein—which I am going to do, on the basis that if I don't do it, it will be done in some way that I probably won't like! It's only

"We're laying plans at the moment. . . . You can't keep a good monster down!"

that one that I really, really, really care about in terms of its remake value—and it'll be kind of fun to have the extra money to do the effects and all that cool stuff.

"So it puts me in the situation of writing both the beginning and the end of Pinhead at the same time.

"I'm excited about it—actually it'll be kind of cool to revisit it once and see if there are things we can do to it which will make it significantly better. I wouldn't wish to direct—I only want to write and be a part of the producing team. I wouldn't want to revisit something that I did as a director, something that I did all those years ago: that would be too, in a way, painful—not painful but weird, difficult, strange."

He wrote a treatment and the following March noted, "The *Hellraiser* treatment has been signed off on by Miramax. They have it in their hands and they like it, and they want a bit more *Hellraiser* mythology, which is music to my ears—it's the first time I've ever heard that request! You know, where do I sign? But they've already signed so that's fine."

The plan then changed, moving the project into the hands of Alexandre Bustillo and Julien Maury to direct and script the project, with Clive producing. The next announcement was that they had been replaced as writers by Marcus Dunstan and Patrick Melton. By October 2008, the cup had passed to Pascal Laugier, and Clive was reported as saying it had become a "reconfiguring" rather than a remake.

Another year, another proposal . . . October 2010 had Dimension announcing that Todd Farmer and Patrick Lussier would be taking on the new *Hellraiser*, with production slated for 2011, with a release date later that year or in early 2012.

Instead, however, the next installment ended up being a rushed-into-production movie, a move that was necessary to keep the studio's rights to the franchise from expiring. This sequel was called *Hellraiser IX: Revelations*, which was released in 2011.

Victor Garcia directed on a shoestring budget and Gary J. Tunnicliffe—who had worked on every *Hellraiser* movie since the third one, providing special effects and make-up effects and designs on each (as well as on *Candyman*, *Candyman 3*, and *Lord of Illusions*), and also wrote, directed, and even donned Pinhead's make-up himself in an unofficial short film in 2004, *No More Souls: One Last Slice of Sensation* (included as an Easter egg on the *Deader* US DVD release)—wrote the screenplay. Because Doug Bradley had declined to take part, the role of Pinhead was played by Stephan Smith Collins.

Clive again almost wrote the next installment when he was asked to reboot the series in 2013. He told *Entertainment Weekly* the following year, "I think the phrase is 'reboot,' although I've never really understood what that meant. I wanted to make sure we sounded some fresh notes. The movie actually begins on Devil's Island. I wanted to fold into the *Hellraiser* narrative something about the guy—the Frenchman Lemarchand—who made the mysterious box which raises Pinhead. I figured, 'Well, what would have happened to him?' He might well have been taken to Devil's Island and I thought that would be a pretty cool place to start the movie."

Again, though, the project came to a halt. Instead Gary J. Tunnicliffe wrote, directed, and acted in the next entry in the series, 2018's *Hellraiser X: Judgment*. Pinhead was this time played by Paul T. Taylor.

In 2021, thirty-five years after Clive assembled his cast and crew in Cricklewood, David Bruckner directed the most recent entry in the series, marking the eleventh movie in the *Hellraiser* franchise.

1996 SACRAMENT

"I am a man, and men are animals who tell stories."

In the spring of 1995, Clive decided that the premise of his next novel, *Sacrament*, would be an important and deeply felt statement about animals—and mankind's place in the world.

"It's a novel which—perhaps more than anything else that I've written—is personal. It's also significantly less fantastical than anything I've done before. It follows the journey taken by the protagonist, Will Rabjohns, who is around my age, happily and contentedly gay and British but who has moved to America.

"Will's business is the study, recording, and documenting of species which are on the verge of extinction. And that's a big issue for me because animals are a big part of my life.

"What I wanted to do," he continues, "was to write about why we need animals, why they're not just a convenience to us, why they're not just the creatures that guard our houses or can be seen through binoculars if you go on safari. They are to do with us, our humanity, and indeed our survival. They're not entertainments, they are part of the holiness of the world. And if we treat them badly and drive them to extinction, then that's a form of evil."

Clive has long lived with animals around him; his home happily runs to the rhythms of their needs as much as his, and he remains in awe of their loyalty and devotion. Contrasting that with the disrespect and cruelty of mankind is a topic that comes easily. The reader's guide, Will, is created as an amalgam of Clive's own experience and that of American photographer and artist Peter Beard.

"*Eyelids of Morning* is one of my very favorite books in all the world and it's a book which I go back to and back to and always find something new. Peter Beard was an *incredible* influence on me—*Sacrament* would not exist without Peter Beard, and his great sense of the tragedy of the natural world. . . ."

Talking recently about how ideas and emotions, such as giving insight into the mind of a dog (as in his 1979 play *Dog* and the short story "Animal Life"), take their time to find the right creative outlet, he agrees: "Oh, I think Lord Fox in *Sacrament* is a perfect example of one of the things that you sit on and that percolate inside you. Because there are some characters you really feel you're channeling and Lord Fox is the best example. Though I'm sure you'll find his speeches are worked

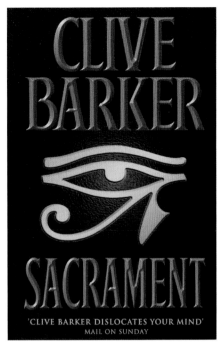

over every bit as obsessively back and forth as every other speech, nevertheless it did feel as if I understood his voice."

With Clive's home now firmly rooted in Beverly Hills, the novel would also serve as an elegy for his life in England, employing the poetic language of loss to mirror not just the extinction of animals but the lost loves, family, and friends left behind.

"It's the book closest to my heart of all the books that I have written, in the sense that it contains all the autobiographical elements. It contains a gay hero, it contains a hero who has relocated from England, Northern England, to here on the West Coast. It contains a passionate, I would like to say, commitment to understand—and devotion to—animals and to the diversity of species. It contains a lot of material about AIDS and about people who have died of AIDS and that are dying of AIDS and what that issue is. So, these are all the things which touch my life. I've lost friends, we probably all have now. . . . It's very much a part of who I am, as a guy, middle-aged, looking at my career, and saying: 'Well, how can I put more meaning in what I do? How can I make what I do deeper, richer, and better?' Will is in the middle of life and he's doing that. He's looking at his life and he's saying: 'I've spent all my time as a creative individual, as a witness. I've been witnessing the world, and now I'm coming to a place where I really want to connect working with all of it.'"

Although he'd freely included gay characters in his work before, *Sacrament* was the first of Clive's novels to bring a gay protagonist front and center. This choice, and Clive's focus on the loss and horror of the AIDS pandemic, were both considered commercially unwise at the time. But Clive held firm, despite concerns from his publisher.

"One of the issues of *Sacrament* is that gay men have witnessed a terrible plague," Clive said as the novel was released, "and are dealing with it in many extraordinary ways. And grief can sometimes open you up to a sense that we have a huge amount to lose on this planet. On a global scale there are species that we can't even name that are being lost. So I've tried to write a book which is optimistic, which eventually reveals a place where the imagination makes a sacred connection between being human, living in the world, and celebrating and preserving the things out there in the world that are not like us.

"I mean, gays are not like the rest of the tribe in several all-important ways," he continued, "and it's always been very easy for people to say, 'Let gay men die of AIDS, they brought it on themselves.' And I think people say the same thing about animals: 'Oh, they're dying out, but they're not like us so if they disappear it doesn't matter.' But it does! It's tough for people to understand that the harm you do to the world, you finally do to yourself.

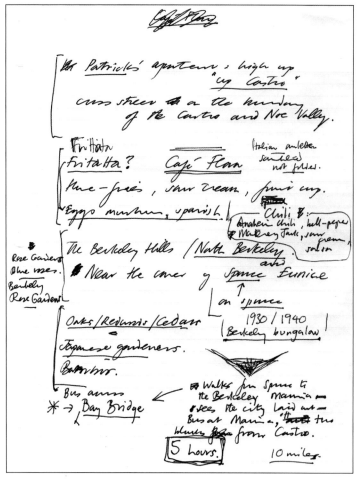

"I've always felt Other, I've never felt like a tribal member. And I think that's at the heart of what I do. I don't feel quite the same and I want to report from the boundary. I'm out there with the Lost Things, and the things that may be lost. And if they are lost, we will be the poorer. Because, to look at this globally, we are, as far as we know, the only point of life in the entire cosmos.

"That's why I'm probably getting more politicized as I get older. *Sacrament* is a call to stand up and be counted, to say, 'I love the world because it's rich and contradictory and paradoxical and strange. I love it because it's beyond me and there's so much I don't know. I don't love it because I want to reduce it and control it.' And that's true of the diversity of people's sexuality, skin color, the animal world, and the diversity of cultural forms. In other words, I think we should always aim to celebrate what's different."

Sacrament captures a somber tone not only in its explicit descriptions of loss but also by communicating a deeper, philosophical sentiment. Its title bespeaks holiness, something to be treasured deeply. Each careful narrative choice, the naming of characters and places—the Domus Mundi—and the words spoken and unvoiced, work to spiral the reader in toward the spiritual as much as the physical. Poetry plays a key role—opening a novel with two set-piece prose poems is a confident move but also a clear signal of what is to come:

> To every hour, its mystery.
> At dawn, the riddles of light and life.
> At noon, the conundrums of solidity.
> At three, in the hum and heat of the day,
> A phantom moon, already high.
> At dusk, memory.
> And at midnight?
> Oh then the enigma of time itself;
> Of a day that will never come again,
> Passing into history while we sleep.

Diversity and variegation are topics that spring to Clive's lips often. He is just as—no, more—likely to excitedly recommend a newly discovered natural history documentary than a groundbreaking movie.

"*Sacrament* began with seeing a film of a polar bear with a mayonnaise jar stuck on his nose and that appears in the book, that image, and that was what it was about. It was about the fact that the receding ice sheet was obliging those polar bears to go to extreme ends to find nourishment and it's a polar bear that starts the entire story in a way, you know: Will almost dies at the paws of a polar bear. That had an influence on me, on my feelings about dangerous animals. We're killing everything. . . . I can't watch David Attenborough programs any longer: he's obliged, because he's an honest reporter and observer, he's obliged to give us the falling note. He cannot, rightly so, make a program which is pure celebration."

Nevertheless, in observing the glorious diversity of the world around us, *Sacrament* moves from the elegiac to the celebratory.

186

"Sometimes my books feel like pieces of a much bigger thing. I think they're all one story: it's 'living and dying, we feed the fire.'"

"The planet is an ark," Clive says, "filled with extraordinary diversity and richness. This takes the form of animals and insects, but it also takes the form of a diversity of human cultures, which are also under threat. You don't need to go to the Antarctic or to the wilds of some jungle to have an epiphany about the extraordinariness of the world. It really is a question of just opening your eyes. And Will, who seems to have open eyes all his life, really realizes at that point: 'Now, wait a second, what I've always done is put a frame around it. Whatever we have done has been looking at the world through a lens. The truest lens is my eye and the truest camera is my soul. Now here I am soul and eye and the world.'"

Reflecting on the novel's villains, Clive observes, "Steep and Rosa were intended to be the Macbeths but I couldn't do it, I didn't have the commitment to that villainy. When I got into Domus Mundi I was confronted with something that I'd never been confronted with before—that there was another subject waiting for me, which was the state of the world, and I wasn't going to be able to address it without doubling the length of the book."

Clive's return to England in the guise of Will gives him the opportunity to explore not just the landscapes of his own life there but also his relationship with his family.

"We discover as we follow his very troubled life," Clive explains, "that the reason for his obsession with animals and extinction can be traced back to his childhood in Yorkshire. It's a story about how we become who we are and how we must deal with what we are by facing up to things, including the things that happened to us in childhood, good and bad."

"My books are filled with thoughts about sons and fathers," he later reflected, "many of which are derived from a very complex and elaborate relationship between my father and myself, based firstly on blood on both sides but also based sometimes on mutual incomprehension. All those things find their way into the books."

Aside from some reflexive reactions to his gay hero, Clive received largely positive reactions to the novel, with a review from *Kirkus* concluding that it was "charged—in its complex development and surprising resolution—with very real, very human emotion. A weirdly absorbing and entertaining tale that offers more disturbing delights from one of our most inventive and risk-taking writers."

Publishers Weekly called the novel "awesome but skewed" but conceded that "even in this fractured tale, Barker presents an astonishing array of ideas, visions, and epiphanies; but they're seen as if through a glass beveled and crazed."

The book's flap copy reads:

Will Rabjohns has everything.

Handsome, famous and revered, he is the world's greatest wildlife photographer: his pictures expressions of the beauty and tragedy of nature at its most raw. But Will is a haunted man, driven to risk his life in pursuit of his art; a pursuit that will lead him to an almost fatal encounter with a polar bear. Fate isn't finished with Will, however. In his coma he remembers and relives the seminal event of his childhood: an encounter with ancient and terrible forces which revealed to him the mystery at the heart of nature. He also relives his bitter-sweet adolescence: the early death of his brother, mythical English summers, the friends he loved and lost . . .

When he awakens, he knows he must return to his Yorkshire home to begin the restorative process of mending his soul, and to confront the kernel of darkness at the heart of his childhood. In doing so, he must rekindle the devotion and faith of that childhood: for he is about to engage in a war not only for his own soul, but for the soul of the planet, and every animal that breathes upon it.

Sacrament is a novel for everyone who ever had a secret, a family and a love of the natural world.

1997 CHILIAD

"The river runs both ways."

First published in 1997, *Chiliad* stands out among Clive's work as a bookend narrative of two parts, distinct yet intertwined.

The novella appeared in *Revelations* (published in the UK as *Millennium*), a collection described by its editor (and Clive's biographer) Douglas E. Winter as walking the fine line between an anthology of disparate tales by ten writers—each representing a decade between 1900 and 2000—and a unified novel sharing neither setting nor characters. "When the final decade was completed," he notes in his afterword, "Clive Barker took on the daunting task of creating a short novel that would 'wrap around' the century and yet remain defiantly a fiction to be read on its own (and, in his hands, majestic) terms."

In discussion with Douglas E. Winter at a convention, Clive spoke about what had driven him to write in a way that leaves the natural distance between author and narrator gossamer thin. "I don't find myself terribly interesting and that's one of the reasons why I write in the mode of trying to escape from the coral that is me. The removal of the limitation that is the self into the place that is the image of things that are boundless: this is the mystical heartbeat of what I do.

"The view, when I look at myself," he continued, "is very familiar to me until I start to look at the places where I think that some of the things that have happened to me might be useful to other people. Talking about being gay in *Sacrament*, talking about depression in *Chiliad*, and talking about middle age in *Chiliad* as well—I wanted to express these things truthfully because I only become interesting to myself when I disappoint myself. If everything is just chugging along just fine, why write about it? There is nothing remotely interesting about that. What is interesting is to be troubled and screwed up and to be dealing with being troubled and screwed up."

Explaining what compels him to write, Clive reiterated: "Fiction for me can only be a means to say, 'How can I understand what is going on in my life better?'"

Some years later, he described *Chiliad* as a confessional. "It is quite short but it is extremely dense, as I describe my mind journeys back and forth through time, encountering along the course of a river, which is the book's spine, other shadowed men like myself, each seeking their own moment

"*Chiliad* . . . is easily one of the darkest pieces of fiction I've ever written."

ABOVE

Limited edition of
Douglas Winter's
Revelations anthology,
which includes the
bookend stories which
comprise Clive's *Chiliad*
narrative. Published by
Cemetery Dance, 1997.

of redemption and release. In many ways it's the most intimate thing I've ever written. . . . It was an immense challenge, and is easily one of the darkest pieces of fiction I've ever written. . . .

"I look back and I think that what I was doing in the Books of Blood was an awful lot more grim and crude, and in a way it was appropriate that it was that way," Clive reflects. "If you do a story called 'The Midnight Meat Train,' you're not going to spend too much time dealing with the poetry of that. But I do feel, where *Chiliad* is concerned, I was really wanting to evoke a poetic life for the piece. And certainly in *Galilee*, where I was talking of romance, and for me a romance requires poetry. So in both cases I was trying for a different quality to the language."

Today, Clive looks back at *Chiliad* with a degree of wonder and retains a certain curiosity about how he was able to marry its gentle, poetic cadences with its sharp commentary—a combination he continues to aspire to in his current writing. His love of phonology has always colored both his poetry and his prose, and comparing *Chiliad* to a new story in progress, he observes: "These are two stories which have *harmonies*. *Chiliad*'s obviously in the end a story about religion and paganism, and whether you see through a plain glass or you see through a colored glass, but they have a lot of echoes of echoes of echoes."

On publication of *Revelations, Kirkus Reviews* observed: "[Winter] has spent seven years assembling this book, looking for genuinely original writing that rises above genre clichés, and he has largely achieved his objective. Clive Barker, in top form, offers two works: the introductory *Chiliad: A Meditation—Men and Sin*, about the thousand years of guilt leading up to this century; and the anthology's wrap-up short novel, *Chiliad: A Moment at the River's Heart*, a parable about guilt that rises magnificently above genre."

When *Chiliad* was published as a stand-alone book in 2014, its flap copy read:

> *Chiliad* consists of two interrelated stories, stories filtered through the melancholy imagination of a narrator perched on the banks of a river that flows backward and forward through time. The first movement, "Men and Sin," takes place in the millennial year of 1000 AD. The second, "A Moment at the River's Heart," occurs exactly one thousand years—the length of a "chiliad"—later as the new millennium approaches. At the heart of these stories are two savage, seemingly inexplicable atrocities, each of which reaches across the centuries to reflect and connect with the other. As the narratives unfold and time becomes increasingly permeable, Barker creates a dark, sorrowful portrait of the ancient human capacity for cruelty and destruction. Writing always with lucidity and grace, he addresses a host of universal concerns, among them the power of guilt and grief, and the need to find signs of meaning in the chaos that surrounds us. In the process, he examines the endless chain of consequences that inevitably proceed from a single act of violence.
>
> At once hugely expansive and deeply personal, *Chiliad* is a compact masterpiece, a resonant reminder of Barker's ability to create fictional worlds that enrich and illuminate our own.

1995– OIL AND COLOR
1998

"Flesh is our indisputable commonality."

"The great thing about painting," says Clive, "is that it can be about everything, and yet you're not demanding any specific interpretation from the viewer. The painting is there, it's what I felt at that given moment, make of it what you will.

"That's very important to me, because the movies clearly are populist pieces designed to stir up an audience and give them some excitement on a Friday night. I hope they last until Saturday morning, but the truth of the matter is that they essentially have to work for an hour and a half on a Friday night.

"The books are large, dense journeys, very layered, and they're the result of eighteen months of me just working to make things as rich as possible. But they nevertheless are going to take the audience on a very specific journey.

"The paintings are for me as an artist—and I hope for the spectator—like stepping out of a labyrinth into open air. It's not a test, it's not a quiz. It may be a puzzlement, but I don't have an answer to it, or if I have an answer, my answer is no more relevant than your answer."

Looking back to when he left school, Clive says, "Painting is always what I wanted to do, before the books, before the movies. But when I got into art college my mother and father said, 'The last thing you do for us before you become an adult: don't become a painter,' so I went and studied philosophy at university instead. But through it all, theatre and then books, I was always doing sketches, then covers for my books and limited editions of this or that. So when I came to L.A., I bought myself a painting studio and that gave me the space and freedom to make a mess and just fuck up.

"Making a mess is the metaphor for my painting. It is a sort of Dionysus/Apollo dichotomy. There is something almost Apollonian about the way I write. It's structured, organized, and rhythmic. Then I crack a beer and I go smoke a smelly cigar and I make a mess. And the pictures are much more eruptive. There's a kind of violence to them, and a messiness, and that's not in the books at all. . . .

"I feel like it's part of my sanity. It's the playing out of the two parts of my nature. It allows my dark side expression and room to be celebrated, particularly if it's a day which contained some pretty frustrating meetings."

ABOVE LEFT
Curated by Clive in 1999 for EMI's Songbook Series, *Being Music* features tracks that he played in his studio as he was painting characters for the Abarat series of books. The CD included a booklet with paintings by Clive and his commentary on what each track means to him.

ABOVE RIGHT
At The Window, 1997.

The Imagination of Clive Barker, presented by Laguna Art Museum at its South Coast Plaza satellite installation in August 1995, Clive's next major exhibition, coincided with the US release of his movie *Lord of Illusions*. For the first time, a number of the pieces exhibited were tied together in a theme as Clive created a series called *The Illusions Suite* comprising eleven drawings related to magic, alchemy, and physical transformation specifically for the show.

With some critics expressing surprise that a museum would curate a solo show from a film director, the organization's director, Naomi Vine, explained, "I was very interested in the way the books and the movies and the paintings all got at the same thing—this incredibly inventive imagination. Barker places the human figure in a frightening context, as well as a very compelling context with strong psychological intrigue. The exhibition really tries to establish a very broad cultural context for the paintings and for the role of imagination in the visual arts. The paintings are really imaginative fantasy. They are very creative. And the role of creativity and imagination in art, as well as in literature and filmmaking, is of great interest to us."

"Different media call forth different things in you," Clive offers. "Paintings are a relatively passive experience, whereas with movies, modern audiences are combative. They say, 'I dare you, scare me.' Movies are the least freeing. You're spending a lot of other people's money, so you're responsible to them, and you're responsible to holding on to a vision which is now being interpreted by many other people and is probably being diluted in that process. Books are next on that rising scale of freedom, because once you've started a narrative line, if you want to be a convincing storyteller, you've got to go where the narrative is leading you.

"The great thing about the paintings is that it's practically entirely an unintellectual business. In a way, they don't answer to anybody.

"There's a particular kind of artist," says Clive, "who doesn't try to scrutinize and perfectly reproduce reality but says, 'Fuck reality.' What I want to do is soften reality in my hands and reconfigure it so that it is my reality, unlike anything you have seen before. A casual wander through the cathedrals of Europe shows you just how long this dark side has festered in the imagination—there are gargoyles everywhere. It's almost as if they are there as reminders of the marginalized, the Dionysian, the panic instinct, that have been shoved to the edges."

In 1996, Clive started to paint new pieces for a planned April 1997 exhibition at the La Luz de Jesus Gallery in Silver Lake, Los Angeles, a gallery with a reputation for hosting "lowbrow" and pop surrealist art. Setting himself no boundaries in the reconfiguration of reality in his images, he experimented with large-scale ink, pastels, and acrylics on paper, all with an erotic or sexual celebration in the characters and their settings.

In the *One Flesh* exhibition that resulted from this work, naked forms—humans, angels, demons, and reconfigured flesh in varying states of arousal—jostled for attention.

"This is the first exhibition which is thematically and visually coherent," he said as it was staged, noting that "the shows I've had previously have been sort of ragged in terms of the way they've been gathered. The *Hellraiser* drawings are a big deal for people; they want to see the drawings and how much the movie's designs are based on them, and I'm cool with that. But at a certain point, I no longer want to be just an extension of my movies. I want people to view these things as objects themselves, not as illustrations for movies."

At the same time, he recognizes that storytelling also plays a part and it's hard not to see his portraits as characters with complex and evolving stories swirling around them. "In the loosest possible sense I think of myself as a narrative painter. If you want to find a story in any of these things, you can, and the story of sex fascinates me, the story of desire fascinates me. It comes up in the books constantly and it feels to me like a subject that's so central to our lives, but is so marginalized, and in painting it's remarkably marginalized."

In his artist's statement for the show he offered:

> Flesh is our indisputable commonality. Whatever our race, our religion, our politics we are faced every morning with the fact of our bodies. Their frailties, their demands, their desires. And yet the erotic appetites that spring from—and are expressed through—those bodies are so often a source of bitter dissension and division. Acts that offer a glimpse of transcendence to one group are condemned by another. We are pressured from every side—by peers, by church, by state—to accept the consensual definition of taboo; though so often what excites our imaginations most is the violation of taboo.
>
> In the series of acrylics on paper works I've made for this exhibition I wanted to explore my own erotic imaginings, not as a series of pornographic tableaux (though some of the pictures reference those scenarios) but as a more fantastical envisioning of the shapes our sexual hunger takes.
>
> These are large, colorful paintings; sometimes tinged with melancholy (as is any business to do with our physical bodies) but often, I hope, celebratory and humorous.
>
> I want to make an exhibition which will be like a sexual carnival—raucous and surreal—designed to engage the heads, hearts and groins of its spectators.
>
> Here, for a time, nothing is forbidden; nothing is condemned, and our flesh—always beautiful in arousal—is portrayed as it transforms into new shapes, reflecting the complexities of our desire.

ABOVE LEFT

Clive in front of his painting *Angels and Demons Dining Together* at the La Luz de Jesus Gallery, which was hosting his *One Flesh* exhibition of works on paper, April 1997.

ABOVE RIGHT

La Luz de Jesus Gallery in California hosted its second exhibition of Clive's work, *The Weird and the Wicked*. Clive and David Armstrong at the gallery, October 1998.

1998 **GALILEE**

"Every family has its secrets."

"What I tried to do," Clive said of *Galilee*, ahead of its 1998 release, "is take what I learned about writing about the real world in *Sacrament* and marry it to what I learned about writing a sort of poetic, almost religious fantasy in *Imajica*. I wanted those to be put side by side."

Galilee is a book of many parts: subtitled as a romance, it is both a love letter to his holiday home in Kaua'i with the titular hero (inspired by his new partner, David Armstrong) and a commentary on how power is held and manipulated. Galilee is a Black man bound by a historical vow to a white family, the Gearys, and also the family's feared foe. The Geary men's connection to Galilee is an abiding source of shame and disgust as they struggle to accept they are jealous of his power, not least the ability to entrance their wives.

"Kaua'i—which is the place where David, my other half, and I go very regularly, and where I made a lot of notes for the book—is an island that awakens a lot of the senses. You step off the plane and the air smells different. The perfume of the island, the smell of the sea . . . it's just so fucking potent! Everything about the island awakens you."

Racial tensions and the American Civil War cast their long shadows over multiple generations of two dysfunctional families, each dynasty wielding very different sorts of power.

"I think as I get older, I see more and more how I have been formed, both negatively and positively, by the dramas, conflicts, and the love of my family," Clive reflects. In *Galilee* he draws a portrait of the reclusive Barbarossa family, who live separate lives in varying degrees of conflict all under one roof, while the Gearys are an extended family held together solely by their common interest—to maintain and expand their wealth and political influence. Although the Gearys would be at home in any novel about fame and wealth, the more enigmatic Barbarossas are a family of divinities; this is where Clive's romance becomes fantastical.

"The older I get, the more interested I am in the subtleties of how fantasy works. My commitment to the fantastique is as immovable as ever; I believe that writers and artists and filmmakers of the fantastic have a chance to describe reality in a much more complex and interesting way than

A STORY OF LOVE, FAMILY, AND BETRAYAL

An astoundingly
different novel
from...

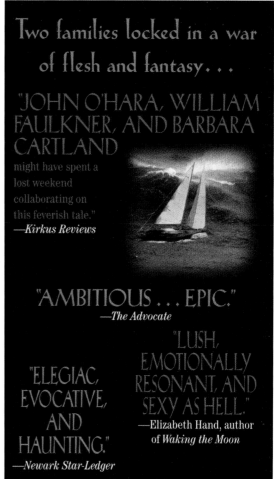

Two families locked in a war
of flesh and fantasy...

"JOHN O'HARA, WILLIAM
FAULKNER, AND BARBARA
CARTLAND

might have spent a
lost weekend
collaborating on
this feverish tale."
—*Kirkus Reviews*

"AMBITIOUS...EPIC."
—*The Advocate*

"ELEGIAC,
EVOCATIVE,
AND
HAUNTING."
—*Newark Star-Ledger*

"LUSH,
EMOTIONALLY
RESONANT, AND
SEXY AS HELL."
—Elizabeth Hand, author
of *Waking the Moon*

so-called realistic writers. For example, the power that dreams have in our lives. The way our lives are constantly affected by and nuanced by things which are not strictly real. Our fantastic lives—that is, our dream lives, the lives of our idling minds—they change, enrich, and develop the so-called realistic part of our lives, and make us much more interesting and complex human beings.

"So when I write a book like *Galilee*, where the fantasy elements are tied incredibly closely to the realism, I find myself studying how I can put just a half twist on reality—and suddenly something very strange is happening. It's not the wild fantasy of *Imajica* or the wild fantasy of *Weaveworld*. But sometimes just a little half twist on something can be every bit as potent as something 'wild.'

"My guess is that with *Galilee*," Clive continues, "the audience is going to get a different kind of pleasure versus what they would get in my previous works. For one thing, it's much easier to relate to some of the chief characters, because there they are, living in our world. And when strange things happen—and a lot of still very bizarre things happen in the book!—hopefully the journeys taken by these characters will still be all that much more accessible."

Clive uses elements of conventional romance: Rachel Pallenberg is an ordinary girl whose Prince Charming seeks her out and whisks her away to a world of glamour. However, that glamour belies a world where wealth is used to shield the powerful from the consequences of their immorality, greed, and abuse. When Rachel rejects Mitchell Geary's possessive and abusive "love" for her, he is stunned.

Galilee, by contrast, is an unusual figure as an alternate "true love" interest for Rachel—he is the absent prodigal son of a family of gods and half-gods who is entrapped by a generations-old vow to the Gearys. His seemingly magical powers of seduction are fueled by a power older than money: story. He engages Rachel with a fable as he has seduced men and women before her, and the power of a storyteller is also part of a larger web being spun across the narrative by the author.

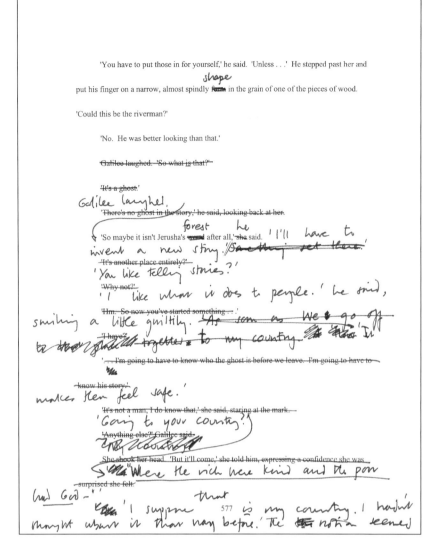

ABOVE

1997 typescript pages
from *Galilee*, hand-
corrected by the author.

The novel takes the form of something like the journal of a writer; readers are told this book is the work of Edmund Maddox, a member of the Barbarossa dynasty who has set out to document the intertwining fates of his family and the Gearys. In that way, the book serves almost as a cautionary tale documenting the highs and lows of writing. "I wanted to write about how I create," Clive explains. "I wanted to tell the story from the point of view of the storyteller. *Galilee* contains innumerable confessions as to my state of mind while I write. Confident one moment, uneasy the next. Filled with visions on a Monday morning. Drained and frustrated by lunchtime."

Using Maddox as a first-person guide, Clive plays the role of a magician who openly reveals how he will construct an illusion while still enticing the audience to watch open-mouthed. Maddox is our inside eye in the Barbarossa family and his self-admitted limitations as a writer, as a journalist, lend him credibility, helping us believe, as he talks of them, that he is indeed a part of a family of gods and demi-gods. He shares his sources as he collects confessions and memories—as fragments of story and style come to him—while weaving a near-omniscient narrative around both families' histories and homes.

The elation and the depression of writing are journaled by Maddox, and it is clear his despair and intellectual compromises are Clive's own when Maddox concludes that "as nothing can be made that isn't flawed, the challenge is twofold: first, not to berate oneself for what is, after all, inevitable; and second, to see in our failed perfection a different thing; a truer thing perhaps, because it contains both our ambition and the spoiling of that ambition."

It's an honest self-assessment of the novel that offers a more restrained central conflict and a subtler use of fantasy than Clive's previous narratives, giving him instead an opportunity to explore a wide array of emotions.

"I wrote the book, and realized that there was so much in the book; so many elements, so many characters—it's set in Samarkand, which is way to the east, it's set in Hawai'i, it's set in New York, it's set in North Carolina, it's set in South Carolina, it's set in all kinds of places. There was just so much going on in the book that what I felt I needed to do was stick it together.

"Maddox Barbarossa," Clive elaborated, "is a cripple, he's a drunkard, he's a cocaine user, he's not a very nice man, and he's wonderful to write—for all those reasons! I'd never done this before;

196

"I guess it's my own
Romeo and Juliet. . . ."

taken on the persona of somebody else and said, 'Well, I'm going to live with this person for'—I guess the last draft took me eight months or nine months—and allowed his personal doubts, his personal convictions and his personal anger to appear on the page."

Kirkus Reviews was intrigued by the cocktail of romance and fantasy, suggesting that, "though its ghoul and demon quotient is comparatively low, this lavishly campy creeper has a legitimate claim to the title of Weirdest Book Yet by the accomplished author of such genre classics as the *Books of Blood* (1988) and *The Damnation Game* (1987). John O'Hara, William Faulkner, and Barbara Cartland might have spent a lost weekend collaborating on this feverish tale of two feuding families whose destinies are catastrophically intertwined."

Armistead Maupin made note of the underlying motifs, writing: "As a writer, I'm always intrigued by Barker's reverence for the power of mythmaking, a theme which pervades much of his work. He sees storytelling as a tool for spiritual growth, a means of making sense of things not just for the reader but for the writer himself. Listen to his narrator in *Galilee*: 'Now I had the answer to the question: what lay at the center of all the threads of my story? It was myself. It wasn't an abstracted recanter of these lives and loves. I was—I *am*—the story itself; its source, its voice, its music. Perhaps to you that doesn't seem like much of a revelation. But for me, it changes everything . . .' The symphonic grace of Barker's prose, his loping, muscular imagination, his sharp eye on the human dilemma—all serve a seamless remarkable whole."

The book's flap copy reads:

Every family has its secrets.

The Gearys are no exception. As rich as the Rockefellers, as glamorous and powerful as the Kennedys, the Geary dynasty has held subtle sway over American life since the Civil War, brilliantly concealing the roots of its influence and the depths of its corruptions.

All that is about to change.

Rachel Pallenberg never dreamed she'd ever meet—much less marry—America's most eligible bachelor, Mitchell Geary. But their wedding is the last time she feels as though she's living a dream come true.

For the Gearys are still at war. Their enemies are another dynasty—the Barbarossas—whose origins lie not in history but in myth, whose influence is felt not in Washington or on the Dow Jones, but in the sensual exchanges of flesh and soul.

When the prodigal prince of the Barbarossa clan, Galilee—who sails the world seldom setting foot on land—falls in love with Rachel, the pent-up loathing between the families erupts in a mutually destructive frenzy. Adulteries are uncovered; insanity reigns.

The secrets are out.

Galilee is a massive tale, mingling the powerful realism of Barker's bestselling *Sacrament* with the dark, genre-breaking invention for which he's known worldwide. The magical eroticism of *Weaveworld*, the chilling rituals of *Hellraiser*, the grand metaphysical visions of the Books of the Art—*Galilee* has room for them all.

POETRY AND PROSE

"Forgive my Art. On bended knees, / I do confess: I seek to please."

"**E**very artist, by and large, has felt that their eyes were wider open than the people to the left and right of them, which I think is the artistic condition," Clive said, in conversation for the publication of *Illustrator II: The Art of Clive Barker* in 1993. "You are seeing, you hope, a little bit more clearly. I think we as a species have to be willfully blind most of the time because it's all very, very painful. It's Eliot, isn't it—'Humankind cannot bear very much reality.' We all have to live in states of limitation to some extent."

Like many teenagers, Clive found writing poetry in school a means of addressing strongly felt emotions in a way that a simple journal entry might not. As Jeanette Winterson writes of discovering T. S. Eliot, "A tough life needs a tough language—and that is what poetry is. That is what literature offers—a language powerful enough to say how it is."

Clive still relishes reciting the poetry he learned as a child both at home and school, including A. A. Milne and John Masefield. It gave him an affinity for phonetics and the musicality of words, which in turn gives his adult prose its distinctive poetic quality. Clive recalls his English teacher, Norman Russell, drawing attention to a piece of homework that exhibited this rhythmic trait.

"The first person who taught me that I did this naturally, and it was a revelation to me, was Norman. I was about fourteen, I wrote a story—instead of compositions we were allowed to write a story. He took one of my stories and he wrote it out again, and it was written in blank verse. And I had no knowledge of doing that, and it was almost completely accurate blank verse. And I know why—we'd been studying Shakespeare; we'd been studying the five-footed line, I had it in my head; I'd probably been reading it before I started to write and there is an element of mimicry in me, which is very dangerous and one of the reasons why I don't read fiction when I'm writing is because I'm a lousy mimic!"

198

'Tell is then.' said the orchard-keeper.

~~Call~~ did. ~~Tell you then~~

"'One part of love is innocence ...'
he said, then hesitated, not certain ~~that this~~ whether this
was the first line or the fifth. He puzzled
over that a moment, concluded that his
judgement was correct, and launched into
the poem afresh, ~~this~~ ~~time~~ ~~with~~ ~~more~~ his
confidence growing with each line, ~~that~~ ~~taking~~ the
deceptive ~~rhythm~~ ~~of~~ simplicity of Mad
~~Money's~~ ~~skill~~ Mad ~~Money's~~ Money's ~~art~~ craft
carrying him along. ~~carrying him on~~

'One part of love is innocence,
'One part of love is guilt,
'One part the milk ~~that~~ that in a sense
'Is soured before it's spilt.
'One part of love is sentiment,
'One part of love is lust,
'One part is the presentiment
'Of our return to dust.'

~~As~~ ~~the~~ The lines finished, he waited
for the judgment of the audience. ~~There~~
was a moment when they simply stared at
him, across the smoky fires, eyes on his

Imitation or not, living in a home where words and music were inextricably linked, as his parents sang show tunes with each other, Clive retained a love of musical narrative. "One of the things I found writing the songs in *Hunters in the Snow* is I've always loved rhyme. Rhyme is poetry's secret weapon; I was, I suppose, a little simplistic in my tastes. I was moved by music, and I want to go onto another thing: the other place I learned poetry was Oscar Hammerstein, who manages to say very, very sophisticated things in very, very simple ways, yes? Two of his pieces deal with racism—*The King and I* and *South Pacific*—'You have to be taught / before it's too late / to hate all the people / your family hate'—now that's pretty strong stuff."

As he grew older, he discovered William Blake and W. B. Yeats and his notebooks became dotted with verse. Some have a lighthearted rhyming humor while others follow a more narrative path, but always his words bear an emotional weight.

> Every story is a journey:
>> out of the light into the dark,
>> out of the air and into the earth,
>> up from the ground and into heaven,
>> Even if the journey leads home again,
>> Can it ever be the same home
>> When the skulls of the travellers
>> Are bursting with Heaven and Hell?

Although Clive's poetry remained largely for his own satisfaction, his distinctive use of language continued to draw comment. Crucial to this is his tendency to read drafts aloud as he reworks them, developing sounds and cadences in his prose that enchant readers. The power of language underpins much of his work, and even in his darkest and most horrific stories Clive introduces phrases that convey profound emotion—as in this opening to a chapter of *The Hellbound Heart*:

> The seasons long for each other, like men and women, in order that they may be cured
> of their excesses.

Occasionally verses surface literally as he gives his characters whole poems and songs. In *Weaveworld*, Cal recites his great-grandfather Mad Mooney's poem and it acts like a spell on the rapt congregation:

> One part of love is innocence,
> One part of love is guilt,
> One part the milk, that in a sense
> Is soured as soon as spilt.
> One part of love is sentiment,
> One part of love is lust,
> One part is the presentiment,
> Of our return to dust.

It is the act of remembering the lines that is critical here for Cal's plotline—and it mirrors how Clive himself delights in sharing verses he has memorized over years of reading. When Marietta wants to seduce a woman in *Galilee*, Maddox knows exactly how to help and reaches for a book of poetry:

> I was a very narrow creature at my heart,
> Until you came.
> None got in and out of me with ease;
> Yet when you spoke my name
> I was unbounded, like the world.

I never felt such fear as then, being so limitless,

When I'd known only walls and whisperings.

I fled you foolishly;

Looked in every quarter for a place to hide.

Went into a bud, it blossomed.

Went into a cloud, it rained.

Went into a man, who died,

And bore me out again,

Into your arms.

Looking at the text of *Sacrament* recently, Clive draws attention to a section of text that makes no announcement at all of its poetic aspiration:

> Communing with the ghosts of heretics and poets he had strode the country from end to end over the years: walked the straight roads where the Behmenists had gone, and heard them call the very earth the face of God; idled in the Malvern Hills, where Langland had dreamed of *Piers Plowman*; strode the flanks of barrows where pagan lords lay in beds of earth and bronze. Not all these sites had noble histories. Some were lamentable places; fields and copses where believers had died for their Christ. At Aldham Common, where Rowland Taylor, the good rector of Hadleigh, had been burnt at the stake, his fire fuelled from the hedgerows that still grew green about the spot; and Colchester, where a dozen souls or more had been cremated in a single fire for a sin of prayer. Then to more obscure spots still; places he'd found only because he listened like a fly at a dying man's mouth. Places where unhallowed men and women had perished for love or faith or both. He envied the dead, very often. Standing in a ploughed field some September, crows cawing in the fleshless trees, he thought of the simplicity of those whose dust was churned in the dirt on his boots, and wished he had been born with a plainer heart.

"This is a piece which stands in many ways completely free of the narrative. It is about the land; it's about England. Now, to me this is not prose in the classic sense, it's the philosophical heart of this book, and I came at this book with a very different feeling: 'Home to England, and the summer almost gone. August's stars had fallen, and the leaves would follow very soon. Riot and rot in speedy succession.'

"*Sacrament* is a book which perhaps more than any other bespeaks its poetic origins; its language is ripe and what I discovered, much to my surprise, frankly, was first that the presence of the characters themselves tended to disappear in these sequences, which indicated to me that I was in a different frame of consciousness. And that I was writing not in the abstract but in an otherness; these segments seem not to be in any way narrative but—I don't know how to describe them—they just speak.

"I do realize that I attempt to write symphonically. I do attempt to bring leitmotifs through and let things go and bring things up again and have chapters where the tempo is short and sharp and swift and then move into longer, more generous sentences.

"Cadence and tone and rhythm and music. You know, every writer worth his salt has a different music and, if you are reading attentively and your heart is open to the reading, then the music goes in and when you put your pen to the paper it's like toe-tapping. I could not write to music because if I was playing jazz or Sibelius they would have completely different effects upon me, and so they are bound to affect the kind of text that I am writing. I very strongly feel the same about other people's writing that, if it's worth a damn, I have to be careful of its influence."

CLIVE AT HOME
AND AT WORK

"Love and Life"

In April 1995, when asked by *Esquire* magazine for a list of his "Top 20 Loves and Hates," Clive put pen to paper and recorded the list opposite.

This list gives an insight into Clive at a point in his life when he had just shot *Lord of Illusions* (but was four months away from its release) and was hard at work on the first draft of *Sacrament*. Notable items on the positive side of the list include film sets but also his new love of oil paint as he worked in his new painting studio at home, his love of Stephen Sondheim's works, and his love of animals, particularly his dog Lola.

Putting the intelligence of animals as compared to humans within a setting of the Big One, the catastrophic earthquake predicted to one day hit the West Coast, Clive had recently written a story called "Animal Life" and had it published in *USA Today*'s weekend magazine in June 1994.

Clive had relocated from London in 1991, moving to Los Angeles with David Dodds, and to be with Malcolm Smith. *GQ* ran a feature in December 1992 about his new life and new location under the headline, "L.A. Gore."

On arrival, he had established a US-based production company called Seraphim, with David Dodds coordinating the day-to-day operations. The team grew, with Clive now working with Anna Miller on film projects. Robb Humphreys was Clive's assistant on *Lord of Illusions* (and appeared onscreen as the demon in Harry D'Amour's flashback). Malcolm Smith and Anna Miller had worked on the Harrowers comics with Clive, and Malcolm had been consulting editor on the Razorline comics, and David would remain the mainstay of Seraphim from the company's inception through to 2004.

The company developed a range of new projects. Over time, Anna Miller left, as did Robb Humphreys (although he would return later, in 2008, to run Seraphim for almost four years). Joe

I LOVE		I HATE
Taboo	1	Feeling my age the morning after
Lola, my German Shepherd: the perfect antidote to Hollywood mind-games	2	Talking about the Big One (in L.A.)
Freezer-thickened Stoli	3	Unforgiving lovers
Readers with well-travelled, loved-to-tatters copies of my books	4	English Sundays
Inventing names for characters and places	5	Hype (and falling for it)
The title sequence from *Barbarella* ("Barbarella, psychedella . . .")	6	"So . . . where do you get your ideas from?"
Miami after a hurricane	7	Critics who haven't read the books they're pronouncing upon
Sex and ritual	8	Natural history documentaries with "aren't animals wacky" music added
Reunions	9	Self-righteousness
Reynard the Fox	10	Lists
"Someone in a Tree" from Sondheim's *Pacific Overtures* (show tune as worldview)	11	Poetry read aloud by actor chappies
Feeling well	12	Stale air
Stories about divinity	13	Bad drag
Conversations with friends	14	Beer, liver, tripe . . .
Silence with friends	15	Forgetting dreams
Film sets before the crew arrives	16	Tears and hiccups
Oil paint (especially blue)	17	Airports (unless I'm coming home)
Beginning . . .	18	Forgetting faces
Twilight	19	Regret
Now	20	Fundamentalists

"I learned many years ago, from Blake and from Lord Dunsany, that there is something marvelous about inventing words."

Daley joined and, later, so did Anthony DiBlasi as Seraphim developed a variety of titles for film and television.

The nature of the setup at Seraphim was a new incarnation of the environment in which Clive revels: an extension of the collaborative, creative hothouse that had been the energy of his group of friends in Liverpool and London and all the film, mime, art, photography, and theatre projects they had undertaken, feeding off each other's enthusiasm and creating individual and collective works.

Clive's sexuality had never been hidden; he had lived as an openly gay man since moving in with John Gregson in Liverpool in the mid-1970s. Clive had moved to London with him, later moving into a home with David Dodds there, then lived with Malcolm Smith in Beverly Hills, but his personal life came to the fore when he did an interview with Charles Isherwood for the February 1995 issue of the *Advocate* magazine. The following month he was the cover feature in *10 Percent* magazine and gave an interview to *Out* magazine. Because he was breaking with an unspoken convention in Hollywood to not be seen as openly gay, other magazines were keen to highlight him; over the next six months *Gay Times*, the *New York Native*, the *San Francisco Sentinel*, *Au Courant*, *TWN*, *Frontiers*, and *Attitude* all ran interviews with him that discussed his sexuality.

As Clive told *Entertainment Weekly* in September 1995, for its feature, "The Gay '90s—Entertainment Comes Out of the Closet": "It just seems like a good time to stand up and be counted. It's important that as many well-known gay men as possible say, 'Yes, I'm gay.' It doesn't turn me into someone who's going to molest your children, folks. It's just an expression of my nature, and you should stop making a big drama of it."

In the spring of 1995, Clive had started work on his novel *Sacrament* (at first called "Last Things"), which features a gay man, Will Rabjohns, as its lead character. Speaking the following year when it was published, he noted, "Will's sexuality is not just an interesting detail, it's central to the theme of the book. But he's also a guy who has lived his life and is saying, 'I don't know what this adds up to.' He captures life on film, but retreats from it. It's one reason I wrote the book because I'm there myself. It was a self-criticism. It was a way to wake myself up, to tell myself, 'Don't just be a witness.'"

Despite successfully working together, notably on comic-related projects, Malcolm and Clive began to grow apart personally. In 1995 their relationship ended and Malcolm moved to Oregon. On Easter Sunday, 1996, Clive met David Armstrong outside the Faultline Bar in Melrose Hill, Los Angeles. They struck up a conversation about their mutual love of art and photography and were later married in November 1997.

Clive's household has always been graced by numerous animals, especially dogs, and Malingo, a green Amazon parrot, joined the family at Christmas 2001 and remains Clive's constant companion in his writing room.

In 2002, a visiting journalist from the *New York Times* described Clive's busy home:

> Barker the impresario is also a bundle of nervous energy, though, and before long he hops up to lead me on an impromptu tour of his three Spanish-style houses, one of which once belonged to the 30's film star Ronald Colman. Barker writes in one of these cliff-side homes; he paints in another; the third he lives in with his partner of seven years, a photographer of erotic nudes named David Armstrong, and sometimes with Nicole, Armstrong's 14-year-old daughter. When you walk into this last house, the cacophony of barks and chirps and squeaks makes it sound as if you've entered a zoo, and to some degree you have—they live with four dogs, tanks full of fish, numerous geckos, a parrot named Malingo and assorted other creatures. Barker particularly wants me to see his rats, some of which he adopted after they'd infiltrated his house. When the rats had babies, he and Armstrong woke up every two hours for weeks to feed them with eyedroppers. "Rats," he says, picking one up and kissing it, "are hugely underappreciated pets."

205

1998 GODS AND MONSTERS

"There are no Monsters here."

"A little while ago," said Clive in late 1996, "a man called Christopher Bram wrote an excellent book called *Father of Frankenstein* which is about the last few months of James Whale's life. James was a great filmmaker who seemed to have a low opinion of the works he made. He directed *Frankenstein* (the original with Karloff), *Bride of Frankenstein*, *The Old Dark House*, and a whole slew of movies including the original movie of *Show Boat* . . . which are all wonderful pictures. In his relatively old age, in his late sixties, he had a stroke and was defuriated. He was a gay man who had been ostracized by Hollywood to some degree. The picture that Bram draws has this man who's really going back over his past and reminiscing about what he had achieved and failed to achieve.

"Bill Condon, who directed *Candyman 2*, was a huge fan of the book, I was a huge fan of the book; I put a quote on the book, so Bill said, 'Do you want to produce this movie if I direct it?' and I said yes. So where we are now is we are trying to get that deal into place. I think it could be very cool. Bill's script brilliantly interweaves the life of this man in the last phases of his life remembering the points of glory, also dealing with the fact of his imminent death."

"Ever since *Candyman 2*," says Bill Condon, "Clive and I had always talked about doing something else. Then I just mentioned to him, 'You wouldn't be interested in doing something that's not based on one of your books, would you?' And, he said, 'Sure!' He was especially excited when I mentioned Whale. I mean, there are such obvious connections between Clive's life and James Whale's. So he generously agreed to become our patron, our godfather—our Coppola, if you will—and attach his name to it and help us get it going. He brought a number of things to this production. First of all, it's as simple as when we met Ian McKellen for the first time, instead of him coming to my little bungalow in Silver Lake, we got to go to Clive's wonderful house in Beverly Hills. I felt like it gave us a certain amount of presence. So, we seemed like we were real and not just Gregg Fienberg, who is the producer, and me. Not that we were two guys up the creek, but being there with Clive, it just sort of made us look like we were more. But that was the smallest thing. It's amazing how delicate these negotiations are and how many times a movie at this level can fall apart,

Ian McKellen Brendan Fraser Lynn Redgrave

gods and monsters

A REGENT ENTERTAINMENT Production In Association with GREGG FIENBERG A BILL CONDON Film IAN MCKELLEN BRENDAN FRASER
LYNN REDGRAVE LOLITA DAVIDOVICH Casting by VALORIE MASSALAS Costume Designer BRUCE FINLAYSON . Music by CARTER BURWELL
Edited by VIRGINIA KATZ Production Designer RICHARD SHERMAN Director of Photography STEPHEN M. KATZ Line Producers JOHN SCHOUWEILER and LISA LEVY
Co-Executive Producers VALORIE MASSALAS SAM IRVIN SPENCER PROFFER Based on the novel "FATHER OF FRANKENSTEIN" by CHRISTOPHER BRAM
Executive Producers CLIVE BARKER and STEPHEN P. JARCHOW Produced by PAUL COLICHMAN GREGG FIENBERG MARK R. HARRIS
Written for the Screen and Directed by BILL CONDON

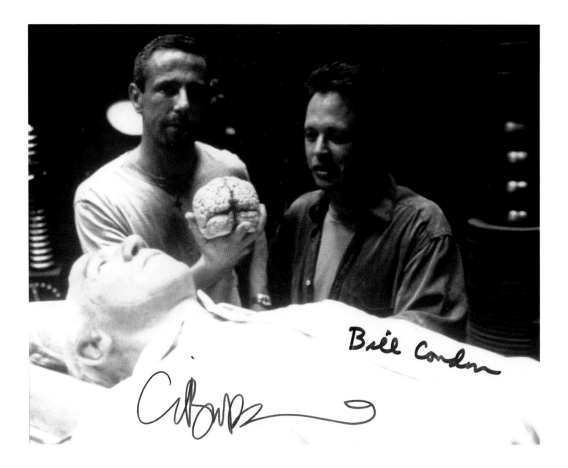

ABOVE

Clive on set with Bill
Condon and a prone
Ian McKellen (as James
Whale), behind the
scenes of *Gods and
Monsters*, 1997.

and Clive was just always there with the right phone call—you know, to kind of keep things going at various points."

"I was a sounding board for Bill at the very beginning of the process," says Clive. "I was then going into meetings with Bill and saying to people, 'Look, you know who I am. Let me introduce you to Bill Condon. He's a really good guy and he's a guy who will deliver us this picture on budget.' What I basically did was offer a portrait of Bill even though he was sitting in the room with us. I needed to get people to understand who Bill was and that I had great faith in him. And later on I sat with Bill and persuaded Ian McKellen to do the picture. I called up Brendan Fraser's agents and said we really want him for the movie. All that behind-the-scenes stuff."

Brendan Fraser agreed to play Clayton Boone, James Whale's gardener, saying later, "I knew that this film had no money, very little time and its working title was 'The Untitled Piece with Ian McKellen' and that's all I needed to know."

Ian McKellen played James Whale, noting, as the movie was released in late 1998, "Whale was born within fifty miles of where I was born. He was an actor for much longer than he was a director; he didn't start directing until he was forty-two. So he's from a world that I understood. And he was a gay man in Hollywood, like me. [The film] is about a man who's dying. He has stopped living, and he's trying to take control of his death, organize it. En route, it's fascinating, because you get a sense of what Hollywood was like, not just in the fifties but in the thirties. It's as good a backstage story as any I've read about what it's like to be a filmmaker."

"Here was a man who reinvented himself, in a way," agrees Clive about James Whale. "Here was a man with a working-class history who turned himself, for a period of time, into Hollywood nobility. He was there at the heart of Hollywood during one of its most glamorous periods and seems to have been, as far as we can understand, pretty out about his life—though I think he ended up paying a price for that. . . ."

Getting an independent movie about the later stages of a gay filmmaker's life financed was not the easiest sell in Hollywood. Clive recalls, "When you're going after very different constituencies—a

"Condon movies are packed with memorable set pieces. I always like the sight of Whale floating in his pool at the end. . . . The resulting effect as [he] elegantly floats, waving goodbye almost, is my favorite shot in the movie."
—Ian McKellen

gay constituency, a horror constituency, an old Hollywood constituency—people would say, 'I don't know who it is for.' The truth is it plays for all three and a whole heap more. It has real crossover potential. Unfortunately, the failure of *Ed Wood* commercially did us a lot of harm. It was a fun movie, but it didn't do its business. So over and over again we went to people with this project and they'd say, 'Oh, it's *Ed Wood*!' And we would say, 'No, no, no, it isn't *Ed Wood*. *Ed Wood* is wonderful, but this is not *Ed Wood*.' That was definitely a problem."

The movie was financed, however, and principal photography started in July 1997. Ian McKellen and Brendan Fraser were joined by Lynn Redgrave as Hanna, James Whale's housekeeper. Lolita Davidovich played Betty, Boone's ex-girlfriend. David Dukes and Kevin J. O'Connor, who had been leads in *Rawhead Rex* and *Lord of Illusions* respectively, also had roles.

Stephen M. Katz was director of photography, as he had been on Bill Condon's debut feature, *Sister, Sister*, as well as on *The Blues Brothers*. Carter Burwell provided the score.

"This is a lovely movie," reflected Clive shortly after its January 21, 1998, debut screening at the Sundance Film Festival. "It's the first movie . . . I've been connected with which should get good reviews from the *L.A. Times* and the *New York Times*. It's a beautifully performed, beautifully paced meditation."

The movie opened in theaters in the US on November 4, 1998, after playing at several more film festivals. It was indeed a critical success, going on to garner multiple award nominations and wins.

Ian McKellen and Lynn Redgrave were both nominated for Screen Actors Guild Awards, Golden Globes, and Academy Awards, with Lynn Redgrave also nominated for a BAFTA. Ian McKellen won Best Actor at the British Independent Film Awards and several other awards, Lynn Redgrave took the Golden Globe for Best Performance by a Supporting Actress, and at the Academy Awards on March 21, 1999, Bill Condon won the Oscar for Best Adapted Screenplay.

Getting financing for a movie about the waning years of a gay man's life had been difficult but, as Ian McKellen noted wryly, "When the history of our sexual morality is written, this will be remembered as the year when an American president became even more popular despite his sex life, and *Gods and Monsters* was nominated for three Oscars."

THE ESSENTIAL CLIVE BARKER

"Stories within stories, worlds within worlds."

*T*he Essential Clive Barker: Selected Fictions was outlined as a celebratory retrospective volume of Clive's written work to date. Tasked with selecting the texts he most wanted to include, Clive explained his approach:

"I went to Kaua'i . . . and I sat in a house beside the beach and I read everything. And I went through it all very slowly and I asked myself in a quiet time, 'What are the most important things for me?'

"I had thought it would be simple to put together. . . . Of course, in your natural arrogance, you believe everything is essential. But when you look at it, you see there are a lot of themes you return to because they answer some deep psychological need. So I was able to see thematic material."

Having made his final selections, Clive said in a UK television interview, "These are my choices, these are my personal visions of what Clive Barker has done which is worthwhile. And I wrote this big essay trying to pull it all together to give people an idea of my obsessions. I think it's a book which catalogues my obsessions.

"If, in twenty years' time, we look at this interview, we're going to say, 'Oh, *that's* who we were,' and in a way that's what it felt like looking at the books and trying to make choices from them. It was a question of saying, 'Well, who was I twenty years ago?'"

Clive's extended essay introduces the collection and answers some of the questions as to how and why he writes:

> People are curious, I think, about how a writer makes a world. The process is assumed to
> be very different from the writing of a so-called realistic novel. In my experience, that's

"The truth is, any intellectual grasp I have upon my fiction, and the context of my fiction, is framed inside a *telling*. I have no means at my disposal but to say: this happened, then this, then this."

true. When I write about places I know—the Hebridean island of Tiree, for instance, in *Sacrament*, or Liverpool in *Weaveworld*, or London or New York—I write quickly, reporting to the page scenes which play out in my mind's eye. I'm almost a journalist. When the narrative is removed to new worlds, however, the rhythm of working changes completely. Very seldom does the scene I'm attempting to create spring immediately into my head. It's misty at first; I have a *feeling* about it, little more. The first exploratory paragraphs are likely to be about that feeling; they seldom make it to a final draft.

The Essential Clive Barker collects his work into thirteen thematic chapters, each briefly introduced by Clive, and brings together whole short stories as well as extracts from his plays and major novels. The choices are indicative of his growth toward a more contemplative depth in his writing.

"I think I've chosen, by and large, things which are perhaps more meditative in tone than I would have done, say, five years ago," Clive says. "Both *Galilee* and *Sacrament* are more meditative in tone and more philosophical in tone and more willing to indulge in digressions in service of metaphysics than previous books. There's metaphysics in *Weaveworld* but it's pretty much subsumed."

Reflecting on the collection, he said, "It gives you that thing that all artists need at some point, a sense of achievement. I think that it is very important that we as artists accept that your voice changes. What I've learned is that many of the things about the work from an earlier time I did not like, but sometimes it's really just about putting it out there. I think it's important to be at peace with that. So when I look at *The Essential*, I look at a lot of work that is very remote from who I am now but also feels, in the nicest way, like a sort of memory of some other fellow I knew once and liked in some ways and disliked in other ways. . . . I don't miss him, and one reason I don't is because he wrote those stories and served his purpose. Part of what allows me to move on is to look back and say, 'I enjoyed that, but I don't want to do that anymore.' I'm infinitely happier than that dark, brooding, and sometimes lonely fellow."

Although Clive shifts seemingly effortlessly from genre to genre—writing a fable one moment, a romance, a fantasy the next—this collection makes it clear that it's all one story.

"I've spent my creative life so far first in the theatre, then on the page, then on the screen, examining what is turning out as I grow older to look like one enormous landscape.

"What I originally thought were different worlds turn out to be one interconnected place. And like a bedspread viewed by a sick child from his pillow, I am very aware that there are colors in various corners which I know very well, but I haven't yet found the ways to get from the blue to the green and from the green to the red.

"I've just begun, and I suppose that's become my preoccupation—the idea that at one point I will see it clearly."

In his foreword to the collection, Armistead Maupin sums up his reaction to Clive's work:

What lingered with me was the absolute authority of Barker's voice. He wrote with the easy confidence of a tribal storyteller, an elder who had seen everything and committed most of it to scripture. And every novel of his I've read since has been imbued with the same quality, the same biblical certitude. Somehow, through an alchemy other writers can only envy, even Barker's most bizarre tales have the ring of history to them, a core of ancient truth that allows us—no, compels us—to follow him anywhere.

1999   **EROTIC SHORT STORIES**

"All channels are open."

In May 1998, Clive drafted a running order for a new collection of short stories. The list contained seven previously published short stories and twenty new pieces, including an untitled Harry D'Amour/Hellraiser story, four autobiographical pieces, two science fiction pieces, called "Berlin" and "Ordinary Joe," and two pieces of erotica, called "Wanton" and "The Golden Bed."

He told interviewers that he was excited to return to the short story format, saying, "I'm working on another collection of short stories for adults. This should be out after *Galilee*. You know, it's great fun! I'd forgotten what fun it is to do stories that you can finish in three weeks as opposed to fourteen months. It's very gratifying to complete material in that time frame. What I'm trying to do in this collection is to cross back and forth across the generic boundaries. You'll have some horror, some science fiction, fantasy, et cetera . . . It's really a reflection of the range of writing that I have been doing in the last few years. I'm also going to be revisiting some of my old mythologies, which will be big fun.

"I had a hard time persuading my publisher to let me do a collection of short stories but my approach was 'Well, I've done *Everville*, *Sacrament*, and now *Galilee*, and they're all huge novels.' So I said, 'Guys, give me a break. I've been a good soldier here, writing these big novels, and having a great time doing it. But I now have twenty really cool ideas for short stories, and I really need to write them. Otherwise I'll go crazy!' Finally they said, 'Go to it.'"

The date 1999 appears on a large number of manuscripts and typescripts as Clive worked on multiple storylines rather than a single novel. A complete draft of "Haeckel's Tale" and a "Valerie on the Stairs" treatment are marked "1999" alongside drafts of an intense story called "Jehovah's Bitch." Clive was also deep into a novella called *Coldheart Canyon*, which he would expand into a full-length novel over the course of 1999.

Alongside these narratives, also dated 1999, are multiple, mostly erotic, complete short stories ranging in length from 120 words ("Whistling in the Dark") to 1,914 words ("Dollie"). The profusion of them—and their different tone from the other short stories—suggested a new project, a collection that would showcase his erotic fiction alongside images from his most recent art exhibitions, *One*

Sloughing off skins during sex.

Flesh and *The Weird and the Wicked*, as well as other previously unpublished artwork. With the Harry D'Amour/Hellraiser story still untitled—and not part of this separate book's contents—Clive titled the erotic collection "The Scarlet Gospels."

"My love for the pornographic," he noted, "or a Lucio Fulci film or a piece of frozen sculpture or something else that is roughly done—is me trying to build a relationship of trust with an aesthetic which is not my natural aesthetic. My natural aesthetic is to be piss-elegant, overthinking, over-polished. *Imajica* is a book where I gave in to all those instincts, and I love that book as a consequence. But this love of the more crude—it's part of the energy of these things, these gouged things, these argumentative things. . . .

"I put out the 'Scarlet Gospels' stuff at HarperCollins. I showed them fifteen pictures, some images that I would build the stories around. They all backed off to the edges of the room. They were appalled. It was fascinating. You would think that something radio-active had just been put on the table. There are very stark things there. I'm very proud of them. . . ."

Taking the project to Callaway Editions, which had produced Madonna's *Sex* book some years earlier, he offered in a draft press release quote, "'The Scarlet Gospels' won't be a safe book. It will appeal, as my fiction and films do, to an audience that wants to explore that fascinating territory between what arouses fascination in us, and what makes us sweat with fear."

Callaway Editions's press sheet said:

Clive Barker—novelist, filmmaker, painter, master of horror and fantasy—turns his hand, for the first time, to a revelatory confessional of his own erotic fantasies. *The Scarlet Gospels*, written in Barker's voice, is also lavishly illustrated with the author's full-color paintings and black and white drawings.

Upon these pages is held the gospel—the gospel according to Clive Barker, that is. Which means readers are in for quite a ride, but a ride that has more to do with descending into darkness than salvation. The all-new stories, or word vignettes, are woven loosely together in a series that resembles dream sequences, and can be read as one convoluted narrative, if the reader so chooses, or as distinct passages. Together the words and pictures create a compelling sexual mosaic.

Barker's best-selling novels contain multi-layered, multi-faceted themes and plots— like threads they weave their way in and out of the narrative. A dark, ecstatic celebration of the flesh, the text here is part hallucinatory, part fantastical, part rational. Barker's imagination draws the reader into a world of forbidden passion where primitive urges are satiated and there are no vices, only pleasures. The primal energy of his stark, erotic, sometimes brutal paintings reflects the more primitive themes of the narrative. Here is the fine line between the sacred and the profane, between "spiritual vision and sinful frenzy."

The intimately sized hardcover gives this confessional the feel of a diary, which, once discovered, is impossible to resist. Intensely colored, intensely written, *Scarlet Gospels* is a fantastic, glittering jewel of exquisite erotica that will open readers' minds to worlds they never knew existed.

"It's confessional and immense fun. I do it without self-censorship. I call it my spontaneous mode."

Clive assembled a package of fifty-six paintings and painted-on photographs and ten texts for Callaway in January 1999 with a note that the book would eventually comprise forty short texts and one hundred images.

"This is cutting-edge Clive Barker," he said about the book later that year. "What I would really like to do is something erotic, and strongly and unapologetically erotic, and comprehensively erotic. I wanted every conceivable element of the human erotic urge; gay, straight, and then some. So what we are constructing is a book which will have about a hundred illustrations, paintings, photographs, and drawings. There will be perhaps forty pieces of fiction, some of them very short, some of them longer, all of them very sexy. The idea is that we will have a kind of compendium of erotica which is both imagistic and literary. I believe it will be laid out in a way which I think will be completely fresh and interesting. I'm very excited by the project because I believe it's going into new territories, not just for me, I'm speaking generally. There's not an awful lot of us that are around making paintings and writing. The chance to do something where you can pull those areas together and make a single statement, using painting, photography, and writing . . . I want to thank Callaway for giving me the chance to do this. HarperCollins has bought the book from Callaway, so Callaway will create it and Harper will distribute it.

"My original editor had rejected it. He thought it was too strong for HarperCollins's tastes. Since that time, it's nearly a year and a half since he said that, the feeling at Harper towards me and my work has changed incredibly for the better. I have a new editor, Paul McCarthy, who is marvelous. There are new people heading up HarperCollins; Cathy Hemming, who is a wonderful lady and really understands my vision completely and what I want to do. She understands the commitment I have to make work which crosses boundaries. As soon as she heard this book was available, she said. 'I want this.'

"This is going to be in many regards an extreme book. There are a lot of eye-popping images and ideas. I have delivered ten or eleven of the short stories and the response is really strong, which is great and what I want. So that's 'The Scarlet Gospels.'"

By late 1999, Clive had turned his attention to writing *Coldheart Canyon* and the remaining thirty or so short stories were set aside. In April 2000, he signed up with Disney for a trilogy of Abarat movies and moved into writing the first of the Abarat books. By January 2002, having been focused on other writing projects in the meantime, the collection had changed and Callaway had exited the project.

Now the projected contents page of "The Scarlet Gospels" contained, in addition to the erotic stories, a number of pieces of fiction from the previously separate short story collection in the works, as well as some nonfiction essays. The artwork pieces were no longer part of the planned lineup. Among the forty-three pieces were two titular stories: "The Scarlet Gospels: Rael's Confession" and "The Scarlet Gospels: The Last Hellraiser Story." The latter of these—posited as a short novella in 2001 and 2002—would be the next of Clive's works to outgrow its original intended length by becoming a novel. Ultimately, the demands of writing this novel and of the Abarat series put the erotic stories—and the collection itself—on ice.

The first part of "Rael's Confession" appeared subsequently in 2003 in David Armstrong's photography book, *Rare Flesh*. The remainder of the erotic pieces, along with other erotic poetry, appeared as the *Tonight, Again* collection from Subterranean Press in 2015.

2001 COLDHEART CANYON

"It is night in Coldheart Canyon, and the wind comes off the desert."

In August 1999, in the midst of writing short stories and starting work in earnest on *Coldheart Canyon*, Clive returned to Liverpool to be with his father, who would soon lose his battle with leukemia. The devastation of his father's death triggered a return of Clive's depression and made writing increasingly difficult.

"In my early twenties I was first visited by a species of profound depression whose shadow I have never completely shaken off. The period after my dad's death was extremely dark. I seem to have in my life periods of great darkness followed by sudden periods of lucidity. Some of that is to do with the fact that I am a dark person in many regards. It's a fact of life. I mean, you lose a parent and you are going to go into the dark times. There's no way of avoiding that. The only way to avoid it is not to love."

Steeling himself to complete UK appearances in support of *The Essential Clive Barker*, by the end of 1999 he was back home and referring to *Coldheart Canyon* in interviews as a short novel. It wasn't many months before he had a full-size novel on his hands that would open with a poignant prologue drawn from the view from his windows in the canyon where he lives in Beverly Hills.

Perhaps it isn't just that the leaves and petals are bitter. Perhaps there are too many whisperings in the air around the ruined gazebos, and the animals are unnerved by what they hear. Perhaps there are too many presences brushing against their trembling flanks as they explore the clotted pathways. Perhaps, as they graze the overgrown lawns, they look up and mistake a statue for a pale fragment of life, and are startled by their error, and take flight.

Perhaps, sometimes, they are not mistaken.

"The original thing had been, I don't know, fifty thousand, sixty thousand words, I suppose," Clive explained, "and it had been originally told entirely from Todd's point of view. It was really going to

"One ripping ghost story, spooky and suspenseful.... A ferocious indictment of (and backhanded tribute to) Hollywood Babylon, depicted through Barker's glorious imagination.... One of the most accomplished, and most notable, novels of the year."

—*Publishers Weekly* (starred and boxed review)

Coldheart Canyon

a hollywood ghost story

"Clive Barker is Hell's anatomist, and with scalpel brilliance dissects Hollywood, twisted gut to heart of Darkness." —Wes Craven

On sale October 2, 2001

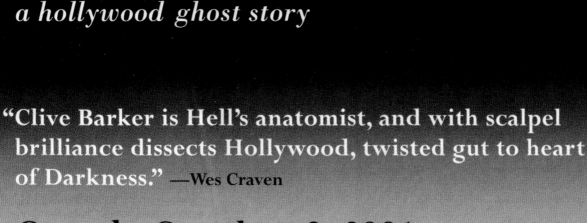

 HarperCollins*Publishers*
www.harpercollins.com

ALSO AVAILABLE FROM HARPERCOLLINS | HarperAudio • PerfectBound e-book

Author Photo ©David Armstrong

"Coldheart Canyon left me with the familiar feeling, a frightening reminder of why I moved away from the canyons of Hollywood to the Valley." —JONATHAN DAVIS

be a very simple book about a rather narcissistic actor in Hollywood who encounters some ghosts and we're not sure at the end of the short story or the novella . . . whether he's really seen them or whether he hasn't. That was the book."

Clive happily admits to loving books that offer a multitude of ideas rather than a single anchoring focus. As the many varied denizens of Hollywood all had stories and secrets and shades of melancholy to explore, he was tempted by more than just Todd Pickett's narrative.

"As I got into it I realized these ghosts are sort of really interesting and I want to write about them because they represent old Hollywood and here I have a chance not only to talk about new Hollywood but also to talk about old Hollywood and to contrast their methodologies and to talk about Hollywood in a much more rounded way than I had originally anticipated. So it was a judgment call made out of ambition, I think, just to tell a better story."

While the characters may seem somewhat familiar to those in Hollywood circles, Clive has remained circumspect about who might have been his inspirations. One character, however, was based on a good friend he'd first met at a convention.

"The gay man in *Coldheart Canyon*," Clive revealed to the audience at the *Los Angeles Times* Festival of Books in 2000, "is a part of old Hollywood. He's my friendly nod to a man I knew very well, Roddy McDowall, who I loved and, as you know, passed away recently. There's a little of Roddy in this character of Jerry Brahms. He's seen the inside of Hollywood, as Roddy has. He was a child actor, as Roddy was.

"Jerry is actually the cultural historian of *Coldheart Canyon*. He's the character who carries the weight of history. His humanity is rooted in this moment he had in his childhood of being a star. And then having that snatched away from him. That's the difference, of course, between him and Roddy. Roddy continued to be a very well-known actor right to the end of his life.

"I didn't realize how much I wanted to say about Hollywood. What's been interesting about writing it is . . . I've got a lot of feelings about this place; very complicated feelings, by no means straightforward feelings at all, a lot of love/hate relationship stuff in there."

Marketed as a "Hollywood ghost story," the novel had the potential to reach beyond Clive's traditional readership, with the glamour of Hollywood past and present set against a promise of darkness revealed. Clive was able to draw upon his own experience not only of working there but more particularly of living in the hills above Los Angeles, such that the narrative navigates its way around the city in the hands of a native rather than a sightseer.

"It does say something about the way the writers and artists are treated. Which I believe is completely true because it's my experience with this place. On the other hand there are times the novel evokes the magic of this place. The magic of California, the magic of the sky, a certain time of day, the smell in the air. The poetry of the book, if you will, lies in its description of landscape, and the bittersweet stuff is very much in the way human beings treat other human beings.

"In this book, as in no other I have written, I move back and forth between a world of wild fantasy and the world I live in. When I look out my bedroom window I see Coldheart Canyon; at night, when the coyotes start to howl on the other side of the hill, I feel a pleasurable shudder of recognition."

Clive gives Willem Zeffer—disenchanted manager to 1920s movie star Katya Lupi—the lines he himself has felt from time to time when Hollywood has been particularly resistant to his ideas:

> He had lived in Paris, Rome and London and briefly Cairo in his forty-three years; and had promised himself that he would leave Los Angeles—where there was neither art nor the ambition to make art . . . and come back to Europe; find a house with some real history on its bones, instead of the fake Spanish mansion [Katya's] fortune had allowed her to have built in one of the Hollywood canyons.

Clive has always shared his life with animals, so following the Northridge earthquake in Los Angeles in 1994 he was prompted to write the short tale, "Animal Life," set in Coldwater Canyon.

"When we enter the world of fantasy—and I'm talking now about horror fiction and invented-world fiction and science fiction too—are we maybe attempting a return, at least imaginatively, to a time when we could look at our pet dog and almost imagine ourselves inside the dog's head? I speak about dogs particularly because I always had dogs when I was a kid, and I still dream of dogs all the time, always with this terrible sense of loss attached, because in your dream state you understand a secret language of some kind, which is lost when you wake. . . . It's like the dream state which is made reference to time and again in fairy stories, of being in the enchanted wood and finally understanding what the birds are saying."

In *Coldheart Canyon*, Clive revisits the closeness of that emotional relationship, writing a moving sequence for Todd and his dog Dempsey. Clive's love of art also comes into play as he injects the power of a single work to encompass a "world of perpetual twilight" directly into the heart of the novel, daring the reader not to believe in its imagery.

Two and a half years after the death of his dad, Clive reflected, "I was sitting in this chair I am sitting in right now, two minutes ago, and I was listening to some music, and I suddenly looked down at my right hand. And my right hand was quietly conducting the music in exactly the way my father used to. I looked at my hand and thought, 'Look at you.' My eyes filled with tears, and I missed him, but he's here with me. We disagreed about ten thousand things, but he shaped me. And his ability to argue and debate is hugely important to me still. His great rationalness, his great calm, and great kindness, all these things I hope I have in some measure."

Publishers Weekly called the novel, "One ripping ghost story, spooky and suspenseful. . . . A ferocious indictment of (and backhanded tribute to) Hollywood Babylon, depicted through Barker's glorious imagination. . . . One of the most accomplished, and most notable, novels of the year."

Meanwhile, Kim Newman—writing for *The Independent*—described it as "big and untidy, like most Barker novels, this is less precious than some, with streaks of old-fashioned gruesome horror, and the author's brand of audacious imagery—Katya appears at one point clothed entirely in live snails. Sometimes, dancing between disciplines, Barker appears to shut out all but an exclusive audience, but here—as the apparent protagonists are destroyed one hundred pages from the end, allowing real people to take centre stage—he tells a story for Tammy Lauper rather than Katya Lupi."

The book's flap copy reads:

> Hollywood has made a star of Todd Pickett. But time is catching up with him. He doesn't have the perfect looks he had last year. After plastic surgery goes awry, Todd needs somewhere to hide away for a few months while his scars heal.
>
> As Todd settles into a mansion in Coldheart Canyon—a corner of the city so secret it doesn't even appear on any map—Tammy Lauper, the president of his fan club, comes to the City of Angels determined to solve the mystery of Todd's disappearance. Her journey will not be an easy one. The closer she gets to Todd the more of Coldheart Canyon's secrets she uncovers: the ghosts of the A-list stars who came to the Canyon for wild parties; Katya Lupi, the cold-hearted, now-forgotten star for whom the Canyon was named, who is alive and exquisite after a hundred years; and, finally, the door in the bowels of Katya's dream palace that reputedly open up to another world, the Devil's Country. No one who has ever ventured to this dark, barbaric corner of hell has returned without their souls shadowed by what they'd seen and done.
>
> Mingling an insider's view of modern Hollywood with a wild streak of visionary fantasy, *Coldheart Canyon* is a book without parallel: an irresistible and unmerciful picture of Hollywood and its demons, told with all the style and raw narrative power that have made Clive Barker's books and films a phenomenon worldwide.

1996– PAINTING THE ABARAT
2002

"There are no words in the Abarataraba."

As he prepared for the *One Flesh* exhibition in 1996, Clive had been intent on painting suitably erotic imagery but, as he recalls, "a funny thing happened. . . . Out of the blue I began to paint rather different kinds of pictures. The first one was of a man in a yellow suit, with a pile of hats on his head and a scowl on his face, standing in front of a nondescript landscape. Except for this fact: there were two strange cats staring at him from a little distance, assessing him.

"The painting seemed to beg for some kind of explanation. So I supplied the man in the yellow suit with the name Kaspar Wolfswinkel, which seemed to match him. He was a thief, I decided; in custody. The hats piled on his head he had stolen, and he was planning to use them to render himself invisible and escape the authorities. And the cats? Well, that was easy. They were there to keep Wolfswinkel from slipping far. In the world of Kaspar Wolfswinkel, I had already explained to myself, cats could see through any spells a minor wizard like Wolfswinkel might throw up.

"The fragment fascinated me. And I wanted to create more."

By the time Clive returned to the La Luz de Jesus Gallery for a Halloween show, *The Weird and the Wicked*, in 1998, there were hints of just how much more. Hanging on the walls of the gallery, alongside painted photographs of male nudes and new erotic work, were more than a dozen small portraits of similarly strange characters.

He toyed with the idea of them illustrating a collection of twenty-four stories he was planning called "Book of Hours" (one for each hour of the day), but the work grew far beyond twenty-four illustrations, most of which were rendered on large 48" × 60" canvases.

"For the next year or so that's what I did," Clive explained later to his publisher, "I painted, and as I painted I let the stories develop in my imagination. At this stage I believe I thought I would write a collection of fairy tales, using perhaps thirty pictures.

"Thirty!

"Little did I know that my imagination had more ambitious plans for the project. Thirty pictures became fifty. Fifty paintings became a hundred.

"The Belgian painter Paul Klee says that drawing is like taking a line for a walk. By this I think he means that you can't plan it. You just follow the pencil. Follow the brush. So that's what I did. And what emerged was like nothing I had painted before in my life. It was as though a whole world of creatures and landscapes and characters had been waiting to be expressed and now had their opportunity. Michael Crichton has that line in *Jurassic Park*, 'Life will find a way.' Well, dreams will find a way too. Imagination will find a way.

"I stopped, and I thought, 'This isn't a book of short stories. This is a whole invented world. Everything I'm painting belongs *in* that world.' "

And that world became known as Abarat.

Clive had known Joanna Cotler, publisher of her own imprint within the children's books division of HarperCollins, since 1991 and in early 1998 he shared his most recent paintings and his outline storyline with her. Together they began to plan how they might publish a series of books set in this new world of Abarat. But the work suggested potential for a wider audience still, and in late 1999, Clive's agent Ben Smith also came up to view the growing gallery of canvases.

"My agent at ICM, who is a visionary fellow, came and saw these paintings and I started to break down to him what the story was. He said, 'This is the new Star Wars,' and I said, 'I don't know about that but I know that I would love to find a movie life for these characters.' So we had thirty-six presentations to studios.

"It became very clear, very quickly, that there were two absolutely major players in all of this: Disney and DreamWorks. Showing those pictures at that time was one of the greatest experiences of my life. What was wonderful was having these folks come into my house, instead of going to them. For the first time in my life they were coming to me. They were coming into my house and looking at the work. And when they came in through the door, instantly they got it. Harvey Weinstein was extraordinarily articulate and wonderful. Mr. Katzenberg was remarkable. He sat on the floor with his legs crossed and said, 'Tell me the story.' It was really quite an exciting time in my life. I was showing myself as I really am, not the horrormeister they had often invited into their ranks, but somebody who dreamt with his eyes open. I think they liked seeing that part of me, and I liked them seeing it."

222

"Barker's art is not the carefully drafted work of, say, Maurice Sendak or Walter Moers. Instead, the rich oil paintings that fill Abarat are muscular, expressionist, often frightening: unconstrained by mimetic realism or cutesy-pie kiddy-lit condescension." —CHINA MIÉVILLE

Having explained the opening arc of the Abarat narrative, April 2000 saw the announcement that Clive's canvases had clinched a deal with the Walt Disney Company, securing the as-yet-unwritten volumes of Abarat for a series of films, merchandise, and an island at Disney World.

Although the printed reproductions in the Abarat books promised to remain striking, Clive was keen to allow the scale and impact of the full-size canvases to be experienced. He booked gallery space at the Pacific Design Center in Los Angeles for a six-week exhibition between September and November 2002, as the first Abarat volume was being released.

For most people, this was the first chance to see the canvases up close, to walk through a wonderland that visitors to Clive's studio had been experiencing for the past six years. He was at his happiest when he could share the paintings with younger readers.

"It was wonderful," he says, "to see people in front of the pictures with big grins on their faces, and this is really, in many cases, people who'd not read the book. There was one wonderful moment when I walked around and saw a boy of maybe five standing in front of the triptych of the islands. Here's a tiny little kid and this enormous canvas and his eyes were huge and I just stood quietly beside him and he didn't even know I was watching him, watching it. And that was worth the effort right there!"

Creating such a large number of near life-size canvases was, however, causing a number of practical problems. For every new character or landscape, a huge oil painting would occupy Clive's studio, needing a space to dry and then space to house it. As his painting studio became swamped, he slowly transformed the top floor of his guesthouse into a walk-in Abaratian gallery.

Guests, friends, and journalists would all marvel at the colorful characters and creatures who greeted their visit and Clive would tell their stories as he walked about the rooms, which became filled with vivid canvases stacked all around.

"Everywhere we look, are the Abarat paintings," enthused one journalist in 2001, who went on to say:
> There's one depicting an elfin creature with google eyes, scoop-shaped ears and little heads sprouting from his thick antlers. There are beings angelic and demonic, plant people and a red-haired goddess and a wise-looking cat with a cavern in its torso. A clown-like figure, electricity crackling around his body, grins savagely. An old man, perhaps an old salt, perhaps a seer, pushes his hands into his coat pockets and looks at us.
>
> It's as if another, more wondrous world has penetrated into ours, emerging from every available inch of Barker's wall space, a world of intense colors, yellows, purples, oranges, inhabited by creatures charming, dangerous, awesome, always surprising. In an alien woods backdropped by golden clouds embedded with stars, a young girl in pigtails gathers stalks, each a thin reed topped by the head of a bird. Elsewhere, a man with hair of flames and sewn lips glowers, and a great stone island in the shape of a head thrusts upward from a dark sea.
>
> Seeing these paintings makes you feel like Dorothy when she opened the door of her Kansas farmhouse to behold the Technicolor Land of Oz."

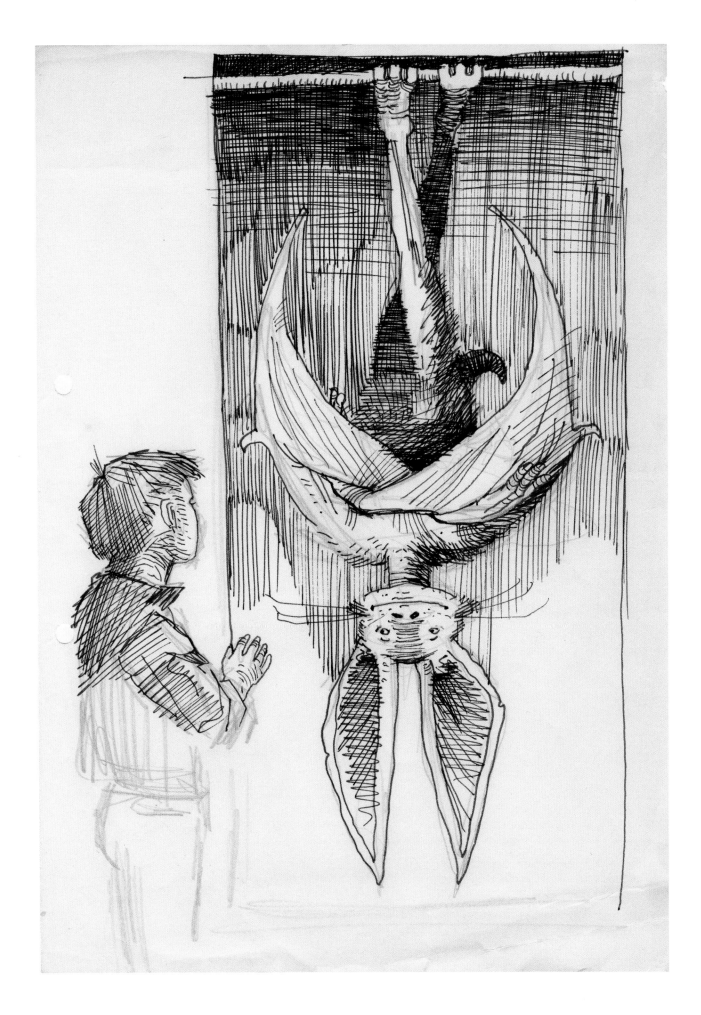

OPPOSITE PAGE
In 1993, Clive worked on a project as a potential Saturday morning cartoon called *Borsch Bat* for Fox television. Although the project never took off, several designs remain.

TOP
Clive drawing at home, 2001.

BOTTOM
In 1997, Scott Bakula (who had earlier played Harry D'Amour in *Lord of Illusions*) visited Clive's home and the pair were captured in this photograph in Clive's art studio.

OPPOSITE PAGE

Christopher Carrion's grandmother, Thant Yayla Carrion—known as Mater Motley—bearing the needle and thread with which she had sewed her grandson's lips together, for daring to speak the word "love," 1999.

TOP LEFT

The fearless warrior, Geneva Peachtree, 1999.

TOP RIGHT

Two Shamans Sharing Thoughts, 2004.

LEFT

Christopher Carrion, who recycles nightmares between his mind and the tank around his collar, is a pivotal character in the narrative of the Abarat. *Christopher Carrion in Old Age*, 1999.

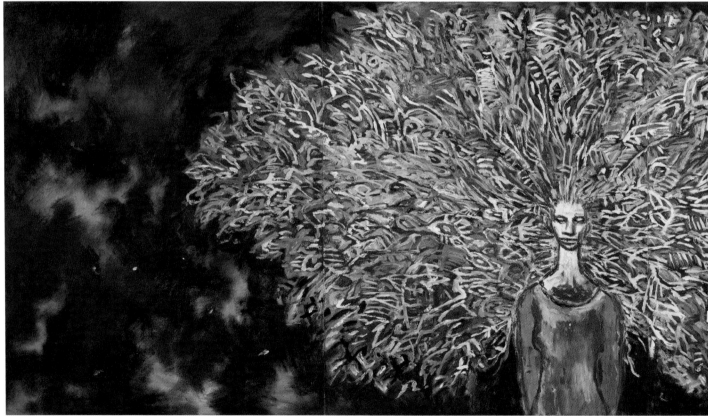

TOP LEFT

The Whisper, pre-2010.

TOP RIGHT

Untitled, a glyph design,
2007.

BOTTOM LEFT

*Woman with Peacock
Hair*, 2004.

BOTTOM RIGHT

*Three Beasts Devouring
Each Other*, 2004.

228

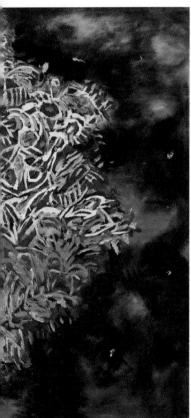

NEXT SPREAD, LEFT, TOP

Demons of Night and Day, circa 1999.

NEXT SPREAD, LEFT, BOTTOM

The Palace of Rain Lantern, 2006.

NEXT SPREAD, RIGHT

Nonce Palace with Dragon Road, 1999.

229

2002 ABARAT

"I dreamed a limitless book."

"I wanted to create a place where I could play almost endlessly and never run out of room."

While at school, Clive had written a number of short tales—including an illustrated fable called "The Wood on the Hill" and a magical fantasy, "The Candle in the Cloud," but earlier still he had drawn an imagined world for "The Impossible Tale of . . . 'Shocking Pink,' " which Clive remarks has "spooky" similarities to the Abarat.

Recalling the stories, Clive says, "Poe—'[The] Mask of the Red Death'—is clearly there and I think some of the shorter pieces of Tolkien, the pieces that went into the Tom Bombadil tales. Those were the first things where I thought, 'Oh—I could do something like that,' because it was short enough to feel I could get my head around it. . . . I remember doing copies of perhaps two or three of the illustrations for one of my father's best pals—Mr. Finkler at BICC—because he liked them so much. And I remember that being quite a big deal because I think he gave me five pounds! It was like the gods had dropped in!"

In the mid-nineties, Clive developed the idea of creating an illuminated Book of Hours—perhaps a series of interconnected stories, each reflecting the mood of an hour—in the spirit of a medieval breviary. The unexpected canvases that had started with the brightly colored wizard sporting a stack of hats on his head spurred his move into realizing this as his Book of Hours.

"I'd been trying to get HarperCollins to allow me to write and publish something along the lines of Narnia—in the sense of it being a collection of books about the same world. I think the publishers had said no about four years before I eventually did the Wolfswinkel painting. My mind had actually been cooking things up for a while, and it just had a passion to make this work somehow. As I had been stymied on the writing part of it, I think the painting side had decided to erupt in its place."

Explaining the conceptual background to his newly imagined world, which would encompass his book of different hours, Clive said, "What excited me about this whole project in the first place—what had brought me to islands and time, and a time out of time and the Fantomaya, and all the various elements—is plugged into my experiences as a child going to Tiree and Guernsey, two islands which featured hugely in my childhood imaginings."

232

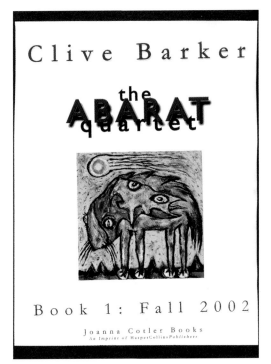

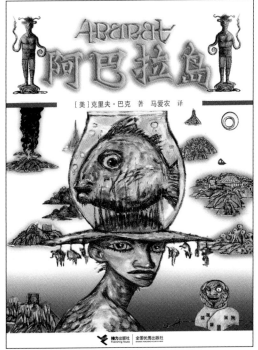

Another island, Kaua'i, one of Clive's favorite travel destinations, had actually first entranced him years before when he was a child. "We only had one album in the house for two years, and it was *South Pacific*, and my mum and dad took me to see it, and it was transformative. The great ache I have for Kaua'i right now is sourced in *South Pacific*, which is where it was shot."

These memories and experiences would culminate in the formation of the Abarat, a visual, temporal, and literary narrative of a world of twenty-five distinctive islands stretching out into an archipelago across the Sea of the Izabella. The appearance of Kaspar was the key that unlocked a period of furious oil painting by night and world-building by day.

His publisher was won over by the sheer body of painted work, which was already spawning ideas in Clive's written notes. His editor at HarperCollins, Jane Johnson, wrote as the April 2000 deal with Disney was announced, "Clive and I have discussed for the last six or seven years now how he might create a new world, a world in which he could set a fantastic epic to rival the worlds of Narnia, Middle-earth, or Oz, an adventure that would speak to the heart of modern readers, readers of all ages. Arenas such as these offer writers and readers alike a unique opportunity to exercise their imaginations, to explore the magical, the heroic, the lost parts of our consciousness, rooted as they are in the bones of human literature, in myth and legend, in the stories humankind has told itself from the beginning of speech."

"Abarat is an archipelago of twenty-five islands," Clive explained ahead of publication. "On twenty-four of those, you're going to find a different hour of the day. On the twenty-fifth island, you're going to find a time out of time, a place where no time exists, and all times exist. A holy moment, if you will."

Clive created a hero who could be relatable for a young adult audience without being overly alien to his existing adult readers: Candy Quackenbush lives in Minnesota, in a town reliant on a single local industry; chicken farming.

"At the intersection of San Vicente and Santa Monica, there's a big sign for a lawyers company called Quackenbush, and I thought, 'That is such a great name. . . .'

"If I can find a voice, if a voice appears quickly, then I know I'm onto a winner. Candy's easy because it derived from Nicole's voice," explains Clive, referencing his daughter. "Nicole is fourteen and smart as a whip and just wonderful, beautiful, and it's impossible to be writing about a heroine, a young heroine, as I'm writing about Candy, without being aware of what I'm being taught by my own

ABOVE LEFT

Joanna Cotler Books' first-look press pack as Clive's Abarat series was announced for publication.

ABOVE RIGHT

Published around the world, Clive's interior artwork was used to create a variety of cover designs for *Abarat*, including this Simplified Chinese trade edition by Jieli Publishing House, 2004.

daughter, you know? She's a marvelous girl and she's taught me a lot about what it is to be alive at that age, in these times—different times to the times when I was fourteen.

"Some are more difficult because they are characters who are almost in a period of change—Malingo was one; the beaten-slave part of it was easy, but when Malingo started to change it became harder to keep the voice and find the voice, crack the voice."

Both *The Thief of Always* and *Abarat* (the first book in the series) introduce our protagonist as bored senseless in school, as Clive chooses to use that liminal space between wakeful focus and sleepy daydream as the perfect time for strange doorways to open. But *Abarat* has an important distinction, as China Miéville recognizes, writing for *The Guardian*:

> Unlike most classics of this kind, *Abarat* starts with a prologue in the fantasyland itself, tracking an incomprehensible conversation between three of its inhabitants, before we meet Candy. In other words, we do not fall down a rabbit hole into the magic kingdom with our protagonist: we know about the magic already, and have to wait for her to catch up. This is a double-edged sword. What is inevitably lost is the first astonishment—the sense of awe as we step out of the Kansas house with our child-avatar into a Technicolor Oz.
>
> But something is also gained. By introducing Candy to what we have already seen, the solipsism of childhood is undercut: there is no room for this to be only a dream. The moral and philosophical stakes are raised: actions have consequences in what must be a real though alternate world.

It was critical for Clive that this world should give him the opportunity to explore something of greater value than a fantasy adventure for its own sake. We're shown common evils like jealousy, greed, and pride but also more insidious ones: the corruption of monopolistic capitalism and the bigotry of fundamentalist politics.

"In this world I can talk about family relations, I can talk about the nature of evil—and that is a central issue in these books, particularly how the knowledge of evil gets passed down from one generation to another."

Yet the novel is also an abundant celebration of diversity, color, love, and courage. As China Miéville concludes:

> Barker is one of the few writers who has altered an entire field: more than anyone since Lovecraft, he has changed the shape, the corporeality, of horror. It is therefore slightly surprising how unhorrific *Abarat* is. There are horrors, of course: but we aren't terrified (except, perhaps, by the hinted-at Lovecraftian presences in the deeps, which will rise in book four, I'd imagine). But even this is related to one of the book's strengths. You cannot have an unearthly

OPPOSITE PAGE

Clive with his painting of the Islands of the Abarat at the Pacific Design Center exhibition, 2002.

ABOVE

Clive with his triptych of Candy Quackenbush and the chickens of Chickentown, Minnesota, at the *Art of Abarat* exhibition in Los Angeles, 2002.

terror who is also a protagonist. In *Abarat*, we spend time inside even "evil" Christopher Carrion's head. And what we therefore lose in terror, we more than make up for in intricacy and empathy. *Abarat* is a sumptuous and lovely thing. With beautiful pictures of monsters.

As Clive moved on to the sequel, he paid tribute to all the work that had gone into creating a volume that incorporated his prose, poetry, and reproductions of over a hundred oil paintings: "*Abarat* is going to be an amazing book. And I say that not just as its creator but as somebody who has stood by and watched Joanna Cotler, which is a subsidiary of HarperCollins, do something exceptional with this book. It's not just a question of what I have given in the way of text and illustrations, it's also a question of what they've chosen to do with the book—they've put it on the best possible paper, they've bound it in the best possible way, and everything about this book is gorgeous."

The book's flap copy reads:

Once upon a world
where time is a place
a journey beyond imagination
is about to unfold . . .

It begins in the most boring place in the world: Chickentown, USA. There lives Candy Quackenbush, her heart bursting for some clue as to what her future might hold.

When the answer comes, it's not one she expects. Out of nowhere comes a wave, and Candy, led by a man called John Mischief (whose brothers live on the horns on his head), leaps into the surging waters and is carried away.

Where? To the Abarat: a vast archipelago where every island is a different hour of the day, from The Great Head that sits in the mysterious twilight waters of Eight in the Evening, to the sunlit wonders of Three in the Afternoon, where dragons roam, to the dark terrors of Gorgossium, the island of Midnight, ruled over by the Prince of Midnight himself, Christopher Carrion.

As Candy journeys from one amazing place to another, making fast friends and encountering treacherous foes—mechanical bugs and giant moths, miraculous cats and men made of mud, a murderous wizard and his terrified slave—she begins to realize something. She has been here before.

Candy has a place in this extraordinary world: she is here to help save the Abarat from the dark forces that are stirring at its heart. Forces older than Time itself, and more evil than anything Candy has ever encountered.

She's a strange heroine, she knows. But this is a strange world.

And in the Abarat, all things are possible.

2004 ABARAT: DAYS OF MAGIC, NIGHTS OF WAR

"Sometimes people should be given second chances."

Clive immediately launched into writing the second Abarat novel after the first was delivered. But with that fluid transition came an unexpected problem.

"I wrote the book, finished the book in November 2002, read the book and didn't like it, and threw it all away, the whole thing, and began again—which I've never done before. So there's *nothing* in the second volume of Abarat as it now stands which faintly resembles that first version. . . .

"It is a six-hundred-page manuscript . . . but I realized my first version was teasing people too much. There wasn't enough delivery as I saw it and I wanted the second book to give you a genuine sense of fulfilment. After all, you will have been through almost a quarter of a million words and two hundred and fifty illustrations. You should have a sense of emotional payback. There should be a sense that some of the storylines have reached some genuine conclusion and I felt that the story wasn't taking the readers far enough: it wasn't giving us enough of a journey to enough of a conclusion to something big enough. And so I thought, 'I don't think this is right or fair. I need to go back and I need to start again and I need to configure this. I want it to go to a much bigger place in terms of narrative, in terms of emotion, and in terms of fulfillment of the narrative promises in the first book.'"

With paintings still coming along by night, he followed their lead and restarted the work, this time with a clearer sense of what the series could be as a whole.

"It was definitely my active intention to bring a number of narrative lines full circle and end some of the stories in the second book so that we could then begin new, fun things for the third book and so that people wouldn't have that sense that really nothing was going to get resolved

236

Un libro senza limiti sognai,
un libro senza coste,
i fogli sparpagliati in grande copia.

In ogni riga un orizzonte nuovo,
immaginati nuovi paradisi;
e stati nuovi, anime nuove.

Una di queste,
nel torpore di un fittizio pomeriggio,
sognò queste parole.
E in cerca di una mano per narrarle
prese la mia.

CLIVE BARKER

until they'd read the quartet. I wanted to really give readers a sense that some things get resolved; new problems arise but there is resolution in the second book.

"You can't do it in movies very often; in movies you very often have the sense of . . . nobody's really dead and nobody really changes—Pinhead looks the same from movie to movie, Freddy Krueger looks the same from movie to movie. I want physical change in the characters I am showing to the audience; I want to watch Candy change as she moves through the islands and experiences things and buys new kinds of clothes to wear, and the same with Malingo and other characters who appear on the page. I really tried to develop their journeys a little bit.

"I don't want this to be a three-book tease with a one-book payoff; I want *each* of the books to pay off some of the narratives and present other strands which are going to grow in complexity and richness and obviously go on. But I think at the end of the second book there's a real sense of 'We were delivered somewhere, we got closure.' There are significant deaths in this book, there are significant changes in this book, there are significant revelations in this book.

"I'm much, much happier with the second book. And so, it was worth it! But that was the other reason why it's taken longer to get here and there have been certain times when I've regretted it . . . but now, having got there, I don't regret it at all—I think it was the right thing to do."

Writing a longer narrative was also giving Clive the opportunity to explore the nature of his main characters in depth. While some have a clear duality that mirrors the underlying nature of the islands of Day and Night, others are more complex and it takes time for this to be revealed in a process that doesn't seem forced.

"It's very different writing a series rather than a novel," agrees Clive, "different in a lot of exciting ways. I'm able to lay little clues in the book which are like seeds which I press deep into the earth of the story which will only flower in later books. If you go back over the first two books, there are lots of clues about Candy, starting with the fact that she has two different-colored eyes. And I try to be very honest with my readers in the sense that I really do try to lay those clues in so that if they come back to the novel they can say, 'Oh yeah, Barker was an honest man there; he gave us the information to make guesses.' There are lots of things in Book Two which will become significant but are almost casual in these early books."

A longer narrative also offers room for multiple complex concepts. The nature of time is paradoxically simple and challenging when each island location is a physical manifestation of a different hour. And a central island of "all time and none" is both nirvanic and horrific in the same instant. Clive's approach remains that of chronicler rather than fantasist, in order to make the world truly exist for the reader.

"I think that's really, absolutely on the nose, I think that's part of my process whereas most, people who write horror, for instance, tend to start in real worlds and darken the real worlds by the monster in the cellar or the monster in the sewer or the monster wherever. I tend to say, 'OK, the real world is the starting place for an investigation into the metaphysical, the physical begets the metaphysical and not the other way around, which would be a classical religious point of view—the metaphysical begets the physical.'

"They—*Weaveworld*, *Abarat*, et cetera—all reference the real world . . . but Chickentown is not as important as Abarat, London is not as important as Yzordderrex; my heart is in the places of dreams. Waking, you come to a rainy London or a rainy Liverpool and you make your peace with that because you know you're going to go to sleep again and dream."

We also get a hint in the second Abarat book of how the world was, and continues to be, created:

"What's the Skein?" Candy said, becoming a little more interested now.

"I quote: '*It is the thread that joins all things—living and dead, sentient and unthinking—to all other things—*'"

Now Candy was interested. She came to stand beside Malingo, looking at the *Almenak* over his shoulder. He went on reading aloud.

"'*According to the persuasive Miss Hap, the thread originates in the Vault at Huffaker, appearing momentarily as a kind of flickering light before winding its way invisibly through the Abarat . . . connecting us, one to another.*'" He closed the *Almenak*. "Don't you think we should see this?"

"Why not?"

"We live in a world in which the Christian mythology makes the creator male, and I get to *play* with that idea and, you know, many of the most powerful people in my life have been women. Starting with my mother who was an Italian lady of great fierceness, my editors have almost always been women, my agents have very often been women.

"The second book of Abarat was, without question, the hardest book I have ever written."

"My grandmother, who died at one hundred and one, was again an Italian lady who was the model for Mater Motley. She's all over the second book. And, this is a completely true story, I was taught as a child a prayer my mother had created to keep my grandmother at bay! That makes a profound mark on a young psyche! So, when it came to creating some forceful power of negation that would stand as a yin to this yang, as it were, it seemed inevitable that I should choose another female so that if it really comes down to the fight, Mater Motley versus this lady, Princess Breath, [it] is going to be quite the thing. I mean, the idea of a woman *breathing out* life seems such a sweetly effortless idea; that breathing is so simple an activity and that with every breath she makes new life and the wind that passes through the islands carries the life into the sea and piece by piece, island by island, the islands are populated. I want to *haunt* the audience a little. . . . I very much want to have people come away with *haunting images* in their heads—the idea of a goddess breathing out life seemed to be a good idea."

In the book Diamanda, one of the Women of the Fantomaya is charged with explaining the metaphysics of the Abarat to Henry Murkitt, who resides in Chickentown:

Anybody can shrug and say life is just some accident of mud and lightning. But Henry, it isn't. And I mean to show you, in the time we have together—whether it's an hour or a day or whatever it is—I mean to show you that you just have to open your heart and look—you hear me, look!—and you'll see every minute a hundred reasons to believe . . . Don't you see we're born into a pattern so huge and beautiful and so full of meaning we can only hope to understand a tiny part of it in the seventy or eighty years we live with breath in our bodies? But one day, it will all come clear.

Days of Magic, Nights of War was awarded a Bram Stoker Award for Best Work for Young Readers by the Horror Writers Association in 2005. Clive was delighted that the book had successfully bridged the gap between many existing and new readers. "It's very nice to come to a gathering which is about horror fiction and yet be able to win for children's fiction—it's *very* nice. I feel like kids understand the dark and sometimes we underestimate their need for the darkness. . . ."

The book's flap copy reads:

Candy Quackenbush's adventures in the amazing world of the Abarat are getting more strange by the hour. Christopher Carrion, the Lord of Midnight, has sent his henchmen to capture her. Why? she wonders. What would Carrion want with a girl from Minnesota? And why is Candy beginning to feel that the world of Abarat is familiar to her? Why can she speak words of magic she doesn't even remember learning?

There is a mystery here. And Carrion, along with his fiendish grandmother Mater Motley, suspects that whatever Candy is, she could spoil their plans to take control of the Abarat.

Now Candy's companions must race against time to save her from the clutches of Carrion, and she must solve the mystery of her past before the forces of Night and Day clash and Absolute Midnight descends upon the islands.

A final war is about to begin. And Candy is going to need to make some choices that will change her life forever . . .

Night comes down upon my heart,
And smothers me in the grief
Let us take comfort, before We part
Life at least is brief.
That at least our lives are brief.

Clive Barker

3.03 a.m. 7th December 2008

Emily Shaw II

OPPOSITE PAGE

Tarrie Cat Army from the Abarat series, painted circa 2003.

ABOVE LEFT

Untitled, 2006.

ABOVE RIGHT

Babilonium, painted in 1999.

LEFT

Manuscript page of one of Clive's poems, December 2008.

ISLANDS

"Places of Magic and Mystery . . ."

"Tiree . . . Guernsey . . . Kaua'i . . . Three islands. Three different worlds. It's almost as though each one of them could have been plucked from a different time.

"Or a different Hour . . .

"In that thought is the beginning of a whole new journey, to a place of visions and imagination, full of the fantastical and the bizarre, yet all rooted in my memories of places I have been and people I have known.

"The islands of Abarat."

William Golding, Arthur Ransome, Enid Blyton, J. M. Barrie, William Shakespeare . . . writers have long understood the enchantment of an island location. The ability to root a story in a self-contained otherworld where conventional rules might not quite apply is invaluable. A specific journey must be taken to reach its shores and, once they arrive, the traveler is held hostage by wind and tide—forces of nature that brook no petition to release them from isolation.

Clive recognized that same allure as a child, holidaying with his family on the Hebridean island of Tiree, and he still mentions its name often, with a hint of a Gaelic burr.

"I spent many summers on the tiny, rugged isle of Tiree, helping my Uncle Hugh bring in the harvest. There are no trees on the island because the wind blows so hard. And when there are storms—which can be ferocious, even in the summer—the biggest waves can break over the island from shore to shore.

"I loved those wilderness summers, walking the deserted beaches and the windswept dunes with just myself for company."

Childhood summers make for particularly potent memories: "I'm in Tiree—there are no books there except books in Gaelic so it's problematic. In the post office there's one of those things that goes round which has paperbacks in it, and in there, there is one Fritz Leiber book—it was sword and sorcery, which is a phrase that he invented—and I'd never heard of it before and it was the only book with a cover that I liked! It was two and sixpence or whatever it was and I picked it up and went home, and there's no television, the radio barely worked so it was a wonderful time to sit on the beach and read. It was a wonderful introduction to him—the fact that it was *there* made it one of those magical moments—why on earth should there be a Fritz Leiber book in Tiree? You know? Fritz Leiber became one of my gods and I had the good fortune to meet him, just the once, and it meant the world to me."

With the island fixed in his mind's eye, Clive drew on it for his first stories. "Very often, the stories of the Books of Blood are based in landscapes I know and obviously 'Scape-Goats' is Tiree . . . atmospheres and imaginings which I have extrapolated from personal experience.

"We would go to Tiree one year and then to Guernsey the next, which is why islands come up so much! And very *different* islands, you know?" Clive would stay with his godparents in St. Peter Port, Guernsey, in an old house which once served as a Nazi headquarters in the occupation of the island.

"When I would go on walks, the bunkers were still there, in some places the guns were still in place, all pointing towards the English coastline. Inside you would find German graffiti on the walls, you know, instructions painted in German. For a kid, this was amazing, you know, really cool. My uncle, my godfather—'Uncle Billy'—had been in the war and was a fervent anti-German and as an act of discourtesy to the Nazi heritage he kept his gardening tools—the little trowel and so on—*in* the rusted Nazi helmet which I used to like wearing on my head. . . . 'You don't know where it's been,' my mum would say! But, I said, 'Bill, I want to wear it on my head, I want to be a bad German,' and so there are a bunch of photographs and you've seen the one of me wearing the helmet in the ruins."

These formative memories of places by the sea—including the dockside of his home in Liverpool—continued beyond childhood, creating something of a preoccupation with rivers, seas, and fluidity.

"My father was an Irishman who worked on the docks. My godfather was a captain and my grandfather a ship's engineer. It is from them that I get my craving for adventure, but instead of using a ship to get to faraway places I use my imagination. . . .

"When I think about the world, I think about the sea. I think the sea—whether the dream-sea of *The Great and Secret Show* or the physical sea as it appears in many of my books—is always the means of carrying me away. My flight into fantasy as a kid was a flight from the world. Now those same mechanisms have become a way back."

After he moved to Hollywood in 1991, Clive found a new island on which to holiday—the "Garden Island" of the Hawaiian archipelago, Kaua'i. There he found the same solace in its uncomplicated seclusion and warm ocean waters, and thus its geography percolated into the stories he was writing. The Geary house in *Galilee* can be found there, as can the Abaratian island of Yzil.

"Princess Breath, the creatrix of the archipelago of Abarat on the island of Yzil, which stands at the Hour of Noon, breathes out lifeforms of every kind. A balmy wind blows through the flowered thickets of that island—the kind that comes off the sea in Kaua'i, my second favorite place in the world after the house in which I'm writing this—and the warm air takes the Princess Breath's creatures out of her arms and carries them out to sea, or to another island, to begin their lives."

Returning from a trip to Europe (and a long flight home), Clive reflected on how all these influences were instrumental in creating Abarat. "Three islands. Three different worlds. It's almost as though each one of them could have been plucked from a different time. They were what excited me about this whole project in the first place—what had brought me to islands, and time, and a time out of time and the Fantomaya and all the various elements that plugged into my experiences as a child going to Tiree and Guernsey. The whole idea of being able to jump through time and then go to a place where time doesn't even exist is something that's very acute right now, being in a state of jet lag! That's the way you feel!"

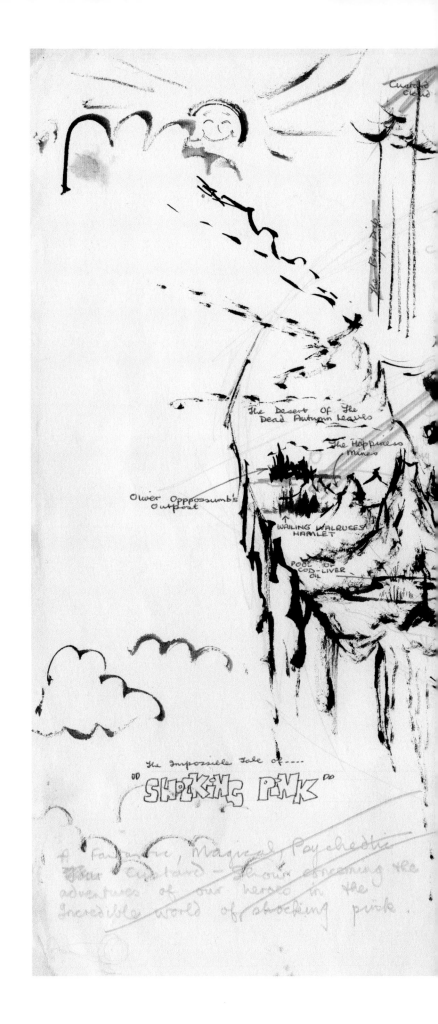

Labels within the illustration:
Cuckoo Cloud
The Desert Of The Dead Autumn Leaves
The Happiness Mines
Oliver Oppossumb's Outpost
WAILING WALRUSES HAMLET
POOL OF COD-LIVER OIL
The Impossible Tale of.....
"OO SHOCKING PINK OO"
A Fantastic, Magical, Psychedelic Tour Custard – Shown streaming the adventures of our heroes in the Incredible world of shocking pink.

THIS SPREAD

An early Barker-imagined world, this July 1969 design for "The Impossible Tale of . . . 'Shocking Pink' " details a world in which the left-hand side is bathed in light from a smiling sun, the right-hand side over the Edge of Tomorrow is in darkness, with the Forever Castle in the top right hand corner.

244

TOMORROW

OF

THE DOMAIN OF
THE LAKE-
KING

Enchanted Forest
of the unicorn
the fairies

Oooooooogle-
Gretins Rubbish
Heap

Custard
Rainbow
JUST THE CITY

Ginger Pop
Springs

Forever
Castle

The Lake of Forgetfulness

Fisherman's Cottages

The Toadstool
Terrors

The Sea-Side

A Thousand Secrets

Winkle Winkles

The Treacle Toffee & Fudge
Factory.
Jeremiah Waffle
The White Knight
guards it against
Fairy Eccles, an
apprentice dragon.

Whistling
Pink
Sand
Beach

The Marsh-
Home of Broken
Biscuit-Bogie Beast.

of the
Cloud Tribe

Volcaniums

Shell Beach

Purple
Pillow Wood

A-They make raft
B-The P.P. People are at war with
the Cloud Tribe, because the Gryphins
need the clouds (they make them out
of candy floss) and the P.D.P. need the
sun (to dry their Purple Pillows)
C-To avoid the Orange-Lolly-On-
A-Stick, our heroes pass C, where
they discover that Hairy Harriet is
a Misunderstood Ogre.

THE CAVE-
DICKERY HUT

The Manure
Plantation

DISMAL
DELTA

The Home of
Hairy Harriet
the Smelly Ogre

VULTURES

ANGE LOLLY-
STICK
OF THE POLUM
EARS

The Realm At
The End Of the World

The Magical
Daisy Chain

DEAD
SAPPHIRE

DOOM

4-7-69 Clive

ABOVE

Fully thirty years later, Clive would design the Abarat—an archipelago of 25 islands, each set in a different time of the day plus the 25th Hour, a Time Out of Time—as realized in this huge 228" × 96" oil painting in 1999.

BOTTOM

On holiday in Guernsey, circa 1962. Wearing an old World War II helmet found abandoned after the occupation of the islands, Clive pulls a gruff face to portray a "bad Nazi."

OPPOSITE PAGE, BOTTOM LEFT

Sharing his love of Tiree on a trip there with his friends: Clive with the group's film camera, 1974.

OPPOSITE PAGE, BOTTOM RIGHT

Clive sketching on a return trip to Tiree, circa 2002.

SPREADING THE WORD, CONVENTIONS, MAZES

"On the road."

Douglas E. Winter's comprehensive biography of Clive, *Clive Barker: The Dark Fantastic*, was published by HarperCollins in late 2001, the better part of a decade after it had been commissioned. A renowned critic and writer, Douglas had previously written another horror master's biography, *Stephen King: The Art of Darkness*, published in 1984, and he'd been one of those enthusing about the Books of Blood at the 1984 Ottawa World Fantasy Convention who had caused Stephen King to dub Clive the "future of horror."

"I've known Clive since before the Books of Blood were published," he says, "and there was a fortuitous relationship between my growth as a critic and his growth as a writer. It seemed almost predestined that I was to become his biographer. He cooperated graciously in the book, principally with interviews and moral encouragement, but he didn't design to advise me. I think he trusted me to write the kind of book that would honor him and, more important, the aesthetics that we hold so dear and in common.

"People like Clive and Stephen King reach an extraordinary number of readers and television viewers and moviegoers, far more than the number reached by the very talented writers who are considered 'literary' but who publish to a much smaller audience. There clearly is something important in what they do. We're talking about novels that have ideas, that echo current anxieties or fantasies or metaphysical dilemmas, and that hopefully do so while telling a good story. That makes these people very powerful influences on our social, political, and metaphysical thought."

In his extensive research he spoke with Clive's parents and other family members, schoolteachers, friends, and publishers in Liverpool and London, as well as his friends and more recent collaborators in the US—all this alongside hours of conversations with Clive himself over the course of many years.

The book had been delayed from an initial planned publication in 1998. "Part of the problem," offered Douglas, "was trying to work with Clive himself. Working with a living writer who is constantly creating and constantly evolving as an artist—you can't pigeonhole Clive; the guy just can't stop creating. There were times when I started to wonder if I could ever find a way to reach an ending for the book that was anything other than an open-ended look into the next few years of work. Fortunately, when I was coming to what I felt had to be the end, Clive was coming to the beginning of the Abarat quartet project, which will consume him for the next few years and is a major junction in his career, so that made for a real strong ending."

Clive said when the biography was published, "I hope that the interesting thing about the book is that it does offer a very truthful portrait of a man who is sort of juggling and trying to work out paths on a spiritual level as he works out a path on an artistic level. I think that what Doug caught was that many of my arguments with myself are metaphysical arguments, spiritual arguments. Debate, confusion, depression. And I've never really hidden any of that stuff, my sexuality or, pretty much, the details of my life. When people asked, and they were the kind of people who legitimately wanted to know, I've never hidden anything—why would I? The interesting thing is seeing Doug put all of that stuff between two covers and I think he's done a brilliant job, an amazing job. I'm amazed at what I've seen some people say about me and I've thought, 'Well, at least now I know. . . .'"

Clive's Lost Souls fan club ceased operations in 2006 after eleven years and its www.clivebarker.com website ceased updates. At Clive's request, the *Revelations* website at www.clivebarker.info, run by Phil and Sarah Stokes since 1998, took over as his official website, having already published a dozen interviews with him. Behind the scenes, Phil and Sarah were also working with Clive on a planned history of his pre–Books of Blood years.

That series, *Memory, Prophecy and Fantasy: The Works and Worlds of Clive Barker*, saw its first volume, *Liverpool Lives*, published in 2009; its second, *Dog Days*, in 2010; and its third, *Masquerades*, which concluded with the end of the Dog Company in 1983, was published in 2014.

The Stokeses also wrote and published a companion book to the Abarat series, *Beneath the Surface of Clive Barker's Abarat*, which featured an extended interview with Clive conducted by his friend Peggy O'Leary's students at Kodiak Middle School in Alaska. The first edition in 2011 was revised later the same year after the publication of *Absolute Midnight*, the third book in the Abarat series.

Also in 2011, *Clive Barker: The Painter, the Creature and the Father of Lies*, a collection of Clive's nonfiction articles, essays, introductions, and liner notes, was published by Earthling Publications in hardcover and signed limited editions.

ABOVE
Clive onstage in a Q&A session at Elf Fantasy Fair at Keukenhof Castle, Lisse, Netherlands, 2004.

Reviewing this collection, the *Los Angeles Times* concluded:

A collection of a writer's prefaces and random prose pieces often feels like the mus-
tard-stained bread crusts on a child's plate after lunch. Nutritive quality? Low. Value?
Marginal. Overall response? Ugh.

That verdict, fortunately, doesn't apply to all collections, especially one by Clive
Barker, a writer perhaps best known for his *Hellraiser* story and Abarat saga. His thought-
ful musings on horror and culture have been collected in *Clive Barker: The Painter, the
Creature and the Father of Lies*.

As varied and unexpected as this material is—editors Phil and Sarah Stokes have culled
material from the last twenty-five years not just from books and reissues but also from DVDs
and press materials—there's still a theme that manages to run throughout. It involves two
c-words: creation and calling . . .

Much of the book is devoted to the *Hellraiser* saga and the novel that spawned it, *The
Hellbound Heart*. But there are plenty of other pieces here showcasing his philosophical
musings on personal identity ("our lives are scattered throughout with periods of unbe-
longing") and poetic meditations on why a writer decides to write horror tales: "We all
hear the call of the dark once in a while: a siren song, inviting us to take a ghost ride into
nightmare." And at other times, Barker is just very candid about what horror writers do:
"We spend our working days making traps . . . that will corner the reader into confront-
ing . . . experiences most of humanity spends its time assiduously avoiding."

The energy and candor he brings to these pieces make this collection hardly an after-
thought. In fact, it's a provocation to read him if you haven't and surrender yourself to one
of those cunning traps.

Publishers Weekly said: "Barker's brain is sensationally splattered throughout the first half in articulate meditations and critical essays on censorship and taboo . . . each revealing another piece of
his puzzling mind."

In 2015, the the Stokeses founded the Clive Barker Archive, with Clive saying, "Phil and Sarah
understand me better than almost anyone on the planet. They have an encyclopedic knowledge of who

"I find nothing more revivifying than coming away from a signing having met with the people who actually put the bucks on the table to actually buy the book. I couldn't write in a vacuum."

I am and what I've done. My relationship with them is one of the great friendships of my life and the permanent placing of my archive with them is a natural culmination of this great, long relationship. They will display many of my works, including handwritten manuscripts, original art, and much more. I am moved beyond words, and I'm pleased to no end to be able to make this announcement here and now."

Fans hungry for news and details about Clive's work could not only dive into Douglas E. Winter's biography and the online worlds of *Lost Souls* and *Revelations* but also interact with Clive himself at various signings and convention appearances. Bookstore staff and convention organizers would consistently report being surprised by the large numbers of people arriving to meet Clive and at the length of time he spent with each, discussing aspects of his work and often adding an original sketch alongside his autograph inside books, on posters, on clothing or other items, and, occasionally, on flesh, which attendees have then had tattooed as a permanent record of their meeting.

Clive has toured extensively for his book, comic, and film releases, reveling in interacting with his audience. His breakout in 1987 with *Hellraiser* and *Weaveworld* was a big factor in the jump from his three-city signing tour of the US in August 1986 for the release of the Books of Blood to a multi-city tour of the US and Canada for *Weaveworld* the following year. Since then Clive continued to tour with each book, at least until late 2011, when he was forced to pause his public appearances due to illness.

He has also been a regular attendee at conventions ever since 1984's Fantasycon in Birmingham in the UK and 1985's World Fantasy Convention in Tucson. He was master of ceremonies at 1988's combined Fantasycon and World Fantasy Convention in London, grandmaster at the World Horror Convention in Atlanta in 1995, and one of the guests of honor at the following year's World Horror Convention in Oregon as well as at the 2006 Fantasycon in Nottingham in the UK. Comic-Con in San Diego was a regular stop-off and 1997's Dragon Con in Atlanta had a mini CliveCon within it, organized by Lost Souls.

Fangoria's Weekend of Horrors was also a regular fixture in his schedule; Clive attended his first in New York in January 1990, through to the Weekend of Horrors hosted by *Fangoria*'s former convention partner Creation Entertainment in September 2011 in Burbank.

"I love going to the conventions and meeting the readers," he offers by way of explanation. "To see their excitement and enthusiasm is fun. It's the exact same thing in the bookstores. Some authors may think that it's a chore, and will only scribble their initials in the book. I try to learn the name of the person I'm signing the book for. The central relationship for me is with my readers. What good is your story if it exists in a vacuum? The readers validate me as an individual. They are absolutely the central focus in my life.

"I feel that the readers are the co-creators of the books they read. The books are created twice. Once, in the imagination of the author while writing the book, and the second time in the imagination of the reader as he reads it. Novels are different from one person to another."

Often alongside him at the *Fangoria* events and in other large-scale conventions were some combination of Doug Bradley, Ashley Laurence, Peter Atkins, Nicholas Vince, Simon Bamford, or other collaborators; these events and festivals presented the perfect opportunity to reconnect with old friends, meet readers and film fans, as well as meet other filmmakers and creatives such as Lucio Fulci and Dario Argento.

Clive also happily accepted an invitation to a 2011 conference at Trinity College, Dublin, titled Dark Imaginer, organized by Sorcha Ní Fhlainn, at which papers on Clive's work were presented by visiting and local academics.

Another chance to experience a Clive Barker "event" came with Universal Studios's invitation to Clive to design a maze for its annual Halloween Horror Nights at its Hollywood theme park, an opportunity that Clive happily accepted three years running. In his first year, 1998, he created, scripted, and designed a maze called "Freakz" in which a caretaker character, General Santiago, guided attendees through twelve rooms, each filled with monsters played by actors. "They were putting twelve hundred people through an hour," Clive noted. "So, you've got all these people, you've got a lot of noise, thirty-five actors coming at you and the walls are moving. Everything that could have been done to scare you was being done at this attraction, and it was great fun to do it. It was very satisfying as well. It was the most popular attraction at the park during that period, which was tremendous. There were lines waiting for an hour or more every night. You could step away from the soundstage and all you could hear was screaming. It was quite funny. I've often talked about the appetite that everybody has for being scared, and here it was, a line of several thousand people waiting to get in just to have the bejesus scared out of them."

The following year, the maze he offered was called "Hell." In 2000, he debuted "Harvest," a trek through a zombie-infested cemetery that was littered with the remains of the dead and the not-so-dead.

"My husband, David, and I designed these things together," Clive said as "Harvest" was staged. "David loves this as much as I do. He really helps me make them, polish them, and is really good at adding the little details which turn a good scene into a great scene. And then we have the great thrill of standing back from the studio and you just hear people screaming. It's great! They come out with shit-eating grins on their faces because there is something completely primal about going into a dark space. You've been in line for an hour or two (last year the line got as long as three hours), and the expectation grows, because all you can hear from ahead is people yelling, laughing, screeching. You're getting closer and closer, and now the screaming is getting really loud and you're thinking, 'What the fuck are they doing to people in there?' You see the people come out giggling and joining the line again. And then you get in! And it smells of smoke and special effects and paint and a little sweat, because people are a little clammy.

"It's just a fun time and then you're really on your own. I mean it's not one of those experiences where you are led by the hand. You move through the space at your own pace. Things are going to hang down on top of you and grab you and whisper obscenities in your ear. You know it will be a fun time had by all."

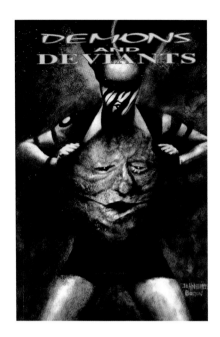

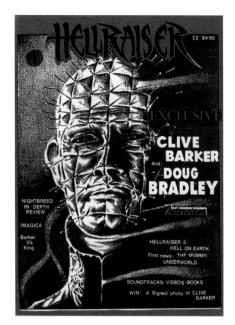

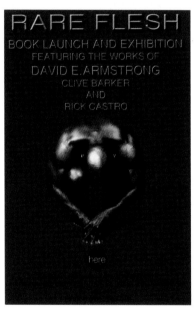

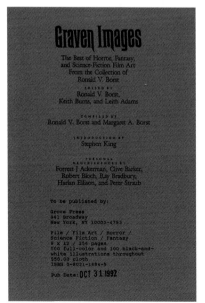

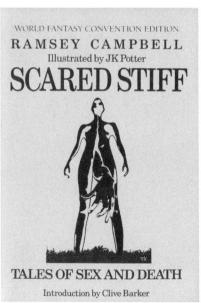

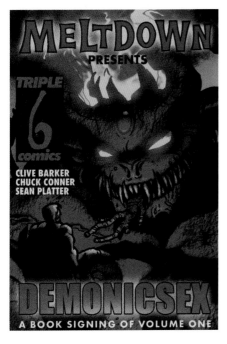

OPPOSITE PAGE

TOP LEFT

John Bolton's cover artwork for the special edition fanzine, *Demons and Deviants*, produced by the Breed fan club, run by Michael Brown, which featured the debut publication of Clive's short story "On Amen's Shore," 1992.

TOP CENTER

Marvel Magazines in the UK produced a new but ultimately short-lived serial magazine, *Hellbreed*, that closed after just three issues, 1995.

TOP RIGHT

The first issue of a magazine from a UK fan club in 1990.

CENTER LEFT

Clive's artwork for *Crazyface*, 1995, used for signed bookplates.

CENTER CENTER

An invitation to a London signing hosted by Starburst and Collins in November 1990.

CENTER RIGHT

An invitation to the launch of *Rare Flesh*, a book of photography by David Armstrong and featuring Clive's poetry, January 2004.

BOTTOM LEFT

A promotional flyer for Clive's book signing in Seattle on the book tour for *The Thief of Always*, December 1992.

BOTTOM CENTER

Clive wrote an essay about the films of the 1960s for *Graven Images*, a book of movie posters. This proof copy lists the strong lineup of contributors. Grove Press, 1992.

BOTTOM RIGHT

Returning the compliment that Ramsey Campbell had given in the first volumes of the Books of Blood, Clive provided an introduction to Ramsey's collection, this pre-release edition being made available at the October 1986 World Fantasy Convention.

THIS PAGE

TOP LEFT

Laminate badge for CliveCon 1, organized by the Lost Souls fan club within the wider DragonCon event in Atlanta, June 1997.

TOP RIGHT

Promotional flyer for the *Hellraiser III: Hell on Earth* preview day event at Golden Apple in Los Angeles, September 1992.

BOTTOM LEFT

Promotional postcard for the January 2006 signing event at Meltdown Comics in Los Angeles promoting *DemonicSex*, for which Clive provided an introduction.

BOTTOM CENTER

The cover of *A Life in the Cinema*, 2000.

BOTTOM RIGHT

In 2000, Clive illustrated *A Life in the Cinema* by Mick Garris, published by Gauntlet Press, with this limitation signature page issued in the Artist's Presentation Edition.

INFERNAL TOYS

"Making monsters."

The Cenobites of *Hellraiser* were first immortalized as model kits by Screamin' Products, which issued a total of eight *Hellraiser* kits between 1989 and 1997. The company produced Pinhead (three versions), Chatterer, Butterball, the Female Cenobite, the Channard Cenobite, and a Lament Configuration box. The Cenobite kits were one-quarter scale with the exception of the final Pinhead, which was one-sixth scale. The first Pinhead model and the Chatterer model were sculpted by Thomas Kuntz; Jeff Brower took responsibility for Butterball and the Female Cenobite, and then followed those with the second Pinhead—complete with a Pillar of Souls—and Channard.

In 1997, sculptor Mat Falls at Sideshow realized Clive's pen-and-ink sketch *Demon Putting Out His Eyes* in three dimensions. The sculpture (which was described as one-quarter scale, suggesting someone knows how big an original demon is . . .) was available in two versions: a vinyl kit and a "fine art" bronze piece limited to twenty copies, mounted on a marble base and with a certificate signed by both Clive and Mat Falls.

Two hundred and fifty copies of a bust of Nix from *Lord of Illusions* were produced in 1996, each numbered and signed in silver ink on its wooden base by Clive and the make-up creator, Steve Johnson.

Series 4 of Todd McFarlane's Movie Maniacs added a Candyman figure into of its lineup of characters in 2001. In a more significant move, given that everything that had been made before had been a sculpture or model of preexisting characters or props, Clive and Todd McFarlane now decided to collaborate on entirely new figures. The first series, Tortured Souls, debuted in July 2001.

"People want to see the monsters," said Clive. "We supply the monsters.

"It's great dealing with Todd because you dispense with the middleman and talk directly to the creator. Todd is about making wonderful things, making things no one has ever seen before. He came along and said, 'Let's do something so scary, so extreme, it'll become a benchmark in horror toys.'

"These are the first toys I've had on the market. I've had model kits and whatnot, but this is a very different order of creation. These are technically amazing and the sheer level of detail is extraordinary. These figures represent the creature that both obsesses you and repulses you simultaneously.

Tom Requiem (Ringmaster?)
Leads the rest of the Parade

"From the first time we met, I knew that we were both kids in grown men's bodies, and that can be trouble —in a good sense."
—TODD MCFARLANE

These are figures you put in a dark place in your house, probably with some votive candles, to haunt a corner in your home. We've really had fun pushing the envelope.

"There's no question that one of my preoccupations has always been the imagery of S/M. That's what I drew on when I created the Cenobites; that's what I decided to draw on when we created Tortured Souls. There's something quite exciting about the fact that these are much, much more extreme reconfigurations of flesh than anything that the Cenobites were. The Cenobites had a little bit of skin pulled here and a nail in there. What we've got is a guy hanging up with his guts hanging out and another guy with an entirely separate face, almost taking imagery from the beauty business, in the sense of the Hollywood change-your-face-and-look-different-tomorrow kind of business.

"On my own I could not have done this. On his own, Todd could not have done this. Together we can. People are grasping for imaginative extremes and they are appreciative of that."

Clive added a backstory to each of the six figures in the first series of Tortured Souls: Venal Anatomica, the Scythe-Meister, Lucidique, Mongroid, Agonistes, and Talisac, each one a character study that would interconnect to create the history of the city of Primordium.

"These characters have been in their time both amongst the greatest and amongst the weakest powers of Primordium. Now we see them transformed, and each of them has new functions. As they are physically transformed, so they are transformed within the world in which they find themselves. I suppose each story is a little morality tale—perhaps that would be the best way of putting it—connected by the theme of transformation.

"You definitely get a feeling of personality from each one. I think that will be strengthened when you have that little piece of backstory because that will also strongly help you create an ambience around them.

"I wanted the world to feel like one of Webster's plays where you've got this kind of effortless fantasy, where in *The White Devil* there's this kind of casual reference to one of the characters being a werewolf. And, you know, nobody makes a big deal out of it. There it is. The feelings that people have in Webster's plays, the profundity of their anger and their need for revenge and their twisted sense of possessiveness over one another, particularly over women, turns them into monsters even if they take human form. I wanted very much for Primordium to be that world and be a place where the least of the creatures is monstrous. Sometimes monstrousness can be beautiful."

Five of the characters were also released as 12" models in 2002 before a second set of figures was released (without further stories) the same year. The six texts were collected into a single volume by Subterranean Press in 2015.

A potential movie project called "Tortured Souls," scripted by Clive with further screenplay drafts by Hans Rodionoff (who had writing duties on the *Saint Sinner* TV movie), was hot news in 2001, but interest at Universal Studios fell away and the project was cold by 2005.

Backstories were again written by Clive to accompany a third series of figures designed with Todd McFarlane in 2004 and later collected for publication by Subterranean Press in 2017. The Infernal Parade was a circus troupe comprising: Bleb and the Sabbaticus and Heeler (a threesome); Dr. Fetter's Family of Freaks; Mary Slaughter the Spike Swallower; Bethany Bled the Prisoner in the Iron Maiden; the Golem Elijah; and their fearless leader, the King of All Showmen, Tom Requiem, with his sidekick Clovio.

OPPOSITE PAGE

Promotional photographs of four *Tortured Souls* figures by McFarlane Toys. Clockwise from top left: Venal Anatomica, The Fix (aka Talisac), Lucidique and The Scythe-Meister, 2001.

261

"What I like about this project," said Clive, "is it's a train—it is six figures all on these almost medieval kind of cart bases with wheels, which can be hooked to one another so you can have this Infernal Parade of monsters, and geeks and freaks and dwarves and all of that good stuff. And I think that these are easily the most beautifully crafted—just on the level of sculpting—of the three sets that I've been involved with Todd on. . . .

"They're a new thing; they're not really horror, it's something different . . . it's what you would see at a freak show. You would see the gorgeous girl doing the burlesque, but you'd also see the man who eats chickens, you know, the geek sitting in the cage—so we've got a nice mixture of the monstrous and the strangely beautiful. . . . They have a different feel, the colors are much warmer; they're much more the colors of carnival—there's browns and reds and yellows, and dancing dwarves and all of that stuff—it's a kind of a Fellini-esque spectacle, if you will.

"Whereas in the *Tortured Souls* novella I was also describing a location—Primordium—here I'm telling something much more like a little fable: backstories which are complete and unto themselves and not connected in quite the same way. These are the stories of who these people are.

"It goes back to me wanting to do circuses since the first time I ever saw a circus, which was when I was five, probably. They used to bring the circus to Sefton Park in Liverpool every, I guess, summer. . . . And the smell of it and this kind of scary ambience of it—the clowns used to freak the hell out of me. These are all very obvious things, but there's something quite powerful about those images and ideas and so we really tried to capture some of that and I think they've done a great job. Of the three sets, these are easily my favorites. Just because they seem to jump much more from a personal dreamscape than the others do."

In 1974, Clive had written a four-act children's story, loosely based on his group of friends, called *The Adventures of Mr. Maximillian Bacchus and His Travelling Circus*. The travelers seem an unlikely

262

Bone Ruff
and Skull Dress for
Queen of Bones

family, staying together for the sake of their collective talent, but have romantic adventures as they travel toward Xanadu, always in search of "more adulation, more applause!" The story, Clive now reflects, "is very close to my heart, rooted as it is in the magical, colorful world of circus performers and their fantastic powers to enchant."

In 2003, NECA Toys entered the fray with a significant, multi-year *Hellraiser* license. With many of the figures sculpted by Kyle Windrix, NECA ultimately released four 7" versions of Pinhead (one in a pewter color), plus more than a dozen other 7" characters, including Frank Cotton and a skinned Julia Cotton. A limited five-thousand-copy diorama of the attic in Lodovico Street with 7" Cenobites was accompanied by a print of a sketch of Pinhead, each one signed by Clive. Then 18" versions of Pinhead and Chatterer were also unleashed, with motion activation, as well as a 13" Channard. A Pinhead bobblehead and several versions of the Lament Configuration were part of the lineup. Additionally, 1,650 copies of a 15" Pinhead sculpt were made, each signed by Kyle Windrix and Doug Bradley. A 7" Pinhead was added into NECA's Cult Classics Hall of Fame in 2006 with an alternate Elliott Spenser head and then issued again, this time without the extra head, in 2009. Later, in 2019, the company also produced an Ultimate Pinhead and a 6" Toony Terrors interpretation.

A set of very different toys was produced in 2005 and 2006: the Jump Tribe, from Art Asylum. Selected from the 240 characters in a series of five canvases painted by Clive in 2004, four colorful creatures—Yaboo, Kungu Nah, Billum, and Twoth—were created as soft plushies. Each creature was accompanied by a new tale written by Clive featuring that creature, printed in a small hardcover book.

Later models have returned to the worlds of *Hellraiser*, including three models from Sideshow, Inc., in 2016 of Pinhead and a Hell Priestess, several Funko Pop! and Funko Dorbz figures of the Cenobites, *Hellraiser III: Hell on Earth* models from Mezco Toyz, and *Hellraiser V: Inferno* boxes from Trick or Treat Studios.

Closer to home, the realclivebarker.com store, run by Seraphim, Clive's own company, collaborated with Cris Alex and Stephen Imhoff on a limited run of Lament Configuration boxes in 2015.

Candyman figures from NECA in 2020, Mego in 2020, and Funko Pop in 2021 joined a first *Nightbreed* figure in NECA's Decker in 2019.

For cosplayers, Trick or Treat Studios made available *Nightbreed* Dr. Decker masks as well as masks of Peloquin, Kinski, Boone as Cabal, Narcisse, and two different Berserkers. Numerous different Pinhead masks have been issued over the years by numerous different manufacturers, and occasionally other Cenobite masks, too, as well as full-length costumes with optional torture tool belts. A Nix mask appeared in 1996.

For those looking for something a little different at Halloween, Clive worked with Disguise, Inc., to create the Dark Bazaar line of costumes and accessories based on both new designs and preexisting artwork. Released for Halloween 2010, each of the costumes came with a "shard" of story from Clive, giving background to the character, so the wearer could discover how Queen Chuffatar became the Queen of Skulls, why the streets of Nakaree are deserted and, who designed Tattu Furio's favorite weapon, the Heartseeker. . . .

Paper masks, half masks, full masks, daggers, and staffs complemented the full-length costumes, and Clive promoted the line in person at the Halloween & Party Expo in Houston in January 2010.

1988– 2006

TELEVISION

"Small screen adventures."

Clive first met Mick Garris in 1988, in Los Angeles. The two men soon began to collaborate on several planned projects: a possible TV series called *Spirit City USA*, a movie adaptation of the Books of Blood story "In the Flesh," and a big-screen version of *The Mummy*. Unfortunately, none of these came to fruition; for a long time the only onscreen evidence of the pair's work together was a cameo appearance that Clive made alongside Stephen King and Tobe Hooper in Mick's feature film *Sleepwalkers*, written by Stephen King.

In 1997, however, Mick brought one of Clive's stories to the screen for the first time in a made-for-television film called *Quicksilver Highway*.

"It came about," says Mick, "when CAA asked me if I would like to write a one-hour pilot for a sort of horror series that John McTiernan, director of *Die Hard* and *Predator*, would direct, and his [then] wife, Donna Dubrow, would produce. She had a deal with ABC to create a series, a kind of ghost hunter series. They wanted me to research urban folktales and true ghost stories from across the country and turn that into a weekly series. That didn't appeal to me a whole lot, but I gave them an idea I had come up with as I cogitated upon their concept.

"I wanted to create a character who is mysterious and interesting and fascinating and enigmatic, who claims to be *only* a storyteller, a strange character with a traveling sideshow of odd stories and odd artifacts. The concept would be a different geographic location across our country each week and he would collect people as he went along and tell them stories that would have something to do with their own lives. Initially what I wanted to do was to put together an ensemble of actors who would be in the stories each week, playing different parts each time.

"They liked that, and the people at ABC really responded well, especially when they learned that I had talked to Steve King about possibly doing his story "Chattery Teeth" as the pilot. So I wrote a one-hour script for them based on Steve's story and came up with the Aaron Quicksilver character."

ABC, however, ultimately passed on the idea, so CAA pitched the hour-long pilot to the Fox network. Smiling, Mick says, "*They* wanted a two-hour movie . . ."—so his next call was to Clive for a story to populate the second hour.

266

MASTERS OF HORROR

Episode #12 - "Haeckel's Tale"

by
Mick Garris

Based on the short story by Clive Barker

PINK PAGES, October 17th, 2005
pages: 57,57A,58,58A,59
FULL BLUE, October 11th, 2005
WHITE-LOCKED, September 22nd, 2005

Masters Productions I Ltd.
8651 Eastlake Drive
Burnaby, BC. V5A 4T7
Tel. (604) 444-1100
Fax. (604) 444-1116

"Some of the funkiest creatures I've done are in *Saint Sinner*."
—PATRICK TATOPOULOS

"I already knew which one I wanted—I said, 'How about "The Body Politic?"' and he said, 'As a film? I hadn't thought about that!'

"The two-hour teleplay is simply the one-hour pilot script with the next script stapled to it—that became our movie."

For both the director and Fox, the key piece of casting for a recurring series was that of the central storyteller, Aaron Quicksilver.

Christopher Lloyd—best known as Dr. Emmett Brown from the Back to the Future movies—was suggested by Lynn Kressel, who had also worked with Mick on *The Stand* as casting director. "She recommended him," he recalls, "because she felt that he was right to play this intelligent and imposing character who is larger-than-life and whose eyes reach into your soul. We never know whether he's good or evil but you get the impression that he has dabbled with the dark side on more than one occasion.

"In the wraparound story for 'The Body Politic,'" explains Mick, "Matt Frewer plays a pickpocket in the middle of a carnival who comes across the 'Quicksilver Exposition of Delightful Horrors' in a tent. Quicksilver tells him a story about talented hands like his, and we go into Clive's story, which I changed a bit.

"The lead character, again played by Frewer, is now a plastic surgeon who's got a great life, a great career. Clive's short story was a wonderful political satire—at least, that's how I read it—about a lower-middle-class tradesman who lives in England. Since we were doing this in the States, I thought an interesting satirical tack would be to set it in Beverly Hills in the land of facelifts and money and privilege. I transformed him into a plastic surgeon because I wanted to enhance the story with a heightened, '90s, L.A. edge. It takes place in the world of vanity and modern America but the situation is pretty faithful to Clive's story."

As with *Sleepwalkers*, Mick included cameos for friends, putting Clive into a scene alongside John Landis, both resplendent in purple operating-theater gowns.

"The purple outfits for all the medical clinic people," adds Mick, "were inspired by *Dead Ringers*. David Cronenberg's sister, Denise, was the costume designer on *Dead Ringers*, and the dramatic red outfits were so perfect for that film—which is my favorite of David's movies—so it's kind of a tribute, only of course ours is a lavender purple, because it's Beverly Hills and it's purple people who attend clinics in that area."

It would be a further five years between the release of *Quicksilver Highway* and the appearance of Clive's next television movie. This new story, *Saint Sinner*, was summarized by the SCI FI Channel in a press release ahead of its October 26, 2002, premiere:

> Only from the twisted imagination of horror scribe Clive Barker could a tale so wild, horrific and disturbingly sexy be spun. For the first time, SCI FI Channel partners with Barker on *Clive Barker Presents Saint Sinner*, an epic story of redemption, suspense and erotic horror . . . *Saint Sinner* centers on a 19th century monk who unwittingly lets loose two female demons upon an unsuspecting 21st century city. The two, driven by a centuries-old appetite, must sustain themselves by feeding on those who fall prey to their sensual charms. To redeem himself, the monk must track them to the present-day and stop them from wreaking deadly havoc.

The storyline—unconnected to the Razorline comic of the same name—had been one of a series of six ideas Clive had crafted for an ultimately unproduced "Shadows and Spirits" series of "movies of the week" with Fox around 1998. The idea was given a new lease of life with a screenplay by Doris Egan and Hans Rodionoff, creature design by Patrick Tatopoulos, direction by Joshua Butler, and a cast that included: Greg Serano as Brother Thomas, Gina Ravera as Detective Rachel Dressler, Mary Mara and Rebecca Harrell as the demons Mukar and Nakir, and William B. Davis as Father Michael. Christopher Lennertz provided the score.

Joshua Butler noted, "We're trying to create, with Clive's assistance and his vision, a new breed of female demon for the screen that we haven't seen before. [They are] incredibly sexually charged, almost drug addicts in the sense that their drug is everything around them, the world around them. Their senses are heightened, and they have to suck the life out of every room they're in, every object they encounter, and every human that crosses their paths. They're just ravenous, ravenous creatures. So ultimately, once that's set up in an almost mystical way, the film really takes off and really commits to the horror of what these two women are doing and the need to stop them."

Hans Rodionoff came onto the project later on for script revisions. "Doris Egan had written several drafts of the teleplay for *Saint Sinner*," he notes, "and she was also doing work on *Smallville* and *Dark Angel*. When they hired Josh Butler as director, he had a lot of things that he wanted to implement, and Doris was juggling a lot of stuff at the time and just couldn't do it in the given time frame. This was about a month before the cameras started rolling, so it was definitely a squeeze. Doris actually did the bulk of the work. She took Clive's idea and expanded on it."

Patrick Tatopoulos, who had provided creature design and effects on *Godzilla* (1998), *Pitch Black*, and *Independence Day*, among others, worked closely with Clive on the look of *Saint Sinner*'s creatures. He notes, "We quickly realized that we were in sync. The design came together really quickly. Clive had a very strong idea of what he wanted to see. Of course, Clive is an accomplished artist and he had a sketch for a creature—which ended up looking very different from that sketch! But it gave us a flavor. Some of the funkiest creatures I've done are in this story."

The next two television projects from Clive's work were both under the banner of the *Masters of Horror* series created by Mick Garris for Anchor Bay Entertainment and broadcast by Showtime.

The first, "Haeckel's Tale," was an adaptation by Mick of Clive's short story by the same name, which had appeared in volume 1 of the Dark Delicacies anthology series in 2005. The episode premiered in January 2006. The cast featured Derek Cecil as Ernst Haeckel, Leela Savasta as Elise Wolfram, and Jon Polito as the necromancer Montesquino. Roger Corman had originally been lined up to direct the story but had to pull out due to a back injury. Instead, John McNaughton took over directing duties.

Clive had earlier noted his enthusiasm for Roger Corman's take on his short story, saying, "I can't wait, particularly because there's talk of Roger Corman directing. . . . I've always been fond of Roger as a person; he's always been very nice to me and I'm hoping he'll be well enough to do it, and if he isn't well enough to do it, then there'll be somebody else at the helm, but I said to Mick last time we spoke, please to hold out for Roger as long as you can because he's a wonderful guy. . . . It might be one of a few things that Roger chooses to do at *this* end of his life and I've always thought of him as a master and the fact is it's a period story and my favorite of his movies are the Poe pictures—it feels like an interesting match."

Roger Corman was also excited, saying "Clive Barker's provocative short story suggests an opportunity to go one step further than Mary Shelley's nightmare masterpiece, *Frankenstein*, in suggesting how closely the erotic drive and the obsession with death are linked." But "I hurt my back, and it was very painful, and I knew that, even though I wanted to do it, I just wouldn't be able to."

The *Masters of Horror* project had grown out of a series of dinners organized by Mick Garris in 2004, as one of the Masters, John Landis, recalls: "There was this television documentary called *Masters of Horror*, and it was about George Romero, Tobe Hooper, Wes Craven, John Carpenter, Guillermo del Toro, and myself, and a whole bunch of horror movie directors. Mick Garris called everybody and said, 'Hey, we should have a dinner and call it the 'Masters of Horror Dinner!' So we met in the Valley last year: Guillermo, Tobe, myself, Sam Raimi, and Carpenter—David Cronenberg was there once . . . a whole bunch of people, and it was very fun, because we got very silly and it was like: 'The Masters of Horror have coffee!' or 'The Masters of Horror order dessert!'

"We've done that four or five times now, with different people every time, but the good thing Garris did was he put together a deal with this company to make a series of movies called *Masters of Horror*—which I think is a really stupid label—where each one of us is supposed to direct a movie, so now we are doing it. They are giving us a budget of $1.5 million for each film, and with that money we can basically do anything we want, as long as it's shot in Vancouver, with the same crew. And it has to be scary, somehow!"

The camaraderie among the Masters was evident. John Carpenter, for example, ahead of his first episode, "Cigarette Burns," noted wryly, "It's a little series we're doing for Showtime. We each have an hour. Each of us has an hour to shoot in ten days. And the first director they got was John Landis. He's now way over budget and way over schedule. So there may not be any more *Masters of Horror*. He may do them in. Dario Argento starts next week. They pushed me later on the schedule because they're going to take all the money out of my show and put it in everybody else's. . . ."

John McNaughton was only too happy to join the team: "When they called me in, the story was already chosen. Clive Barker had written the short story and gave it to Mick Garris, who wrote the screen-play. I made some notes on the script and there were a few minor changes, but it was already in good shape. I chose the actors; in fact, I brought in two actors I had worked with before. Because we shot in Vancouver, most of the cast came from Canada, and my episode was in fact the last one shot there. . . .

"It's different from anything I've done. We have a scene in a graveyard with this naked dead woman who's surrounded by dozens of zombies. When I look at the episode, there are a number of scenes that really remind me of paintings I like, because art is a great influence in my style as a director and storyteller. So I have a whole store of paintings in my head, and I look at them when I need an influence for a certain scene."

"It was," says Clive, "if you'll excuse my French, fucking marvelous. 'Haeckel's Tale' is a story that I'm very proud of, and they did a magnificent job with it, particularly since it was a period piece and the FX are amazing. It's pretty intense stuff, and that pressed me to push even further with the

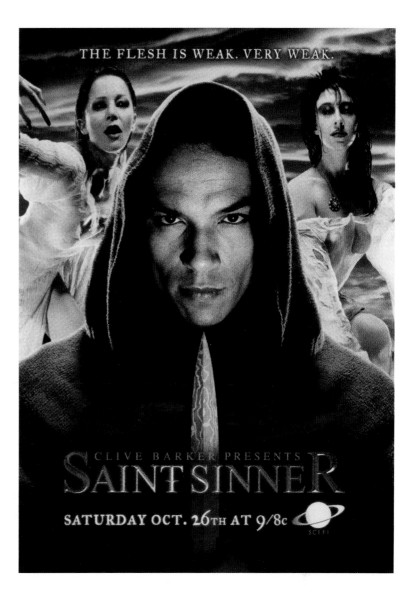

second story, so the erotic elements in 'Valerie on the Stairs' are probably extreme."

Season 2 of *Masters of Horror* saw Mick Garris both adapt and direct Clive's story 'Valerie on the Stairs.' Clive rewrote his 1999 fiction treatment to update it for the show, still planning to turn it into a complete short story in time. "I gave him that forty-five-page treatment and said, 'I know there are going to be things in this story that you are not going to be able to get on to the screen, primarily for financial reasons, but I want that stuff in the short story, so I gave you everything,' and I completely trust him to make the right choices as to where he's going to put the money. Mick, God bless him, said it was the first time he'd received a forty-five-page treatment for a sixty-minute teleplay!

" 'Valerie on the Stairs' is about a house which has been given by a now-dead writer, a failed writer, over as a kind of hospice for failed writers. They take rooms and they can stay there and the moment they get a piece of work published, they're out, OK? I think in the story there are nine rooms; it's a big house and nine fervent and fevered and desperate imaginations working each in solitude can do strange things to houses. . . .The thing that's fun about it is it's about writers and it's about the agony of it, really; it's about the pleasure of it and it's about the things that haunt you.

"I think it probably would have been a long short story, even maybe shading into a novella . . . with a large erotic element—and it was really the fact that the erotic elements of 'Haeckel's Tale' had worked, I thought, so very well; the casting of the girl was amazing, and the scenes involving her in the cemetery were, I thought, very intense and certainly a benchmark, really—you hadn't seen that on television for sure! I liked this mingling of the erotic and the horrific and I had this other idea and when I say I'd been dawdling around with it, I mean I'd been dawdling around with it for probably five or six years—very clearly it needed to get used up and what better place for it?"

Tony Todd and Christopher Lloyd both made return visits to Clive Barker stories as the Beast Othakeye and one of the writers in the house, Everett Neely, respectively. Tyron Leitso played the central character, Rob Hanisey, alongside the object of the writer's dreams, Clare Grant as Valerie. Howard Berger and Greg Nicotero provided special make-up effects, as they had done on *Lord of Illusions*.

The episode aired on December 29, 2006, and was well reviewed as one of the strongest in a strong series.

ABOVE

Promotional postcard for the *Saint Sinner* TV movie for Sci-Fi Channel, directed by Joshua Butler and starring Greg Serano as Tomas Alcala, Gina Ravera as Rachel Dressler, Mary Mara as Munkar, and Rebecca Harrell Tickell as Nakir, with William B. Davis as Father Michael, 2002.

> # "I never ever lose fascination with villains and the idea of speaking an entire novel with the voice of a villain has been, I suppose, just a pleasure, a holiday!"

2007 MISTER B. GONE

"Burn this book!"

In 2007, expectations were running high for a story—"The Scarlet Gospels"—that had long been gestating from a short entry in a proposed collection into a major novel. But that spring, Clive announced instead that he would be releasing an entirely unrelated story—*Mister B. Gone*—for Halloween.

"The rumors are true!" he posted in an online blog. "*Mister B. Gone* is a short horror novel—slightly longer than *Thief*, but intended for an adult readership—that tells of the discovery of a demonic 'memoir' penned in the year 1438. It consists of one copy only that has been buried by an assistant who worked for Johannes Gutenberg of printing press fame."

Clive had been writing "The Scarlet Gospels" for some time and explained that he'd needed to write *Mister B. Gone* as a "breath" before plunging into the final draft of the longer novel. Writing in the first person helped to distinguish it from anything else in his mind.

"I didn't want this to be a tale of a demon in Hell, I wanted this to be a tale of a demon amongst men and women, observing their ways, observing evil, observing human evil. I suppose I want to show as many ways [as possible] that the demonic side of us manifests itself and so, towards the end, he says, 'I'm giving you a treatise on evil here, I'm showing you all the ways that you use your powers against one another, in threats and seduction, physical threats sometimes, sometimes mental manipulation.' I hope it's a very powerful narrative as a consequence because you can read it as being a story of the devil you don't want to know or you can actually decode it and find all kinds of other levels way below."

HarperCollins created an aged look for the book, printed in period-style fonts on yellowed paper to sell the idea that readers had a fifteenth-century volume in their hands, and the Halloween release date tied to the pitch that this was a return to full-on horror fiction for Clive.

Clive wrote a "Dear Reader" note in a promotional envelope of press materials that read:

I've always wanted to write a book that will play with the reader in a way that has never been tried before.

Enter Jakabok, a vicious, demented, and blood-thirsty demon. He was an occupant of hell for many years, and he knows how to cause every kind of mischief; grief, anguish,

and agony are his food and drink. But Mister B., as Jakabok likes to be called, is no longer an occupant of the underworld. He's in this book.

Let me be clear: Mister B. is not in this book as Scarlett O'Hara is in *Gone with the Wind*. The terrifying Mister B. will be possessing this book, watching you from its words. He can feel the pressure of your fingers on the pages, he can hear your breath and your mutterings, he can also hear your heart quicken. That's what he loves most: the quickening heart, the clammy hands. Any proof that the terrifying tales which he tells are working their dark magic.

You see, Mister B. has ambitions, and he'll use every trick he knows to get what he wants from you. He'll entertain you with his stories of the war between heaven and hell that is going on around us all the time; he'll threaten you with horrors only those who've seen the depths of the underworld could possibly know. He'll even throw in some gallows humour when he's in the mood.

But what does he really want? And what is he prepared to do to you to achieve his ends? The book has plenty of answers. But to get to them, you'll need to read, and with every page you turn Jakabok comes closer to you. Closer, ever closer. Tasting the sweat in your fingertips as it sinks into the page where he waits.

Welcome to the world of Mister B. He is delighted to meet you. Really he is.

Clive's focus on the evil demon, Jakabok, and the Halloween presentation distracted many readers and critics from his underlying look at the power of language. Literally, the book uses three small words—burn this book—to influence the way the reader turns the pages. Historically, Gutenberg's movable-type press remains a touchstone for the democratization of the written word.

Speaking to IGN.com as the novel was released in October 2007, Clive reflected: "I wanted *Mister B. Gone* to be a celebration of the word and what the word can do. And, indeed, what it can't do. In a way, at the ripe old age of fifty-five, I'm still playing in a sandpit—albeit of my own, peculiar concoction—which contains words and colors and ideas."

The book's flap copy reads:

> *Mister B. Gone* marks the long-awaited return of Clive Barker, the great master of the macabre, to the classic horror story. This bone-chilling novel, in which a medieval devil speaks directly to his reader—his tone murderous one moment, seductive the next—is a never-before-published memoir allegedly penned in the year 1438. The demon has embedded himself in the very words of this tale of terror, turning the book itself into a dangerous object, laced with menace only too ready to break free and exert its power.
>
> A brilliantly and truly unsettling tour de force of the supernatural, *Mister B. Gone* escorts the reader on an intimate and revelatory journey to uncover the shocking truth of the battle between Good and Evil.

2003– PAINTING IN THE
2012 MIDNIGHT HOUR

"What would you see if you could peek inside the mind of Clive Barker?"

In 2004, Clive began a promotional tour across the US in support of the second book of Abarat, *Days of Magic*, *Nights of War*. Previous book tours had involved bookstore signings and media interviews, but the different nature of Abarat led him to add new types of events.

Over the course of 2004 and 2005 these included live painting demonstrations at Amazon's corporate headquarters in Seattle, at the West Hollywood Book Fair, at Storyopolis (a dedicated children's bookstore in Los Angeles), at the *Los Angeles Times* Festival of Books, in Toronto at the *Rue Morgue* Festival of Fear, and at Tower Records in Sherman Oaks, California.

In Chicago, in October 2004, alongside a small weekend exhibition of selected Abarat canvases at the city's Museum of Contemporary Art, Clive led a workshop painting session with children at the Humanities Festival.

His next one-man show was far more extensive and was timed to mark another artistic step forward. Running from December 8, 2005, to January 28, 2006, at a new venue, the Bert Green Fine Art gallery in Los Angeles, the exhibition, *Visions of Heaven and Hell*, took its theme from a new art monograph, published in October 2005 by Rizzoli.

The publisher's press material said:

What would you see if you could peek inside the mind of Clive Barker, creator of such classics as *Weaveworld*, *Hellraiser*, and *Candyman*? Would you dare look?

Crack open *Visions of Heaven and Hell* and you have unlocked a Pandora's Box of images that are certain to stay inside your head. For more than twenty-five years Barker has awed

ABOVE

A selection of Clive's oil-on-canvas paintings in storage, April 2009.

fans and critics alike with his groundbreaking works of fiction, but what few know is that the heart of his fantastic worlds lies in pictures. Now, for the first time, this book brings out from the dark depths more than 300 of Barker's most stunning drawings and oil paintings. This artwork renders with expressionist fervor some of our most primal passions—good, evil, and all that's between. From the graphically terrifying to the ecstatically sensual, *Visions of Heaven and Hell* takes you on a journey through unexplored and forbidden realms.

As with the earlier Pacific Design Center exhibition, presenting the canvases as works of art—not as illustrations of a story—was an important statement of intent.

"My pictures are not illustrations," he said, "because they precede the literature, they precede the words, so they cannot, by definition, be illustrations, because they don't illustrate anything.

"The Abarat as a narrative is me as a storyteller creating reasons for these things to exist—but it's not the true reason," he stressed. "They exist of themselves: I am giving them a literary life, but a literary life is not a painterly life. A painterly life is completely separate.

"I'm producing pictures at quite a rate now," Clive said in 2006, "and I have the experience of going through paintings as they are taken away; I say, 'Take this away before I fuck with it, just take it away,' and I will not go to the gallery house for maybe a week or ten days and I will say, 'What is that?' Obviously I know it's my handiwork, I have a vague sense of where I was when I was making it, but when a gentleman was here recently talking to me about Prometheus not only stealing fire . . . for humanity, but also his blood producing flowers from the earth, which was something I didn't know, it turned out both images were included in this painting that I had finished two weeks before I met him. . . ."

As the subject matter of Abarat grows darker in the third volume, the whimsical lightness of some of Clive's early canvases is superseded by flaming images of destruction, villains threatening

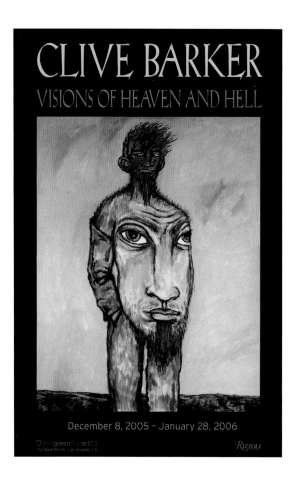

CLIVE BARKER
VISIONS OF HEAVEN AND HELL

December 8, 2005 - January 28, 2006

bertgreenfineart
102 West 5th St., Los Angeles, CA

RIZZOLI

"Painting is not a puzzle. Painting is red and yellow. Painting is filling the brush with something that looks so tasty you feel like you could feed off it for a thousand years, then slapping it on the canvas and feeling an immediate emotional rush from it."

psychological terrors, and unfiltered depictions of apocalyptic events. One such image, *The Stitchlings Howl*, reflects the intensity and horror of Mater Motley's campaign to conquer the Abarat through fear, intimidation, and force.

"The books are going to have pictures that are frightening, embodiments of things still to come. *The Stitchlings Howl* is one of the grimmest pictures in the book and I just wanted to show total heartlessness, a total lack of humanity. I wanted to say: this is what it would be like to be surrounded by stitchlings, to have the whole canvas—from top to bottom of the painting—completely gray and brown pigments, no release, no compassion, no morality. Because if you think of the great heartless war machines of the twentieth century—the Nazi war machine will obviously be uppermost/topmost of mind—that would be what the stitchlings are about. Yes, they are these things, these bits of cloth and flesh, filled with mud; so were the Nazi war machines. They are relentless, terrible things. I've actually painted a couple of pictures of them which may not even make the cut of the book because they're vicious."

Further solo gallery exhibitions were mounted at Bert Green's gallery in November 2007, November 2009, and January 2011; at Packer Schopf Gallery in Chicago in January and October of 2008; at Sloan Fine Art in New York in April 2008; at the Crown Gallery in Carlisle, England, in July 2011; and at the Mars Gallery in Chicago in October 2011. He also had a joint show with Myron Conan Dyal at the Otis College of Art and Design in Los Angeles in August 2008.

Clive had become less publicly visible as he endured a series of five operations between 2008 and 2010 to remove recurring throat polyps (benign, but debilitating because they restricted his oxygen intake). Reenergized after the last of these, he hosted the Los Angeles Museum of Contemporary Art at his home one evening in mid-June 2010, allowing a new audience to witness up close the profusion of canvases stored in the studio, and to see Clive at work on a piece that he created as the evening progressed.

2011 ABARAT: ABSOLUTE MIDNIGHT

"Rise, all of you! And give me my Midnight!"

In December 2005, while also working on *The Scarlet Gospels* novel, Clive described the difficulties of keeping both the third and fourth Abarat novels in balance.

"All the files of notes that I've kept for story elements have 'Abarat III and IV' written on the front of them and that's in part because I haven't yet figured out where I'm going to take the break in the story and it's partly because there is a *shit-load* goes on in these books. . . . And I sort of am, in a way, thinking of those two books as one huge run-up to a massive climax."

As the year drew to a close, Clive made the difficult decision to extend the scope of the narrative from the planned four-volume series to five.

"I had two weeks over Christmas where I sat down with myself and examined what I knew I wanted the narrative journey, the shamanistic journey, that Candy Quackenbush takes from being an errant schoolgirl in Chickentown to being what she will become at the end of what will now be the fifth and final book of the Abarat series. And I realized I couldn't get it in four books; I couldn't get the *characters* in four books! . . . You've known from the beginning how much I've been in service to the energies of this book—the paintings came along when I didn't expect them and when I started to create a world round them, the world began to proliferate at a speed that I had never experienced in my life before. And I have grown to love this world, probably more than any other that I've created and I want to serve the rising scale of this drama and the conflict and the revelation of what Candy is, of what Abarat is, of what it is to us, as human beings, what we are to it. I don't want to rush it.

"This is, in one sense, the closest thing I will do to my idol Blake's work in the sense that it's a marriage of my painting and my poetry and my writing and it's for all audiences and it's metaphysical and it's comical and it's demonic and it's of Heaven and Hell and all things in between and if I'm going to do that, man, I've got to do that the best way I can and I'm not going to fuck it up. That was what the conclusion of that fourteen days was; it was 'You know what, Barker? You can't do this in four books—own up!'

"It was a huge relief, because I saw the bigger engine, and there must have been a part of me that knew the bigger engine was there all along. . . . The obvious thing is, I now have a middle book—I have a wheel and I have a hub of a wheel."

That relief was short-lived; Clive was struggling to juggle *The Scarlet Gospels*, various film projects, and Abarat all at once. He elected to take some time off to visit Hawai'i for a short break in February 2007. On his return, he resolved to work on something that would be a break from the pressures of his other projects; this would be the short novel *Mister B. Gone*. With that book complete and delivered, he at last returned to Abarat in June 2007 but found many of the project's complications remained.

"It's very hard in the abstract to describe what the challenge is but you will see immediately what I've been trying to tackle, which is this elaborate dance of characters who are playing out some kind of middle eight, like in a song, and it's got to be beautiful and it's got to be seductive and it's also got to be at times really, really scary, because we are showing the first signs of where Mater Motley gets her magic from and we are seeing the book of the Abarataraba and the stakes suddenly become much, much higher."

If the second volume of Abarat was the most difficult to write for exclusively creative reasons, Clive found himself describing the third in equally harsh terms—this time for reasons rooted in the real world.

"I've had some personal things going on in my life," he said, "which are nothing to do with the book which have been sort of sad and hard to deal with, and frightening sometimes. And I've had to spend more time dealing with stuff. . . . I love doing this and it has annoyed me intensely that it has taken me so long to write the third book. And it's nothing to do with the book, in the end, it's to do with some things that I don't really have any control over, which are other people and their own issues and their own troubles."

In early 2009, Clive had endured the painful breakup of his relationship with his husband, David, and the fall-out from this was difficult both in practical and emotional terms. The turbulence of these events threatened an already overdue deadline with his publisher—and undoubtedly intensified the dark and apocalyptic plot of the third Abarat book.

Usually, Clive waits until he's happy with a final draft of a book before he shares more than a treatment with his publisher. Given the length of time it was taking, he instead delivered an early-draft manuscript of *Absolute Midnight* in August 2009, seeking early notes that he was on the right track.

"I want it to be a book about all of us. . . . I didn't want this to be about a very special girl, I wanted it to be about a girl who could be anyone and even though she seems to have some elements of uncertainty in her nature, we're going to discover that we all have those uncertainties in our nature, at least to some extent, and then the question is how do we deal with them?"

After a long wait for these edits and notes, when they arrived in mid-2010, Clive faced a critical six-week deadline in which to turn the draft into a final edit for print—without the usual iterations in between. "It was draft upon draft upon draft, all squashed into six weeks, and four hours of sleep a night—I was sleeping under the desk, because it was the shortest possible distance between me and the work."

Clive was also dealing with a terrible loss: the death in August 2009 of his young friend and mentee, Justin Brown. Justin had spent many hours with Clive recounting his experiences of military tours in Iraq and his insights had informed the conflicts within the book.

Abarat: Absolute Midnight is dedicated to Clive's then-new partner, Johnny Raymond, and to Robb Humphreys and Mark Alan Miller, all three of whom supported Clive in his Herculean effort to pull the final draft over the line.

Despite leaving him emotionally drained, the third Abarat volume ultimately delivers on Clive's hopes for it, in terms of the darkness of its material and the scope of the narrative, speaking directly to his personal philosophies of the power of both language and color. As evil comes into ascendancy, Abarat's characters—both heroes and villains—are severely tested and primed for further complexities to be revealed.

"One of my biggest ambitions for these books," Clive said ahead of publication, "is that I would take the clichés, if you will, of fairy tales and the clichés of heroic fiction, epic fiction, and I would turn them upside down."

The book's flap copy reads:

"I know that many of you here have waited years for this Hour," Mater Motley said, using that voice that, though it was barely conversational in volume, was somehow heard everywhere. "The waiting is over. Tomorrow there will be no dawn. Only midnight, absolute and eternal."

And so begins a new chapter in the epic story of sixteen-year-old Candy Quackenbush and her journeys through the world of the Abarat, where every hour is an island in one eternal day, and nothing is as it seems.

Candy travels through the Abarat from island to island and across the sea with an unlikely band of friends: the escaped prisoner Malingo the Geshrat, the quarrelsome John Brothers, who all share the same body but never the same opinion, and the many other colourful characters they meet along the way.

The problem is that trouble finds Candy wherever she goes. And soon she discovers a secret plot, masterminded by the diabolical Mater Motley, who is obsessed with becoming Empress of the Islands. Her method is simple. She will darken the skies, putting out the suns, moons and stars. She will bring Absolute Midnight.

ABOVE LEFT
Untitled, pre-2011.

ABOVE RIGHT
Mater Motley, 2005.

OPPOSITE PAGE,
BOTTOM LEFT

Leading the Way, circa
2006.

OPPOSITE PAGE,
BOTTOM RIGHT

Imagination, pre-2010,
used as the cover of
Clive's non-fiction
collection, *Clive Barker:
The Painter, the
Creature and the Father
of Lies*, in 2011.

1990- **VIDEO GAMES**
2009

"Be ever vigilant, or the Undying King will walk the earth once again."

The earliest video games based on Clive's work were released in 1990, both based on the movie *Nightbreed*. Made by Ocean Software, you could play as Boone as he dealt with the Sons of the Free, a masked Decker, and other hazards on his descent into Midian to free the Breed and release the Berserkers.

It would be another decade before a game involving Clive would be released, although he did collaborate with Virgin Games on a planned version of the Ectosphere (the world introduced to Marvel comic readers in *Ectokid*) in the early 1990s.

Clive Barker's Undying was released in 2001. Clive actually came late to the project; he was asked to provide an edge to a partially developed first-person shooter game running on the Unreal Engine as a known piece of software (developed by Epic Games). The game was originally based on an earlier Steven Spielberg project that promised arcane magic, supernatural abominations, and ancient horror.

"DreamWorks was looking for a partner to develop the story, the creatures in the story, and bring it to conclusion," he notes, "This was a great way to see the bones of the thing and then be invited to put the flesh on it.

"They had done some of it and I said, 'Make it more weird.' I've written hard on the story because my first responsibility, I felt, was to get the story part of it right and be sure that the story made emotional sense. That seemed to be the heart of the problem. Once we'd done that, then we could start to fiddle with design and first up was character, because that's really what an audience is going to respond to."

The main character was Clive's first focus. "We had this fellow called Magnus. Count Magnus Wolfram. Who was bald, tattooed, looked like a comic book hero. And I got them all in a room, and I said, 'Look, does anyone in this room know a count? No. Does anybody in this room know anybody called Magnus?

No. Does anybody really want to be in this guy's skin? Since this is a first-person play, why would you want to be in this man's skin? Why would you want to play as him?' And so we threw him out, and I said, 'Look. You've got a gay man in charge here. Bring me somebody I want to sleep with. Bring me somebody fabulously sexy.'

"Brian Horton, about ten days later, sent me the character that now appears on the screen. Who was wonderful; he's everything I wanted. He was just the right kind of character. He seemed like somebody you would want to be, somebody you would want to play, whose skin you would want to occupy for a period of time. Even if he was going against the hordes of hell, at least he was going to do it with a smile on his face.

"Next up was environment and I did nothing with the monasteries and the walls of the manor, as that fell to the designers completely, and, with Oneiros, I just said that I want to make sure that its depths are as vertiginous as possible. It can't just be a pretty piece of Lovecraft. It's got to have a weird kind of logic to it, which it's got."

Although he was working in new environment, Clive was fascinated by the process of creating a strong narrative:

"In a way, it does go back a bit to the Books of Blood, the feelings I had when I wrote those books, which was that there were no rules. There are some things in this game that are just outrageous. Ambrose, particularly in his transformed state, is really just disgusting. I also think, if you look at this game, it's designed like a movie, it feels like a movie. It's not brightly colored like a Pokémon game; it has sepias and grays and occasionally eruptions of red.

"I think, in a way, you can tie Undying to Edgar Allan Poe or H. P. Lovecraft. Some of the landscapes definitely bring to mind some of the weird, inter-dimensional spaces that Lovecraft evoked, while once you get inside the house, and you see all the twisted, messed-up family, you're in Poe territory, the same territory that informs the House of Usher. So I think we paid our dues to our literary forebears and then moved on into something wilder."

Clive also lent his vocal talents to the game—recording the voice of the black sheep of the family, Ambrose.

Undying's producer, Brady Bell, looked back at the collaborative process and reflected on what had the potential to be a difficult project, teaming up with someone with little understanding of game-building:

"We approached Clive with a first pass at our story and environments already in place. He took the story, punched holes in it, taught us how to improve it, and went to work on additional character

ABOVE

Clive collaborated with Electronic Arts/ DreamWorks Interactive to work on the narrative for the *Undying* game. Cover art and logo for the game, which had its US release in February 2001.

287

"Technology is moving along at such a speed that we will have engines that will create novels in the form of games . . . and I want to be there when it happens."

design with our artists. It's been an ongoing process where the team has benefited far past our expectations. Without question, what attracted us most was Clive's diverse talent. On our team we have a guy who studied literature, one who graduated from film school, and a troop of artists and animators from various professional backgrounds. Clive Barker is the only person we could all honestly say we've been professionally inspired by. That's more rare than people think."

The game's synopsis reads:

Set in Ireland of the 1920's, players take on the role of Magnus, who has been summoned to an ancestral estate by its lone descendent, Jeremiah. Death has claimed Jeremiah's four siblings, all of whom have been reanimated and now intend to slay their living brother, the last of the family. To save his friend and unravel the horror that has befallen Jeremiah and his family, players must embark on five perilous quests. The quests will take players to 10 areas of the game including the ancestral estate, a destroyed monastery, the Eternal Autumn and the cursed city of Oneiros. Players will have to defeat each of the evil siblings in his or her individually corrupted and demonic environments in order to grasp the greater scope of the horror of *Clive Barker's Undying*.

Along the way players will also encounter more than 20 enemy creatures, but will be able to avail themselves of 16 spells (eight defensive and eight either miscellaneous or offensive), including the destructive Skull Storm and reality-bending Mindshatter. In addition, there will be eight weapons for players to use in the game including dynamite, a shotgun, Tibetan War Cannon and The Scythe of Brennus. The game will also feature a special spell called Scrye that will allow players to see or hear clues and back story that are not apparent to the naked eye.

In 2005 Clive collaborated with Majesco Entertainment and Tiger Hill Entertainment on a planned game called "Demonik," with models created by Marvel artist David Finch, saying:

"I enjoyed my *Undying* time and I'm enjoying this too. It's not, as you know, my strength; I am not a player and yet that in some ways is fun because I'm learning as I go and it's always nice to learn a new thing. It's a big pool of people, there's a lot of people involved, but I like that too; it's collaboration. My day is spent, as you know, in solitary endeavors, so sitting with these guys and solving problems and getting some designs together [is wonderful]."

Explaining the plot, Clive continued, "It's essentially a revenge motif, it's a demon summoned that you are controlling, summoned to carry out revenge on your behalf and the question is, are you actually going to do it or aren't you going to do it? It carries some moral weight, which is fun. The first thing I did when I sat everybody down was quote Gauguin, who said, 'Life being what it is, one seeks revenge,' and everybody nodded sagely and everybody around the table had to tell me who they would want revenge upon—it was amazing! Wives, old boyfriends, there was no end to it, so that's actually been fun too."

The project was canceled due to financial difficulties, but with the importance and reach of great storytelling in the burgeoning games industry becoming clear, Clive saw the possibilities for a story idea he had been mulling for some time: *Jericho*.

The Abyss of the First-Born for End of Game. (side view)

First Born

"'Demonik' got canceled, which was a bit heartbreaking for me, because I put a lot of work and love into it and I got to work with David Finch, who's an extraordinary artist, and that was wonderful. But it's very seldom I get involved in something that doesn't, somehow or other, come together—finally. It may take years, but finally I'll get there. And the other thing is, it just makes your appetite for the next thing more acute, so when we decided to do *Jericho*, there was a real hunger in me to get back to the gaming arena and to do something that was genuinely intense and threatening and hopefully had a narrative that was intriguing and a little bit off the beaten track."

Working with Alchemic Productions and MercurySteam, Codemasters released *Clive Barker's Jericho* in 2007 as a squad-based first-person shooter. The unfolding narrative was perfectly suited to making the linear journey through game levels—with chapters of the story equating to the developing locations and slices of time—an immersive horror experience.

ABOVE
Clive's sketch of The Abyss of the Firstborn for *Jericho*, 2007.

As well as supplying the story, complete with an epic enemy, the Firstborn, Clive was involved at all levels of the design, providing sketches as shorthand to communicate ideas for the designers: "It's certainly useful to be able to 'talk' in both words and pictures," he said.

Strongly aware of the cinematic strengths of the game, Clive called on composer Cris Velasco—who had been working on "Demonik" when it was canceled—to create a soundscape that would further engulf the player in the world of *Jericho*, a project that Cris relished: "When I read Clive's books I really believe in these characters and get wrapped up emotionally in what's happening to them. It's just a simple step to take these emotions he's elicited from me and translate them into music. I've always felt that the worlds he creates have been begging to have music written for them, and with *Jericho* I finally had the chance."

Alongside artistic elements there were technical challenges for MercurySteam as advances in gaming led players to have ever-greater expectations of their experience. Designer Raul Rubio, elaborated: "Perhaps the biggest challenge was to merge the tactical action with the horror genre. It's difficult to create tension with six elite soldiers armed to the teeth supporting you. . . . Players do expect that enemies smell you when approaching from behind; they do expect that monsters turn around if you shine torchlight on them; [they] do expect that patrolling enemies warn [their] pals when spotting you. And, of course, they do expect that enemies can dodge all the obstacles while in the middle of a battle. And all this while the AI manages a six-member squad able to take cover, work as a team, help other team members when they are in trouble, and take care of themselves looking for advantageous positions.

289

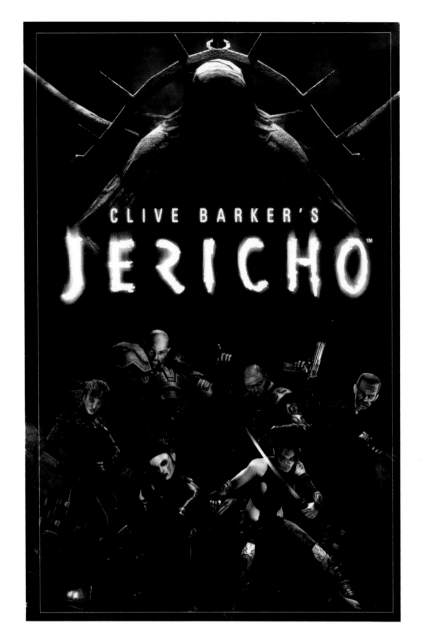

Jericho's AI is possibly one of the things we are most proud of. We usually joke, saying that *Clive Barker's Jericho* won't be remembered for its AI, which is wonderful."

Clive remained impressed by both by the talents and the teamwork, working in what was a relatively new medium for him, which he noted at the game's presentation in Madrid.

"It is important to emphasize: the making of a game is not the work of one man. Even though my name is above the title, I was not alone in this huge endeavor.

"I have worked with the guys at Mercury-Steam over a period of years now, developing, sending drawings backwards and forwards, sending ideas backwards and forwards, always trying to push the envelope, always looking for the taboo, the forbidden. Always trying to find images that have not been seen before. This is hard. In gaming there is a tendency, as there is in every other art form—and it is an art form— for games to resemble the games that came before them. So we have a lot of games that look as though somebody had been reading *Lord of the Rings*, a lot of games that suggest someone saw *The Matrix*, and while, of course, you can never be completely new because it's not the nature of the human imagination to be able to push out everything that you know, wherever we found something in the work that looked too much like something else in somebody else's work, we threw it out.

"The folks at MercurySteam have been extraordinary in their patience with my desire and ambition for this game."

Jericho's backstory reads:

In the beginning, God created the Firstborn . . .

According to certain Gnostic and Apocryphal texts, before Adam, before Eve, there was the Firstborn, God's first abortive attempt at creating a being in his own image.

In a remote desert in the Middle East, near the cradle of all civilization, the earth was wounded. The presence of the Firstborn continued to fester, eon after eon, breaking down the fabric of reality as human civilization flourished around it. The prophecy states that the Firstborn will break through into our world several times. With each appearance, it will ride disease, corruption and perversity like an all-consuming wave until seven mystics sacrifice themselves to drive it back into the Abyss . . .

The Firstborn has made previous attempts at escape, always returning to the spot of its conception. Due to the immense power contained within it, this piece of earth has

"It's like Russian dolls, spaces within each other, and trapped inside each space is a slice of time where the warriors of good have gone against ultimate evil and have lost."

been contested for thousands of years by conqueror after conqueror, each with his own agenda for the Firstborn.

On its first appearance, seven Sumerian priests entombed the Firstborn within a holy ziggurat and guarded its prison until the desert and their enemies consumed their great civilization and the site was lost. The Roman Empire was the next landlord, the Crusaders the next . . . on and on until the present day. This is the bedrock on which the modern city of Al-Khali now stands.

Every time the Firstborn is banished, it takes with it a larger piece of the earth to add to its realm, the Pyxis. Whenever it next returns, those layers of time and space overlap with reality, creating a place out of place, a time without time. Like a Chinese puzzle box, the city of Al-Khali has been transformed by the Firstborn into layer after layer of time and space. The further you go into the city, the further back in time you travel until you reach the point of origin, the moment the Firstborn came into being.

The Department of Occult Warfare was founded in WWII to investigate reports that the Nazis were pursuing the development of supernatural weaponry. At first, the D.O.W. was concerned only with analysis, poring over reports and intelligence gathered by the Office of Strategic Services. But soon it became clear that Hitler, guided by the mystical Thule Society, was not only obsessed with procuring a supernatural advantage, he was actually succeeding.

Thereafter the D.O.W. began taking a more active role in the war, working closely with their British counterparts on missions ranging from the acquisition of powerful supernatural relics to psychic assassination.

It is now the most powerful and clandestine special forces unit in the U.S. arsenal.

Fresh from his experience with *Jericho*, Clive wrote an introduction to editor Bernard Perron's *Horror Video Games* book in 2009, offering both insights and a warning about the medium, one that he had been keen to avoid in plotting the game:

"In an earlier time, this audience would have been satisfied with the wonders of Ray Harryhausen's wonderful stop-motion monsters and Raquel Welch's pneumatic breasts in *One Million Years B.C.* or had their gonads tickled by the stylized sex games of comic books (all those tight-fitting garments that reveal everything and show nothing; the vast array of phallic weapons and monstrous vaginal dimension breaches). Now the audiences that would have lapped up Raquel and her dinosaurs are immersed in far more murky territory and it is serious stuff.

"Why? Because unlike the audiences for earlier adventure epics involving exquisitely beautiful women, abominable tortures, and fantastically grotesque monsters, these players are involved—*profoundly, intimately involved*—in the action. They do not sit, as I did, seven days in a row, watching every performance of *One Million Years B.C.* in my local cinema in Liverpool. They are locked away in their rooms with sugar- and caffeine-stoked energy drinks engaging in battles with *Dark Forces*. This is not remotely the same kind of experience that I had watching Harryhausen's masterpiece. These players are defining their own kind of heroism, or, more perniciously, being drawn into an identification with evil. Let us not dismiss the power of these stories too lightly. *They tell lies.* The most monstrous lie, of course, is the merciless contempt that they stir up for otherness; the ease with which something other than the human is demonized, and reduced, and made fodder for the gun-wielding player who stands anonymously behind the screen.

"Is this not very dangerous territory?"

2003–2020 BOOKS OF BLOOD MOVIES

"The dead have highways."

In 2003, Clive formed a new production company called Midnight Picture Show with an idea to produce a series of independently made films of his work, primarily drawing on the thirty stories in the Books of Blood, only four of which had yielded theatrical or television movies at that point: "Rawhead Rex," "The Yattering and Jack," "The Forbidden," and "The Body Politic."

After making *Lord of Illusions*, Clive had decided to focus on writing and producing rather than directing, but over the next ten years he faced a frustrating cycle: again and again he would develop a project with his team at Seraphim—which would then seem poised for production at an interested studio—but then would end up unmade, having fallen into limbo. The decision to go it alone was very much born of this disappointing process.

In particular, a three-picture deal at Spelling Films was dropped in 1998 when the company decided to exit theatrical features to concentrate on television projects, and then a deal for six "movies of the week" at Fox fell away shortly afterwards.

Speaking to the planned approach with Spelling, Clive noted, "This was an attempt to sort of go back to first principles. The first principles are what I consider to be the golden age of low-budget horror films. I think some of the best work was done by people who were not bound by massive budgets. They weren't making huge studio movies. They were making offbeat, modestly scaled, modestly budgeted, personal movies. Cronenberg was doing that. Wes Craven was doing that. I feel that horror fiction on the screen is best when it takes risks. The more conservative it gets, the less interesting it gets, the less scary it gets. I think one of the things we have increasingly lost is the risk element. I'd like to get some of that back."

THE MOST TERRIFYING RIDE YOU'LL EVER TAKE

THE MIDNIGHT
MEAT TRAIN

A press release announced Clive's new move: Clive Barker, Joe Daley, Anthony DiBlasi and Jorge Saralegui launched Midnight Picture Show in 2003. Prior to this, Saralegui was Executive VP of Production at 20th Century Fox from 1996 where he was involved in the conception and production of such big budget successes as *Speed*, *Independence Day*, *Broken Arrow* and *Alien: Resurrection*. Through his own production company, Saralegui produced *Red Planet*, *The Time Machine*, *Queen of the Damned* and *Showtime*. The team produced Hal Masonberg's movie *The Plague*, filmed in 2005 and released in 2006, but it was not a happy experience for either Clive or its director. "He did a tough job on a very tough schedule," says Clive, "but there were things that I begged for at the end, for the producers to throw in some extra money towards Hal so that he could go back and do a couple of extra days' shooting, but they shook their heads and that was the end of that. It is not a movie I am pleased with or proud of—it feels compromised and Hal got in his car and drove away before the picture was even locked. . . . There were some great scenes—there really are some great scenes—and the central notion is wonderfully perverse and apocalyptic but I don't think Hal served his script how Hal-the-screenwriter imagined it. It was not the movie I read and that Hal pitched to us—a real shame—as the script was just so damn good."

The new group also now sought out a writing team to adapt the Books of Blood. First up was *The Midnight Meat Train*, and Clive commented: "It's the first movie we're going to do and it's scary as shit. And the reason it's the first movie we're going to do is to sort of put our mark in the sand. It was always—from its title onwards—'OK, here we go: I'm not here to make you laugh, I'm not here to reassure you . . .' I always thought that was a strong horror title—you know, like *The Texas Chainsaw Massacre*: there are two words in that title, 'chainsaw' and 'massacre', and the two words 'midnight' and 'meat'—they are words that signify you're going to see some no-holds-barred horror."

Jeff Buhler adapted the story: "In the short, we're inside Leon's head, so we know what he's thinking and feeling as he observes the city around him. Film wouldn't have easily allowed us that luxury, so I decided to reinvent the protagonist as a photographer, whose observations could be visually communicated to the audience through his work. I felt that it would also give us the visual tool to observe Mahogany, and what he does."

ABOVE

The poster for Ryûhei Kitamura's Book of Blood adaptation of *The Midnight Meat Train*, starring Bradley Cooper as Leon, Leslie Bibb as Maya, and Vinnie Jones as Mahogany, 2008. The film's limited theatrical release was a frustration for Clive.

"I love physical stuff. I knew we had a huge fight scene at the end; it was going to last twenty minutes. I knew it would be with Vinnie Jones, so I knew it was going to be amazing."
—BRADLEY COOPER
on *The Midnight Meat Train*

Even with a strong screenplay in hand, the production was far from smooth. For an extended period, Patrick Tatopoulos, who had created the creature effects on *Saint Sinner*, was attached to direct his first feature. The planned October 2005 start date was pushed to the summer of 2006, which again was disrupted. Finally, Ryûhei Kitamura took the directing reins and the film was shot in March and April 2007.

Bradley Cooper plays Leon Kaufman; Leslie Bibb plays his girlfriend, Maya Jones; Brooke Shields is Susan Hoff, the icy gallery owner encouraging Leon to work harder with his photography; and Vinnie Jones is the implacable, efficient Mahogany. For the second time in a Clive Barker movie, Ted Raimi plays a character who gets brutally killed (having also been a victim in *Candyman*). Clive's own artwork featured on the walls of the movie's Negative Space Gallery.

"I was like a kid in a candy store any time we filmed the scary bits," said Bradley Cooper. "The one thing that did make me cringe was the pierced Achilles tendons, having severed my own five years ago playing basketball. . . .

"Ryûhei is a true auteur. His vision is unique as well as his storytelling technique. And he does all this without ever raising his voice. He also seems to love what actors bring on their own to the roles. He guides you when you need it while always enlisting his confidence in your own ideas."

After the film was shot, however, politics at Lionsgate pushed the movie into a minimum contractual release of just one hundred screens in the US.

"The first sign," said Clive, as those plans were in play, "that there might be something not right in the state of Denmark was when Lionsgate tried to take the word 'Meat' out of the title, which would have made it *Midnight Train*, which would be like taking 'Massacre' out of *Texas Chainsaw Massacre*. I went apeshit! What most disappoints me is that the audience might not get to see this movie on the big screen, with all the subtleties you get in a theater, including the awesome sound mix. The whole idea was that this movie would literally take you on a ride into darker places —and it does."

Speaking to Mick Garris, Ryûhei Kitamura said, "It was very heartbreaking because it was my first American movie. And I was very proud of the movie. And the last I heard was, you know, they got so excited and they even set a release date. I still remember . . . 2008 . . . May 16. That's a very good day. Hot summer day. They were confident with the movie. And they released the trailer. . . . I still remember, when I went to Arclight Cinema to see *Rambo 4*, the trailer was there. I was like, 'WOW.' And then . . . all this craziness happens."

"It frustrates me because we would have had a trilogy out of this," says Clive. "I set to work to develop, in note form from way back, the backstory of the City Fathers. The other movies were not just taking place in this city but in other parts of America. They were connecting up the story of underground activity, which is America-wide. It would have climaxed with a meeting of all the stations, all of the lines. I had this massive plan in my head. The absence of a theatrical release was . . . not

294

only were we losing the chance to exhibit the picture the way it should have been shown, but also we were killing the chance of getting a real horror trilogy that would be constructed picture by picture."

The second movie from Midnight Picture Show was constructed from the opening and closing stories, "The Book of Blood" and "The Book of Blood (a Postscript): On Jerusalem Street" As producer Joe Daley noted, "The *Book of Blood* script was written by John Harrison (our director) and Darin Silverman. Clive and I met John after we watched the first part of *Dune* (2000) on the Sci-Fi Channel—we were blown away by what he had done on that miniseries and that was the beginning of our friendship. John also wrote a draft of 'Abarat' when the project was set up at Disney."

Shooting in Edinburgh from December 2007 to February 2008 with an FX shoot in London in March 2008, *Book of Blood* starred Jonas Armstrong as Simon McNeal and Sophie Ward as Mary Florescu.

"It was very important," said Clive, "that we had two performers who were fearless in terms of not being afraid of exposing their feelings or their skins, and we were blessed, let me tell you. We have two, firstly, exquisitely beautiful young people, and two people who have been absolutely fearless in terms of what they've presented to the camera. I doubt that there is a sexier horror movie out there. . . .

"I'm very aware that Mary also has something in common with *Hellraiser*'s Julia—that is, she's a woman who has a completely dysfunctional love life and is reaching out to the comfort of somebody who she can trust and love, even though he's a cheat and a liar. I think that's kind of interesting."

John Harrison added, "*Book of Blood* has been compared to *Hellraiser*—I'm not exactly sure why, it's a very different story. I happen to love *Hellraiser*, so it's not deliberate on my part to try and mimic that movie. I'd say, if anything, what I was really trying to do was mimic the kinds of movies that I grew up on that were more based on suspense and tension and atmospherics than on in-your-face horror:

ORIGINAL DIRECTOR'S CUT

CLIVE BARKER'S
BOOK OF BLOOD

THE DEAD WILL NOT BE SILENCED

ADMIT ONE
SPECIAL SCREENING
FRIDAY, JULY 24, 10 PM – GASLAMP 15 THEATRE
701 5TH Avenue, San Diego, CA 92101
AVAILABLE ON BLU-RAY AND DVD SEPTEMBER 22

ABOVE

Ticket to a screening of *Book of Blood*, directed by John Harrison and starring Jonas Armstrong as Simon McNeal and Sophie Ward as Mary Florescu, at ComicCon, San Diego, July 2009.

movies like the Val Lewton movies or Robert Wise's *The Haunting*. I guess you could say maybe some of the contemporary analogies would be *The Others* or *The Orphanage*. But I suppose because it takes place in a single house and the third floor happens to be the portal to the other side that there are comparisons."

In other roles, Clive Russell plays Wyburd and Paul Blair plays Reg Fuller. Doug Bradley and Simon Bamford both appear too.

The completion of the film coincided with a hard time for the film industry, with the financial crash of September 2008 hitting release schedules that fall. Instead, the film aired as a Syfy (formerly known as Sci-Fi Channel) exclusive in the US in September 2009 before being released to DVD there and in other markets.

The third Books of Blood movie made by Midnight Picture Show was *Dread*, based on Clive's short story by the same name. As the press release issued on October 15, 2008, announced:

Principal photography has commenced in the UK on *Dread*, the eagerly-awaited new instalment in Clive Barker's Books of Blood franchise, with Anthony DiBlasi at the helm, directing from his own screenplay based on Barker's original short story. Hot new US talent Jackson Rathbone (*Twilight*, *S. Darko*) heads the cast in *Dread* which marks the second collaboration between the UK's Matador Pictures and LA-based Midnight Picture Show.

Joining Jackson Rathbone in the young cast line up are rising British talent Shaun Evans (*Being Julia*, *Telstar*, *Princess Kaiulani*) and newcomers Hanne Steen and Laura Donnelly.

Dread is a psychological thriller centering on three college students who study other people's fears. As the study progresses, one of the students begins to seek salvation from his obsession by exploiting the terrors of his fellow participants.

As Jackson Rathbone, who plays Stephen Grace, noted: "I hate to call it a horror film because it's really more of a psychological thriller. Clive Barker's known for those horroristic elements, and it was more of a humanistic story. . . . I was considering doing the project so I gave it to a friend of mine to read. He read it, and he got to the end and was like, 'Dude, it made me want to vomit.' So I was like, 'Yup, doing this project. That's awesome. . . .' One of the things I like is when different worlds collide. With the *Twilight* films, you have the horror element of the vampire, but it becomes more of a romantic action film with the vampire falling in love with the girl. With *Dread* it's kind of the same thing. Clive Barker's world is usually more of a mythical gothic world, but *Dread* is more of a personalized psychological thriller instead of a horror. It has the horror elements, but it's much more of a person-to-person drama."

Shaun Evans, who plays Quaid, said, "Quaid is on a mission to exorcise his own demons. He has seen his parents killed by an axe-wielding maniac, and that image is ever-present in his subconscious. His involvement in the experiments is not therapy so much as wanting to isolate his dread in order to get rid of it. It's when he accepts that darkness in him that the main *Dread* plot kicks in—for Quaid realizes it's a significant part of his life, and recognition doesn't signal closure. The one figure that decimated his family is bigger than his parents. So it has taken on godlike proportions, and that's what I found so interesting about *Dread*'s story, because what it says about real life is important to me. You want to know where your fear is coming from by exploring it in others. Horror films showing people going wrong on the inside are my favorites, because you start looking at those around you, wondering what they could be truly capable of."

Of all the stories in the Books of Blood, "Dread" is the only one without a fantastical element, as all of Quaid's experiments happen in the real world.

"The story is centered," says Anthony DiBlasi, "around characters that you encounter in day-to-day life in a world that we live and breathe every day, and that for me is why 'Dread' is one of Clive's most terrifying tales. It shows you that monsters aren't always born, sometimes they're made. And they walk among us and they usually look just like you and me. . . . I categorize *Dread* as a coming-of-age horror/thriller. The main characters are that age when they're finding their way into adulthood. So I explore a lot of aspects of finding love, finding adventure, finding sex."

Recognizing how the movie adaptation could have fallen into the same category as the Saw "torture" movies, Clive pointed out: "It's a completely different thesis. Firstly, of course, we came twenty years earlier! I just have to say that for the record! Saw's thesis is a very different one, however. Firstly, it's a revenge thesis. Secondly, Quaid is essentially researching fear, he's researching the nature of dread and Jigsaw in *Saw* is not interested in that, he's interested in watching people break down. He's interested in watching the test—testing their ingenuity, if you will, when there's a bomb attached to their testicles. And that's a very different idea. I'd be surprised if the writers of *Saw* hadn't read 'Dread,' but who am I to know . . . ? And the tone—I'll give you an example. One of the memorable things for many people in 'Dread' is the meat—you know, the girl who will not eat meat being left with a piece of meat which is slowly decaying and becomes more repulsive. As the days go by and as she becomes more desperate you know her chance of being nourished by it becomes more disgusting—that isn't the stuff of *Saw*. I don't know what *Saw* would do in place of

"It turned out well and I'm very happy with it, but my timing was impeccable as I finished it just when the stock market crashed."
—JOHN HARRISON
on *Book of Blood* (2009)

that—probably something like put a bomb in the food or something. But this is much more about that, I'd like to think that *Dread* is an elegant movie about terror and at times it will be brutal and, of course, it's rooted in things that are very close to me: I went deaf for a period in my life and I know what that terror's like and I am disgusted by certain kinds of meat, to the point where I'd actually throw up at the sight of it. . . ."

The movie screened theatrically in the US for the week of January 29, 2010, as part of After Dark Horrorfest 4, before appearing on DVD in March 2010 in the US and in other countries.

Following the three Books of Blood adaptations, Midnight Picture Show dissolved. Anthony DiBlasi continued his association with Seraphim until 2011, when he left to direct his next movie, *Cassadaga*, and Joe Daley also left the group around the same time.

Further Books of Blood would remain unfilmed until a new collaboration between Clive and Brannon Braga resulted in 2020's *Books of Blood* for Hulu, directed by Brannon and cowritten with Adam Simon.

Brannon Braga explained the development process: "It was a dream come true. We would meet like *Tuesdays with Morrie*: every Tuesday at three, I would go to Clive's house and sit with Clive Barker for three hours. And we recorded these sessions. And I have hours and hours of recordings with Clive talking about horror and the philosophy of horror and all this stuff. It was just fascinating. You're sitting with Clive Barker; his artwork is all around you. And he's brilliant. And he's just fascinating to talk to. And you just know, I spent a lot of time just kind of listening.

"It did start, very initially and very briefly, as a TV anthology concept. But we realized that these stories would work better in slightly shorter form as an anthological film. Then it was about choosing the three stories that we wanted to do, and picking an anthological structure. We kind of looked to *Pulp Fiction*, which is not a horror movie but an anthology movie, in terms of how the stories could stand alone, cross-pollinate, and make it cohesive as a film."

Once again "The Book of Blood" and "The Book of Blood (a Postscript): On Jerusalem Street" were adapted for film, but this time they were woven together with two new stories developed by Clive for the movie. The cast featured Britt Robertson as Jenna, Freda Foh Shen as Ellie, Nicholas Campbell as Sam, Anna Friel as Mary, and Rafi Gavron as Simon.

Regarding the two new stories, Clive noted: "There have been, over the years, these stories accruing in my head, and I really had no one to tell them to. And along comes Brannon and I say, 'Hey Brannon, I've got some other stories—maybe we should be thinking about these too?' and he said, 'Bring 'em on!'"

Britt Robertson says, "The ending of Jenna's story was the thing that attracted me most about her. I've read articles about psychological warfare and what it does to someone's mind, when you manipulate a situation and things get very dark. I was very intrigued by that. But also, there was this

ABOVE

Ryūhei Kitamura visits Clive to discuss designs for *The Midnight Meat Train* ahead of filming the movie, 2007.

idea that Jenna was incapable of existing in her own spaces. You hear about her fleeing college and she flees her family, but really the thing that she was trying to escape was herself and her own mind."

About Brannon Braga's direction style, Anna Friel says, "Brannon is very, very focused and concentrated on the monitor. He'd know exactly what he wanted and would say, 'There's your character; go with it.' It was very, very collaborative and supportive, so it made it quite a joy."

As lead actor Jonas Armstrong had experienced in *Book of Blood*, now Rafi Gavron bore the need to have his flesh inscribed by the dead: "So that was a couple hundred thousand dollars' worth of makeup. It was one of the best prosthetic teams in the world. They are amazing and the kindest people and very patient with me, because it was seven hours of makeup in the morning. I had to wake up at four, and then we only got to shoot for about six or seven hours, which was very kind of them, because it was so uncomfortable. It was a latex suit that covered my whole body; I couldn't really go to the bathroom properly. It suffocated my body, because my skin couldn't breathe, really, and then it got really cold and really hot. So Anna fed me Snickers bars the whole time, and I was grumpy the whole time, but it was so worth it because of the way it looks. . . ."

2006– IMAGINING MAN
2009

"A different lens."

Clive has always been a photographer of the male form, from his early shoots with Doug Bradley, Philip Rimmer, Peter Atkins, Graham Bickley, and others in the 1970s, through to the sessions he used to produce painted photographs in the 1990s and early 2000s. Some of these were shown in his 1998 exhibition, *The Weird and the Wicked*, and he contributed a similarly modified cover image in 1999 to Caitlín R. Kiernan's book *Silk*. Beginning in 2006, however, Clive became inspired to embark on a new sustained photography project: instead of painting on photographs of men, he would photograph painted men.

Clive had undertaken bodypainting before, including in public settings at *Monsters!* for Junker Designs at Bluespace in October 2004 and, on a larger scale, at his own *Zoomen* opening at the Bert Green Fine Art gallery in January 2006, when he had painted four men and a woman.

The premise of the *Imagining Man* project was to ask his models what they would choose to be in their imagination, then to paint their bodies to represent these dreams, desires, and ambitions.

He wrote himself the following note:

> The greatest love story in history is that of the imagining man with the man whom he imagines.
>
> 3.54pm 14th June 2006

Sometime later, in 2019, discussing the compilation of the Imaginer art book series, he reflected on his more recent abstract works on paper and canvas:

"I don't think abstraction would have appeared in my work unless I'd started to decorate men. Occasionally I'd decorate people with representation but very seldom. Almost always I'm designing things on them; I'm clothing them, actually, paradoxically, in paint! And the first thing I'd say is, 'What's your favorite color?' when they came in through the door, you know, and then we'd start to speak about being clothed in the color that they like. I was very excited when I looked back at the pictures because by using light and very often filtered light—filtered through some kind of lattice or mesh—onto the model, along with the paint, there are at least two layers of removed-ness from the naked man—and that's why *Imagining Man*

300

"I'm trying to find a way to represent men that's . . . going to catch the eye in a different way, in a way that'll make people look at the body in a different way."

is the right title. Because if it was just shooting them naked it would be called *Photographing Man*—right?

"What I always was trying to do was say, 'Let me bring these beautiful men, these beautiful souls, into my world, photographically, so that people can see there's a continuity between my erotic art and an aesthetic appreciation of what these men wear and the painting.'

"When I think about the eighty-nine thousand photographs that I took in the three years of photographing for *Imagining Man*, I'm aware that, firstly, they're not sexual, not primarily sexual. I'll often shoot the face of my model, very, very few shots do not contain his face, and there are almost no shots, almost no shots in eighty-nine thousand, which emphasize his penis, which is a pornographic view.

"Pornography means the study of the life of whores; that's the translation. *Imagining Man* is not the study of the life of whores. For one thing I'm painting them, so I'm turning them into something which isn't quite human anyway, and pushing them towards design."

A number of the photographs were exhibited in an online Tumblr gallery, at the Dirty Show in Detroit in February 2009, at Bert Green's gallery in Los Angeles in November 2009, and at West Hollywood's Erotic City during L.A. Pride in June 2013.

NEXT SPREAD, LEFT
A sequence of images to show Clive painstakingly painting his model to create a character ahead of an *Imagining Man* shoot, May 2007.

NEXT SPREAD, RIGHT
One of the resultant images shot by Clive in his Beverly Hills studio, May 2007.

301

In November 2009, Clive exhibited a number of his most recent *Imagining Man* photographs as part of an exhibition at Bert Green Fine Art in Los Angeles, including a number of the following images. *Spirit*, 2009.

Vision, 2009.

Palette, 2009.

Vampyr, 2009.

2007- **CLIVE'S HEALTH**

"Out of nowhere, something strange."

At one point in early 2007, Clive suffered a period of complete exhaustion that disrupted his schedule for several weeks. He recovered, but in addition to this episode, he found he was losing his voice on regular occasions and having difficulty breathing when active for long periods.

In March 2008, Clive issued a statement that said:

> Over the past couple of years at signings, people have often come up to me saying, "Your voice doesn't sound too good, are you OK?" So, to all those people who have shown me kindness and concern, I would like to say, "Thank You." There was an issue—I have had polyps on my throat which has constricted my breathing and affected my voice—and this has just recently been addressed, with great success. I am feeling far healthier and more energetic! I may be a little less talkative for a short while, but it's all good news and I want to make a point of thanking all of you who have shown concern— it has been much appreciated.

Unfortunately, this was not the end of the medical issue, as the polyps recurred several times, with Clive having a series of operations between 2008 and 2011 to remove them. Despite the success of the surgeries, the return of the polyps were just as debilitating for Clive's breathing each time. He also underwent hernia surgery in this period and, on top of that, began to experience pain in his writing hand and severe pain in his legs that prevented him from working on large-scale oil paintings and on his *Imagining Man* photography.

Physical pain aside, this period took an emotional toll on Clive as well. He was open in a talk at the 2009 Sitges Film Festival about the desolate loss he felt after the death of his friend and mentee Justin Brown. Clive also lost his mother, Joan, who had been a powerful daily influence on him, to cancer in 2011, which affected him greatly.

In January 2012, in an event that has impacted him ever since, Clive suffered toxic shock, had three heart attacks in the ambulance on the way to the hospital, was in a coma for eleven days, and was considered unlikely to live by his doctors.

Speaking in March that year, at home but weak, in answer to how he was doing, he said, "Not great. Eight weeks ago I was in a coma and I'm just grateful to be alive, you know? I'm very lucky. Fifty percent of people who go into hospital with toxic shock die.

"I had a four o'clock appointment with the dentist. It was exploratory, to see what they wanted to do. It wasn't anything. There was a little bit of bleeding, there was some blood, so obviously they pierced something. I got home, I didn't feel great, a bit woozy, then I have no memory of anything. . . . I have no memory of anything until twelve days later, fighting to pull the tubes out of my throat. I had three tubes down into my lungs, to inflate them and keep them going, because my system had completely turned off.

"Now the doctor was saying to me, 'This is the third time you've done this—if you do it a fourth time you'll die.' And I was terrified—I didn't know who these people were—they wore masks—it felt like I was being tortured. I kept trying to ask, 'Why?' but couldn't because of the tubes in my throat. . . . It was horrible, let me tell you, it was horrible. There was nothing about it that was revealing or insightful or pleasant. It was a nightmare.

"When I left the hospital, three separate doctors who'd worked on me said, 'You should not be here. There's no way somebody who's as ill as you were when you came to us—you'd already had three seizures in the ambulance on the way down to Cedars-Sinai,' which, you know, is only five minutes' drive. I don't remember any of this—I was unconscious, but I had three seizures, each one of which should have killed me, and they had no expectation of me coming out again alive, and my poor friends, you know, my loved ones in the house, God bless them, they were sitting by my bed, trying to bring me round by talking to me for eight hours at a time. I remember nothing—well, I have some snatches of things that are too horrible to talk about, that I don't want to talk about—maybe I will one day, but not now. . . .

"I had a relapse later, here at the house, about a week after I got home, which was horrible. I suddenly felt—well, my vital signs went down, rapidly—not very nice, you know?

"Now, weeks later, I'm exhausted. I'm exhausted right now and most days I'm exhausted, you know? I've lost twenty-five pounds; it's taken a toll, a huge toll, but: first thing, I'm alive; secondly, the flood of wonderful, wonderful things from readers and film people and people who just love the work is just incredibly inspiring to me—hundreds and hundreds of them—and it's been important to me to get the message out—'I am going to live.'

"I'm still very weak and it's frustrating, not getting out of the house. I feel very vulnerable to everything; I feel like skins have been stripped away from me. . . . I'm in a very dark place, which is common after comas, apparently. You know, my life was going along reasonably well and then suddenly nothing—my life stopped—and I woke again almost two weeks later, not knowing who I was or where I was or what had happened."

Eighteen months later, in September 2013, it was clear that the recovery was going to be a long and painful process. "It's a long, slow trek," said Clive. "They said it would take two to three years when I came out of hospital—I've only left the house five times since I left the hospital. Some days I'm fine and other days I'm not. I am getting better—it's hard to judge. I haven't been sick a lot in my life; I've not been sick and unable to get out of bed. There are days when this conversation just wouldn't have happened; I just wouldn't have the wherewithal to do it. I keep coming back to all the doctors saying when I awoke, 'You should not be alive. . . .'

"It's a wake-up call that makes me realize that (a) I'm very lucky to be alive and (b) I need to take that gift and not betray it by pretending that I'm all tough and ready to get back into work again like nothing ever happened. God gave me a gift and I will pay homage to that, resting and sleeping and conserving my energies and getting well."

The long recovery period kept Clive largely confined to a single room in his house that became both his workspace and sleeping area. Although he had had three houses next to each other—one his residence, one an office for Seraphim that also housed his painting studio, and one a guesthouse that stored many of his finished paintings—he ended up selling the guesthouse in 2012. He was bedridden for long periods and unable to walk next door to the Seraphim house, going there only once in the five years before that house was also sold in 2017, leading to largely remote interaction between Clive and the team at Seraphim.

"Everything that's happened in the last few years has happened in this room; I haven't been able to work anywhere else, because, you know, [I've needed] to be close to a place where I could lie down. I've made, um, three hundred paintings in this room I guess in the last few years. I've written a lot of stories and they're in first draft mainly, and I've written a lot of poetry, which has become very important to me in this time because poetry is a short form for me—you know, I'm not writing *Paradise Lost*—and so in a breath of energy, in a short time of energy, I can perhaps set something down and it's worked very well for me."

By 2018, the entire Seraphim team had departed and Clive was recovered enough to start attending large-scale conventions again, traveling to events in Dallas, Chicago, Atlanta, New Jersey, and Las Vegas—his first public appearances outside California since 2011.

This enforced absence had led to speculation about his health, his capacity to work, whether he would ever recover, and whether it was something like AIDS or drug addiction that was keeping Clive out of the public eye—because surely he was recovered from toxic shock by now?

Responding to this, he said in January 2019, "There have been certain people who've known me who decided that they would give up on me, if you will. And they started to pass the rumors around that I was very, very sick and would not live, or that I was incoherent, my mind had gone

"My obsession's my writing, my obsession's my art, and if that's my sickness, well, so be it. But I really would like to think that, well, it's a price paid, I guess, it's a price paid."

as a consequence of the sickness I'd had and that I would never write again or create again. And a number of other unpleasant rumors—none of which are true. It's been a long journey to get healthy . . . and the fact that I am getting better at all is a wonderment—the doctors meant it back in 2012 when they said, 'He's going to die.' They really weren't joking. As my father was fond of saying, though, when we passed Smithdown Cemetery, 'A lot of people are jealous of me in there, you know!'

". . . But it's been very demoralizing to discover that some of the people that I trusted and loved were amongst the people who said these things—even though they fully understood that I was not incoherent and I was not stopping writing and so on. So it's been important to me to get out into the world—as somebody said, was it Twain? I'm not sure—'Reports of my death have been greatly exaggerated!' Clive Barker is alive and well and living in the fantastic lands he's always lived in, from which there will come novels and short stories and eventually films.

"I've been busily working away at lots of stuff for a while, and even though it's been a long and frankly painful process to get well, the alternative was wretched. And I am well-er literally by the day—and so, my love and gratitude and thanks—and a promise that the Clive Barker that perhaps they thought had, if not passed from the world permanently, had certainly moved into retirement is neither retired nor dead!"

A year later, in 2020, he reflected, "For what has turned out to be years since the toxic shock, I have been in various states of unwellness; I've been close to death twice, I had a second coma, I've lain in bed for how long? I don't know, a year, two years, I don't know, unable to walk, unable to walk next door, to my house next door. None of this is catching, none of this was viral or anything like that, I was just very, very, very sick. When you lie in bed and you literally can't get out of bed for a very long time, your legs start to weaken because they're not being used and, you know, when you're sick you're in defiance constantly.

"One of the things which troubled me—the only thing that really troubled me—about death was being parted from those I loved and not finishing the work. That drove me to a sort of crazy frustration on those days when I simply couldn't work, which unfortunately was a lot of those days; I just didn't have the energy to—it sounds silly doesn't it—but the energy to put pen to paper.

"I think, given our social media age, word got around from a couple of sources who were, I thought, my friends, that I would never be in a public venue again because I was incoherent, intellectually erased, that I would have nothing to give because I wasn't there anymore.

"One person made my situation seem even worse than it was; he made sure people 'knew' that I was intellectually incapable now, that I would never again write, that I would never again be a creative, cogent person—this is devastating to even say now, honestly.

"These are very hard things to hear. The fact that they came from friends—people I thought were my friends, and one in particular—was devastating. I don't want to underestimate, in terms of my being ill, the effect of that. It would be wrong to say that it was simply the sickness which was destroying me; it was the knowledge that something that I had built over the better part of my lifetime was being destroyed behind my back. . . ."

2004– A RETURN TO COMICS
2017

"A completely nihilistic story."

After the demise of the Razorline imprint in 1994, Clive's work was absent from new comics and graphic novels for a decade, until he contributed to a collection by Voltaire called *Deady: The Malevolent Teddy*. Clive's story, "The Waiting Room," in which the titular bear falls asleep and experiences a nightmare, came immediately after a story by Voltaire, in which Deady meets Clive Barker himself at Dragon Con and unleashes some variant middle-management Cenobites.

In 2006, Clive contributed a storyline called "Field" to the third issue of *DEMONICSEX*, the adult magazine detailing graphic "Satanic Tales of Transformation and Possession." Involving phallic crop circles on a Kansas farm, a gay orgy in the field, and four-hundred-foot-tall demons, the ten-page story was told without words, in art by Sean Platter.

In 2005, *The Thief of Always* was adapted as a three-part comic book by Kris Oprisko and illustrated by Gabriel Hernandez for IDW Publishing in a first collaboration with its editor in chief, Chris Ryall. Chris went on to adapt *The Great and Secret Show* over twelve issues between March 2006 and May 2007.

Clive noted that "when Chris came to me with the notion of adapting *The Great and Secret Show* for comic books, I was enthusiastic, but cautiously so. I had seen another of my large novels, *Weaveworld*, violated in its adaptation many years before (through no fault of the adaptor, Dan Chichester) and the memory still stung a little. But Chris is immensely persuasive and he was determined that the epic narrative of *The Great and Secret Show* could be told in a series of twelve issues without losing the novel's scale. When he laid it all out for me, and shared the vision, I agreed."

The glorious artwork of the comic books was the work of Gabriel Rodríguez with colors by Jay Fotos. Variant covers for each of the issues were printed, featuring black-and-white pieces of Clive's artwork, several of which had been drawn for the original 1989 limited edition of the novel. This was an extensive and thoughtful adaptation, as evidenced by Chris Ryall's notes added to the later collected edition of the full graphic novel in one volume. Together, writer and artist buried a wealth of references and clues that rewards repeated reading of the adaptation.

CLIVE BARKER'S
SEDUTH

COMES WITH
3-D
GLASSES

Signed
EDITION

WWW.IDWPUBLISHING.COM

00112

8 27714 00105 1

> ## "When we look back at the recent history of horror, no other writer has shook the pillars of fear like Clive Barker. He rewrote the book on how we scare each other."
> ## —STEVE NILES

Following these two adaptations, in October 2009, IDW published Clive's first all-new stand-alone comic in fifteen years. *Seduth* was Clive's original concept that he then cowrote with Christopher Monfette, with art and color again done by Gabriel Rodríguez and Jay Fotos, respectively. A 3D conversion was done by Ray Zone for a special version of the comic that came with 3D glasses. A cover variant featured a new piece of Clive's art, painted for this edition.

Clive's notes say, variously, that *Seduth* is "A Completely Nihilistic Story," "A Surreal Story. A Story by Fellini or Buñuel. This is not Superman. This is Burroughs," and uses "the idea of Peter Beard's diaries as a narrative device."

Christopher Monfette described the process: "Clive came to me, quite literally, with nothing . . . which is to say he wanted to create a piece about the essence of nihilism. Foolishly, I had expected a story—manageable, straightforward, perhaps a bit messy—and what I received was a five-dimensional jigsaw. . . ."

The IDW press release stated:

> In *Seduth*, Barker tells the tale of celebrated architect Harold Engle, who first glimpses the small cloud of darkness inside a glittering, priceless diamond. But he can't possibly be aware of the terrible plague contained within. *Seduth* follows Engle on a surreal journey through murder and madness to the very heart of existence and a terrible, impossible choice—to unravel the very fabric of the world, or to save it?

The IDW graphic novels were collected together in various hardcover and softcover editions and translated into foreign editions in a major push for Clive's return to comics.

His next outlet was a new take on the *Hellraiser* mythos with the first of a run of stories published by Boom! Studios between March 2011 and January 2014. The series, titled *Hellraiser*, was overseen by Matt Gagnon and Chris Rosa at Boom!. Its first installment was a prelude issue written by Clive with Christopher Monfette called "At the Tolling of a Bell." Complete with art by Leonardo Manco, this eight-page issue was released electronically as a free download.

Clive and Christopher also collaborated on the first eight issues together, which were split into two distinct story arcs: first came "Pursuit of the Flesh," with art for issues 1–2 by Leonardo Manco and art for issues 3–4 by Stephen Thompson; then came "Requiem" (issues 5–8) with art by Stephen Thompson, Jesús Hervás, and Janusz Ordon.

Clive continued to provide storylines, cowriting subsequent issues with his Seraphim team: Anthony DiBlasi on issue 9, Robb Humphreys on issues 10–11, and Mark Alan Miller on issues 12–20, across storylines titled "Heaven's Reply," "Hell Hath No Fury," and "Blood Communion."

Variant covers were created for each issue, with Tim Bradstreet and Nick Percival as the principal cover artists, although Clive also contributed art for a variant cover for issue 1.

Anthony DiBlasi left Seraphim after issue 9 to film *Cassadaga* and subsequent movies. Robb Humphreys left Seraphim in early 2012 after issue 11, and after Clive's toxic shock illness, which led to Mark Alan Miller taking the reins at Seraphim.

Together, Mark and Clive contributed the story "Closer to God," illustrated by Jesús Hervás, to the first *Hellraiser Annual* (a special additional issue featuring bonus content for the series), which

Death is never be pretty. But often on occasion, beautiful. At least I thought so.

④

Looking down at a corpse.

was released in March 2012 alongside "My Enemy's Enemy," written by Brandon Seifert with art by Michael Montenat.

Brandon wrote the next four issues, subtitled "The Road Below," with art by Haemi Jang, before cowriting with Clive for the final twelve issues, subtitled "The Dark Watch," with art by Tom Garcia and Korkut Öztekin.

Brandon also wrote "Good Intentions" for the second *Hellraiser Annual* in October 2013, with art by Jesús Hervás. Clive's story in the annual, cowritten with Ben Meares, another of the current Seraphim team, was "Something to Keep Us Apart," with art by Janusz Ordon. Artist menton3 provided the cover.

Looking back over both the earlier Marvel run and the more recent Boom! series, Clive observed, "The comic books have been in many cases rather brilliant and actually really taken the mythology to new and interesting places, so I'm very proud of the comic books in a way that I'm not really proud of the many sequels to the movie. . . . I've been, I'd like to say, a major part of the comic book creation, but I think that's pretentious of me. I think in a way the comics have to tell their own tales through the people who write and paint them."

In a subtle shift, Clive had no storylines in the six-part *Hellraiser Bestiary*, published by Boom! between August 2014 and January 2015. Several stories were written by various combinations of Seraphim's Mark Alan Miller, Ben Meares, and Christian Francis, alongside stories by Victor LaValle, Christopher Taylor, Ed Brisson, Lela Gwinn, Michael Moreci, Valerie D'Orazio, and Christopher Sebela.

Later, in 2017, Seraphim self-published two further collections of all-new, stand-alone stories inspired by the Hellraiser universe in two *Hellraiser: Anthology* volumes. Both were edited by Ben Meares, with cover art—as well as the art for three of the stories—provided by Daniele Serra.

Between May 2014 and April 2015, Boom! also published a new series of *Nightbreed* comics. The twelve issues were credited as "Story by Clive Barker" and written by Marc Andreyko. Art was by Piotr Kowalski, Emmanuel Xerx Javier, and Devmalya Pramanik, with color by Juan Manuel Tumburús.

Marc Andreyko noted: "Whenever you work on someone else's properties, you want to do right by them and you hope they're cool. Clive has been a real dream collaborator. It's been a real honor and thrill to not disappoint him. . . . We both love this property so much, we're like little kids playing dress-up. . . ." Of the Breed themselves, he offered, "Some of them are mad, some of them are gentle souls cursed to be in these bodies. Some of them are warriors, some of them are mothers. Some of them hate who they are and want to destroy other monsters. It's just an embarrassment of riches."

For many, the most significant title in these new comics came between May 2013 and August 2014 in the form of a brand-new Clive Barker series called *Next Testament*, published by Boom!.

Written by Clive with Mark Alan Miller, the plot involves a character named Julian Demond who has unearthed someone calling himself Wick and claiming to be the vengeful God of the Old Testament. "And now that God is back, God help us all," proclaimed the press release. Haemi Jang created the distinctive art throughout; covers were by Goñi Montes, except for issues 1 and 12, which had variant covers featuring Clive's artwork.

The central character of Wick arose from one of Clive's *Imagining Man* photography sessions around 2007 or 2008, during which he had painted his eventual cowriter in the divine colors that Wick bears in the comic art.

As Mark Alan Miller recalls, "Head to toe, I was painted in tribal-looking blue and red and yellow and all these earth-tone paints. We're standing there and Clive was just free-associating these paintings. When he finished, we both stepped back and said, 'Who is this guy? He needs a story. . . .' Clive said, what if he was part of the original trinity and he'd been banished and the other two were still out there free and this guy is like God and the Devil rolled up in one?"

The storyline, which had originally been called 'New Genesis,' rather than *Next Testament*, had been percolating for some time, with Ross Richie, the CEO of Boom!, noting that "the funny thing about Clive's 'New Genesis' is that it was actually what we got together with him for. *Hellraiser* came out of the 'New Genesis' discussions. We were talking and talking, and he felt very comfortable. So he said, 'Let's hold on this idea. Why don't we do *Hellraiser* instead?' And he's so proprietary on *Hellraiser* that it felt so good. The first time I went over to his house, you think about 'What's this meeting going to be about?' and in your wildest dreams there's no way you think you're going to get *Hellraiser*. Not right out of the box. So we were talking about doing original projects first, but it's funny how the timing works out."

Comic book artist Grant Morrison, known for their work in the DC Comics universe, said, "*Next Testament* delivers a twenty-first-century sequel to the Bible itself! Blasphemy, Grand Guignol, apocalyptic human drama and the return of a vain, easily bored, and casually genocidal deity who might just be the God we deserve. I'm a believer!"

Wes Craven described it as "a daring and totally original work. Our perception of the reality of God is limited only by our ability to imagine him. The good news is, God is not dead. The bad news is that in a spectacular explosion of dark genius, Clive Barker and Mark Miller have now imagined him in a frightening new way, and heaven and earth will never be the same again."

Award-winning genre writer Joe R. Lansdale added, "Weird and wonderful, Clive Barker keeps finding stuff in his brain that the rest of us wish we could find. Cool art. Cool story. You need this."

Prolific comic book artist Warren Ellis declared, "Clive Barker remains a vital and protean mythmaker."

The collected editions of the comic featured introductions and essays by Victor LaValle, Rodrigo Gudiño, Thomas F. Monteleone, Jonathan Maberry, Doug Jones, and Liam Sharp.

Clive notes, "I would say that it's a surprise that it was responded to so popularly. We had anxiety about the religious content right from the beginning and it turned out to be something that people were interested in; they wanted to talk about God. Or opine about God, should I say. . . ."

A novelization of the series called *Clive Barker's Next Testament* was written by Mark Alan Miller and published by Earthling Publications in 2017, and the comic itself was given an innovative release as a motion comic by Madefire Studios.

Impressed with the motion-technology platform, Clive planned a series of twelve new adaptations of the Books of Blood for the platform. The first was an adaptation of "The Book of Blood" by Mark Alan Miller and illustrated by Sam Shearon, with a score by Cris Velasco, released in October 2014. The others, including "The Midnight Meat Train," adapted by Ben Meares and again illustrated by Sam Shearon, which would have been the next to be released, sadly fell by the wayside.

THE SCARLET GOSPELS
AND HEAVEN'S REPLY

"Your job is to witness.
To see and remember."

Pinhead, as embodied and portrayed by Doug Bradley, was absent from *The Hellbound Heart*, in which the lead Cenobite was instead a figure whose "voice, unlike that of its companion, was light and breathy—the voice of an excited girl. Every inch of its head had been tattooed. . . ."

From his first appearance onscreen in *Hellraiser*, though, the Lead Cenobite's image, demeanor, bearing, language, and intonation would forever be emblematic of the movie.

Clive had contributed plotlines and occasional lines of dialogue for the character in movie sequels and in comic books, but—before setting down a few exploratory pages towards a sequel to *The Hellbound Heart* in 1993—he had not written a literary life for Pinhead.

It would be another five years before he would start to talk about the idea that would result, almost twenty years later, in Pinhead's first appearance in book form.

In 1998, Clive announced that he had begun a short tale that would pit the Cenobite against his recurring hero, Harry D'Amour. Initially titled "The Last Hellraiser Story," then "The Lazarus Requiem," it would appear finally as a novel called *The Scarlet Gospels* in 2015.

The journey from 1998 to 2015 is one that charts an evolving text, expanding from a short story within a planned collection to a longer novel, then to an epic before its progress was punctuated by personal issues and serious ill-health and being stripped back into a leaner novel that excised significant pieces of the mythology that had entered its draft narrative.

THIS SUMMER,
RAISE SOME HELL

CLIVE BARKER
THE SCARLET GOSPELS

HELLRAISER IS BACK

ABOVE
UK paperback edition of *The Scarlet Gospels*, featuring cover art by David Mack, 2016

Having explained in several interviews in 1998 that he came up with the title "The Last Hellraiser Story" because he intended to kill Pinhead in its pages, he set about recording a suitably apocalyptic end for his creation.

The need to write a second version of Abarat's second book, having thrown one version away, and then a diversion into writing the *Tortured Souls* screenplay put the drafting of Pinhead's confrontation with Harry D'Amour on the back-burner. And yet, "this Hellraiser story, *The Scarlet Gospels* one, which began as a modest little tale," he said in 2004 as it began to gather pace again, "it's now ninety thousand words and counting! And so it's now actually a short novel. . . .

"What happened was I *lightly* introduced Jesus into the narrative, thinking I could get away with a quick mention and out again, you know? Actually it was Joseph of Arimathea that I introduced—who brought the Holy Grail actually back to Cornwall, to a tin mine, according to fable. And that sort of got me excited about the narrative in a whole new way and I realized I couldn't finish my man, Pinhead, off in a tale that also has room for Joseph of Arimathea without really dealing some.

"What I hadn't realized until I started writing was how passionate I felt about the character of Pinhead. I suppose part of it is that I had become very familiar with the image—like everybody has— the toys, the game, obviously the films, and so on. But when I actually went back and wrote about him, wrote in his voice, as it were, I realized that he became more interesting than he had a chance to be in most of the movies. . . . I think he is quite a complex character. He isn't Freddy Krueger; he isn't Jason Voorhees; he is something more eloquent and possibly elegant. And so I really wanted to explore this character and really give him a chance to speak one last time—very eloquently."

As the narrative continued to expand, it became clear it would be a stand-alone novel in its own right. In 2006, Clive explained: "My original thought was that I would simply tell a tale of closure that was the size of the tale which introduced him—thirty thousand words—and then I thought, 'That does him a terrible injustice, because we are teased over the films with a sense that there is some huge structure there in which he belongs, in which he has a significant part, and how can I write that, how can I bring him to his final act without first taking him, taking my readers, through what that system is—in other words, taking them down to Hell and showing them what the Order of the Cenobites are and where he belongs in them and what the consequences of rebellion on his part might be, and so on and so forth?'

"So many of the journeys that I've taken in the last few years have taken me to such diverse places, and sometimes very sad places; *Sacrament* has such sadness in it, certainly, and I think the stuff I did for *Chiliad*, that was pretty melancholy stuff. Abarat has brightened me and painting brightens me, and when I'm bright, I can go into the dark places more comfortably. It's only when you're actually in a really, really dark place that the idea of getting up in the morning and going into these dark places yourself is really overwhelming. It becomes almost beyond me. It had become beyond me particularly after my father's passing, to go into those very dark places. It's one of the reasons I'm having such a good time with Abarat; the lighter tone of Abarat, the brightness of Abarat, it was a willful stepping away from the subdued tones and the cruelty and the violence and the almost arbitrary death that were part of my earlier horror fiction and now it's very much back on the page in *The Scarlet Gospels*."

Clive took another extended break from the novel, setting it aside at the beginning of 2007 to write *Mister B. Gone*, then moving onto *Abarat: Absolute Midnight* rather than returning to the Hellfire of *The Scarlet Gospels*, saying in 2008: "To be very honest, I had a grim period in my life where a lot of very dark things happened and the idea of going back and doing the fourth draft of a 250,000-word book with so much death around me was just a little too much for me at that point, so I did what I knew was best for my psyche. And I think that's one thing probably I never talk about, which is the fact that, because I treat this stuff with respect, it has an effect upon me, and it would be stupid of me to minimize it and say, 'Well, you know, it's inconsequential.' It isn't inconsequential; these things affect me deeply."

Approaching the novel again in 2009, having already discarded a plotline in which a thirteen-year-old Harry D'Amour at his Catholic boarding school met Pinhead, he decided to also excise the Holy Grail storyline. Instead he wrote that narrative as a separate draft novel called "Grail," dated July 2009. These simplifications decided upon, he set about the novel again before being called onto writing *Absolute Midnight*'s final draft in the summer of 2010.

Mark Alan Miller edited the book over an extended period, including after Clive's toxic shock in January 2012 and through Clive's subsequent period of recovery—this at a time when Mark was also working on the Boom! *Hellraiser* comics and taking over the leadership of Seraphim following Robb Humphreys's departure.

In a break from Clive's relationship with HarperCollins, *The Scarlet Gospels* was sold in an auction to St. Martin's Press in October 2013 and published in May 2015.

The book's long gestation had accumulated great expectations along the way, not least of Clive's promised enfolding of the Grail storyline and his discussion in interviews of the sheer volume of pages of the handwritten manuscript in its earlier drafts and the story's epic nature.

It was published as a novel of a little over one hundred thousand words, less than half the size previously mentioned by Clive. Despite some positive reviews, including novelist Michael Marshall Smith's observation in *The Guardian* that the story "was meticulously framed, endlessly inventive and spun with rollicking good humour," readers and reviewers who had followed the creative journey of the novel over many years and had anticipated a more complex, nuanced narrative had a more mixed reaction.

The book's flap copy reads:

> For nearly thirty years the Hell Priest—better known to us by his descriptive mantle of Pinhead—has been one of the most recognizable and famous characters in the pantheon of horror. Acclaimed literary icon Clive Barker brings him back with the final chapter of his narrative begun in *The Hellbound Heart*, closing the circle on the Cenobite mythos for all time.
>
> Long-beleaguered detective Harry D'Amour ("The Last Illusion," *Everville*), investigator of all things supernatural, magical, and malevolent, has been battling his own personal demons for years. When he happens upon a Lament Configuration—a deeply intricate puzzle box that is rumored to open a doorway to Hell itself—his own demons are replaced by the real thing as he finds himself caught in a terrifying game of cat and mouse that is bloody, disturbing, and brilliantly complex.
>
> These words are Hell's untold scripture: *The Scarlet Gospels*, the long-awaited horror epic as told by the undisputed master of the form.

At the same time that he was reworking *The Scarlet Gospels* and writing "Grail," Clive wrote the opening sections of another Hellraiser book, entitled "Heaven's Reply." The novel opens with a setup about the Big House, on Île du Diable, Devil's Island, in the Salvation Islands, the former French penal colony, where Philippe Lemarchand's spirit exists.

The opening chapters recount how Kirsty, our heroine from *The Hellbound Heart* (using the alias Christina Beckford, "the name she had been using since she'd had her problems with the Kryos that had pursued her from the Wastes through Paris"), receives a letter in the mail from a doctor of theology in Minnesota, Joseph Lansing. Describing the final page of the correspondence, Clive's manuscript reads, "There were other ways to cross a threshold, Lansing had remarked, besides solving some antiquated puzzle box. And the way he heard it, one of those ways was going to become apparent soon."

Kirsty recalls the events at the house on Lodovico Street with Rory Cotton, his wife, Julia, and brother, Frank, and the Cenobites. She returns to look at the house where it happened and encounters, on the recently tree-trimmed sycamore-lined street, an obscene-talking demon, a Runner. Returning home, she calls Dr. Lansing a first time, after which she hears a single tolling bell as a news story on the television tells of a seven-year-old girl in Tokyo, Miyoko Naka, who has folded paper into an origami box. Hearing it, Kirsty recalls another box:

> She thought of Frank, whose desire to know more, taste more, own more of the world's supply of experience than was his right to possess, had brought one of the boxes Lemarchand had fashioned into the house on Lodovico Street. Kirsty had held it in her hand. It had been heavy, she remembered. Her hand still knew its weight as though the

"I simply want to tell an apocalyptic tale in which Harry will meet the forces of Hell."

flesh of her palm would always be haunted by the holding of it. But it had just been a box, a tool in the hands of its corrupted commissioner.

That creature went by many names. To those foolish or suicidal enough to indulge in insult, he was called Pinhead. It was an idiot name, Kirsty had thought so the first time she'd heard it, and had not changed her opinion since. But no doubt those who had first used the name, had done so believing it would somehow dilute the power of the beast. But no. The Pinhead was a toxic flower by any name.

Besides, like most of the entities that haunted the Wastes, the Cenobite owned more than one name. Many demons had half a dozen or more. Pinhead had been given his name from the ranks of nails that were driven in a symmetrical pattern over his entire head by some cruel baptismal hammer, from the line of his jaw up over his dour and weary face to the spot at the base of his naked skull where a hook kept the flesh taut. But he went by several other names. He was the Tailor of Nightmares and Satan's Suit-maker.

He was the Infernal Pope and Lord of the Last Light. And most commonly, The Cold Man. She speaks with Dr. Lansing again who says that he has heard, "in the air," the same way that "millions are getting the news," and that "people are folding bits of paper and are listening to the bell from the Wastes," that she has had an encounter with a foul-mouthed athlete that afternoon. He also knows where The Cold Man is—he's on Devil's Island. . . .

Forty hours later, Kirsty arrives on the island. At the hotel, she meets the owner, Madame Rembert, who knows exactly who Kirsty is. . . .

These opening chapters were submitted to HarperCollins in May 2010 as an indication of Clive's overall idea, but the remainder of the text was set aside when he fell ill.

The unfinished typescript was picked up by Mark Alan Miller in 2015, prior to the publication of *The Scarlet Gospels*. In 2018, after Subterranean Press published the revised text as a novella under a new name, *Hellraiser: The Toll* by Mark Alan Miller, Mark said, "I was going through the archives and I found the notes on 'The Toll,' and I asked Clive if I could have a crack at it after all these years. I talked about it with my friend and collaborator Christian Francis and he's the one who actually pointed out that it could work perfectly as a bridge between—in its first incarnation—*The Hellbound Heart* and the *Gospels*. So I thought about how to do it, and then sort of backwards engineered it from there and made it my own."

After sharing his first draft of "The Toll"—which edited Clive's text and added an ending—with the hosts of *The Clive Barker Podcast*, it was pointed out to him that it wasn't really a sequel to *The Hellbound Heart*. "Pinhead isn't even in *The Hellbound Heart*," Mark says, "so *The Scarlet Gospels* can only really be a sequel to the film rather than the book. It was Ryan Danhauser and José Leitão who read an early draft that still had elements unique to *The Hellbound Heart* and pointed them out to me. When I realized they were right I did a rewrite of 'The Toll' that specifically folded in the film mythology rather than the book's version."

HARRY D'AMOUR

"I am you and you are love and that's what makes the world go round."

Although Clive's work circles from time to time around certain themes, it's less common for him to be drawn to a single character with the same persistence. But private investigator Harry M. D'Amour has been conspicuous in his ability to serve multiple narratives and has a particular talent: he serves as a witness, regardless of whatever strangeness might be put in front of him. That appeals to Clive, because that sense of journalistic integrity is exactly how he feels about his own work:

"I don't think I create a lot, I think I witness a lot. I witness a lot that is being put into my mind's eye by . . . I don't know what.

"I've always had a passion for film noir," he admits, "and that reflects itself to some extent in my work. There are an awful lot of gangsters, whores, pimps, hustlers, and druggies wandering around my stories and, in some cases, even being the heroes and heroines of the story. The other thing I get from film noir is the element of mystery. A lot of my stories have some kind of puzzle element in them, a sense that something has got to be unraveled and eventually be made understandable."

Harry is introduced in "The Last Illusion" in volume 6 of the Books of Blood as the man equipped to solve those puzzles, in a story followed swiftly by "Lost Souls," published later the same year in the Christmas 1985 edition of London's *Time Out* magazine. Although Clive had written noir-inspired pieces such as *Nightlives* and *The Damnation Game*, the possibilities offered by setting his private investigator against demons proved particularly tempting.

"I like Harry," Clive offers, "because I'm a great [Philip] Marlowe fan, in the hard-boiled tradition. But I also like the collision of the hard-boiled with the fantastical—it's almost as if they shouldn't really mingle because one is so much about the real world."

"The Last Illusion" only teases the possibilities of a more extensive story in its mentions of Harry's past, whereas "Lost Souls," being set later, features a Harry who has since become well versed in dealing with the uncanny and even demons "from the Gulfs." The latter story introduces

Norma Paine, a character who proves vital as Harry's confidante, guide, and friend. Despite her blindness, she sees the world of the dead clearly and offers Harry a grounded relationship in his uncertain world.

In 1987, Harry continued to offer new narrative opportunities for Clive's next film project. "Harry D'Amour: The First Adventure" (later titled "The Great Unknown") was intended as the first of a trilogy but remains unfilmed. It follows the story of Harry's introduction to the world of the Metacosm and the dark forces that reside there, as he is charged with defending the world against a planned invasion. Norma is again Harry's touchstone and she shows him her vision of New York with ghosts and aliens walking by—most just watch us for amusement, she explains; but some from the Metacosm are harmful, while others protect us.

Harry embodies here all the relatable characteristics for which he remains popular in other works: his dysfunctional home life is almost nonexistent; his disorganized office doubles as his apartment; he barely survives from one contract to the next, and it's little surprise his chaotic life prevents him finding a meaningful partner. Yet his innate integrity is obvious and an unselfish sense of fair play is central to his appeal. Even in the darkest of situations he retains his dry humor, laced with a certain abiding charm. Revisiting an image from Clive's early short film, *The Forbidden*, there's a telling indication that Harry is nevertheless a creative soul, as the takeout containers on his messy desk have been shaped into sculptures and the tax bills folded to create origami figures. (The motif of an intricate paper puzzle enclosing more in its folds than the sheet from which it is fashioned would play out some years later in *The Scarlet Gospels* in the hands of the High Priest of Hell, Pinhead.)

The Harry screenplay "The Great Unknown" echoes ideas that would eventually find their way into other stories—the Metacosm would become familiar to readers of the Art books, and another character, Lucia, bears more than passing resemblance to Rachel in *Cabal* as she conjures visions and mutable forms. Animate murals bring to mind the walls of Midian, and Clive would later revisit that motif in the haunting opening sequences of *Coldheart Canyon*.

A closing image of two lovers embarking on a new adventure together against a background of stars is again reminiscent of the final scene of *Cabal*, but Harry remains a more nuanced character than those in the story of the Nightbreed. His motivations are multilayered; the worlds he walks in and the adventures he has are more complex and all the more engaging for it.

By the time Harry appears on the screen in *Lord of Illusions* in 1995, he has already lived the events of *Everville*, in which he is introduced to readers in an art gallery as "a well-made fellow in his late thirties, with three days' growth of beard and the eyes of an insomniac." Harry's reason for being there? He's been immortalized by his friend Ted Dusseldorf's painting, *D'Amour on Wyckoff Street*, which depicts Harry in Brooklyn, "where one sunny Easter Sunday almost a decade before Harry had first been brushed by infernal wings." We learn more of Harry's backstory—his relationships with his mentor, Father Hess, and with Norma, who offers her explanation of his singular abilities: "You're a good man, Harry, an' that's rare. I mean really rare. I think something moves in you that doesn't move in most men, which is why you're always being tested in this way."

For the movie, Scott Bakula was cast as Harry D'Amour, who is described in the screenplay as "handsome, open-faced, mid-thirties. Needs a shave. And—though we'll later find out he is a man with a great sense of humor—he's looked happier." We see him first in his New York apartment, which has "strange mementos of Harry's adventures on the shelves and walls; piles of box-files, magazines. A wall covered with yellowed newspaper clippings." A fresh copy of the *New York Post* has the headline, "Private Eye in Brooklyn Exorcism Drama," and the article recounts that "Harry D'Amour, who describes himself as a private detective, has been linked with occult activities on several occasions."

In a key flashback, the movie shows us an exorcism with a small boy and a winged demon to further establish Harry's credentials in dealing with the otherworldly.

"He's the Harry I've had in my head for years—no word of a lie," Clive said about Scott Bakula as the film was released. "When he stepped onset, in costume for the first time, which happened to be into his apartment, the set for his apartment, I thought, 'This is wonderful—this is the man I've been writing about for years,' and that's a real thrill to see an actor so beautifully embody somebody that you've been writing about for such a long time—it's a real thrill. I have to say, they used to say that thing on posters: 'So-and-so is so-and-so.' Well, Scott Bakula is Harry D'Amour, and it really sends a shiver down an author's back."

"I've travelled a long way with Harry D'Amour," he wrote in 1996, for the liner notes on the *Lord of Illusions* LaserDisc:

> I've not made the road very easy for him. His destiny, it seems, is to be in constant struggle with what might be loosely called "the forces of darkness," though he claims he'd be quite content investigating insurance fraud. His reluctance is, I trust, part of his charm. He's not a Van Helsing, defiantly facing off against some implacable evil with faith and holy water. His antecedents are the troubled, weary, and often lovelorn heroes of film noir—private detectives with an eye for a beautiful widow and an aversion to razors. It therefore seems perfectly appropriate that Harry finds his way onto the cinema screen, where his world can intersect with that of the Grand Guignol horror movies I've had the pleasure to create hitherto.

Attempts to follow *Lord of Illusions* with a sequel, "Vipex," and then a TV series came and went, although a project with Harry at its core remains a possibility. The detective endures, never far from Clive's writing desk or his thoughts.

In 1998, Clive noted that he had started a short story that would put Harry D'Amour and Pinhead together. Over time it grew to become *The Scarlet Gospels*, which was published in 2015. The novel

"Harry D'Amour's a character who's in a way almost an alter ego for me; a guy who's drawn over and over again to the dark side, to the supernatural, to the occult. He tries to resist it but somehow or other it's in his karma, he can't do anything about it. He can't help himself. These things come find him, and when they come he has to deal with them. I sometimes feel that's true of the stories that I make and the images I make. They come unbidden, a lot of them in dreams. I know how Harry feels, in other words."

set aside the non-canonical appearance Harry made, alongside Pinhead, in the Boom! Studios comic book *Hellraiser* series (2011–2014); instead it advanced Harry's story—and Norma's and several of his friends'—in epic and transformative ways.

Clive's plotting for the unfilmed "Vipex" screenplay indicates that Harry had once been in the NYPD. *The Scarlet Gospels* adopts this backstory as well, expanding it:

> Harry D'Amour had never wanted a life like this. He'd attempted to make a normal life for himself, a life untainted by the secret terrors whose presences he had first encountered as a child. The keeping of the law, he had reasoned, would be as good a bastion as any against the forces that stalked his soul. And so, lacking the smarts and the verbal dexterity required of a good lawyer, he became instead a member of New York's finest. At first the trick seemed to work. Driving around the streets of New York, dealing with problems that reared from the banal to the brutal and back again twice in the same hour, he found it relatively easy to put to the back of his mind the unnatural images that stood beyond the reach of any gun or law that had been made.

Part of the novel recounts Harry's dramatic last night of active duty and his first meeting with Norma, which happens when he reports for counseling. Although a plotline in which a thirteen-year-old Harry was to have encountered Pinhead was excised from the final draft, *The Scarlet Gospels* does recount the litany of demons Harry has faced across the years since leaving the force and becoming a private investigator—before sending the present-day, forty-seven-year-old Harry on his most metaphysical journey yet: entering Hell itself.

Taking place several years after the conclusion of *Everville*, the events of *The Scarlet Gospels* deliver Harry to a place where he can take up the role planned for him by Clive in the third and final book of the Art trilogy—not least of which is his bearing witness, over the course of the epic and metaphysical narrative, to an event that Clive promises, if revealed, will shake human understanding and beliefs. . . .

Harry, our commonsense, practical, brave hero, will continue to act as our guide and companion as we journey into that unknown.

But why the name D'Amour?

Clive's answer: "Love, in all its complexity and its darkness and its ambiguity and its contradiction, is actually a lifeline to our higher selves. That sense, that knowledge, is underrated: the fact that love is a way to touch the divine in ourselves."

POETRY IN PRINT

" 'I'm a poet,' the young man said, 'and it's my job to remember the sadness of things.' "

OPPOSITE PAGE

Manuscript page of Clive's poem.

In 2001, Clive's then husband, David Armstrong, created a series of striking photographic images for publication. *Rare Flesh*, as the collection was titled, offered Clive an opportunity to collaborate with David and share his poetry in a more prominent way than he had to date.

In an interview for his fan club in 2003, he reflected, "David's photography has been something that I've watched going on over the period of the last several years, often because my painting studio is right next door to his photography studio. . . . I liked very much the idea of being inspired by photographs my other half was taking as a starting-off place for words—that seemed like a really interesting idea."

Clive found the project challenging. It demanded that he marry his words with David's images, but it also elicited some anxiety about the emotional exposure inherent in publishing his verse.

"I agonized probably more over these words than just about anything else I've ever done, partly, because they needed to be very short. You don't want to spread too far into a page, which has got a photograph on it. So you need to have a kind of density of intention and a density of form."

Meanwhile, Clive had been writing *Abarat*, whose very opening lines are a poem: "I dreamed a limitless book. . . ," which declares that the author expects the reader to understand both how his stories come to be and how they are told.

Throughout the Abarat volumes there are differing kinds of verses—some are scattered freely throughout the text, others at natural breaks between chapters of narrative—and they remind us that this is both an imagined place and a real one. Poets, named and unnamed, are credited as authors, often with no plot-purpose other than to hint at the vast unseen history and geography of this world.

Characters who express great joy are given lighthearted songs and nonsense verse—betraying Clive's love of Edward Lear and Spike Milligan—which have captured the imagination of readers young and old:

~~Our skin~~
~~We go~~

God, I heard, created skin,
~~Fo~~ For sac to put our innards in,
And then, ~~y~~ because the sack was
                                    blind,
~~&~~ Cut eye-holes in ~~his sack~~ (O God was kind!)
He put ~~a~~ a nose there, and a mouth,
And made some other littles holes south
Of ~~nose~~ where our faces are,
                          to weld
And gave us ears, ~~to stop~~ not despair
from being trapped inside e our ~~heads~~,
With all ~~a~~ our fears, our sweats and
                                    dreads.

And here we are, ~~a sack with hole,~~
                        we hole-y sacks,
With ~~holes~~ bone for heads, and arms
                                and backs,
Going about ~~a~~ the world ~~it's~~ ~~than~~ odd—
As though we were the mirror of God.

"I think if ever there were a naked art it's poetry."

> O woe is me!
>
> O woe is me!
>
> I used to have a hamster tree.
>
> But it was eaten by a newt
>
> And now I have no cuddly fruit.
>
> O woe is me!
>
> O woe is me!
>
> I used to have a hamster tree!

Nonetheless, poetry also serves a hugely important tonal task, bearing the weight of intense emotions or concepts that might overly weigh down the main narrative.

> Night comes down upon my heart
>
> And smothers me with grief.
>
> Let us take comfort before we part,
>
> That at least our lives are brief.

The Abarat series brings Clive closer to one of his great heroes, William Blake, by enabling him to use art and poetry together to create a multifaceted whole.

"Let's look at this in the context of 'Tyger, tyger burning bright,/In the forests of the night,' which, everybody knows, is in one sense an incredibly simple series of images: here is a tiger burning bright in the forests of the night, 'What immortal hand or eye framed thy fearful symmetry?' In other words, how were you made, how is it possible you were made? Is it possible that the same hand that made you also made the lamb? Well, yes, it is, says Blake, it is very possible and on one level that is an incredibly simple idea—the tiger is terrible and magnificent and fearsome, and the lamb is gentle and soft and vulnerable, but God made them both. But now, take away the thesis of the poem and you first look at the words, and the words have this energy. You can say, 'Tyger, tyger burning bright,/In the forests of the night,' and it's an invocation. I defy anybody to say those words don't feel different on a Monday to the way they do on a Tuesday. There's something about those words which is almost infinite."

The growing sophistication of the themes underpinning Abarat can be seen as the paintings and poems shoulder a growing philosophical implication. "As I move through the series," Clive says, "everybody will see me pushing hard to make those connections between the visual and the literary tighter and stronger and more significant."

World creation has always offered an opportunity to generate names and places with unfamiliar words—a task that Clive greets both eagerly and painstakingly. In a more abstract way in Abarat, Clive also uses the musicality of an unknown language to write magical incantations that operate for the reader solely through sound and tempo.

> Ithni asme ata,
>
> Ithni manamee,
>
> Drutha Iotacata,
>
> Come thou glyph to me.
>
> Ithni, ithni,
>
> Asme ata:
>
> Come thou glyph to me.

Asked by young Abarat readers if he suffers with writers' block, Clive replied, "I don't know a writer who doesn't. I write poetry. I free my mind of the constraint of prose by writing poetry. In fact, certain of the poems that I've used in Book Two, certainly, were poems which began because I was blocked and I couldn't write. When I block it's usually because I don't know where the story is supposed to go. And instead of writing and taking the wrong road, I sort of hang around and in that waiting time I write poems. If you're going to write, I really recommend that—it really works well—Stephen King does it as well, by the way. . . . You don't have to show the poems to anybody; [they can be] just for you and you alone. But on the other hand you might find something comes along that you really, really like. So, it's completely your decision but it is a great way to loosen up your feelings, if you will."

More recently, Clive has been collating his poetry for publication, sharing some of it online: "I've written a lot of poetry which has become very important to me in this time because poetry is a short form for me—in a breath of energy, in a short time of energy, I can perhaps set something down and it's worked very well for me."

> The presence of this breath.
> The presence of the stratosphere.
> The presence of the void.
> The presence of presences.
> The presence of those not present.
> The silence of their bodies.
> All silences.
> All voids.
> The presence of this breath.

"The larger they get, the more I wrestle. But I tend to believe that if I have to wrestle I should chuck it out. I don't think it's wastage: I feel it's me listening to my instinct. I feel like a tap dancer, I feel I can sound almost maudlin in my sense of not wanting to claim this for myself but it's gifted to me, in a way that the prose is not."

Clive quickly returns, though, to the subject of those writers who inspire him. "There's also Yeats—who is a great hero of mine—a lot of his poems are named for the first line of the poem—'When You Are Old and Grey and Full of Sleep'—so you get a list of Yeats's poems, particularly *The Complete Yeats*, the contents pages are *heartbreaking* if you look, because you've just got this wonderful sense not only of the glories you're going to discover when you open the book, but also just because he was so masterful, just an eloquence in those first lines.

"Poetry does something that nothing else can do: it uses the language that we're using now and turns it to a different purpose. And it enhances our sense of our own capabilities, I think," Clive says, offering the final three lines of "The Wandering Aengus" by Yeats as an example:

> And pluck till time and times are done
> The silver apples of the moon,
> The golden apples of the sun.

"There's no words in those lines which are unusual or weird, or poetic even, right? What makes them work is their arrangement on the page and the rhyme."

2013– IMAGINER
PRESENT

"Conduit"

OPPOSITE PAGE
A 2020 promotional poster for Imaginer, an eight-volume, limited edition series of books published between 2014 and 2020, presenting over six hundred of Clive's paintings in full color.

In October 2013, the West Hollywood Library hosted an exhibition of Clive's art and literary work. The following month, the Century Guild gallery in Los Angeles staged the first of three solo shows of Clive's work that it would curate and host over the next two years. Solo exhibitions at Alexander Salazar in San Diego in July 2014 and Galleri Oxholm in Copenhagen, Denmark, in February 2015 were also organized by Century Guild.

Another solo art show was staged at the CoproGallery in Santa Monica in August 2016.

The Imaginer series, a Century Guild project to collect hi-resolution archival images and present them in a collection of art books, was taken over by Phil and Sarah Stokes in 2015, with the eight-book series published between 2014 and 2020. Each volume's print run included one thousand regular-edition copies and one hundred limited-edition copies (signed by Clive).

In private during that period, spurred on by a frustration that the slow pace of his recovery was preventing him from painting large-scale oils and confining him to his bed for long periods, Clive devoted his artistic energies to creating hundreds of small new pieces. He committed to using less physically demanding media, including ink on paper and a brush or a branch from the garden, or even his fingers; or a mixture of paints and ink, sometimes loaded into eyedroppers.

"I've been through really the darkest time of my life," he noted in August 2015, "but I am definitely healing now. And although I see a doctor more often than I would like, we're getting there and I've just produced sixty-five paintings for Abarat 4 and 5. These are not the same scale as the others, simply because I can't stand to do oil paintings yet—I will eventually, but standing for a length of time, it isn't practical. So I'm doing these in oils but I'm doing them on oil paper, which is sort of a pastiche of oil canvas and paper—which has the texture of canvas but is in fact as light as paper."

Clive also returned to pen-and-ink character portraits worked in dense, fine lines and pastel work on more portable sketchpads.

"If I'm sitting with a pen and a small piece of paper, I can intensify the experience and actually live within the bounds of a nine-by-eleven piece of paper and a Pentel or whatever it is. I love doing

IMAGINER

THE CLIVE BARKER ARCHIVE

"Clive Barker is a mapmaker of the mind, charting the furthest reaches of the imagination." —Douglas E. Winter in the *Washington Post*

the sumi-e brush loaded with ink, it's great fun to do, but I can't—how I'm sitting right now—I can't get a fully loaded sumi-e brush and expect to paint with a large piece of paper on my knee, I mean it's just not plausible.

"This has been a time when I've tried to come to terms with the limitations of my body. I'm not allowing it to dictate the kind of work that I was going to be able to make in the future, even though I'm very aware that I won't be producing any more *Beautiful Moments*. Just by the very nature, the ambition of that picture, I did it all on my own, and God knows it was a kind of madness, probably. I couldn't do that right now. Will I be healthy enough to do that in the future? I most certainly hope so! I'm certainly striving for that. You do one thing, then you move on to another thing—the size means nothing at all."

Clive also found an urgency to represent not just ideas of narrative or character but the sense and emotion of a moment, and found himself creating dozens of multicolored abstract pieces that he understood little better than he had understood the arrival of the earliest Abarat characters in oil.

In 2016, he noted: "In the first three or four months of this year I've done three hundred and some-thing works on paper—painting at night on your knee is to turn yourself into a Technicolor expression of your own, because the paint goes everywhere. . . . There's no way of stopping it, you know? It's messy and the floor around us, where I am right now, is testament to how messy it is, because you just can't handle twenty little bottles of paint and brushes and water and then a large piece of paper on a board on your knee—with dogs hovering around and a parrot screaming at you!—but I got so profoundly depressed, so profoundly angry with myself that I was allowing the problem to dominate my access to something that was very important to me. And so I thought, well, let's do this, and if they're not good, even if only one in every ten is good, then that's the one they'll see.

"It turned out as time went by that I found new methodologies. I produced pictures that were small, obviously, but very, very, very intense, so that they could sit perfectly happily with one of the canvases in *Imaginer*. A lot of them are abstract, or semiabstract, which is a completely new adventure for me. There's something very interesting about transferring my subconsciousness from representation to abstract, and it says something about where my head is.

"I've actually been liberated in a weird way by the freedom of being able to do in some cases smaller pictures, obviously, and in other cases also slightly more abstractive pictures. I am finding the abstract use of color to be empowering, curiously, and this is I think because I don't have to tell a story. What I have to do is identify a character's *emotional* life, and there's something a lot more pleasurable about that than there is somewhat didactically going through a narrative which I already have in my head."

"It feels as though after illness and silence I'm finally back . . . back where I was. It's been a tough time. But I'm well now. And strong now. And writing like crazy."

PERSONAL LIFE

"True artists cast no shadow."

A visit to Clive's writing room today reveals someone racing to catch up with the many projects that his illness left adrift. Character sketches for film and book projects litter the drawing table overlooking the palm-framed garden. Drafts of new short stories jockey for attention alongside manuscript pages for the fourth and fifth books of the Abarat series. Extensive plot outlines for *The Third Book of the Art* are also in evidence, as are hundreds of poems being collected for publication. Two other novels are here, one of which, *Deep Hill*, leans heavily on Clive's concerns for global climate issues:

"When I started this book in this form," he said in 2019, gesturing to the manuscript, "I wasn't sure I was going to live long enough to write another book after this. I no longer have that fear, but nevertheless my anxiety about voicing my profoundest concerns about the way we treat each other and the planet we live on had to be stated in this book because I might not ever have a chance to state it again. And really this book is driven by the fact that we are doing some terrible things to the world we live in and to each other that seem to me even more terrible than the things that used to terrify me when I was ten and I want, very much, to put those concerns into a book."

The man Clive credits for his recovery and continuing well-being has long been an artistic inspiration as well as the composed center in an otherwise busy household.

As we looked at a particularly serene painting together for Imaginer, Clive said, "This is a very important painting for me—because of its sheer minimalism, you know, a plain face and a plain egg, a balancing act if you will—and in part because it has Roman's face in it and obviously he's the man I adore. He's the most beautiful man I ever met, and he has an incredible calm, right?"

Clive was married to Roman Stelmach in a quiet ceremony at home in July 2019 and the pair complement each other completely. In recent years, Clive's creative strengths have returned as his home life has felt more settled and his energies are all focused on new and upcoming projects.

"The opening of *Sacrament*," he reflects, "says we are animals who tell stories. And then it goes on to say why we tell stories, and that's because, if we didn't, we wouldn't understand ourselves.

"There's a quote I love which says, 'On good days, you're concerned about going out into the street because a bus might strike you and you might not finish the great work. And on bad days you hope a bus strikes you and you won't have to finish the great work.' I think that says it all."

"Barker will never be confined to a 'genre' —that most condescending of literary labels—having grasped something basic about his art: when the horrific and the humane coexist believably in a work of fiction, the reader's experience of each is heightened."
—ARMISTEAD MAUPIN

MERCURIAL: AN AFTERWORD

"I write, I draw; I draw, I write; it's all interchangeable."

How to communicate that which exists only in our minds is an abiding question for any artist. How to best express, say, that thrill as the first autumn wind dashes through laden golden branches—does that demand a rush of adjectives, a swirl of color, a timpanous orchestral phrase, or a virtual reality amalgam of sensory inputs?

No sooner than he had made his name as a writer, Clive offered his talents as an artist, creating the detailed horrors of the cover art for the six volumes of the Books of Blood. Scroll forward and he's a fantasy novelist, with fluid brush and ink work to match, and then a film director, leaping forward from homemade 8mm and 16mm experimental shorts straight to the Hollywood-funded hit *Hellraiser*. The answer, perhaps, is that different ideas demand different media.

In 2000, Clive offered this thought: "I've been making plays and paintings and films and writing stories for twenty-five years. One of the things I love about making fantasy and horror is the chance to be protean, to have many faces. If I've got another twenty-five years, I'd like to be as unrecognizable to myself and to readers as I am, looking back, over the last twenty-five years. . . ."

In the years since, his work has certainly changed, but he remains recognizable to readers as a force for radical storytelling and image-making.

At an early stage in Clive's career, journalists were quick to latch onto his mercurial talent for working in multiple media. "Renaissance Man" was the go-to moniker for profile pieces, but Clive shrugs off this label, insisting instead that he's only ever looking for the best way to communicate that flash of vision in his mind's eye, the emotion in his heart.

"My enthusiasm as an artist is not rooted in any particular medium, but in the act of imagination. I am motivated by the images and scenes which arise from my subconscious."

"One of my great idols, Noel Coward, was asked, 'How did you manage to maintain your popularity through the years?' His answer: 'Darling, it's very simple. You always pop out of another hole.' I take that to heart. Whenever they think they've got the hole you'll pop out of, you find a new one. If they think you're a horror novelist, you go write profanity. If they think you're writing a thousand words of profanity, you go write a kids' book. If they think you write for kids, too, you write something horrific. It drives the publicists crazy."

But he admits that the models for his confidence to "have a go" at new means of expression came from the works of Jean Cocteau and William Blake: "These guys didn't make a distinction between what they did. There's a certain artificiality—and it's a pretty modern phenomenon—about the way we divide our endeavors up. If you, a writer, are also expressing yourself as a painter, you're still the same person. The manifestations of my interest in the world will be many and multifarious. So my attitude always is that I don't look too closely at myself and my processes. Most times, I just get the heck on with it. I want to have a crack at that, so it's: 'Let's see what we can achieve.'

"So I write, illustrate, make movies like *Hellraiser*—oddly, that's more French than English. The English don't like polymaths; they prefer you to do one thing well."

And the continuing development of digital skills in filmmaking has ignited the possibilities for adapting novels previously considered "unfilmable." Clive often analyzes the ways that different adaptations succeed (and fail) to successfully navigate the narrative structures. Given his particularly visual method of writing prose, the prospect of his most beloved novels being granted a new life onscreen is strong.

"I very seldom create a story or a novel without having drawn the characters first, even if they're very simple sketches; I need to know what it all looks like. . . . I need to know the geography of a house before I write about it. . . . I draw, I make little maps, you know a top-view of a house, so that I can locate 'OK, the stairs are there,' you know? It matters to me only because—and this is something I've said before—I don't think of myself while I'm writing as a writer, I think of myself as a journalist, reporting on something I'm seeing. . . . It's happening in my mind's eye and so the best thing to do, for me at least, is not think about the words but think about the images and use the words to describe them. . . ."

So, with the ability to create prose, poetry, art, photography, film, and so much more, perhaps the only thing we can be sure of is that whatever comes next from Clive, it will be a surprise.

I hope to
die a failure;
for if I die
a success then
I did not aim
high enough.

C.B. 5/10/96

AUTHORS' NOTE: ON CREATION

"There are countless wild imaginations in this world, but there is just the one Clive Barker." —OWEN KING

On the odd occasion that our names have cropped up in the text of this book, we've mostly referred to ourselves in the third person, our default position as documentarians rather than protagonists. Encouraged, though, both by Clive and by the team at Abrams as they worked alongside us on this book, we've endeavored here to put some context around who we are and how (and why) we work with Clive.

Art—creation—speaks to us all: it's a means of communication between the higher parts of us that we barely understand, as well as being rooted in sensations of pleasure, puzzlement, curiosity, and all the emotions that make us human.

Each of us finds our own beacons that, to extend the metaphor, broadcast on our personal wavelength: artists, musicians, writers, poets, actors, directors—as well as politicians, religious leaders, and advocates for change—that "speak our language" or "speak to something within us."

On encountering such beacons, it's a natural human response to find ourselves reading, watching, listening to, and exploring these particular creatives, visionaries, and leaders more attentively: seeking out their work; digging deeper.

When a person who engages us in this way is living, creating, and developing in our own time we are both blessed and cursed to follow their work in real time. Blessed because we can quiz them about their means and methods, cursed because we have less ability to generate perspective: we can be too close, mired in information overload, to make proper sense of what we're seeing created before us.

For our own experience with Clive Barker's work—and it was his work that "spoke" to us, long before we ever met the man who has become our great friend—it intrigued us that someone creating work that was so well regarded by some but deemed dangerous or subversive by others had seemingly "come from nowhere." Thankfully, Clive appeared happy to chat to journalists of every stripe if he could talk about his loves—of William Blake, of Goya, of philosophy and comics. We began to seek out these interviews and take note of their content.

In 1998, we constructed a website—*Revelations*—where we could organize what we found—primarily using verbatim quotes from Clive and his various collaborators in film and theatre—to see if it might coalesce into something that helped us to connect the threads that had intrigued us. Our entry-point into his work had been the written word, but his films and then, sometime later, his artwork when we got to see the sweep and profusion of it, gave more weight to the threads and we began to see themes. There was a worldview that was beyond fiction and simple entertainment: it made us think; it challenged us on a metaphysical level as well as in the gut.

At that point, despite being online in the new world of the World Wide Web, we were working solely for our own pleasure, using the underlying architecture of a website simply to document our progress and discoveries. We were mildly surprised to find that the phrase "if you build it they will come" proved true, and we began to receive queries and create friendships with like-minded readers.

We'd met Clive at signings for several years previously and were fully paid-up members of the Lost Souls fan club when we started on a plan to interview him formally for the Revelations site. Following a first foray in November 1998 at a public Q&A at Liverpool's Everyman Theatre, the same venue where he had staged some of his earliest theatre work, and with the assistance of Clive's team at Seraphim in Los Angeles and at HarperCollins in London, we sat down with him for a two-hour interview at London's Dorchester Hotel in September 1999. Titling it "Leitmotifs and Dark Beliefs," the Revelatory interviews were up and running.

Like countless other interviewers have recounted over the years, we found Clive to be a generous and fascinating conversationalist; speaking with him is always both an intellectual and an emotional joy.

Spurred by reading the interviews, alongside the news and information we collated and presented on *Revelations* from every source we could locate, the more the queries from others came. Clive's assistant at Seraphim, David Dodds, was kind and meticulous in helping us share timely news of events, press releases and new projects to readers who were increasingly using the web to inform themselves. Clive's friends also started to get in touch, among the earliest being Pete Atkins to clarify and correct an interpretation we'd made on one of his *Hellraiser III* quotes and to offer us his "Building the Beast (In Stages)" essay on the making of *Hell on Earth* for publication on the site.

As we continued to follow Clive's forward momentum, we retained the persistent query about what led him to his breakthrough publishing deal. Our interest was creative rather than biographical. When Stephen Jones's *Shadows in Eden* had been published in 1991 it had piqued us no end. Steve's inspirational work combined full-length conversations with Clive's friends and colleagues about all his projects to date, illustrated with Clive's artwork, photographs and peppered with snippets of quotes from Clive's own book of press clippings—some of which shone chinks of light onto his earlier work. But we wanted more. So many people had written about *Hellraiser*, the *Books of Blood*, *Nightbreed*, *Candyman*, and all the "famous" projects, but we wanted to know about what came before, what led to those projects—what *didn't* we know that could help us to better connect the threads?

Away from the website, we resolved in 2002 to write an essay on the pre-Books of Blood years. With the working title "Ecstatic Disorder," we wove together facts gleaned from asides in interviews alongside artwork and words from Clive. We printed a copy as the first draft came close to completion and tentatively handed him a copy for his thoughts or notes. Our conversations (continuing interviews for Revelations and correspondence by letters and email) had become semi-regular and he suggested that we spoke more often, to fill in the gaps in our essay.

Almost every Friday lunchtime for several months in 2004, Clive would take a break from his morning writing stint to chat about those "old days" with us. It became increasingly apparent to all three of us just how relevant the projects at school, at university, and beyond were to his continuing creative concerns. Clive also encouraged his earliest collaborators to add thoughts, with Julie Padget (née Blake), Doug Bradley, Pete Atkins, Olly Parker, Les Heseltine (now better known as Les Dennis), Helen Clarke, his schoolteacher, and many others all offering insights though interviews. Taking our cue from the central motif in the Books of The Art, we renamed the essay project "Memory, Prophecy and Fantasy" and what had been a modest essay became an ongoing series of books. With three volumes published to date, we've still not quite reached the period of the Books of Blood release and we intend to continue to explore further . . .

We succeeded Lost Souls as the "official" source of Clive's news and updates on the internet in 2006 and maintain the *Revelations* site at www.clivebarker.info to this day. At the same time, Clive asked us quietly and privately late one night on one of our visits to stay with him if we were "in it for the long haul" and whether we would be the guardians of his works should anything happen to him.

We said "yes" without hesitation. We formalized this in 2015 with the www.clivebarkerarchive.com resource and the subsequent establishment of The Clive Barker Archive as a formal entity to hold Clive's archive for the long term, to make it available to academics and researchers and to publish work from it. Since 2017, we've been in near daily contact, speaking by phone two or three times a week.

Clive loves to collaborate and we have different ways of working together depending on the project. We often work by phone, given that Clive is based in Beverly Hills and we are in London. This works just fine for discussions of written work, but nothing beats a face-to-face chat over several mugs of tea, and looking at artwork in particular works far better in person than onscreen: for the Imaginer project for example, which collected high-res captures of Clive's paintings in eight large-format hardback books, we would arrive at Clive's house on a periodic basis, bearing print-outs, and spend happy days comparing prints to the original canvases. Selecting the paintings to include in each volume involved back-and-forth discussions of each one, seeking out the relationships between them.

The archive is very much a live animal and gives other creatives access to materials not previously available—licensing artwork for use in print, movie, and TV projects, or written work for editors and publishers. Over time, our plan is to create a physical setting to extend access to students and in-person visitors.

In the same way that our tentative steps in 1998 created something to help us connect the dots in Clive's metaphysics, the archive has given Clive a clearer view into his own working notes and papers to allow him, in some cases, to make connections that have inspired new creative works. While he's been working on a collection of poetry, the archival process has located and retrieved previously uncollected material from within boxes of written notes or on the back of other paperwork, making verses he wrote many years ago available for possible inclusion. In this sense the archive is very much a working research hub.

It has been our pleasure and privilege to become Clive's friends and collaborators. It has led us to explore pathways we might not otherwise have followed and building the archive has enriched our lives over many years. That work is ongoing as we simultaneously look forward with Clive to new and upcoming projects whilst looking back to secure legacy projects for those who come after us, curious to understand his creative life.

I've written my fair share of Forewords and Afterwords for other people's books over the years, and have invariably found the process very pleasurable.

So I assumed this Afterword would be no great challenge.

I was wrong.

Strictly speaking it isn't my book. It was researched and written by Phil and Sarah Stokes, who are my friends, my archivists, often my most insightful critics, and are now my biographers. What makes this book so exceptional is that each chapter unveils a fresh collection of photographs, most from my private collection, which Phil and Sarah have been locating, identifying, and now showing our readership for the first time.

You can understand how I might have assumed that to write a short curtain speech after such a spectacular show would be no more difficult than writing about Ramsey or Steve.

But the book, which is hopefully in your hands as you read this, isn't like the books I've written commentaries about to celebrate the work of writers I admire. This is me writing an Afterword for a book that has my life as an artist as its subject. The tone of admiration that marked the Foreword I wrote to 'Salem's Lot would sound grotesquely self-congratulatory if I were to write this in the same tone. And there's an even trickier problem that arises from the memories that so many of the images in the book stir up. A few of the pictures are standard movie posters. But the bulk of the pictures you've been looking at are reminders of innocent and often intimate moments caught when the subjects were not even aware that the shot was being taken; or, if they were, never assumed it would become a telling part of a story that is really about a number of friends who, rather than losing touch with one another as life took them off along different roads, kept working together as the years went by, so that now, as I creep towards my three score years and ten, I find—to my great delight—that I am still working on projects with people I've known and loved for forty, even fifty years.

So I find, in all honesty, that the most emotionally potent card that might normally be played in a brief piece such as this is not going to match the truth. For the future is not a blank page. The lives recounted here continue, not least my close friendship with Phil and Sarah.

I very much hope this deliriously diverse collection of plots and plans and inexhaustible, unextinguishable ambitions will keep us together, making pictures and movies and books.

As Winston Churchill remarked, in a very different context.

"This is not the end. It is not even the beginning of the end.

But it is, perhaps, the end of the beginning."

BIBLIOGRAPHY

PRIMARY SOURCES

The published works of Clive Barker.

Unpublished works by Clive Barker held by the authors, Phil and Sarah Stokes, in The Clive Barker Archive.

The published works of Phil and Sarah Stokes.

Correspondence with, and interviews by, the authors, Phil and Sarah Stokes, with Clive Barker and others quoted in this book, 1998–2022.

SECONDARY SOURCES

Publisher production materials, press releases, and other marketing materials for each of Clive's books.

Studio production materials, press releases, and other marketing materials for each of Clive's films and films related to Clive's works.

Accomando, Beth. "Lord of Illusions." Interview at San Diego Comic-Con, 1995.

Alexander, Chris. "John Harrison Talks Book of Blood and Composing the Score for George Romero's ...Of the Dead." *Blood-Spattered* (blog), March 3, 2009.

Allen, Bruce. "Something Wicked Comes to Oregon." *New York Times*, November 20, 1994.

Anonymous. WB Authortalk – Waldenbooks, 1986.

——. *Video Business*, January 18, 1988.

——. "The One on One: Clive Barker." *The One* 25 (October 1990).

——. *Times Literary Supplement* review of *Imajica*, 1991.

——. "Opening the (Puzzle) Box of Delights." *Comic World* 9 (November 1992).

——. "Rising Star." *Samhain* 35 (November/December 1992).

——. "Video World Classic: Nightbreed, Video World." *Festive*, December 1992.

——. *Clive Barker on the Art of Clive Barker.* Documentary, Bess Cutler Gallery, 1993.

——. Exclusive interview with Clive Barker, creator of the Hellraiser series. *Video Business*, April 23, 1993.

——. "Clive Barker: Hellraiser IV and Lords of Illusion" at www.Gigaplex.com, 1995.

——. "The Gay '90s - Entertainment Comes Out of the Closet." *Entertainment Weekly* 291 (September 8, 1995).

——. Review of *Sacrament*. *Kirkus Reviews*, May 15, 1996.

——. Review of *Sacrament*. *Publishers Weekly*, July 1, 1996.

——. *Lord of Illusion*, Home Cinema Choice, September 1996.

——. Review of *Revelations*, edited by Douglas E. Winter. *Kirkus Reviews*, April 15, 1997.

——. Review of *Galilee*. *Kirkus Reviews*, May 15, 1998.

——. "Gods and Monsters." *Bent*, November 1998.

——. "Clive From New York" at www.McFarlane.com, February 13, 2001.

——. "Tortured Souls on Screen" at www.McFarlane.com, February 1, 2002.

——. "I, Patrick." *SFX* 97 (November 2002).

——. Masters of Horror! at www.KillerMovies.com, February 11, 2005.

——. Interview with Clive Barker, *The Thief of Always* graphic novel, Book 3, IDW, May 2005.

——. "Masters of Horror" supplement. *Daily Variety*, July 13, 2005.

——. Q&A: Clive Barker's *Jericho*, online for Xbox 360 print magazine *Readers Only* at www.oxm.co.uk, February 13, 2007.

——. "A New Novel - Mister B. Gone" at Clive Barker's MySpace blog at www.myspace.com/clivebarkerbooks, May 10, 2007.

——. Review of *Coldheart Canyon*. *Publishers Weekly*, June 20, 2011.

Athey, Ron. "Dissections." *Honcho* 124 (June 1997).

Atkins, Peter. "A Dog's Tale." In *Clive Barker's Shadows in Eden*, edited by Stephen Jones. Lancaster, PA: Underwood-Miller, 1991.

——. Screenplay of *Hellraiser III: Hell on Earth*, May 8, 1991.

——. *The Astonishing Doug Bradley, Secret City: Strange Tales of London*, the 1997 World Fantasy Convention book.

——. Appearance at the Hellraiser Reunion panel, Monster Mania 5, May 20, 2006.

Auden, Sandy. The Auden Interviews at www.thealienonline.net, January 2002.

——. "Definitely Chickentown." *The Third Alternative* 40 (Winter 2004/2005).

August, Kim. "Explorer from the Far Reaches of Experience." *Pharr Out!*, 1998.

Azzopardi, Chris. "Scared Stiff." *Between the Lines* 1706 (February 5, 2009).

Babouris, Bill. "Addicted to Creativity (Part 2)." *Samhain* 71 (January 1999).

Baby Doc. Review of *Hellraiser*. *Venue*, September 11, 1987.

Bacal, Bacal. "Lord of Illusions - A Fable of Death and Resurrection." *Sci-Fi Entertainment* 1, no. 5 (February 1995).

——. "A Touch of Quicksilver." *Shivers* 42 (June 1997).

Barker, Clive. Appearance at the Canadian Booksellers Association Gala Tribute event, June 8, 2007.

——. Online Q&A for *Hollywood Spotlight* at www.RealHollywood.com, June 23, 1998.

——. Talk at Kepler's Books, Menlo Park, California, December 2, 1992.

——. Talk at the Fangoria Weekend of Horrors, Los Angeles, May 17, 1992.

Transcribed in *Coenobium* 7 (1992).

——. Introduction to *Nightbreed*. Nightbreed US Video, Media Home Entertainment, 1991.

——. Talk at Leapcon 1995, the Quantum Leap convention, February 18, 1995.

——. Online Q&A for *People Online*, July 30, 1998.

——. Statement to *The Geraldo Rivera Show* on *Candyman 2*, March 8, 1995.

——. Abarat Tour Q&A talk, Seattle, Washington, September 24, 2004.

——. Appearance at a Jericho press event with Mercury Steam, Casino de Madrid, Spain, October 10, 2007.

——. Audio commentary on the *Lord of Illusions* unrated laser disc, MGM, 1996.

Beeler, Michael. "Clive Barker." *Cinefantastique* 30, no. 2 (June 1998).

——. "Gods and Monsters." *Cinefantastique* 30, no. 11 (December 1998).

——. "Hellraiser IV – Bloodline." *Cinefantastique* 27, no. 2 (November 1995).

——. "Lord of Illusions - Filming the Books of Blood." *Cinefantastique* 26, no. 2 (February 1995).

Bentzen, Cheryl, and Stephen Dressler. "From the Dog Days to Bloodlines." *Lost Souls* 3 (1996).

——. "Confessions." *Lost Souls* 2, no. 1 (April 1999).

——. "Confessions." *Lost Souls* 3, March 1996.

——. "Confessions." *Lost Souls* 5 (October 1996).

——. "Confessions." *Lost Souls* 9 (November 1997).

——. "Confessions." *Lost Souls* 10 (June 1998).

Bergal, Gilles. Interview, Mater Tenebrarum, 1985.

Bergman, Jason. "Clive Barker's Undying Interview" at www.SharkyGames.com, February 21, 2001.

Bernstein, Abbie. "Hooked on Candyman 2." *Fangoria* 139 (January 1995).

Berry, Michael. "Birth of a Barkerverse." *Wizard* 25 (September 1993).

Billow, Marjorie. "Set Piece." *Film Monthly*, July 1989.

Bissette, Stephen. Introduction to *Clive Barker, Illustrator*, by Clive Barker and Fred Burke. (Arcane/Eclipse, 1990).

Black, Amber, and Tim Trautmann. Interview, *Review*, 1996.

Boisvert, Eric S. Fantasia 2009 interview with John Harrison at www.Fangoria.com, July 15, 2009.

Bradley, Doug. "Pinhead's Progress." 112 (July 1992).

——. *Sacred Monsters: Behind the Mask of the Horror Actor*. London: Titan, 1996.

Bradley, Mike. "Ghoul Britannia." *The Times – Metro*, October 31–November 6, 1998.

Brady, Wayne. *The Wayne Brady Show*, Fall 2002.

Bragg, Melvyn, and Daniel Wiles. *The South Bank Show*, May 1994.

Braynard, Matthew, and Chris Morris. "The Well Rounded Interview - Brady Bell" at www.Well-Rounded.com, 2000.

Brekke, Joe. "Inside the Mind of Clive." *The Tribune* (San Luis Obispo, CA), October 15, 2000.

Briggs, Joe Bob. "Sex in the Attic with Devilhead Slime." *Dallas Observer*, October 1, 1987.

Brown, Michael. "Clive Barker 1973–1993: Bess Cutler." *Dread* 9 (January 1993).

——. "Rawhead Rex - The Creator." *Dread* 6 (1992).

Bryce, Allan ——. "Bee Movie Monster!" *Video World*, August 1996.

——. "Clive Barker." *Video Monthly* 1, no. 5 (July 1990).

——. "Hellbent on Horror." *Photoplay* 38, no. 9 (September 1987).

Burke, Fred. *Illustrator II*. Eclipse Books, 1993.

Chainsaw, Billy. "My Bizarre Life." *Bizarre* 50 (September 2001).

Cherry, Brigid, and Brian Robb. "Peter Atkins: Hellbound Writer." *Starburst* 131 (July 1989).

Cherry, Brigid, Brian Robb, and Andrew Wilson. "Weaveword" *Nexus* 4 (November/December 1987).

——. "Weaveword." Nexus 5 (January/February 1988).

Christie, George. "The Great Life." *Hollywood Reporter*, November 17, 1987.

Clayden, Martyn. "Hell's-A-Pop-Pin." *Video World*, July 1993.

The Cleaver. *Slaughterhouse* 1, no. 4 (1989).

Colin, Fabrice.: "Clive Barker." *Lire Magazine Littéraire* 1H (March/April 2021).

Collis, Clark. "Clive Barker Is Back from the Dead." *Entertainment Weekly*, October 2014.

Coltrera, Francesca. "Clive Barker's Aim: A Mixture of Horror and Fantasy." *Boston Herald*, February 11, 1990.

Conner, Jeff. "Bloody Books Coming Soon." *Scream/Press/Release* 1, no. 4 (September 1985).

Cooper, Dennis. "Fuck the Canon." *LA Weekly*, Literary Supplement, August 31–September 6, 2001.

Crowther, Robert, Jr. "Interview from the Dark Side." *Hiatus*, March 1, 1990.

Dadomo, Giovanni. "Blood Lines." *Time Out* 723 (June 28–July 4, 1984).

Decker, Sean. "The Crazy Train." *Fangoria* 275 (August 2008).

DiBlasi, Anthony. Abarat 2 promotional CD ROM sampler, Joanna Cotler Books, June 2004.

Donovan, Katie. "Hard-Working Fantasy Man." *Irish Times*, May 30, 1995.

Dr Drew and Adam Carolla. *Loveline*, May 15, 1997.

Drenth, Sophia. "Illustrating Mr Barker." *Albedo One* 30 (August 2005).

Dressler, Stephen. "Confessions." *Lost Souls* 12 (January 1999).

Dubin, Zan. "Horrormeister Barker Turns Imagination Loose on Canvas." *Los Angeles Times*, August 22, 1995.

——. "Laguna Museum Enters the Grisly World of Clive Barker." *Los Angeles Times*, June 26, 1995.

Dziemianowicz, Stefan. "Other Voices Other Realms." *Washington Post*, October 27, 1991.

Ebert, Roger. "Hellraiser." Chicago Sun-Times, September 18, 1987.

Edwards, Phil. "Hair-Raiser." *Crimson Celluloid* 1 (January 1988).

Ellard, Andrew "Mr Flibble Talks To. . ." at www.RedDwarf.co.uk, January 26, 2001.

Elliott, David. "Lifestyles of the Sick and Skinless." *San Diego Union*, September 18, 1987.

Ellison, Harlan. "Can We Talk?," transcript of a 1988 KPFK Los Angeles radio appearance, Midnight Graffitti, Winter 1994/1995.

Ferrante, Anthony C. "Barker Looks Back." *Bloody Best of Fangoria* 12 (September 1993).

——. "To Surrender Hell." *Fangoria* 151 (April 1996).

Ferrante, Anthony C., and Rod L. Reed. "A Tribute to the Hellraiser Series." *The Dead Beat* 3 (1993).

Fielder, Miles. "Renaissance Man." *The Scotsman*, September 18, 1999.

Fohr, Craig.: "Confessions." *Lost Souls Newsletter*, September/December 2000.

——. "Confessions." *Lost Souls Newsletter*, March 2002.

——. "Confessions." *Lost Souls Newsletter*, August 1, 2003.

Fohr, Craig, and Kelly Shaw. "Confessions." *Lost Souls*, March 2001.

Fowler, Christopher. "The Long & The Short of It" at www.ChristopherFowler.com, March 11, 2012.

Gaiman, Neil. "He Ain't Heavy." *Knave* 17, no. 6 (1985).

——. "The Face Fits." *Knave* 17, no. 7 (1985).

——. "Tales of Terror." *Penthouse UK*, May 1985.

Ganahl, Jane. "Hell-Raiser on a Spiritual Quest." *San Francisco Examiner*, August 11, 1996.

Garris, Mick. Post Mortem - Ryuhei Kitamura, the Post Mortem Podcast, April 2018.

——. Quicksilver Highway audio commentary, Anchor Bay DVD, 2005.

Garris, Mick, and Joe Russo. Post Mortem - Clive Barker, the Post Mortem Podcast, Episode 119, April 28, 2021.

Gibson, John. "The Fantasy Man Has No Illusions." *Evening News* (Edinburgh), August 26, 1989.

Gilbert, John, and Mark Salisbury. "Faces of Death." *Fear* 22 (October 1990).

Goldstein, Patrick. "Hellbound's Horror-Fiction Lion." *Los Angeles Times*, December 28, 1988.

Graham, Bob. "A Demon for Work." *San Francisco Chronicle*, February 22, 1999.

Grainger, James. "The Cannibal Express." *Rue Morgue* 81 (August 2008).

——. "The Science of Fear." *Rue Morgue* 81 (August 2008).

Greenfeld, Karl. "The Lost Boy." *Blue*, August 1997.

Grosser, Marty. "A Piece of My Mind." *Previews* 3, no. 1 (January 1993).

Hancock, David. "Playing Undead." *The Times, Midland Metro*, September 2, 2000.

Hansom, Dick. "To Hell and Back." *Speakeasy* 102 (September 1989).

Harris, Joanne. "Rebuilding Asgard." In *The Writer's Map*, edited by Huw Lewis-Jones. London: Thames and Hudson, 2018.

Hasted, Nick. "Clive Barker." *Creature* 5 (1985).

——. "The Great and Secret Donny and Marie Show." *The Independent on Sunday*, November 8, 1988.

Hemmerich, Thomas. "Clive Barker on the Phone." *That's Clive!*, March 29, 2005.

Henry, William A., III. "Magic Powers." *Time*, March 19, 1990.

Higgins, Bill. "Barker, DreamWorks Play Games." *Variety*, April 27, 2000.

Hobson, Louis B. "Bogy Barker." *Calgary Sunday Sun*, November 8, 1987.

Hodgson, Clive. *Underworld* preview, 1985 London Film Festival program.

Hogan, Hogan. "The Hell It Is." *Melody Maker*, March 19, 1988.

Holland, Christopher. *The Art of Horror* documentary, 1992.

Horton, Robert. "Wordsmith Also Directs Relentless Horror Film." *The Herald* (Washington), September 23, 1987.

Howe, David. "Barker USA." *Starburst Yearbook 1991/92*, Special No. 10.

——. "Hellraiser." *Starburst* 110 (October 1987).

Hughes, David. "Whom God Destroys." *Dreamwatch* 56 (April 1999).

Humphreys, Robb. *A Gathering of Magic, Behind the Scenes of Lord of Illusions*, documentary, 1995, on unrated laser disc, 1996.

Hunter, Stephen. "Hellraiser Is Not Unlike a Feather in the Throat." *Baltimore Sun*, September 22, 1987.

Isherwood, Charles. "Lord of Illusion." *The Advocate* 675 (February 21, 1995).

Jarvey, Paul. "Creator of 'Pinhead' Believes Imagination Is Key to Success." *Telegram & Gazette Worcester*, September 11, 1992.

Jaworzyn, Stefan. Review of *The Damnation Game. Time Out*, 1985.

——. Nightbreed – Preview. *Horrorfan* 1, no. 3 (Fall 1989).

Johan, Rizal. "Bradley Cooper Talks About His Role in Midnight Meat Train." *The Star*, August 5, 2008.

Jones, Alan. "Blood and Cheap Thrills." In *Clive Barker's Shadows in Eden*, edited by Stephen Jones. Lancaster, PA: Underwood-Miller, 1991.

——. "Clive Barker's Nightbreed." *Cinefantastique* 20, no. 1/2 (November 1989).

——. "Dread." *Fangoria* 289 (January 2010).

——. "Hellfire and Location." *Film Review*, April 1992.

——. "Hellraiser III and Me." *Shivers* 5 (February 1993).

——. "How Fox Bungled Nightbreed per Clive Barker." *Cinefantastique* 21, no. 1 (July 1990).

Jones, Stephen. "Clive Barker: Anarchic Prince of Horror." In *Clive Barker's Shadows in Eden*, edited by Stephen Jones. Lancaster, PA: Underwood-Miller, 1991.

——. "Clive Barker: Raising Hell in London." *Monsterland* 17 (Fall 1987).

——. "Editor's Note, May 1989." In *Clive Barker's Shadows in Eden*, edited by Stephen Jones. Lancaster, PA: Underwood-Miller, 1991.

Joy, Nick. "Hell to Pay." *Shivers* 57 (September 1998).

Judell, Brandon. "Hell's Angel." *10 Percent* 3, no. 13 (March/April 1995).

Kaan, Gil. "Clive Barker: A Renaissance Man of Gothic Proportions." *Genre* 86 (October 2000).

Kane, Eugene. "Pain and Pleasure Film." *Milwaukee Journal*, September 1987.

Kane, Paul. "Dyed in the Flesh." *Rue Morgue* 81 (August 2008).

Kay, Laurie. Q&A with Clive Barker. LA Times Festival of Books, April 29, 2000.

Kaye, Don. "How Hulu's Books of Blood Movie Taps the Mind of Clive Barker" at www.DenOfGeek.com, October 7, 2020.

Keough, Peter. "Clive Barker Wishes You a Hellish Little Holiday." *Chicago Sun-Times*, December 25, 1988.

Kermode, Mark. "Lost Be My Tribe." *Monthly Film Bulletin* 57, no. 681 (October 1990).

King, Larry. *The Larry King Show*, October 11, 1988.

Kleffel, Rick. Interview with Clive Barker at *The Agony Column*, www.bookotron.com, September 1 and 2, 2008,

Kuntzman, Gersh. "Clive Paints It Black." *New York Post*, November 20, 1993.

Kurtz, Frank. "Cutting the Razorline." *Hero Illustrated* 2 (August 1993).

Lacey, Liam. "In World of Skinless Bodies, 'Weird' Means Really Macabre." *Globe and Mail*, October 31, 1987.

Lackey, Mike. "The Clive Barker Interview." *Marvel Age* 107 (December 1991).

Lamanna, Dan. "Clive Barker's Lurid Fascination." *Cinescape*, January 1995.

Landon, Christopher. "The Many Lives of Clive." *The Advocate*, January 18, 2000.

Lawson, Terry. "'England's Stephen King' Goes for the Gore with Gusto." *Dayton Daily News and Journal Herald*, September 18, 1987.

Lee, Luaine. "Bakula's 'Leap' to 'Lord of Illusions' No Easy Trick." *Los Angeles Daily News*, September 1, 1995.

Levatino, Christian, and Victor Mendoza. *Lost in the Labyrinth*. Seraphim documentary on the Anchor Bay Hellbound DVD, 2000.

——. *Resurrection*. Seraphim documentary on the Anchor Bay Hellraiser DVD, 2000.

Linehan, Graham. "Ripping Yarns: Clive and Dangerous.: *Hot Press* 12, no. 20 (October 20, 1998).

Lloyd, Nigel. "Clive Barker – Lord of Illusions." *SFX* 16 (September 1996).

Lopez, Brein.: Barnes and Noble stage presentation at the LA Festival of Books, April 25, 2004.

Loretti, Nicanor. "John McNaughton Rejoins the Masters." *Fangoria*, January 27, 2006.

Lupoff, Richard, Richard Wolinsky, and Lawrence Davidson. Transcript of an interview on KPFA, San Francisco, *Science Fiction Eye* 4 (August 1988).

MacCormack, Patricia. "An Eviscerator and a Gentleman." *Terrorizer* 126 (December 2004).

MacCulloch, Simon. "Fantasycon X." *BFS Newsletter* 12, no. 3 (Winter 1985).

Mackenzie, Angus. "Brush Strokes in Blood." In *Pandemonium*, edited by Michael Brown. Eclipse, 1991.

Maldonado, Kristen. "Hulu's Books of Blood Cast on Interweaving Dark Storylines & Brutal Horror Make-Up" at www.TheFanClub.com, October 7, 2020.

Mansfield, Richard. "A Hell of a Day." *Video – The Magazine*, April 1988.

Marlowe, Chris. "Barker Hears Call, Creates 'Jericho' Game." *Hollywood Reporter*, July 18, 2006.

Martin, John. "Hellwriter." *Samhain* 10 (August/September 1988).

Martinez, Ed. "Candy Carnivale." *Coenobium* 14 (Summer 1995).

Matherson, Nigel. "The Watermelon Factor." *Savvy* 1, no. 3 (1994).

Maupin, Armistead. Foreword to *The Essential Clive Barker*, by Clive Barker. New York: HarperCollins, 1999.

McCormick, Carlo. "Meet Pinhead's Daddy." *Paper*, April 1993.

McDonagh, Maitland. "A Kind of Magic." *The Dark Side* 45 (April/May 1995).

McIntyre, Gina. "The Damnation Gang." *Wicked* 3, no. 2 (May/June 2001).

McKellen, Ian. E-Post Q&A Correspondence at www.McKellen.com, 1999–2006.

Miéville, China. "Candy and Carrion." *The Guardian*, October 19, 2002.

Miller, Mark Alan. E-mail to *The Clive Barker* Podcast at www.CliveBarkerCast.com, September 26, 2017.

Monfette, Christopher. Leaves on the Story Tree, 2008.

——. Mega-Interview with Clive Barker at www.IGN.com, October 11, 2007.

Moreno, Johnny. "JoBlo Visits the Set of The Hangover" at www.JoBlo.com, May 1, 2009.

Morris, Janet. "Raising Hell in Hollywood." *Film Review*, November 1991.

Nazzaro, Joe. "Weird Fantasy." *Starburst*, Special No. 76, 2006.

Neilson, Robert, and Des Doyle. "Clive Barker." *Albedo One* 3 (1993).

Newgen, Heather. "John Carpenter on Masters of Horror" at www.ComingSoon.net, May 7, 2005.

Newman, Kim. "Book Review: Tricks and Treats from the Country of True Lies." *The Independent*, August 18, 2001.

——. "Clive Barker." *Interzone* 14 (Winter 1985/1986).

——. "Hell on Earth." *City Limits* 398 (May 18–25, 1989).

——. "Living Hell." *New Statesman*, July 18, 1986.

Newport, David. Underworld at Limehouse, Denholm Elliott Stars, *Screen International*, February 23, 1985.

Nicholls, Stan. "A Strange Kind of Believer." *Million* 13 (January/February 1993).

Nutman, Philip. "Bring on the Monsters!" *Fangoria* 87 (October 1989).

——. "Clive Barker: The Dark Fantastic." *Fangoria* 214 (July 2002).

——. "Clive Barker - Lord of the Breed." *Fangoria* 91 (April 1990).

——. "Gangsters Vs. Mutants." In *Clive Barker's Shadows in Eden*, edited by Stephen Jones. Lancaster, PA: Underwood-Miller, 1991.

——. "Hammering Out Hellraiser." *Fangoria* 65 (July 1987).

——. "Hellraiser III - Welcome to Club Dead." *Fangoria* 110 (March 1992).

——. "If You Knew Clive Like We Know Clive." *Fangoria* 78 (October 1988).

Nutman, Philip, and Stefan Jaworzyn. "Meet Clive Barker." *Fangoria* 51 (January 1986).

O'Leary, Peggy. Kodiak Middle School, Alaska, 2009 and 2010.

Olson, Lee, and Dick Crew. "Masters of Fantasy." SciFi Channel, July 19, 1996.

Owchar, Nick. "Clive Barker: The Painter, the Creature, and the Father of Lies" (review). *Los Angeles Times*, August 10, 2011.

Pannifer, Bill. "Serious Maggots." *Stills*, February 1987.

Pascale, Anthony. "Brannon Braga on 'Books of Blood' and Bringing Horror to 'Star Trek: The Next Generation.'" www.TrekMovie.com, October 5, 2020.

Phegley, Kiel. "Richie & Sablik Discuss the Evolution of BOOM!" www.ComicBookResources.com, March 6, 2013.

Piccoli, Sean. "Lock Up the Kids / Ex-Boy's Revenge." *Washington Times*, December 16, 1992.

Pouncey, Edwin. "Bookworms - Dark Star of Horror." *Sounds*, August 31, 1985.

Power, Ed. Clive Barker interview: "I Woke Up from a Coma, and Everything I Owned Was Gone." *Daily Telegraph* at www.Telegraph.co.uk, November 26, 2020.

Radish, Christina. "Britt Robertson on the Hulu Horror Film 'Books of Blood,' the Twists and Turns, and That Ending" at www.Collider.com, October 7, 2020.

Rhodes, Peter. "Clive's Chilly Work." *Birmingham Evening Mail*, April 16, 1984.

Richardson, John H. "Hellraiser Rises Above the Norm with Scary Images." *Sacramento Union*, September 23, 1987.

Riley, Joe, and Peter Trollope. "Clive: A Happy Horror Writer." *Liverpool Echo*, March 23, 1984.

Ringgenberg, S. C. "A Man for All Seasons." *The Comics Journal* 171 (September 1994).

Robb, Brian J. "Games Without Frontiers." *Fear* 6 (May/June 1989).

Roddick, Nick. Review, Screen International, June 13, 1987.

Ryan Rotten. Interview with Hans Rodionoff at www.CreatureCorner.com, December 4, 2002.

——. "The Midnight Meat Train Trilogy" at www.ShockTillYouDrop.com, February 13, 2009.

Ruby, Jamie. Books of Blood Press Day – Anna Friel and Rafi Gavron at www.SciFiVision.com, October 7, 2020.

Russo, John. *Scare Tactics*. New York: Dell Publishing, 1992.

Russo, Tom. "Razorline." *Marvel Age* 126 (July 1993).

Salisbury, Mark. "Chains of Love." *Fear* 3 (December 1988).

Scapperotti, Dan. "Candyman." *Cinefantastique* 23, no. 4 (December 1992).

Schleir, Curt. "The Future of Horror Is Here: His Name Is Clive Barker." *Inside Books*, November 1988.

Schwartz, Jeffrey. The Candyman Mythos documentary on the Candyman DVD, 2004.

Schweiger, Daniel. "Bernard Rose's Demons of the Mind." *Fangoria* 118 (November 1992).

——. "Candyman: A Nightmare Sweet." *Fangoria* 117 (October 1992).

Semel, Paul. "Clive Barker" at www.Gamespy.com, December 13, 2000.

Seward, Keith. Clive Barker's Eye, Clive Barker: Paintings & Drawings 1973–1993, Bess Cutler Gallery, March 19–April 24, 1993.

Shaw, Kelly. "Confessions. *Lost Souls*, February 2002.

Sheehan, Henry. "Clive Barker and His Visions of Horror." *Orange County Register*, August 14, 1995.

Shinnick, Kevin G. "Monster Maker." *Scarlet Street* 30 (November 1998).

Sillito, David. Interview at the *Gods and Monsters* premiere, March 25, 1999, Odeon, Leicester Square, *BBC Breakfast News*, March 26, 1999.

Smilin' Jack Ruby. "Clive Barker: Part Two" at www.Fandom.com, December 13, 2000.

——. "Clive's Busy, Busy, Busy, Busy Year" at www.13thStreet.com, July 12, 2001.

Smith, Martin. Interview at the LA Times Festival of Books, April 25, 1998.

Smith, Michael Marshall. The Scarlet Gospels review, Continues the Hellraiser Story in Unsettling Style, The Guardian May 13, 2015

Spence D. "Clive Barker's Jericho: Soundscapes from the Dark Beyond" at www.IGN.com, September 17, 2007.

Stanley, John. "'Hellbound' / Sex, Horror Twine in Evil Sequel." *San Francisco Chronicle*, December 18, 1988.

Steinberg, Scott. *Clive Barker Talks About Jericho*, podcast at www.DigitalTrends.com, September 26, 2007.

Strauss, Bob. "Barker's Searching for a Higher Plane." *Fresno Bee*, October 25, 1987.

Streitfeld, David. "Who's Afraid of Clive Barker?: The Titan of Terror and His Studies in Dread Reckoning." *Washington Post*, September 30, 1987.

Stroby, W. C. Review of *Imajica*. Fangoria 109 (January 1991).

——. "Trust Your Vision." *Writer's Digest*, March 1991.

Sweeting, Geoff. "Shades of the Illusionist." *Ex Cathedra* 4 (May 1995).

Tarbuck, Liza. "Fantasy Man on The Big Breakfast." Channel 4, September 24, 1999.

Thesiger, Wilfred. *Arabian Sands*. New York: Dutton, 1959.

Tomlinson, Anthony. "Hell's Scribe." *Shivers* 53 (May 1998).

Tracy, Kathleen. "Clive Barker Gives Disney a Nightmarishly Edgy Kid Flick Rep." *KidScreen Magazine*, May 2001.

Truitt, Brian. "Clive Barker Pens 'Next Testament' of Biblical Horror" at www.USAToday.com, May 27, 2013.

——. "Nightbreed Series Returns to Monstrous Midian." *USA Today*, May 4, 2014.

Trussell, Robert. "Grisly Excesses Rob Hellraiser of Its Horror." *Kansas City Star*, September 18, 1987.

Tucker, Ken. "One Universe at a Time Please." *New York Times*, February 11, 1990.

Tuttle, Lisa. "Every Fear Is a Desire, September 1988." In *Clive Barker's Shadows in Eden*, edited by Stephen Jones. Lancaster, PA: Underwood-Miller, 1991.

Twelker, Eric. "Crossing Over" at www.Amazon.com, January 2001.

Waddell, Calum. Bernard Rose talks Amusement, Snuff, Etc. at www.Fangoria.com, August 31, 2005

——. "Lord of Illusions." *SFX* 194 (May 2010).

Wallace, Jason. The Bookends Interview at www.TheBookPlace.com, October 1999.

Warren, Bill. "The Quicksilver Highway to Horror." *Fangoria* 163 (June 1997).

——. "Shining Quicksilver." *Fangoria* 164 (July 1997).

Watt, Mike. "Saint Sinner." *Cinefantastique* 34, no. 6 (October/November 2002).

Weaver, Tom. "USHERed into History" at www.Fangoria.com, January 9, 2006.

Webb, Dan. *Clive Barker's Jericho*, podcast at www.xbox360achievements.org, September 27, 2007.

White, Lesley. "A Knight at the Pictures." *Sunday Times*, March 7, 1999.

Whittle, Peter. *Salome and the Forbidden*, documentary, Redemption, 1995

Wiater, Stanley. "Clive Barker: Master of the Fantastique" at www.Amazon.com, 1999.

——. *Dark Dreamers*. Novato, CA: Under-World Miller, 1990.

Williams, Owen. "For Whom the Toll?" At www.ScreamHorrorMag.com, March 1, 2018.

Wilmington, Michael. "Hellraiser: Intelligent It Is, Tasteful It Is Not." *Los Angeles Times*, September 18, 1987.

——. "Hellraiser Weds Sex and Death, Imaginative Stomach-Turner." *Arizona Republic*, September 19, 1987.

Wilson, Staci Layne. Interview at the Bram Stoker Awards, June 28, 2005, at www.About.com.

Winter, Douglas E. "An Artistic Escape." Transcript of an interview at DragonCon 1997, *Lost Souls*, July 1997.

——. *Clive Barker: The Dark Fantastic*. New York: HarperCollins, 2001.

——. "The End: An Afterword." *Millenium / Revelations*, 1997.

——. "Give Me B-Movies or Give Me Death!" *Faces of Fear*, 1985.

Winterson, Jeanette." Shafts of Sunlight." *The Guardian*, November 15, 2008.

Wooley, John. "To Hell and Back." *Tulsa World*, September 13, 1992.

Worley, Rob M. "Saint Sinner Brings Barker Horror to SCI FI" at www.Comics2Film.com, September 11, 2002.

Yablonski, Linda. "Clive Barker: Bess Cutler Gallery." *Artforum*, April 1994.

Yeats, William Butler. "The Song of Wandering Aengus." In *The Wind Among the Reeds*, by William Butler Yeats. London: Elkin Mathews, 1899.

Zaleski, Jeff. "The Relaunch of Clive Barker." *Publishers Weekly*, October 1, 2001.

NOVELS

The Damnation Game (1985), *Weaveworld* (1987), *The Great and Secret Show* (1989), *Imajica* (1991), *The Thief of Always* (1992), *Everville* (1994), *Sacrament* (1996), *Galilee* (1998), *Coldheart Canyon* (2001), *Abarat* (2002), *Abarat: Days of Magic, Nights of War* (2004), *Mister B. Gone* (2007), *Abarat: Absolute Midnight* (2011), *The Scarlet Gospels* (2015)

SHORT STORIES / NOVELLAS / COLLECTIONS

Books of Blood volumes 1–3 (1984), *Books of Blood volumes 4–6* (1985), "Lost Souls" (1985), *The Hellbound Heart* (1986), *Cabal: The Nightbreed* (1988), "Coming to Grief" (1988), "Whose Line is it Anyway?" (1988), "On Amen's Shore" (1992), "The Departed" / "Hermione and the Moon" (1992), "Pidgin and Theresa" (1993), "Animal Life" (1994), "A Story With No Title, A Street With No Name" (1995), *Chiliad: A Meditation* (1997), *Six Destinies / Tortured Souls* (2001), "The Wood on the Hill" (2001), *The Infernal Parade* (2004), *Jump Tribe* (2005), "Haeckel's Tale" (2005), *The Adventures of Mr. Maximillian Bacchus and His Travelling Circus* (2009), "They're Mad, They Are" (2012), *The Candle in the Cloud* (2013), "A Night's Work" (2013), "Dollie" (2013), "Afraid" (2015), *Tonight, Again* (2015)

NON-FICTION

The Painter, *The Creature* and *The Father of Lies* (2011, revised edition 2018)

ART

Illustrator volume 1 (1990), *Illustrator volume 2* (1993), *Visions of Heaven and Hell* (2005), *Imaginer volume 1* (2014), *Imaginer volume 2* (2015), *Imaginer volume 3* (2016), *Imaginer volume 4* (2017), *Imaginer volume 5* (2017), *Imaginer volume 6* (2018), *Imaginer volume 7* (2019), *Imaginer volume 8* (2020)

SELECTED EXHIBITIONS

Bess Cutler Gallery, New York (1993), Laguna Art Museum, CA (1995), La Luz de Jesus, Los Angeles (1997, 1998), Pacific Design Centre, Los Angeles (2002), MCA Chicago (2004), Bert Green Fine Art, Los Angeles (2005–2011), Packer Schopf, Chicago (2008), Sloan Fine Art, New York (2008), Otis, Los Angeles, (2008), Crown Gallery, Carlisle (2011), Century Guild, Los Angeles (2013, 2014), Alexander Salazar, San Diego (2014), Galleri Oxholm, Copenhagen (2015), Copro Gallery, Santa Monica (2016)

GAMES

Nightbreed: The Action Game (1990), Nightbreed: The Interactive Movie (1990), Undying (2001), Jericho (2007)

GRAPHIC NOVELS AND COMICS

Primal (1992), *Night of the Living Dead* (1993), *Deady: The Waiting Room* (2004), *Field* (2006), *Seduth* (2009), *Next Testament* (2013–2014), *Tapping the Vein* (1989–1992), *Hellraiser* series (1989–1994 and 2011–2015), *Nightbreed* series (1990–1993 and 2014–2015), *Jihad* (1991), *Weaveworld* (1991–1992), *The Yattering and Jack* (1991), *Dread* (1992), *Son of Celluloid* (1991), *Revelations* (1991), *The Life of Death* (1993), *Rawhead Rex* (1993), *Razorline: The First Cut* (1993), *Ectokid* (1993–1994), *Saint Sinner* (1993–1994), *Hokum & Hex* (1993–1994), *Hyperkind* (1993–1994), *Pinhead* (1993–1994), *The Harrowers* (1993–1994), *The Thief of Always* (2005), *The Great and Secret Show* (2005–2006), *Age of Desire* (2009), *The Book of Blood* (2014)

POETRY

Rare Flesh (2003)

ANTHOLOGY

The Essential Clive Barker (1999)

THEATRE

Voodoo (1967), *Inferno* (1967), *Neongonebony* (1968), *The Holly and The Ivy* (1970), *Is There Anybody There?* (1972), *Hunters In The Snow* (1973), *Salome* (c. 1973), *A Private Apocalypse* (c.1973), *The Scream Of The Ape* (1974), *The Fish Bride* (1974), *Poe* (1974), *The Egg* (1974), *Grunewald's Crucifixion* (1974), *A Dream* (1974), *The Wolfman* (1974), *A Clowns' Sodom* (1976), *Day Of The Dog* (1977), *The Sack* (1978), *The Magician* (1978), *Dog* (1979), *Nightlives* (1979), *The Comedy of Comedies* (unstaged, 1980), *The History Of The Devil* (1980), *Dangerous World* (1981), *Paradise Street* (1981), *Frankenstein In Love* (1982), *The Secret Life Of Cartoons* (1982), *Crazyface* (1982), *Subtle Bodies* (1983), *Colossus* (1983)

FILM / TELEVISION

Salomé (1973), *The Forbidden* (1978), *Hellraiser* (1987), *Nightbreed* (1990), *Lord of Illusions* (1995), *Nightbreed – Director's Cut* (2014), *Hellraiser II: Hellbound* (1988), *Hellraiser III: Hell On Earth* (1992), *Hellraiser IV: Bloodline* (1996), *Candyman* (1992), *Candyman 2: Farewell To The Flesh* (1995), *Hellraiser* franchise, *Candyman* franchise, *Underworld (Transmutations)* (1985), *Rawhead Rex* (1986), *The Yattering and Jack* (1986), *The Body Politic* (1997), *The A–Z of Horror* (1997), *Saint Sinner* (2002), *Haeckel's Tale* (2006), *Valerie On The Stairs* (2006), *The Midnight Meat Train* (2008), *Book of Blood* (2009), *Dread* (2009), *Books of Blood* (2020), *Motörhead – Hellraiser music video* (1992), *Gods and Monsters* (1998), *The Plague* (2006)

IMAGE CREDITS

Artwork and photographs by Clive Barker.

Additional artwork by Simon Bisley, John Bolton, Paris Cullens, Bastien Lecouffe Deharme, Les Edwards, Scott Hampton, Dave McKean, P. Craig Russell, Tristan Schane, Daniele Serra, and John Totleben.

Additional photographs by David Armstrong, Joan Barker, Leonard Barker, Susan Bickley, Murray Close, Tom Collins, Dovedale School, Anne Fishbein, John Greenwood, James Kay, Onie, Keith Payne, Quarry Bank School, Philip Rimmer, and Phil Stokes.

Promotional and production material from Aldwych Theatre, Arcane Comix, Bent-Dress Productions, Bert Green Fine Art, Bess Cutler Gallery, Boxer Graphics, Éditions Bragelonne, Cemetery Dance, Charter Books, Codemasters, Collins, Joanna Cotler Books, Dark Delicacies/Fool's Press, deviantART, Dimension Films, Disguise, Inc., Eclipse Books, Eclipse Comics, Electronic Arts/DreamWorks Interactive, EMI Records Ltd., Fangoria, Fantaco, Fifth Avenue Entertainment, Fontana, Gauntlet Press, Golden Age Collectables, Ltd., Golden Apple, Jon Gregory, HarperCollins, Here Lounge, IDW, Jieli Publishing House, Lakeshore Entertainment, Lions Gate Entertainment, Inc., Lions Gate Films, Macmillan Publishers, Madefire, Marvel Comics, Marvel Magazines, Masters Productions I Ltd., Matador Pictures, McFarlane Toys, Meltdown Comics, MGM, Midnight Picture Show, Morgan Creek Entertainment, New World Pictures, Chris Priestley, Pan Books, Phantom Press, Pocket Books, PolyGram Filmed Entertainment, Prism Comics, Rizzoli/Universe, Rue Morgue Festival of Fear, Sci-Fi Channel, Scream/Press, Screamin' Products, Inc., Seraphim, Seraphim Ink, Shueisha Bunko, Sonzogno, Sphere Books, Starburst, Titan Books, Toshiba Entertainment, Trans Atlantic Entertainment, Triple 6 Comics, Underwood-Miller, United Artists, Vestron Video, and Zehrapushu, Inc. held by the authors, Phil and Sarah Stokes.

Thanks to Clive Barker and to Jane Abbott, Peter Atkins, Doug Bradley, Cliff Holmes, and Julie Padget for images from their collections. All other material held by the authors, Phil and Sarah Stokes, and The Clive Barker Archive LLP.

Our thanks too to Clive and Roman for their love, friendship, and hospitality; to Cameron and Jamie for their patience; and to the many, many friends we've gained along the way through our work with and about Clive. Special mentions for Stephen Jones, whose *Shadows in Eden* inspired us back in 1991, and Rodolphe Lachat for guiding this book.

CLIVE BARKER'S

DARK
WORLDS

ISBN 978-1-4197-5846-1
LCCN: 2022933591

© 2022 Phil and Sarah Stokes

Texts: Phil and Sarah Stokes
Cernunnos logo design: Mark Ryden
Book design: Benjamin Brard

Published in 2022 by Cernunnos, an imprint of ABRAMS.

Printed and bound in Italy
10 9 8 7 6 5 4 3 2 1

ABRAMS The Art of Books
195 Broadway, New York, NY 10007
abramsbooks.com

In the Hills, the Cities had
the dubious distinction of being
the most scorned of those *stories* [contained
in *The Books of Blood*. Nobody
liked it. ~~My~~ Not my agent, or my agents'
assistant; my editor, not nor ~~my~~ her
~~editor~~ assistant. The repeated
objection was that the conceit
of the story was so far beyond
the parameters of the believable
that no reader would embrace
it. The story would be laughed
off the page, I was told. //